I0576322

Ethnosensitive Dimensions
of African Oral Literature:
Igbo Perspectives

Ethnosensitive Dimensions of African Oral Literature: Igbo Perspectives

EDITED BY

Afam Ebeogu

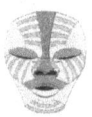

AFRICAN HERITAGE PRESS

NEW YORK   LAGOS   LONDON

2017

AFRICAN HERITAGE PRESS

First Edition, African Heritage Press, 2017

Copyright © Afam Ebeogu, 2017

All rights reserved. No part of this publication may be reproduced or trans-mitted in any form or by any means, electronic or mechanical, without permission in writing from the publisher.

Library of Congress catalog number: 2016944457

Cover Designer: AHP

ISBN: 978-1-940729-19-0

Dedication

To all Teachers, Researchers and Scholars of African Oral literature whose views and publications have contributed in no small measure in giving authenticity to African Literature.

Acknowledgements

Seven essays in this book were originally published either in journals or books mainly outside Africa, except for one which was published in Nigeria. We hereby express our indebtedness to these original sources:

"Old Wines, New Bottles, What Connoisseur?: Dimensions of contemporary Nigerian Oral Literature" in *Lore and Language* 7/1 (1988) pp 61–75.

"Of Progress and Distortions: A Pattern in the Panegyric Ethos in Igbo Life and Culture" in *Lore and Language* 8/1 (1989). pp. 81–94.

"The Feminist Temperament in Igbo Birth Songs" in Umea papers in English No. 15 *(Power and Powerlessness of Woman in West African Orality)*. Eds R. Granqvist and N. Inyama, Umea 1992, pp. 43–62.

"The World of the Lullaby: The Igbo Example". *Research in African Literatures* 22.2 (Summer 1991), pp. 43–62.

"The Dead Can Bite: Continuity in the Legend of the Visiting Dead in a Nigerian Igbo Community" in *Woman in the Academy: Festchrift for Professor Helen Chukwuma*. Eds. Seiyfa Koroye and Noel Anyadike. Port-Harcourt: Pearl Publishers 2004, pp 447–465.

"City and Transcity Folk Literature: The Dramaturgy and Rhetoric of Oral Advertisement of Medicine in Nigeria". *Lore Language 11 (1992–1993), pp. 45–67.*

"*Njakiri, The* Quintessence of Traditional Igbo Sense of Satire" in *Spoken in Jest.* Sheffield: Sheffield Academic Press for British Folklore Society Milestone series 1991, pp. 29–46.

These essays are being republished in this volume because of our conviction that the original sources of their publication had rather restricted circulation whereas this volume will enable the Nigerian reader to have easy access to the essays.

We also express our profound gratitude to Uzor Nwokocha who allowed us to use both his computer system and his typist, Bright Okereke, in the initial typesetting of this book.

Notes on Contributors

Afam Ebeogu is a Professor of English in Abia State University, Uturu, Nigeria.

F.U. Okoh teaches at Nwafor Orizu College of Education. Nsugbe, Anambra State, Nigeria.

Chinwe Nwizu is a Lecturer in the Department of English Language and Literature, Abia State University, Uturu, Nigeria.

Francis Chima is a Ph.D. Student of Abia State University, Uturu, Nigeria.

Isidore Diala is a Professor of English, Imo State University, Owerri, Nigeria.

J.O.J. Nwachukwu-Agbada is a Professor of English at Abia State University, Uturu, Nigeria.

Isaac Udoh teaches in the Department of English Language and Literature, Abia State University, Uturu, Nigeria.

Chinyere Nwahunanya is a Professor of English, Abia State University, Uturu, Nigeria

Dr. Ogbonna Onuoha and **Ugochukwu Ogbonnaya** teach in the Department of Linguistics and Communications/Igbo. Abia State University, Uturu.

Dr. G.I.N. Emezue teaches in the Department of English Language and Literature, Abia State University, Uturu.

Emma Ngumoha is a Professor of English, Abia State University, Uturu.

Table of Contents

Ethnosensitive Dimensions of African Oral Literature: Igbo Perspectives

Preface

Ethnosensitive Dimensions of African Oral Literature: Igbo Perspectives is a collection of nineteen essays selected and structured in such a way as to represent all the genres of African Oral literature, from the poetic genre to the rhetorical genre. These essays are arranged in such a way that the reader, whether he is a casual reader, a student or a researcher is able to apprehend, in one sweep, all the various aspects of the subject. Part One of the book is introductory, and includes three essays that are of a general kind, touching all aspects of the genres, while Part Two includes six essays concerned with the poetic genre. Part Three, made up of two essays, concerns essentially the prose genre while Part Four, of two essays, treats the drama genre. Part Five, made up of three essays, addresses the rhetorical genre, and Part Six has three essays that cut across all the genres. Below is a prefatory comment on all the nineteen essays.

Chapter One of *Part One*, entitled "Old Wines, New Bottles, what Connoisseur?: Dimensions of Contemporary Nigerian Oral Literature" is an attempt by Afam Ebeogu to present a succinct summary of the state of the scholarship on Oral Literature in Nigeria. It traces the origin of the scholarship on oral literature from its earliest state in Europe to the present situation in Nigeria, examining the implications of the ethnocentric imperatives of the scholarship in relation to the nationalistic demands of the Nigerian nation-state, ultimately opting for a healthy dialectic between the two. The author then makes some recommendations on the nature of the pragmatic processes needed for an effective teaching and study of oral literature in Nigerian higher educational institutions.

Chapter Two, Isaac Udoh's "Text and Context of African Oral Performance", is an updated statement of the fact that one of the factors which inevitably comes to the fore in discussing African Oral Literature of whatever genre is the issue of text and context. He makes it obvious that that literature cannot be assessed on the basis of its text alone as one would written literature. Rather, text goes hand-in-hand with context of the literature, for "context ... is the enfolding scaffolding with which a text is rendered". This is because Oral Literature is a performance in which the moment of actualization of the text involves many constituents—the personality of the performer, the nature of the occasion, the presence of histrionic elements, the audience factor and other factors associated with the ambience of performance. These then determine the context of the literature.

Chapter Three is F.U. Okoh's "Flexibility of Oral Art in Relation to Modern African Society", which reveals that the expanse of the oral art includes not only the purely traditional arts obtainable in purely traditional societies of Africa, but also manifests in contemporary society in written novels, poems and plays, in the performance arts and in mass media like radios and televisions. In these forms, the author argues, oral art retains not only quintessential forms but are also adapted, remodeled, revised and mediated upon to suit contemporary experiences.

Chapter Four introduces the essays of *Part Two*, dealing with the poetic genre. Chinwe Nwizu's "The Motif of Praise in the African Oral Tradition" discusses praise poetry as it manifests in some African oral songs, particularly pure panegyric, elegiac songs and chants, and religious songs and chants. The author argues that the tendency to eulogize the actions and characters of persons, animals and things is characteristically human, and that a great deal of these eulogies is evident in African cultures. She uses texts of such praises to illustrate her argument, and concludes that "praise raises the tone of an oral poem, beautifies it and makes it more appreciable".

Chapter Five continues with the issue of praise in African oral poetic tradition, and here Afam Ebeogu, in "Of Progress and Distortions: A Pattern in the Panegyric ethos in Igbo Life and Culture", studies the nature and character of panegyric poetics in relation to the Igbo of pre-colonial, colonial and post-colonial cultures. He argues that praise names among the Igbo were fuller, richer, more reflective of the culture's attitudes to life, and more stanzaic in form in the colonial situation than they are now, because of the corrosive acquisitive and somewhat anarchic tendencies in the colonial and post colonial eras that tend to reduce the quality of panegyric poetry. Using praise chants and abundant epithets from the Igbo culture, he shows how the contemporary Igbo praise names have tended to bastardize the achievement values of the Igbo people.

In Chapter Six, "The Content, Form and Performance of African Oral Elegies", Chinwe Nwizu studies forms of elegies which include dirges and lamentations performed at moments of loss, death and other afflictions. These songs or chants, as the case may be, reveal "every aspect of human existence, associations, relationships, exploits and expectations". She identifies these elegiac forms as being panegyric, religious and consolatory, and examines a number of these forms as they manifest in different occasions, revealing various human attitudes. Her study reveals amazing levels of qualitative poetry, and concludes that "the content, form and performance of African oral elegy remain an integral aspect of African oral heritage". While handling the topic, "Satire in Traditional African Oral Poetry: the Edda Igbo Example", in Chapter Seven, Francis Chima uses the opportunity to pick holes with some earlier scholars of African oral poetry who may have held certain positions on traditional African oral poetry based on apparently inadequate depth of field research. His recent researches on satiric practices among Edda Igbo enable him to make some valid and fresh revelations on that aspect of African oral poetry. He concludes by saying that "... before the end of this 21st century, if nothing serious is done to record the half-dead satire in traditional African oral poetry, we shall only have them in the nearest future as fossils for study in oral literature departments in our own African Universities".

In Chapter Eight, entitled "Poetry of Occasion I: The Feminist Temperament in Igbo Birth Songs", Afam Ebeogu takes a feminist perspective of Igbo birth (or maternity) songs. He discusses the songs using four classificatory typologies—of situation, medium, form and theme—to establish that these songs qualify as authentic folk poetry, and that they reveal evidences that these women performers use the songs to express uncommon feminist views, in spite of the fact that the Igbo society is in many ways male-chauvinistic. This perspective, aided by authoritative references from past and contemporary social anthropologists on the Igbo, brings to the fore the fact that feminism has always existed in traditional African set-ups, even though the tendency is to regard it as a contemporary phenomenon.

Chapter Nine is entitled "Poetry of Occasion II: the World of the Lullaby (the Igbo Example)", and here Afam Ebeogu studies the lullaby as a heuristic and pedagogic form of oral poetry, asserting that even though this oral form "among the Igbo exhibits some qualities of the doggerel, it also exhibits a serious views of life that is firmly anchored on Igbo culture". He identifies two types of lullaby, the "overt" and the "covert", attributing to them two types of rhythmic formats: "the fast-rocking rhythm" and the "slow-rocking rhythm". He concludes that "although the occasion for the performance of lullabies and the mode of their rendering may suggest a qualitatively low-grade poetry, they actually constitute a serious oral repertoire and deserve serious scholarly attention".

Chapter Ten is the first essay in *Part Three*, and entitled "The African Oral Narratives: The Folktale". Here, Francis Chima studies a genre that has been much discussed and at times misunderstood in the scholarship of African Oral Literature. He raises the fact that the word "folktale" has been used by scholars to refer to all prose genres in Africa. But he distinguishes the folktale as not meaning myth, legend and some other prosaic narrative modes that are not fictionalized. Rather, folktales are fictionalized and are of two types: the simple ones that are meant for children, and the complex ones that are aimed at the adults. All these are "such stories in American oral narratives that involve humans, animals, spirits, etc. designed to serve the purpose of addressing social vices, and mirrowing the people's world view, among others". He studies these stories in relation to their texts, structure, setting and themes, and concludes by recommending that scholars of the African folktale should devote their attention on the individual-narration of the tales, and their imaginative output.

The study of contemporary legend is a thriving activity in Europe and Africa; ghostlore scholarship constitutes a fascinating aspect of this study. Afam Ebeogu's "The Dead Can Bite: Continuity in the Legend of the Visiting Dead in a Nigerian Igbo Community", which is the eleventh chapter of this book, is an attempt to situate this scholarship in the African environment. The chapter examines this rather unusual but dominant oral narrative tradition as it manifests in an Igbo village of the past and present, in relation to the popular "hitchhiker" tradition of the Western world. He examines eight ghost stories recorded verbatim in Igboland with respect to their content, themes, style and setting, and concludes that the stories "have motifs that are fundamentally universal and primordial".

Part Four is concerned with the drama genre and in Chapter Twelve, entitled "Negotiating the Hegemonic: Ritual and Mythological Recuperation in Irobi's Drama and the Soyinka Model", Isidore Diala presents what can be regarded as "applied folklore scholarship" by studying four plays of an Igbo playwright, dramatist and scholar, Esiaba Irobi, in relation to traditional Igbo dramaturgical experiences. He predicates his study on the famous argument of Professor M.J.C. Echeruo who, way back in 1971 in "The Dramatic Limits of Igbo Rituals", had argued that for modern Igbo dramatists and playwrights to write and practice authentic African drama, they would need to do what the Greeks of old did: force the story (plot) out of its myth in order to create drama out of ritual. Diala's argument is that Esiaba Irobi has done just what Echeruo had suggested, for his "exultation of folk literature and beliefs makes them the compelling background of his art.... Irobi's fascination with the drum language, masking and the state of possession, which they include, is consistent with his abiding interest in the idiom of religious ritual,... his abiding theme is the role of ritual in the rebirth of the society", and in writing his plays, like *Nwokedi*, Irobi "demonstrates his apprehension of the dramatic potentials of Ekpe as dance-drama as well as its dramatic limits". Diala's argument seems to be that this model, which the Nobel laureate Wole Soyinka had eminently practiced using Yoruba mythology as his basis, would bestow authenticity to modern African dramatic practices.

In Chapter thirteen, "A Type of Popular Secular Theatre: The Dramaturgy and Rhetoric of Oral advertisement of Medical Products in Nigeria", Afam Ebeogu studies the advertisement of some medicines by itinerant drug-sellers in Nigerian cities and luxury buses. In a typically folkloristic tradition, he has been able to observe the theatrics and record the verbal accompaniments of this performance, and he discusses them in relation to the traditions of the popular theatre and Brechtian aesthetics. He concludes that this "folk performance remains a transmitter of a rhetorical and dramaturgical tradition, and provides telling evidence which shows that forms of folk art or oral literature are a dynamic product of the socio-economic consciousness of an era".

Chapter Fourteen introduces *Part Five* which deals with the rhetorical genres of African oral literature. The Chapter, written by Ogbonna Onuoha and Ugochukwu Ogbonnaya, is entitled "Rhetorical Genres of African Oral Literature: The Idiom, Puzzle, Tongue Twister and Pun". Here, these two scholars of Igbo Linguistics and Literature guide us into the nature of these genres that are aspects of Igbo oratorical skills and practices, giving examples of their linguistic peculiarities. These genres are revealed as adding beauty and richness to Igbo speech practices, philosophy and verbal wisdom, for which reason they deserve more scholarly attention and research than have been the practice in Igbo, and generally African, literary and linguistic studies.

In Chapter Fifteen, "Proverb Yield in the Igbo Field: Why Are We So Blest?", J.O.J. Nwachukwu-Agbada authoritatively discusses the state of this rhetorical genre, the proverb, in the African society, with particular reference to the Igbo world. According to him, if "new proverb coinages continue to roll out from the Igbo proverb mill", it is because for the Igbo, the proverb fulfils a lot of functions—six in all—and they include the functions of "amplification, authoritativeness, education, rhetoricism, image-building and aestheticism". He shows how, though the proverb is an ancient conversational formula, it is still quite relevant and protean to the contemporary Igbo world, and may remain so for quite some time to come. The chapter has a lot for the reader somewhat overwhelmed by the ancient and contemporary Igbo person's penchant for this form of lore in African life and literature.

Afam Ebeogu's "*Njakiri*, the Quintessence of the traditional Igbo Sense of Satire" (Chapter Sixteen), is an attempt to discuss the constituents of traditional humour in respect of the Igbo culture. He uses texts recorded in appropriate contexts to extray the Igbo satirical *njakiri*, and, comparing it with other classical and neo-classical satirical traditions, argues for the uniqueness of this Igbo quintessential rhetorical comic practice. He concludes that: "as long as Igbo writers from the Igbo culture … continue to draw their resources of rhetoric and humour from … 'the language of men', so long will they capture in the rhythm of their dialogues and expressions nuances of *njakiri*".

Part Six opens with chapter seventeen, and attention is turned to some literary folklore practices that cut across genres. Studies in oral literature in the last four decades or so have established that the epic tradition, originally thought to be absent in African oral traditions, is not alien to that continent. Chinyere Nwahunanya, in "The Role of Women in Three Epics: A Feminist Reading of *Sundiata, The Ozidi Saga* and *The Mwindo Epic*", assesses the tradition of the epic in Africa, and comes to the conclusion that women play significant roles in establishing the epic stature of the leading epic heroes. He argues that this is unlike the situation in many of the novels written by African authors. A feminist reading of these epics is thus necessary in the overall study of African oral literature.

Chapter Eighteen, "Essential Stylistic Features of Oral Literature", discusses a pattern of linguistic peculiarity which oral art embodies. G.I.N. Emezue takes style "to be the way artists employ the subtle nuances of their language to make meaning and communicate intensions while also exhibiting their individual peculiar artistry". He proceeds to look at some purely linguistic stylistic aspects of oral literature, like parallelism, repetition and refrains, and paralinguistic features like ideophone, rhythm and musicality. He is able to conclude that the oral artist uses stylistic features not only to entertain his audience but also to communicate in a special way with them.

In Chapter Nineteen, "The Researcher and African Oral Literature", which is the last chapter of the book, Emma Ngumoha emphasizes that "the search for knowledge in oral literature exposes the scholar to rigours and problems that a scholar of written literature may avoid", for "the problem of oral literature study is … that of conducting research in an area which is not easily empirically recoverable in addition to being 'evanescent'". He guides us into an ultimate knowledge of aspects of the folkloristics that are inevitable in the life of the ardent scholar of oral literature.

You are invited to have a pleasurable reading of these essays, most of which draw their materials for discourse from the Igbo life and culture, thus indicating that an ethno-sensitive perspective of African Oral literature is inevitable.

PART ONE: INTRODUCTIONS

Chapter One

Old Wines, New Bottles, What Connoisseur?: Dimensions of Contemporary Nigerian "Oral Literature"

Afam Ebeogu

The presence of "Oral Literature" in the syllabuses of most liter-ary-based departments in Nigerian universities and institutions of higher learning has become such a pervasive feature that there is a danger of our losing a sense of how recent this field of scholar-ship is in Africa. There is obviously a real danger of fossilization of the content, conception and methodology of imparting the sub-ject—a fossilization that is typical because, every so often, we tend to grab wholesale current trends of thought that breeze their way in from across the European continent, and proceed to perpetuate them, their benefits and their pitfalls, as if we in Africa were agents of the dispersal of intellectual traditions that originate from else-where. We accept that there is a universality in knowledge and schol-arship; a universality that concentrates on fundamental truths, and de-emphasize the over-localisation of experiences and phenomena. But, in the same vein, we must take cognizance of the relevance of some kind of knowledge and associated scholarship to particular situations, and be more wary of trying to disseminate concepts, even if very scientific concepts, without modifying and adapting them to specific environments.

When the study of folklore,[1] with emphasis on folk literature, be-came a very serious affair,[2] there were particular reasons for this. It is generally agreed that in Europe of the middle nineteenth century, the two powerful social, economic, political and literary movements which came to be known as "nationalism" and "romanticism" encouraged

3

a very serious scholarly interest in the life of the "the folk" who came to be recognized as a vital segment of the society whose interest could no longer be ignored in an overall scheme that aimed at the evolution and survival of the nation. The ends of folk studies then were fairly functional, as witness the often mentioned fact that the Finnish epic, the *kalevala,* arose from, and helped to forge, a feeling of nationhood amongst the multifarious dialect groups of a colonially dominated Finland. Having performed this specific function in Europe, folklore[3] scholarship was soon to degenerate into almost mere pastime, what Richard Dorson deprecatingly called an "antiquarian hobby or storage enterprise", ("Is Folklore a Discipline" 203), especially in the so-called democracies or capitalist states where acknowledged scholars in the field could boast of the use of folklore for "knowledge and insight" (Williams 213). It was essentially in this state that the scholarship almost entirely as an enterprise invaded Africa in very recent times, and the earliest scholars in the field tended to see the study of oral literature as an essential medium for exploring "traditional Africa". So preoccupying had been the interest of such big names in African oral literature as Ruth Finnegan and S. Babalola in the textual and formal analysis of African oral literary genres that the very important issue of methodology in both research and teaching had tended to assume marginal attention until recently.[4] In many ways, it can be said that these "traditional" attitudes persist, especially when it comes to the scope and ideological orientation of the syllabuses in the universities, and the actual research and teaching methods.

It is only in the light of the above that we can appreciate the reactions against established tendencies which are beginning to grow. Broadly, one can describe some of these reactions as being radically Africanist, some as being indignantly nationalistic, and others as ideologically political. There is no mutual exclusiveness in the above identification; indeed, what we recognize is a rather complex situation besieged by inherent contradictions, and we will attempt to pick our way carefully through the marsh.

Of obvious significance is that there is now in Nigeria a crop of very serious scholars of Oral Literature who prefer to call themselves folklorists, so that their area of specialization in folkloristics becomes folk literature rather than just oral literature. This group does not feel bound by the traditional, purist approach to the study of oral literature; and this is captured quite expressively by even such a genuine scholar of African Oral Literature as Ruth Finnegan when she admits her prejudice against what she calls the "unfortunate term", *folklore*, "which I prefer to avoid, for its inherently misleading associations" (*Oral Poetry* xi).[5] It is gladdening to observe, in passing, that Finnegan's most recent approaches to the study of oral literature are quite folkloristic, and the fact that she acknowledges her indebtedness to the rich work done by this group of modern scholars in folklore suggests that her bias is against the origin of the term itself rather than against the methodologies and motives of modern folklore scholarship.

The serious commitment of modern scholars of folk/oral literature in Nigeria is to be seen in their attempt to broaden the areas covered by that scholarship beyond the narrow confines of the traditional approach, with the result that such genres of literature as proverbs, slang, aphorisms, obituaries, myth, jokes, slogans and so on which had been regarded as some kind of sub-genres of literature, are now fully acknowledged as encompassing a significant spectrum of folk sensibility. Focus on folk art has revealed that literary consciousness among the folk is intimately connected with other aspects of folk life and thought, so that to begin to understand who and what constitute folk culture is to begin to appreciate the presence and humanity of a large percentage of the Nigerian population who very often occupy only a peripheral position in the consciousness of policy makers and implementers. Thirdly, this serious interest in folklore scholarship has also led to the bringing together of many scholars from various parts of the Nigerian nation in the recognition of a common point of interest, a common basis for interaction. It has become obvious to these scholars that though they belong to different ethnic groups that form the Nigerian state, and that though, most often, their ethnic cultures provide the bases for folklore studies and specialization, there are many similarities between these various cultures; their researches have usually become proof of Chiek Diop's argument in favour of a fundamental unity which most black African cultures share. (Diop, *The Cultural Unity of Negro Africa*).

The attempt by many of these Nigerian contemporary scholars of folk literature scholarship to create a common forum of interaction led to the formation of the Nigerian Folklore Society in 1980. Since then, the society has been holding annual congresses, and one picture that emerges from the themes of these congresses, at least in very recent times, is the concern by the society to use the forum of the conferences to emphasize a Nigerian national consciousness.[6] In the address delivered by the President of the society during its 4th Congress, the nationalistic commitment that led to the origin of folklore as a discipline was emphasized, as was also the need for those who formulate development plans for the country to consult regularly with folklorists for a better perception of the social, ideological and political needs of Nigeria.[7] The communiqué after the congress

> recognized the urgent necessity to develop the enormous human and material resources of Nigeria to create a nation in which individuals and social groups can realize their aspirations of freedom and fulfilled existence. To this end, Congress calls on the various governments to increase investment in the modernization of institutions so that they can promote a culture of humanism, fairness, and national consciousness. Congress also urges scholars *and cultural administrators to explore sources* of indigenous thought and creativity in order to guarantee the autonomy and sovereignty of the country's development process. (*Folklore and National Development*, xiii).

A good number of the titles of the papers in oral or folk literature presented at some of these conferences make it clear that most of these scholars of folk literature perceive their discipline as an important tool in de-emphasizing ethnic prejudice, encouraging tolerance of ethnic diversities and recognizing the common factors that bind the Nigerian ethnic groups together. For example, it has been argued that a thorough examination of the concept of heroism and leadership in many Nigerian legends, myths and folk stories might be a useful beginning in the attempt to fashion an indigenous political system on which the concept of leadership and heroism is thoroughly rooted on indigenous antecedents.[8] It has been claimed that

> Through references to the people, [Igede] poets use poetry to foster unity among the Igede and their other audience in Nigeria. Their resources are the myths, legends, folktales, anecdotes, proverbs and other established modes of expression in Igede. The involvement of the poet in the task of national integration with the grassroots populations deserves attention (Ogede 1)

This writer has also argued that radio and television programmes like the "New masquerade", which tap their resources from folk imagination, language resources, sense of humour and satire, can be a veritable instrument for arousing a feeling of oneness, operating essentially on a psychological level, amongst the various groups of the Nigerian peoples who watch the programmes. (Ebeogu "Media Comedy").

There has therefore been a very deliberate attempt by folklore scholars to stretch arguments, even, at times, to the point of the ridiculous, in order to prove that folklore scholarship has an essential fundamental value in identifying indigenous models from which a Nigerian national consciousness, unity and pride, can be evolved. It has happened before with other countries; why not with Nigeria, the arguments tend to affirm with clinching finality.[9]

One of the tendencies characteristic of these contemporary folklore studies is the attempt to define and redefine the concept of the folk so as to accommodate the dynamics of social change characteristic of all societies. Whereas the word has been used in various contexts to mean "popular", "peasant", primitive", "ordinary", "common people" (Lord 6–8), it may also just mean "people in general" (*The Advanced Dictionary*, 385). The tendency had been for students of oral literature to regard the producers of such literature as "traditional people" who live in the rural areas or the "countryside", and who remain essentially resistant to the perversions of urban culture and modernism.[10] But, as Richard Dorson admits (*Folklore and*

Fakelove 46), the word "folk" no longer applies just to "country folk", though Dorson's attempt to associate folk culture with "traditional culture" creates additional problems. Instinctively, people tend to associate "traditional" with "indigenous". And, as the earliest scholars of folklore, whether anthropologists or literary people, recognized, these people are of necessity the most authentic producers of folk art in the sense that such art is in their blood—they are in control of it; they know to what malleable limits they can subject it, and they do not strain themselves in order to posses and own it, making it part of the very parameters that define them, as a cultural group.

But the contemporary situation would not accept as still legitimate that attempt to confine "traditional" modes of life and vision to "the villages". Most of our urban communities and groups are quite traditional, if not in settlement patterns, at least in attitudes, allegiances, sentiments, cultural associations and clubs.[11] Oral art is very much current in this world of "urban traditional" culture. This very large population of people and groups in our cities is part of the folk. Rather than presenting a very definite articulation of the folk, therefore, one might just be content to identify the characteristics of the folk: they are associated with indigenous culture—they either practice, identify with, understand or appreciate customary practices and values associated with traditional modes of life and vision; they form a very high percentage of the population of the country; a significant proportion of that population is in the rural areas; they possess a creative consciousness which guarantees a tradition of art on which basis distinctive aesthetic values can be formulated; ultimately, they tend to possess a common language or lingua franca with which many of them identify, and to which some of them can become very parochially attached. Most contemporary folklorists would identify with the above view, and their area of specialization as folklorists is often determined by a combination of some of the factors enumerated above.

The need by folklorists to define or redefine "the folk" of contemporary Nigerian society has also been motivated by other factors than the attempt to identify special areas of scholarship. The issue of the objective of folklore studies has always been a dominant source of polemics, and even acrimony, among folklorists. For example, in the United State of America, there has always been exchange of verbal crossfire between "bourgeois scholars" and "radical academics" as to the purpose of folklore scholarship; the one insisting on "knowledge and insight" for its own sake, the other unapologetically insisting on the ideological use of folklore for the liberation of the oppressed masses from elitist and hegemonic leadership (Williams 237). This familiar scenario in academic circles is, naturally, re-enacting itself on the Nigerian scene. Amam Amkpa has gone so far as to question the motives behind the formation of the Nigerian Folklore Society:

> We are yet to understand the philosophy that inspired the gang up. Could this information be inspired with the need to investigate our folklore, myths, legends to help us understand the present and to enable us abolish (sic) a future of cultural, political and economic domination of our people? We will want to be optimistic in this sense and hope this forms the basis of this gang up. However we should equally be concerned about the limits of such a formation questioning the hegemony (17).

G.G. Darah's researches among the Urhobo argue that, in the purely indigenous Nigerian societies before the advent of colonialism, oral literature in the society was not only a product of the ideological orientation of that group but also indicative of the nature of that ideology (See Darah, 182–207). Indeed, it becomes obvious that to the Marxists scholar, there ought to be no confusion over the real definition of "folk", or rather that the confusion is understandably characteristic of the tendency by "bourgeois scholarship" to create a mystifying aura around scholarly concepts in order to escape from the responsibility of confronting certain implicit ideological issues. "The folk" are no less than "the masses", with all the Marxist ideological connotations which the word evokes; the mass of common people who ought to be the cardinal focus of all policies of governments but who, most often, are oppressed and dispossessed by the exploitative policies of the bourgeois governments and imperialist

dominations. For the Marxist then, the folk must be defined ideologically, for that is the only way to really know who they are, in the
context of the materialist dialectics which identify them in relation to
their economic base in society.

No matter what might be the intellectual and ideological preferences of most of the scholars of folk literature, they all seem to
accept the fact that folklore research "implies the interrelated social,
intellectual and material aspect of culture in their ethnic context".
(Degh 34). Most of the big names in folk literature scholarship in
Nigeria are experts in the folk literature of particular ethnic groups
in the country.[12] Indeed, when some scholars argue about the use of
folklore for the purpose of arousing national consciousness and fostering national unity, the argument is most often only notional rather
than illustrative, and when it is illustrative, most of the illustrations
make a case for ethnic nationality rather than state nationality, even
if, understandably, the supposed argument is that what is valid to the
ethnic nation can be applied at the level of the state as a nation.

A few illustrations here will suffice. When some scholars of
folklore studies argue about the value of the legend of Oduduwa
(Osinowo) or Ogun (Adekoya, "Myth and Unity" 9) in fostering unity among the Yoruba, it is difficult to see how such myths can foster
unity among Nigerians. When another scholar examines the Bayajida myth as a significant factor of hegemonic control amongst the
Hausa, (Karaya 12), we know that the problem is peculiar to the
Hausa nation. In the same vein, another scholar has tried to show
how the reference for the Ala deity in traditional Igbo society ensured a great deal of discipline in that society (Ugonna 273–295).
Even if it is possible for contemporary Igbo society to go back to the
worship of this deity, it can only bring discipline to those who accept
her—and they would necessarily be Igbo—but not to the Nigerian
nation with its legion of ethnic deities to whom only small ethnic
nationalities can pay allegiance. This writer once examined the feminist tendencies in Igbo birth songs, and proceeded to suggest that
the medium of such similar songs is still legitimate for expressing
feminist views in contemporary Nigeria society (Ebeogu, "Feminism

and Oral Literature", 43–62.) The study would have been more folk-loristic if the author had the linguistic and cultural competence to examine similar birth songs in other Nigerian ethnic groups in order to arrive at a proposal based on sound comparatist analysis.

The impression one gets after reading some of these presentations is that there is a large gap in social and academic interaction between the critics of folk literature and the practitioners of that literature; between this special kind of audience and the creative performers who may not have thought of that audience as part of the genuine consumers of their art or people with whom they share the same criteria for aesthetic appreciation. Every folk artist performs within the context of some folk tradition and idiom which have conditioned his creative sensibility. Those who form part of that society which has informed his art are his immediate audience, and it is their aesthetic reaction to his art that constitutes part of the critical appreciation of his performance. The folk scholar who approaches any folk artist for a discussion of or information about the performer's art must first of all identify socially, linguistically and psychologically with the tradition which nurtures the creative vision of the artist. When that scholar begins to insinuate interpretations which are outside the aesthetic frame-work of the performer's literary tradition, or to mount suggestive pressures as to the direction in which the object of the composition and performance of his art should lean, the artist is likely to become cautious and uncooperative. If a folk artist willingly decides to use the medium of his art to evoke sentiments that are likely to draw sympathy from the folk consumers of that art in favour of state policies, that decision must be properly motivated and the performance must be in the context of an economic and socio-political system from which the artist does not feel alieanated.[13]

While the Hausa folk singer, Alhaji Mammam Shata, composes a piece of folk poetry on farming amongst "Northerners"—the Are-wa—and only alludes to the Operation Feed the Nation when he calls farming a "war of today" (Yahaya, 149–151), an Igbo ballad singer, Udekwe Omambala, devotes a track of an LP gramophone record to a eulogy of the OFN programme, going as far as naming General

Olusegun Obasanjo and Governor Atom Kpera, then of Anambra State, as the chief architects of the programme at the national and state levels. Both compositions are on the same subject, but the artists court different kinds of emotional responses from different audiences—the Hausa-speaking and Igbo-speaking audiences. Whereas the Hausa poet emphasizes the dominant position of farming to a group he identifies as "Arewa", which "theme" forms the whole chorus responses in the performance, the Igbo poet seeks effect for his topic by making a humorous jibe at the fact that the reason hunger dominates in his (Igbo) society is because every able-bodied person, including women who for that reason find it difficult to get husbands, have gone to school and so nobody is left to do the farming. While Alhaji Mammam Shata lauds the traditional farming ability of his society, in relation to the OFN programme, Udekwe Omambala criticizes the white collar job preferences of his own society, but also in relation to the OFN programme. It becomes obvious that both poets, who are Nigerians, have different folk audiences in mind even while the subject of their song is the same. Would it really be argued that both poets aim at arousing a national consciousness simply because they sing in support of a government programme? Is the vision of the Hausa poet of his society not more positive and less critical than that of the Igbo poet who raises a fundamental issue about the destiny of a people whose career aspirations are not often related to the provision of the basic economic need of their life—food.

It is no doubt the ethnic base of most folk art which has led to a situation in which most folklorists in Nigeria focus their interest on particular areas of folklore study in their own ethnic groups. The mere fact that they are linguistically equipped to record their collections in their own mother tongues and to transcribe from such authentic collections is in itself a justification for their choice of the cultures for their studies. As Bascom has observed, folk literary collections

> must be recorded in the African language, and should be presented with the African text, a literary interlinear translation, and a free but nevertheless faithful translation must once more

be driven home, because without the African text it may be impossible to say how accurate the translation is, how much a tale has been rewarded or re-written, or even whether or not it only a summary. (28)

But having undertaken his researches, recorded and described his folk literary materials in his own mother tongue, the Nigerian folk-lorist still has the problem of making his scholarship accessible to other Nigerians who do not share the values of his ethnic culture nor understand his own mother tongue. If he is a teacher of oral litera-ture in any Nigeria's institutions of higher learning whose students are drawn from diverse ethnic groups in the country, the folklorist has the problem of carrying home the message of certain verbal il-lustrations in the English language, no matter how faithful the trans-lations are.[14]

We can therefore appreciate why, even though a good number of the literary departments in some Nigerian institutions of higher learning claim to teach African Oral literature, what is most often essentially taught, in terms of scope and continuity, is the oral liter-ature of the dominant ethnic group in whose domain the institution of higher learning is situated, an observation which an American visiting lecturer in one of Nigeria's premier universities made in one of the conferences of the Nigerian Folklore Society (Ward 750).

In a situation such as that described above, what chance has folk/oral literature of de-emphasizing ethnic loyalty even while it arouses ethnic consciousness or, in other words, of serving the interests of the ethnic group without jeopardizing those of the state? The ethnic orientation of folklore scholarship seems inevitable, as long as most folk groups in the country relate to particular ethnic communities. What both students and teachers of folk/oral literature in Nigeria have to do is to try their utmost not to promote the study of the folklore of any particular ethnic group to the detriment of national consciousness and unity. For example, students and scholars of folk literature should be encouraged to learn Nigerian languages other than their own and, in any case, to undertake studies in folklore in folk groups other than their own. Each higher institution of learning in the country offering courses in folk literature should be able to recruit lecturers in the field from different ethnic groups, and these institutions should develop well co-ordinated exchange programmes in research and the teaching of folk literature. The need for a comparativist focus in the study of folk literature in a country like Nigeria, seeking to evolve a national consciousness out of divergent pulls of ethnic loyalties, cannot be overemphasized (see Okpewho, "Comparativism and Parochial Imperative").

Furthermore, scholars of folk literature should strive to establish greater rapport with the performers of the literature, so that a meaningful and useful dialectic between the creative and the critical faculties can be cultivated. These folk performers, for example, should be invited to higher institutions of learning and centers of culture to perform on a regular basis, in an atmosphere that is devoid of elitist conditioning. This will create opportunities for students in the discipline always to revalue their theoretical postulations in the light of empirical evidence. It is a situation like this that is likely to influence folk performers into forming broader visions of the concept of the folk-visions that will encourage the possibility of seeing the whole Nigerian people as one folk audience. In this connection, folk artists should be encouraged to avail themselves, more than ever before, of the resources of the electronic media for the dissemination of their art; in this way, they will be reaching a larger audience. Of greater significance too is the realization by these performers that their mother-tongues do not always have to be the medium of their performance. A non-ethnic rooted language, like Pidgin English, commands a great deal of folk appeal, especially in urban centres, and there is no reason why a folk performer cannot avail himself of the resources of that language medium.[15]

A programme that aims at cementing national consciousness in Nigeria through a courtship of folk sensibility must involve the various governments in the country in a very meaningful way-more meaningful ways than just getting artists to compose and perform politically motivated slogans and songs in support of questionable party or government policies. Federal and state governments should create centers of culture or arts councils where they do not exist, and finance such centers adequately. Scholars and departments of folk literature also need reasonable institutionalized sponsorship for effective research and teaching. Governments, in co-ordination with universities, should establish and run viable publication units for effective dissemination of research findings. If the more technologically and scientifically advanced countries of the world like Soviet Union and the United State of America can invest huge sums on folk scholarship, even when the level of national consciousness in their countries is very high, there is no excuse for a young country like Nigeria, seeking to build a self-reliant and independent nation on the basis of indigenously derived resources, doing any less than that.

Finally, we must accept the fact that national consciousness can only be solid and lasting if it derives from folk consciousness. And the only way to make folk consciousness national is by instituting a system of government and politics which has the folk as the centerpiece of development policies. The folk cannot have a national consciousness when they do not identify emotionally and patriotically with the nation, and when they remain largely alienated from the mainstream of government action. When the folk become convinced that the main objective of government is their welfare, then the quest for national consciousness in Nigeria will be more than half-realised. The role which folklore scholars have to play in all this scheme should by no means be marginal but, for that role to be effective, these scholars must undertake a self-re-examination of their commitment to their discipline; they must face the truth of the uneasy dialectic between ethnic commitment and national allegiance: they must approach their discipline with dispassionate, detached and scientific logic. While some of the old wines are still tasty, some have gone sour; the brewers of the kind of art that is rooted in folk imagination must think of new products that will appeal to the tastes of more complex Nigerian connoisseurs.

NOTES

1. We use the expression "folklore" here rather than "oral literature" because we share Richard Dorson's view that "the great bulk of oral literature is traditional, but a mass of folklore falls outside oral tradition: the realm of belief, ritual festival, the field of art; the topic of medicine, and other subjects such as folk costume, folk cuisine, folk crafts" (*African Folklore, 17*)

2. For a historical perspective on the origin and trends in folklore scholarship in general, and oral literature in particular, see Richard Dorson, "Africa and the Folklorist", *African Folklore*, 3–72; Ruth Finnegan, *Oral Poetry*, 30–46; Albert Lord, "Perspectives on Recent Work on Oral Literature", 1–24.

3. For the origin of the expression "folklore", and the attitudes it evoked, see Richard Dorson, "Is Folklore a Discipline?", 203.

4. As examples of opinions that emphasise the issues of relevance and methodology in the study and teaching of Oral Literature in Nigeria, see Isidore Okpewho, "The Relevance of Oral Literature Study in Africa". Okpewho's anthology of African poetry, *The Heritage of African poetry*, is quite useful not only because of the currency of the opinion on African Oral Literature expressed in the introduction to the book, but also in the fact that most of the English translations of African oral poems appear very faithful to their originals—though quite expressive translations, their oralness is not lost. On issues of methodology, see O.L. Okanlawon "On Problems of Oral Literature Research in Nigeria Today", 73–84. Ruth Finnegan's *Oral Poetry: Its Nature, Significance and Social Context*, (1977), is also remarkable for its comparatist scope, currency of opinion and sociological perspective on oral poetry.

5. See also pp. 30–37 of the book where the author associates the origin of "folklore studies with the "Romantic and Evolutionist Theories" of oral literature which tended to see the discipline as some kind of antiquated genres and "fast-perishing relics".

6. For example, the theme of the Congress of the Nigerian Folklore Society in 1984 was "Folklore and National Development", and in 1985, it was "Folklore and National Integration".

7. An address of the national president of the Nigerian Folklore Society, Prof. D. Abdulkadir, at the fourth congress of the Nigerian Folklore Society held at Ile-Ife, Dec. 17–21, 1984 on *Folklore and National Development*.

8. See, for example, Gbolade Osinowo, "Folk Heroes and Nationalism", (79–90); Olowo Ojoade, "Ethnic Stereotyping in Nigerian Folklore: A Factor of National Development" (143–180); E.O. Kofoworola, "Concepts and Changing Factors of Creative Developments in the Myths and Legends of Nigerian Folklore", (181–209); Ode Ogede: "Oral Poetry and National Integration: the Example of Igede Poets Odeh Igbang and Michah Ichegbe"; Afam Ebeogu: "Media Comedy for Nigeria's folk: the example of the adventures of the 'Masquerade' Drama *Group*".

9. See particularly Olowo Ojoade: "Folklore: an agent of national Integration in Nigeria", where the author makes references to states like Finland, China, Germany and the U.S.S.R. which have utilized the propaganda value of folklore in achieving the high degree of national feeling characteristic of these states.

10. See Ruth Finnegan's very analytical treatment of the complexities of "oralness" of cultures in *Oral Poetry*, 16–24; 246–261.

11. G.I Nwaka has given an insightful socio-historical analysis of this phenomenon of urbanization of the traditional, with regard to the Igbo, in his "Urban and Industrial Culture in Igboland: The Crisis of Adaptation", *Igbo Socio-Political System*, 47–63.

12. Isidore Okpewho is the only Nigerian folklorist we know of who is fluent in at least three Nigerian languages. His comparatist approach to folk scholarship is well-known and attested to by his publications, especially his three most authoritative books in the area: *The Epic in Africa, Myth in Africa, and African Oral Literature: Backgrounds, Character and Continuity*.

13. See Part Three of Uchegbulam Abalogu, Garba Ashiwaju and Regina Amadi-Tshiwala, eds., *Oral Poetry in Nigeria*, 247–258, titled "The Emotional Elements in Traditional Poetry". The two articles there, present an argument that validates our contention.

14.This writer, as a final-year undergraduate in Nigeria's oldest university, was taught Oral Literature by one of Nigeria's most informed professors in the field. Much as the professor tried to illustrate, in the English language, some characteristics, genres and stylistics of African Oral Literature, he had on numerous occasions to perform certain genres, like chants and incarnations, in his own mother tongue. Their appreciation of the total stylistics of the genre illustrated was therefore severely limited.

15. For some of the sources of folk characteristics of Nigerian Pidgin English, see Bernard Mafeni, "Nigerian Pidgin", London, 95–112.

WORKS CITED

Abalogu, Uchegbulam, Garbo Ashiwaju and Regina Amadi-Tshiwala. Eds. *Oral Poetry in Nigeria.* Lagos: Nigeria Magazine, 1981. Print.

Adekoya, Olusegun, "Myth and Unity", Paper presented at the 5th Congress of the Nigerian Folklore Society, Ahmadu Bello University, Zaria. Dec. 2–5, 1985.

Amkpa, A.D. "Hegemony and Drama: the Crisis of Nigerian Literary Drama". Paper presented at the 5th Conference of the Nigerian Folklore Society, Ahmadu Bello University, Zaria, 2–5 Dec, 1985.

Babalola, S.A. *The Content and Form of Yoruba Ijala.* Oxford: Clarendon Press, 1966. Print.

Darah, G.G. "Igho Sh'emu Sua: A Note on the Capitalist Ideology of Urhobo Oral Literature". *Theory and Practice* (Journal of Nigerian Academy of Arts, Science and Technology). 2 (1977). 187–207. Print.

—. "Oral Literature". *Nigeria: Peoples, States and Culture before 1800.* Falola, Toyin & Adeniran Ed. Lagos: John West, 1982. 4–12. Print.

Degh, Linda. "The Study of Ethnicity in Modern European Ethnology". Oinas, Felix. Ed. *Folklore, Nationalism and Politics.* Columbus: Slavica, 1978. 9–17. Print.

Diop, Cheik. *The Cultural Unity of Negro Africa.* Chicago: Third World Press, 1978. Print.

Dorson, Richard. ed. *African Folklore.* New York: Doubleday, 1972. Print.

—. "Is Folklore a Discipline?" *Folklore* (Autumn, 1973). 10–22. Print.

Ebeogu, Afam. "Feminist Temperament in Igbo Birth Songs". *Power and Powerlessness of Women in West African Orality.* Umea papers in English 15, 1992. 43–62. Print.

—. "Media Comedy for Nigeria's Folk: the Example of the Adventures of the 'Masquerade' Drama Group". *Nigeria Magazine* 55. 2 (April–June 1987). 1–12. Print.

Finnegan, Ruth. *Oral Literature in Africa.* London: Oxford University Press, 1970; Cambridge: Open Book Publishers, 2012. Print.

—. *Oral Poetry: Its Nature, Significance and Social Content* Cambridge: Cambridge University Press, 1977. Print.

Hornby, A.S., E.V. Gatenby and H. Wakefield. *The Advanced Dictionary of Current English*. London: Oxford University Press, 1963. Print.

Karaya, Laikudi. "Myth and the Formation of National Consciousness: the Bayajida as Myth". Paper presented at the 5th Congress of the Nigeria Folklore Society, Ahmadu Bello University, Zaria. Dec. 2.5, 1985.

Kofoworola, E.O. "Concepts and Challenging Factors of Creative Developments in the Myths and Legends of Nigerian Folklore". *Folklore and National Development*, 181–209.Ife: Nigerian Folklore Society, 1985.81–99. Print.

Lord, Albert. "Perspectives on Recent Work on oral Literature". *Oral Literature (Seven Essays)*. Ed. Duggan, J.J. Edinburgh and London: Scottish Academics Press, 1975. 9–17. Print.

Nigerian Folklore Society. Folklore and National Development. Proceedings of the 4th Congress of the Nigerian Folklore Society, University of Ife, Ile Ife, Dec. 17–21, 1984. Print.

—. *Folklore and the Challenges of Integration.* Proceedings of the 5th Congress of the Nigerian Folklore Society, Ahmadu Bello University; Zaria, 2–5 Dec; 1985. Print.

Nwaka, G.I. "Urban and Industrial Culture in Igboland: The Crisis of Adaptation". *Igbo Political Systems.* Paper presented at the 1985 Ahiajoku Colloquium. Owerri: Ministry of Information, Culture, Youth and Sports, 1985. 47–63.

Ogede, Ode "Oral Poetry And National Integration: The Example of Igede Poets Odeh Igbang and Micah Ichegbeh". *Folklore and the Challenges of National Integration.* Ife: Nigerian Folklore Society, 1985. 171–191. Print.

Ojoade, Olowo. "Ethnic Stereotyping in Nigerian Folklore: A Factor of National Development". *Folklore and National Development,* Ife: Nigerian Folklore Society, 1985.143–180.

Ojoade Olowo: "Folklore an Agent of National Integration in Nigeria". Paper presented at the 5th Congress of the Nigerian Folklore Society held at Ahmadu Bello University, Zaria, 2–5 Dec., 1985.

Okanlawon, O.L. "On Problems of Oral Literature Research in Nigeria Today". *Nigeria Magazine 146* (1983). 73–84. Print.

Okpewho, Isidore. *African Oral Literature: Backgrounds, Character and Continuity.* Bloomington: Indiana University Press, 1992. Print.

—. "Comparativism and Parochial Imperative: an African Literature Dilemma". Paper presented at the 5th Ibadan Annual Literature Conference, July 29–Aug. 1, 1980.

—. *Myth in Africa.* New York: Columbia: Cambridge University Press, 1983. Print.

—. *The Heritage of African Poetry.* Harlow: Longman, 1985. Print.

—. "The Relevance of Oral Literary Study in Africa". Paper presented in the Institute of African Studies Seminar, University of Ibadan, 27 March, 1977.

Osinowo, Gbolade. "Folk Heroes and Nationalism". *Folklore and National Development,* 79–90. Print.

Ugonna, Nnabenyi. "Ala and Discipline in Igbo Society". *Folklore and National Development,* 273–295. 283–289. Print.

Ward, Barry. "Some observations on the Teaching of Folklore: North American and Nigerian Models". *Folklore and National Development,* 1985. 743–755. Print.

Williams, J.A. "Radicalism and Professionalism in Folklore Studies: A Comparative Perspective". *Journal of Folklore Institute* xi. 3 (March, 1979). 131–140. Print.

Yahaya, Ibrahim Yaro. "Traditional Poets as Moulders of Public Opinion: The Hausa Poet". Abalogu et. al. *Oral Poetry in Nigeria.* Lagos: Nigeria Magazine, 1981. 149–151.

Chapter Two

Text and Context of African Oral Performance

Isaac M. Udoh

Implicated in the assessment of text and context in oral performance is an understanding of the social system within which the text, the performer and performance function. This social system incorporates a gamut of masks, costume, music, festival, masquerade, ritual performance, funeral, initiation ceremony, mime, impersonation and the moment. In these, the bent, proclivity, aspirations, attitude of mind, language, fears, social relationships, philosophical disposition, logic and worldview, of a people are brought to the fore and explored for their potential to mitigate and effectuate life as it is.

Oral literature is a product of and a vehicle for the revelation of the heritage of societies. It is a vehicle for the affirmation and refutation of reality and a means for achieving transcendental reality. As a performed and aural activity, oral literature exists for the moment; that moment when creativity bespeaks the life and existence of a people. It is that moment when all else come to a halt in the celebration of man. Oral literature is not only about performance, which is "stylized movement, characteristic rhythm, highly trained speech and voice, and studied gestures" (Awoonor 70), but an aggregation of the oral creative text and the condition within which that text is created and related and enjoyed, and, all of these taken together, creates a link which aids the accretion of all the elements in society.

At the heart of oral literature is its orality. That is the whole gamut of the performance of an oral text before a live audience. Performance is often said to be an activity that is contrived, realized, achieved, created; an activity that is achieved within a social context and this context determines its realizability and the performer's flights of creative exuberance. It is what engenders and enhances creativity in oral literature. It is different from the private moment of Wordsworth's "Perfect recollection in tranquility". It is a boisterous concourse wherein history mingles with tradition, culture jostles with religion, and education, entertainment and information coalesce for the rapprochement of the past, the present and the future.

Oral literature incorporates self-constitutive activities that are at once deliberated and spontaneous in their conception and delivery. Since oral literature does not aim at mere entertainment, but also the codification of beliefs, culture and experiences, its creation is aimed at the enablement of existence.

In the African context, orality was the vehicle by which a great majority of people "regulated themselves, organized their present and their pasts, the means by which Africa made its existence, its history long before the colonial and imperial presence of the west manifested itself" (Gunner 1). The African 'spoke' his experiences and recorded them on the tables of his heart from where they were transferred from one generation to another by word of mouth, unlike his Western counterpart who had the privilege of writing, and ultimately printing, with which to record his experiences. By the spoken word he regulated himself and did not need tomes to exact order in the society from which he evolved.

He created oral performances which interpret the make-up of the society while also allowing for the verbalization of the social order, thereby giving body and active presence to the social thoughts which percolate to form the fabric with which the social condition is woven and governed. The text of these social thoughts of society is created out of the social condition and, whether oral or written, functions to relocate the past and the future in the presence in order to teach lessons, thereby demonstrating the historicality of the oral text. Oral literature as a constitutive activity functions to mediate and cement social relations and ties at all the existential levels.

THE TEXT

The text of oral performance does indeed exist, even as there exists one for written literature. But whereas the one for written literature remains the same from age to age, that of oral literature is unstable and evanescent.

A text is loosely defined as a written material that is connected with learning, with the impartation of knowledge. In this statement the word 'written' is highlighted, and it tends to negate the possibility of applying it to oral literature. But 'written' is not restricted to a physical medium like a book. We know that ideas, concepts can be written on the tables of one's heart. It is in this light that we appreciate the text in oral literature. The 'writtenness' of an oral text is invisibly present in the mind of people and it is from this well that it is constituted and presented.

Again, whereas the text of written discourse is fixed and visibly tangled, the oral text becomes visible only at performance, and even then, only as echoes richocheting in the minds of the recipient audience. It must be emphasized here that the oral text is usually very precise in its demands; it cannot be divorced from its moment of realization and that moment of realization unveils a framework of expectations and assumptions which, in concert with various accompaniments—gestures, rhythm, a store of formulas and themes and composition techniques (Lord 99), the performer's intricate rallying with his audience, tonal shifts and emphasis—conduce to invigorate the text into what it is.

Ruth Finnegan observes that:

> Oral literature is by definition dependent on a performer who formulates it into words on a specific occasion—there is no other way in which it can be realized as a literary product ... without its oral realization and direct rendition by a singer or speaker, an unwritten literary piece cannot easily be said to have any continued or independent existence at all (2).

The text therefore, is not a finished work. It can never be finished. The oral text has an evenascent presence, always evolving, always

being mitigated by the moment, by the occasion; that moment of ac-
tuation, of activation, where the intangible presence is fused into the
tangible. The text is therefore devoid of life or lifeless until it is shaped
and given life by the performer at the moment of performance. For
the text, performance is not a moment of creation; it is a moment *not
unlike after God had modeled man out of sand and whispered breath into him and
man came alive.*

The text, therefore, because it is ever-evolving, always being
shaped, always metamorphosing to suit and address the moment, is always pliable and thus, evinces an amorphous proportion. For instance,
the oral text of the *Sundiata* epic has a basic form that stretches chrono-
logically form beginning, to middle, to the end. Between the beginning
and the end there are concourses of experiences depicting various ris-
es and falls in the lives of the characters as shown in diagram 'A' below:

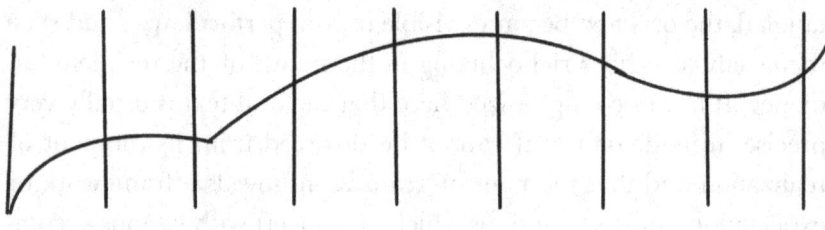

A. Beginning   Middle   End

'A' may represent the basic text which celebrates the life, time, exploit, and triumphs, of the Maghan Sundiata. Any rendition seeking
a chronological recitation of his life would usually unveil as in 'A'
above.

We however know that the oral poet/performer is not bound
by the chronological rendition which the fixity of written discourse
imposes on the writer/reader. Performance is activated and actuat-
ed by prevailing concerns and the performer is allowed the liberty
of choosing any episode/section of the existing form with which to
pass comment on the dominant concerns of the material moment.
He is at liberty to begin a performance at the middle of the text, if

such would help address the concerns of the moment. Thus, the text performed at moments 1, 2 and 3 may present as follows:

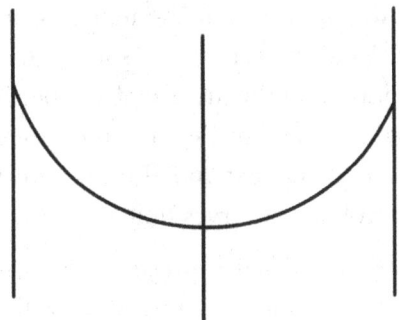

B. Moment 2

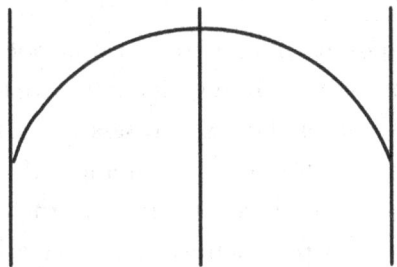

C. Moment 2

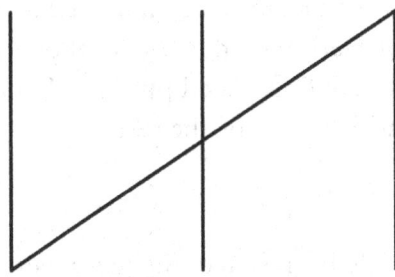

D. Moment 3

The texts of the three moments are all taken from the original Sundiata form, but each evinces a uniqueness that is determined by 'the moment' and the personality of the performer.

As much as we can say that the text of oral literature is amorphous, it is an eclectic literary piece subject to the vagaries of the moment of rendition and the artifice of the performer. Robust articulateness and flights of creative exuberance are germane in the creation and evolution of the text and also the determinants by which is created. F.B Akporobaro observes that:

> Because it is a performed expression, the artistic qualities of the given form are intimately bound up with the given social occasion in which it is performed and the performing skill of the artist himself. The emotional tones, pitch changes, ... which the reciter can bring into play in the course of his performance are often lost completely in the written version which has no life or phonological aesthetic possibilities (4)

Albert B. Lord, emphasizing that "an oral poem is not composed *for* but *in* performance" (13), highlights the contribution of spontaneity in the rendition of the text, possessed and goaded by the particular experiences of the material moment the performer creates. Even where what he renders is taken from the communal pool, his virtuosity and robust articulateness differentiates his text from that of others. That particular text performed becomes and interpretation of that moment in time and distinct from other texts modeled after other moments.

We must pause to mention that text which is presented to the audience is not presented in vain. That is, it has a purpose to it—any of entertainment, information and education—and as such it must be constrained to fulfill its stated purpose. How well this is done is dependent on the formatics of the text.

THE CONTEXT

As have already been stated, the text relies on the moment, the context, for its realization. Context has been defined as meaning "outside the text". Context is said to be the situation, events, or information which are related to something and that help you to understand it better. Ventilated, while text is the inside of something, context is its outside knowledge or condition that adds to and deepens knowledge of the text. In oral literature we cannot talk about 'context' without performance. The 'con' of text can only be experienced during performance, it is here that additional information like historical or biographical facts, dominant social concerns, the occasion marked, are attached and allowed to ventilate the text to present a fuller more vibrant material to the audience. Context, therefore, can be said to express the living condition of the text in performance.

Context of performance reveals an interpenetrating range of presentational formatics which are partly psychological, linguistic, social, cultural, traditional;, etc, all of which constitute the totality of experience. When all of these are thrown into the mix, they task the attitudinal as well as the technical suavity of the performer in a revelatory moment where the past, the present and the future of given societies are laid bare.

Bronislaw Malinowski avers that, "the text ... is extremely important, but without the context it remains lifeless ... the story is vastly enhanced ... and given its proper character by the manner in which it is told" (219). Context is the moment; the material moment in time that a literary event that is contrived and realized takes place. It is at that moment that a literary text containing a sliver or a whole corpus of a people's experiences is experienced. It is often said that a literary text comes alive as we experience it. The "experiencing" is the moment; the context, the ambience, within which the text, incorporating a people's experiences, is made to come alive.

Context therefore is the enfolding scaffolding with which a text is rendered; it could be a state of mind—happiness, sadness,—it could be a perceptible condition—war, plague etc; it could be biographical, timing or personality. Whatever it is, it enhances and enriches the verbal narrative. It is context that situates experience, especially where that experience is not an original one; an old, usual and common-place experience can be better appreciated if it is contextualized. The meaning of a text can change as its context changes. For instance, Okonkwo's (*Things Fall Apart)* personality has undergone radical transformation over the decades as the society moves farther among from the conditions that created him. Where he had, perhaps, six decades ago, been valorized as representation of the brave, thoroughbred African ideologue who would rather die than participate in an offensive change, today, because of a deeper and better perception of the psychological make-up of man, in some quarters he is perceived as a weakling, who takes the easy way out rather than face the demanding task of negotiating an unfolding unfamiliar terrain. It can be argued that the change in perception is occasioned by context. Today, shifting interest, change in surrounding, culture, education, historical contexts have mandated a re-reading of Okonkwo's personality.

We had earlier stated that context expresses the living condition of the text in performance. The "living condition" here demonstrates the prevailing social, cultural, political, religious etc, conditions that a text must very well be modeled on. If literature is said to be a mirror, a presentation, a reflection, of the lived-life, what it mirrors or reflects or represents is not static. It is very much like the views a passenger gets as he travels in a car through the countryside; he remains in a static position within the cab but the view is ever-passing, adding and deleting, as the car moves on. This therefore percolates to indicate that, like man in the car, the text of oral literature may remain static because of communal ownership, but the ever-evolving revelatory audience of the enfolding human condition gives it at once a hue that is transient, that is reflective of the moment and markedly related to that environment.

THE PERFORMANCE

Ruth Finnegan avers that performance "lies at the heart of the whole concept of oral literature" (28) and the oral text—poetry, narration, drama—has no existence outside its performance. Unlike written literature with its fixity, its one lone reader and independence, oral literature is a vibrant flexible, context-dependent artistic form which emphasizes the audience, the nature of the audience, the environment within which the oral text is appreciated (context), the performer, his personality and the resources available to him at the place and moment of performance.

The moment of "performance is a moment of creation for the (performer)" (Lord 14), a moment where, with a neutral blank piece of narrative experience, (the text), the performer, aided by his dramatic ability and narrative skill, creates a socio-cultural context within which issues of importance are related.

Okpewho (42) posits that:

> It is ... in the study of performance that we are able to see the essential character of oral literature as distinct from written literature, that is, as an art form *created in the warm presence of an audience as against the cold privacy of the written work (The Oral... 42 Emphasis mine)*.

It has been stated earlier that performance is a contrived, realized, achieved and created endeavour. It is a subjective activity wherein an individual brings alive before an audience, the history, culture and tradition of a people in order to entertain, educate, and inform them. It is a stylized activity that is not carried out in vain but aimed and directed at the elucidation of germane concerns and the imposition of some form of order on the chaos of given society.

Performance as a realized, contrived, achieved and created activity is variegated and the multi-colouredness is effected by issues of age of the participants, the occasion, setting, the time of day, the audience, the accompaniment, if any, and so on. No two performances can be the same. It is a context-determined activity and its is realized "within the only context where it is meaningful, before an audience" (Okpewho, *African Oral 42*). The audience is a strong factor in performance and determinedly affect the performance. Okpewho asserts that, "The excellence of a song is not determined by the results of a single performance: rather it is influenced by the audience atmosphere (rapport, indifferences, hostility) within which it is performed at any one time" (*The Epic 51*).

The audience is therefore greatly implicated in the performer's walk towards excellence. If he views himself as a public performer, working for the audience, he has an eye for that audience, consciously crafting each performance to please and excite it. He is pivotal in what Okpewho refers to as "the drama of the moment" *(The Epic...* 53)*; employing all the resources at his disposal to regale his audience and impart valuable knowledge. The public performer is an electric, dynamic character who, being caught up by the drama of the moment, is goaded into an exuberant delivery by a consciousness of the responsibility of his office as historian, reciter, entertainer, educator and informant. Djeli Mamuodou Kouyate, the performer in D.T. Niane's *Sundiata* asserts:

> I teach kings the history of their ancestors.... Listen to my word, you who want to know ... By my mouth you will get to know the story of the ancestor of great Mali... (1)

This is purely imperious! As we listen to him, we see an elaborated expansiveness to his knowledge, his ability and the breath of the canvas he paints. His words evoke mysteries, and a mythical ambience which imposes him pointedly on the psyche of his society. His delivery is dramatically acute and revelatory and thus heightens the acceptance of his message. Whatever joy results in a rendition of this nature results from the performer's blending of various factors to create harmony.

Harmony in performance is achieved through the performer's awareness of the three categories in oral literature: textual knowledge, contextual knowledge and performance knowledge. The first two are usually appreciated by both the audience and the performer while the third reside principally with the performer.

During performance, the performer accumulates, combines, recombines, models and remodels, his material in order to present a refined artistic experience (Lord 26). The product he produces is at once a product of what he already knows and what he has created anew, a recombinant variety that is at once known to the audience and brand new; there is pure delight in hearing an old phrase rendered in an entirely new and refreshing manner and this evolves a vital and evocative imagistic literary experience.

Further, composition, generally, and oral performance, specifically, is based on usefulness and necessity; usefulness of the occasion and the necessity of the performance, at the one level, and usefulness and necessity of the materials at the disposal of the artist, at another level. The relevance of the occasion impinges on and affects performance, the choice of images, concerns, tone, language and even the mood evoked.

Again, performance is based on timing and sociability. During performance paralinguistic resources such as gestures, body movement; multimedia, such as material paraphernalia like costume, musical instrument; material culture, shared generic conventions of performance, socio-cultural conventions; cultural norms and practices; social interaction, local vocational and climatologically factors, combine to enliven and broach communality and integration. The artistry of the performer is not his own alone—the ornamentation, richness and human touches of character which he employs—are a product of "communal entertainment and collective artistry" (Bauman 69).

He approaches performance with a percolating knowledge, what Thomas Dubois calls "native hermeneutics" (246), of the occasion and audience. It is a sense-pattern developed by the audience, and the performer also, since he is usually a member of the audience's community, to arrive at or construct meaning. Shared experiences and worldview, communal ethos and background, furnish extra-textual blocks with which the audience appreciates and accesses the interpenetrating maze of ricocheting artistic snippets evolving before their very eyes.

The performer taps into the resources at his disposal to arrive at aesthetic experience during performance. They include: nature of the performance/occasion, the person of the performer, memory, talent, audience effect—visual and aural—music, formulae, ventilation, etc. All of these are props which he maximizes to great effect.

He also has the aesthetic resources of the performance environment; the warmth and pyrotechnics of the crackling and glowing embers resulting from the bonfire, the elements, the chirping of birds and insects, all of which are external to the narration, but which are available to the performer to be used to captivate and retain the audience attention as well as the transfer of cognitive experience (Sekoni 139).

CONCLUSION

We must here reiterate that the text, the object of perceived experience, in oral literature relates to the external universe and is constrained to reflect that external universe in order for it to be truly situated. As much as we cannot experience experiences outside of a setting, so also can the text not be seen or experienced without the context. Context aptly dresses experiences and imposes a perceptible state or scaffolding to it, framing and projecting it within acceptable and available ambience. And oral performance is seen to be not merely a "distinctive sign" of a given social condition or moment but a potential means of exerting pressure upon or transforming social conditions and power relations (James 470).

Oral literature, like its written counterpart, ultimately aims at the transfer of cognitive experience. The text, context and performance in oral literature are implicated in the transfer of cognitive experience. They do not individually achieve this; because they exist in a coterminous relationship; they are able to objectify experience, relate the experience to the external world and project it in an aesthetically acceptable manner. How well this is done exemplifies oral literature.

WORKS CITED

Abrams, M.H. *The Mirror and the Lamp: Romantic Theory and the Critical Tradition.* Oxford: Oxford Univ Press 1971. Print.

Akporobaro, Fred B.O. *Introduction to African Oral Literature. Revised Ed.* Ikeja: Lagos: Princeton Pub. Company, 2012. Print.

Awoonor, Kofi. *The Breast of the Earth: a Survey of the History, Culture and Literature of Africa South of the Sahara.* New York: Nok Pub International, 1975. Print.

Bauman, Richard and Charles L. Briggs. "Poetics and Performance as Critical Perspectives on Language and Social Life". *Annual Review of Anthropology.* 19 1990. 59–88. Print.

Dubois, Thomas A.. "Native Hermeneutics: Traditional Means of Interpreting Lyric Songs in Northern Europe". *Journal of American Folklore.* 109. 235–66 1996, Print.

Lord, Alfred B. *The Singer of Tales.* Cambridge, Massachusetts: Harvard Univ. Press, 1960, Print.

Finnegan, Ruth. *Oral Literature in Africa.* Oxford and Cambridge: Claredon Press and Open University Books Publishers, 1970 and 2012. Print.

—. *Oral Poetry: its Nature, Significance and Social Context.* Cambridge: Cambridge Univ. Pres, 1977. Print.

Gunner, Liz. "Africa and Orality". *The Cambridge History of African and Caribbean Literature* 1. Abiola Irele and Simon Gikandi. Cambridge: Cambridge Univ. Press, 2004. Print.

James, Deborah. "Music of Origin: Class, Social, Category and the Performers and Audiences of Kiba, a South African Genre". *Africa* 67. 3 (1997). 454–75. Print.

Malinowski, Bronislaw. *Myth in Primitive Psychology.* New York: Norton. 1926. Print.

Niane, D.T. *Sundiata: An Epic of Old Mali.* London: Longman Group, 1965. Print.

Okpewho, Isidore. *African Oral Literature: Backgrounds, Character and Continuity.* Bloomington: Indiana University Press, 1992. Print.

—. *The Epic in Africa: Toward a Poetic of the Oral Performance.* New York: Columbia University Press, 1979. Print.

—. ed. *The Oral Performance in Africa.* Ibadan: Spectrum Books, 1990.

Onuekwusi, Jasper A. Fundamentals of African Oral literature. Owerri: Alphabet Nigeria Pub, 2001. Print.

Chapter Three

Flexibility of Oral Art
in Relation to Modern African Society

F.U. Okoh

INTRODUCTION

Three key terms require definition in this topic. These are flexibility, oral art and modern African society. This is necessary so as to clear the ground on which the discourse will germinate and to place the issues in proper perspective. It will also foreground these terms and point the direction in which the discussion will go. In the *Longman Dictionary of Contemporary English*, flexibility is entered as "the ability to change or be changed easily to suit any new situation". This implies the quality of changing to suit a new situation. The change is usually necessary because of the change in the situation.

Oral art has been qualified by different names. Some scholars have called it traditional literature, orature, folk literature, folklore and oracy. Okpewho defines oral art or oral literature simply as "literature delivered by word of mouth" (*African Oral Literature, 3*). Their production and consumption is usually simultaneous. It is preserved in the memory of the performer and passed down from one generation to another by word of mouth. Oral literature comprises forms like folktales, riddles, parables, proverbs, songs, witticisms, panegyrics and so on which are composed, transmitted or communicated by word of mouth. "Modern African Society" refers to the post-colonial period or the post-independence Africa. The thrust of this chapter is to demonstrate how oral art in Africa has changed in order to suit the changes in modern African society. Put in another way, it is to examine the extent to which oral art has readjusted to modern African society.

THE CONCEPT OF ORAL ART OR FOLKLORE

Oral art can be known as folklore, which is a more embracing term. Folklore, morphologically speaking, is a compound word derived from 'folk', meaning 'people', and 'lore', signifying knowledge, information related to a particular or certain group of people. The word was coined by William John Thoms in 1846 in a letter he wrote to *The Athenaeum* under the pen-name, Ambrose Marton. Before his usage of this term, the nomenclature "popular antiquities" was employed to designate the same issue. Folklore is also often referred to as oral tradition, orature, oral literature. This concept is multi-disciplinary in nature. As a result, scholars in linguistics, anthropology, sociology, literature, art, mythology, rites, rituals, religion, theology, philosophy, aesthetics, custom and belief, cosmology and so on are all interested in folklore and even tenaciously clutch and cling to it as belonging to them. However, it "squarely falls into the domain of the folklorist" (Ezugu 10). Arising from the multi-disciplinary nature of the matter, there are divergent views and definitions. For instance, Maria Leach's *Standard Dictionary of Folklore, Mythology, and Legends* contains twenty-one definitions. It is important to observe that there is no one comprehensive definition of the term. The study of the materials constituting folklore is known as folkloristics. Even though the earliest works on folklore by the Grimm Brothers on household tales appeared in 1812, this does not negate the fact that folklore is as old as mankind.

William Bascom, an anthropologist, defines folklore as

> ...a part of culture but not the whole of culture. It includes myths songs, legends, tales, proverbs, riddles, the texts of ballads and other songs, and other forms of lesser importance, but not folk art, folk dance, folk music, folk costume, folk medicine, folk custom, or folk belief ... All folklore is orally transmitted, but not all that is orally transmitted is folklore. (7).

Another folklorist, Samuel P. Bayard, disagrees with Bascom on his exclusion of traditional belief and custom. Perhaps, a more interesting definition relevant to our work is that by Alan Dundes.

According to him,

> Folklore includes, myths, legends, folktales, jokes, proverbs, riddles, chants, charms, blessings, curses, oaths, insults, retorts, taunts, teases, toasts, tongue-twisters, and greetings, and leave-taking formulas (e.g. see you later, alligator). It also includes folk costume, folk dance, folk drama (and mime), folk art, folk belief (or superstition), folk medicine, folk instrumental music (e.g. fiddle tunes), folk songs (e.g. lullabies, ballads), folk speech (e.g. slang), folk similes (e.g. blind as a bat), folk metaphors (e.g. to paint the town red), and names (e.g. nicknames and place names). Folk poetry ranges from oral epics to autograph—book verse, epitaphs, latrinalia (writings on the walls of public bathrooms), lime-ricks, ball bouncing rhymes, jump rope rhymes, finger and toe rhymes (to determine who will be "it" in games), and nursery rhymes. The list of folklore forms also contains games; gestures; symbols; prayers (e.g. graces); practical jokes; folk etymologies; food recipes; quilts and embroidery designs; house; barn, and fence types; street vendors cries; and even the traditional sounds used to summon animals or to give them commands. There are such minor forms as mnemonic devices (e.g. the name Roy 6 Biv to remember the colors of the spectrum in order), envelope sealers (e.g. S.AK—sealed with A Kiss), and the traditional comments made after body emissions (e.g. after burps or sneezes). There are such major forms as festivals and special day (or holiday) customs (e.g. Christmas, Halloween and birthday). (5).

The list is almost all inclusive, but it is by no means comprehensive. MacEdward Leach states that "folklore is the generic term to designate the customs, beliefs, traditions, tales, magic practices, proverbs, songs, etc, in short the accumulated knowledge of a homogenous unsophisticated people" (10). However, it must be observed that not only unsophisticated people have folklore. As an art form, folklore is usually transmitted orally and is stored in the memory of the teller. This implies that the death of any performer shuts down a whole library of oral forms. Another fact to note is that even when it is recorded, folklore remains what it is (Ezugu, 14).

Okpewho writes that

> The word folklore implies much more than just literature and in some quarters underplays the literary aspect of what the folk do. It was first used by Englishman, William John Thoms, in a letter he wrote to the *Athenaeum* at a time when the study of traditional culture was attracting a lot of attention in Britain and Europe.... Oral literature—which comprises riddles, puns, tongue-twisters, proverbs, recitations, chants, sons, and stories—represents only the verbal aspect of folklore. (*African Oral Literature. 4*).

Okpewho's concern is with making the distinction between folklore and literature. He argues that oral literature is just the verbal aspect of folklore, adding that folklore comprises traditional methods of cooking, architecture, medicine, and dressmaking as well as religion or ritual, art, instrumental music, and dance. He ends by stating that "The total body of information which a community possesses about all these things is its folklore" (5).

Alo asserts that "The African tradition of oral literature is as rich in content and variety as that of any other major cultural areas, folk or civilized, past or present. Proverbs, riddles, song and drama text, poetry, praise names are significant parts of African Oral Literature" (12). The various categories of African oral literature have a rich content and are of various forms. These are also important and culturally informative and full of the corpus of knowledge of the folk. Folklore, folk literature or oral literature can be brought squarely under the purview of folklorists. Ezugu, from this perspective, states that

> folklore can be defined as pleasurable *verbal* and sometimes *written* and *performed* works of art of the people with aesthetic value geared towards memorization, instruction, and delight. Its ultimate protection against abuse or bastardization is the people (16).

This definition introduces some interesting insights. Folklore comprises verbal, written and performed works. It also supports the view that recorded materials remain folklore. According to Ezugu, "Recorded folklore remains folklore all the same" (14). He cites the narrative Igbo examples of 'Ojiadili' legend and 'Enenebe-Ejeghio-lu' and adds that "folklore is receiving a lot of attention in writing since the twentieth century especially in the study of the cowboy, the mountaineer and the Negro" (14). Amos Tutuola's stories: *The Palmwine Drinkard, My Life in the Bush of Ghosts, Simbi and the Satyr of the Dark Jungle, Feather Woman of the Jungle, The Brave African Huntress and The Wild Hunter in the Bush of Ghosts* remain African folklore though they are all published. Recording them preserves the past for the future generation. This also enriches and enhances the growth and development of modern literature. In the light of this Ezugu maintains that

> Before long many elements of our folklore would have been put into writing; this notwithstanding, they still remain our folklore. It is not the medium (oral or written) that gives them classification; it is their origin and whose property they are: the folk ... creative African writers are free to draw elements from all these and use them creatively in their poetry, drama or prose, folklore forms part of our traditional inheritance. If we read between the lines, we find some folkloric elements in the novels of Chinua Achebe, Elechi Amadi, Wole Soyinka, Ayi Kwei Armah, Ngugi Wa Thiong'o (18–10).

Another interesting dimension is the protection of folklore. The people are always prompt in ensuring that these materials are not abused or bastardized. Any instance of such is quickly corrected collectively or individually, irrespective of the person, place or occasion involved. This is done unapologetically and it is never taken as insulting. Some of the problems associated with African folklore are those of identification, propaganda and documentation.

FLEXIBILITY OF ORAL ART IN RELATION
TO MODERN AFRICAN SOCIETY

Modern African Society refers to the pos-independence era of life in Africa. This is a period in which the colonial masters have handed over the administration of African countries to Africans themselves. The white man has left but he has left behind his education, religion and other reminders of his own culture. The colonial masters and their burden have been eased off the shoulders of the people but certain attitudes and vestiges of the white man are still there. This had brought about many changes in the political, social and religious life of the people. For instance, in the area of education, there has been a drastic change from the traditional informal apprenticeship system of education to the western formal system of education. This formal system of education has influenced almost every facet of life in Africa. Modern African writers who have been beneficiaries of this system of education have bent the oral forms of folklore to serve their purpose in their writings.

Okpewho has identified at least four ways by which African writers rework materials from the oral tradition in their works. These are classified as:

(i). Tradition preserved—the transfer of oral art to a literature tradition, e.g., Thomas Mofolo's *Chaka,* Taban Lo Liyon's *Fixions;*

(ii). tradition observed—the transfer of concepts and motifs from the literate to the oral tradition, incorporating same within in the latter—e.g. Fagunwa's *The Forest of a Thousand Daemons,* J.P. Clark's *Ozidi Saga.*

(iii). tradition refined—The tales in their old forms are dropped; only their figures are adopted for the essences of values they embody. Wole Soyinka's works evince this practice most.

(iv). Tradition revised—Old mythic traditions are revisited with a view to furnishing a new visions (*Myth in Africa,* 155–221).

It is, therefore, not surprising to find in the works of African writers aesthetic forms from their traditional heritage. In the novel genre,

Chinua Achebe's works, *Things Fall Apart, No longer At Ease*, and *Arrow of God* are exemplars of this practice. In the novels, there is a fluid and healthy admixture of elements from the oral tradition of the Igbo with the formal and technical considerations of this Western genre. There is a frequent recourse to folklore like proverbs, riddles, jokes, witticisms, aphorisms, folk-tales, and so on. In these works, there is also a heavy reliance on festivals. The living and the dead are known to mingle very freely in festivals, since these are considered the highest communal interaction between these spheres of existence. Masked spirits were often also in attendance. Nnolim in his "Folk tradition and Achebe's Novels" has highlighted the significant position of masked spirits thus:

> For the masked spirit in traditional Igbo society was a vehicle of much more than manners: it was the repository of what was sacred, mythical, mysterious, cultural, superstitious, and supernatural in Igbo culture. It was the throbbing centre of its folk tradition and folk ways (35).

Nnolim even identifies, in Achebe's novels, a reliance on folkloric structures. He asserts that *"Things Fall Apart, Arrow of God and No Longer At Ease* seem each to be based on the folkloric formula of 'exile and return', which formula offers the basic bipartite structure of the novels" (40). The precursors of the narrative genre in African literature had also based their works on the oral tradition. Thomas Mofolo's *Chaka* (1925), Peter Nwanna's *Omenuko* (1938), and Amos Tutuola's *The Palmwine Drinkard* (1953) were all made possible because of the oral tradition that informs them.

In the genre of poetry, poets like Kofi Awoonor, J.P. Clark,. Okot p'Bitek, Wole Soyinka have enriched their poems with elements from their respective folk traditions. Awoonor, especially, has relied heavily on the dirge traditional of his native Ewe of Ghana, and has drawn his images from this source. Awoonor himself has acknowledged his source when he wrote that " The Ewe dirge has fascinated me as a complete form. Its use of the elegiac tone, statement exhortation, and prayer combine into a totally effective poetic medium" *(The Breast of the Earth,* 202). This attitude is highly effective in one of Awoonor's earliest poems, 'Songs of Sorrow'. J.P. Clark, in his poems, borrows very artistically from his native Ijaw imagery and idiom.

Perhaps, a very significant poet here, is Okot p'Bitek. His *Song of Lawino* is based on Acoli tradition. The images and idioms are taken directly from the Luo as recorded during the Gulu festival in Uganda. In an interview with Robert Serumaga in London, February 1967, Okot p'Bitek had this to say about his work:

> When I was doing my work on the oral literature of the people of Northern Uganda, I first got my inspiration. I found that the poetry was rich, the oral literature was full-blooded, the dance was wonderful and the music just inspiring; and I couldn't just stop; I just wanted to go on, and this was the great inspiration behind the Gulu festival ... (*African Writers Talking,* 150).

Nwoga sees in p,Bitek's poetry "the impact of his culture on his imagination" (32). According to Gerald Moore:

> Okot p,Bitek lends fire, imagination and tragic passion to this traditionally minded heroine ... (who) uses the image of traditional Acoli funeral and dancing songs, rather as Achebe's elders use proverbs, to give her song depth within the culture and enable it to drink from the abundant spring of inherited experience (*The Chosen tongue* as cited in Nwoga, OCMAP, 32).

Another very significant poet in this tradition is Wole Soyinka whose poetry borrows heavily from the Yoruba pantheon and mythology. He is one poet who has consciously and unapologetically nominated Ogun as his own Muse. In Okpewho's estimation,

> Soyinka himself has done more than any other African writer to make the symbols of traditional African Mythology the basis of his creative work: in various plays, novels and poems, especially his poem *Idanre* ... he had made the Yoruba god of iron, Ogun ... his ideal of the revolutionary artist constantly involved in the struggle to correct society. (*HAP,* 21).

African poets cultivate this practice, first and foremost, out of an awakening consciousness and cultural nationalism. They are aware of their rich traditional and artistic heritage. They are also aware of the violence done this heritage by Western and Islamic cultures, and the urgent need to preserve the indigenous artistic forms from further assault and extinction. Nwoga even foresees a hybrid poetic idiom arising from the symbiotic association of the oral and the western traditions ('Obscurity and Commitment 35). This development is natural judging by the fact that literature as a written activity came with the colonial masters who dictated the canons. There is, therefore, a conscious or unconscious marriage of elements from both the oral and western traditions in the works of the African writers who had directly or indirectly been exposed to the Western and Islamic systems of education. Though this trend is common to all the genres, the major thrust of this work is to investigate it in modern African drama.

Modern African drama is still experiencing some growth and development. Many playwrights and theatre practitioners are experimenting in a bid to Africanize, or at least give their works an African identity. Banham in *African Theatre today* has put it succinctly that "it is inevitable that in looking at African theatre today, we should be aware that it has developed in recent years under diverse influences, but equally we should be satisfied, to note that its basic Africanness is re-asserting itself" (1). This position finds support in Ogunba's submission that "What is being argued, however, is that it is only in the past few years, particularly since independence that drama has become properly established in many African stages" (xi).

Osofisan in 'The Origins of Drama in West Africa' defines modern African drama as the one "whose medium remains the language of the former colonizing powers, and whose techniques are borrowed from the European state" (11). Awoonor's statement that "modern drama and stagecraft in Africa owe its basic impetus to the introduction of European dramatic technique" (306) is in agreement with Osofisan's definition. This is to be expected since the dramatists had attended mission schools where plays had been dramatized using western techniques. Also, those of them who had been to university were further grilled in Shakespeare and Moliere. Conscious efforts were made, especially in Anglophone Africa, to discourage African theatre forms like dance, drumming, songs, music and so on. African traditional theatre forms such as rituals, dances, and story-telling, were left to go unheeded. In fact, the colonialists, especially the Christian missionaries, denounced these forms as barbaric and devilish'. Nwoko in 'Search for a New African Theatre' (462) makes the same point. The phenomenon of cultural superiority and suppression was also true in the other sub-regions of Africa. In 'East African Drama', Peter Nazareth writes that the numerous reasons responsible for the inability of indigenous African drama forms to lead directly "to the creation of a rich, modern East African drama ... can be traced to one root cause". 991–92).This cause, he maintains, is colonialism. B.L. Leshoai laments that "few people understand the damaging effect that the white man's religion has had on the development of drama in Africa" (115–116).

Drama did not fare better in North Africa than in the South, East, and West. Islamic religion and culture arrested the growth and development of drama in North Africa. According to Omotosho in 'Arabic Drama in North Africa', "...Islam, the religion of the Arabs, which is said to be generally against any and all forms of representational art ... is the most important and the most relevant factor responsible for the inability of the 'fleeting moments' of Arabic literature to lead to the development of any form of drama whatsoever among the Arabs"(*Theatre in Africa*, 137). This was the situation in the colonial, or pre-independence era.

When at last some of these nations became independent, the need for cultural emancipation arose. The dramatists contributed their own quota of cultural nationalism by deliberately integrating artistic forms of the oral tradition within their works. Nwoko, Adelugba, Osofisan all have appreciated and encouraged this development.

NARRATIVE FLEXIBILITY

Oral forms are also flexible in terms of structure and medium. In the works of some modern African writers, we find certain popular folktales adapted to suit their own purposes. One of such writers is the Ghananian playwright, Efua Sutherland. She has demonstrated a consciousness of the need for a consistent and continuous blending of elements from the African oral tradition with those of the West in the dramatic creations of contemporary African playwright so as to indigenize this genre of literature. In her major works to date, she has persistently explored and exploited the essential properties of her Akan culture. In *Foriwa*, for instance, she adapts a well-known folktale of the people. The tale narrates the story of a pretty and proud girl who would not marry any man chosen by her parents, but who ends up choosing a young handsome stranger. The young man later turns into a python and swallows up the girl. The moral here is that young girls who disobey their parents in such matters, which require experience and wisdom, would have only themselves to blame when the chips are down. This particular folktale is very popular and widespread in most African societies. In some of the versions, the stranger becomes a skull, spirit, or some other funny creature. Ama Ata Aidoo, another Ghananian playwright, has also adapted this tale in her play, *Anowa*, in which the heroine Anowa, rejects her parent's choice of a husband. She makes her own choice of a husband, Kofi Ako who, incidentally, practices witchcraft. He has mortgaged his sexuality and virility for his own personal wellbeing and this costs them their marriage. The marriage is fruitless and she is alienated from both her parents and husband. Other African writers like Amos Tutuola, J.P. Clark and Flora Nwapa have also built on this structure from folklore. Sutherland also subverts a traditional festival—the path—clearing festival in *Foriwa*. This treatment is, however, symbolic in the sense that it is a metaphor for the expediency of the revitalization of some aspects of the traditional and outmoded life in Kyerefaso. In *The Marriage of Anamsewa*, Efua Sutherland adapts and re-works the Akan story-telling tradition known as

'Anansesem', which she has imaginatively recoined 'Anansegoro'. Ananse is the chief character in most Ghanania folktales, something similar to the Tortoise or Hare in other traditional African societies. The play re-enacts the oral narrative through the medium of the Western stagecraft and techniques. It is good to note that whether oral forms are written or spoken they remain basically folklore. It is not the medium that necessarily determines their nomenclature but the fact that they belong to the people, the folk.

FLEXIBILITY OF ORAL ART IN THE PERFORMING ARTS

Another area where the flexibility of oral art can be observed is in the performing arts, especially music and dance. In the music of musicians like Osita Osadebey, Oliver de Coque, Ebenezer Obey, Sunny Ade and so on, we find oral forms made to serve their purposes. These forms include proverbs, parables, folk narratives, witticisms, innuendos, praise epithets etc. Osadebey, for instance, infuses his music with a lot of wise sayings which convey deep philosophical statements about life. He also employs folk narratives which teach deep lessons. Oliver de Coque employs praise epithets in his music. Prominent and wealthy members of the society are singled out and praised in the lyrical notes and to the accompaniment of drumming and dancing. At other times, clubs, societies and other groups of wealthy and powerful persons are eulogized. Yoruba musicians like Ebenezer Obey and Sunny Ade sing the 'orikis' of prominent members of society. These forms have been brought into modern African music from their traditional roots.

There are also dance and music performances which have been uprooted from their ritual bases. These include the Ijele masquerade performances and the Ohafia/Abiriba war dances, the akuko-na-egwu among the Igbo. The most prominent among these is Mike Ejiagha's ballad forms in which he makes far-reaching philosophical statements and teaches great lessons. This trend of bending oral art to serve modern realities can be observed in the modernist tendencies in the Yoruba Alarinjo theatre. The Alarinjo is a travelling theatre.

It relies heavily on folktales, oriki, song, dance, praise epithets, storey telling, the riddling game and so on.

ORAL ART AND ELECTRONIC MEDIA

Another interesting development is the recording forms in the electronic media. Modern science and technology have also influenced oral art in Africa. Some of the folktales now live not only in the memory of their tellers but also in electronic media like CD, DVD, MP3, television, computer and so on and so forth. It must be stressed that this is a happy development as it serves to preserve the materials. It should be emphasized that though materials have been recorded they still remain art at base. They belong to the people; they are folk art or folklore.

CONCLUSION

This chapter has examined flexibility of oral art in relation to modern African society. It reflected how modernity introduced through western education had affected oral forms in Africa. Oral art has adapted to this society in terms of medium. Some of the works have since passed from the oral to the written medium, implicating the element of fluidity or what some critics have termed the oral-to-written transformation. There has also been some kind of narrative flexibility where different writers introduce variations in their own versions of the same tales. This trend was also observed in the performing arts where oral art forms are infused in the music of our popular musicians. It has also been seen in the electronic media as some of these forms have now been recorded and documented. These changes are not detrimental but auspicious to these oral forms as they help to preserve and perpetuate them.

WORKS CITED

Abrams, M.H. & Harpham, G. *A Glossary of Literary Terms* (8th ed.). Boston: Michael Rosenberger, 2005. Print.

Alo, L.K. 'Oral Tradition As History'. *An Encyclopedia of The Arts*. Vol.61

(2006). Print.

Awoonor, K. *The Breast of the Earth. New York: NOK Publishers Int.,* 1975. Print.

Banham, M. *African Theatre Today.* London: Pitman Publishing Ltd, 1976. Print.

Bascom, W. 'Folklore and Anthropology', *Journal of American Folklore, 66 (1953). 283–90. Cited in Ezugu,* 'Folklore in Africa, unpublished Book Chapter 7.

Cosmo, Pieterse, ed. *African Writers Talking.* London: Heinemann, 1978. Print.

Dundes, A. *The Study of Folklore.* New Jersey: Englewood Cliffs, 1965. Print.

Leach, M. ed. *Standard Dictionary of Folklore, Mythology and Legend.* Cambridge: Harper & Row, 1972. Print.

Leshoai, B.L. 'South African Theatre'. *Theatre in Africa.* Oyin Ogunba and Abiola Irele Eds. Ibadan: Ibadan University Press, 1978. Print.

Longman Dictionary of Contemporary English. Essex: Pearson Education Ltd., 2003. Print.

Moore, G. *The Chosen Tongue.* In Nwoga D.I. 'Obscurity and Commitment in Modern African Poetry'. *African Literature Today.* Repr. 1982. Print.

Nazareth, P.: 'East African Drama'. *Theatre in Africa.* Ed. Oyin Ogumba and Abiola Irele Ibadan: University Press, 1978. Print.

Nnolim, C. 'The Form and Function of Folk Tradition and Achebe's Novel". *Ariel* 14.1, (January 1983). 35–47. Print.

Nwoga, D.I. 'Modern African Poetry: The Domestication of a Tradition'. *African Literature Today 6* (1982):. 10–22. Print.

Nwoko, D. 'Search for a New African Theatre'. *Drama and Theatre in Africa: a Critical Source Book.* Yemi Ogunbiyi Ed. Lagos: Ministry of Culture and Information, 1981. Print.

Ogunba, O. and A. Irele, ed. *Theatre in Africa.* Ibadan: Ibadan University Press. 1978.

Okpewho, I. *African Oral literature: Background, Character and Continuity.* Indianapolis: Indiana University Press, 1992. Print.

Okpewho, Isidore: *The Epic in Africa: Towards a Poetics of Oral Performance.* Indianapolis: Columbia University Press, 1979. Print.

—. *The Heritage of African Poetry.* London: Longman, 1985. Print.

The Heritage of African Poetry. London: Longman. 1985. Print.

Omotosho, K. 'Arabic Drama in North Africa'. *Drama and Theatre in Africa: a Critical Source Book.* Yemi Ogunbiyi Ed. Lagos: Ministry of Culture and Information, 1981. Print.

PART TWO: THE POETIC GENRES

Chapter Four

The Motif of Praise
in the African Oral Poetic Tradition

Chinwendu A. Nwizu

INTRODUCTION

The art and act of praise, in all its ramification, remain a major aspect of verbal interaction among people in any given culture or society. Ms. McClure in her *Notes* acknowledges that

> To praise means to express admiration, give homage and proclaim the positive attributes of someone. Praise can be found in many cultures. These poems are created so that the young people in the tribe know who they are, who their ancestors are, why they are loved, and what special gifts they bring to the tribe and the world". (http://msmcclure.com?page id=9329)

Praise has always manifested orally in diverse contexts, it could manifest in songs and chants, it could be in ordinary conversations of dialogues: it could manifest itself instrumentally through drum-beating. It is commonplace knowledge within the confines of oral literature that songs, chants and renditions are predominantly the genres or poetry in African oral tradition. That is to say that praise poetry is a significant and central aspect of African oral poetry which exists in different African culture. The interest of this essay is to illustrate, ascertain and authenticate that the concept of praise is a running motif in African poetic tradition. Illustrations and examples of songs would be drawn from repertoire of African oral poetry from diverse African backgrounds. McClure further explains that

> In Africa, praise poetry has served as a form of oral documentation. Professional poets carry and recall the narratives detaining

the history of the people, the great leaders, and their outstanding achievement. It is not unusual for African praise poetry to be performed accompanied by instruments. These poems began typically as oral poems that were either sung or chanted. (http://msmcclure.com?page id=9329.

Praise is that act of expressing a heart-felt admiration towards something of someone using suitable words and imageries to express the conceptions of ideas in mind. This is usually done verbally by words of mouth, songs, or chants or praise, or it could be performed through the playing of instruments. Eulogies are part of human appreciation and development in every given culture. It has becomes a tradition in all cultures for encomiums to be rendered and showered on someone or something as a sign of admiration, recognition, acceptance and encouragement. Barine Saana Ngaage explicates as thus: "praise poetry is a means of adoration, education and promotion of the ideals of a people. It does so from the positive perspective of eulogy and not from the negative perspective of satire that questions and condemns anti-social behavioural traits in people" (178). As a result of this, praise has remained a motif running through all forms of African oral poetic tradition irrespective of their classifications.

According to M.H Abrams, "motif is a conspicuous element, such as type of event, device, reference or formular, which occurs frequently in works of literature" (177). He further explains that "the term 'motif' or else the German 'liet motif' (a guiding motif), is also applied to the frequent repetition, or complex of images" (177). Summing up the views of Abrams implies that any such issues which re-occur, or run through works of African oral poetry is a motif. However, the implication now is that "praise" as a phenomenon or action recurs in virtually all forms of African oral poetry. African poetry manifests in various forms and types which are strongly determined by the theme explored and exhibited in them. The manifestation of praise in the African oral genre is protean.

PRAISE POETRY/PANEGYRIC

The motif of praise is predominantly in the domain of the pan-egyric "praise" or "court" poetry. This type of oral genre is purely the act of singing the praise of the king or the aristocrats in the court of a king or monarch. It is a recognized and developed sub-genre of oral poetry. It has a long history of existence, usage and significance in the African oral lore and heritage. This is why Ms. McClure explains that,

> To praise means to express admiration, give homage and pro-claim the positive attributes of someone. Praise poetry can be found in many cultures... These poems are created so that the young people in the tribe know who they are, who their ances-tors are, why they are loved, and special gifts they bring to the tribe, and the world. (http://msmcclure.com?page id=9329.

The praise of human beings is paramount, but praise may be sung or rendered in honour of any other thing as long as its useful-ness has not been affected. Mapange and White aver that praise-po-ems do not only deal with chiefs and with kings. 'Any person may be praised for his skills or his personality' (7). In the same vein Okpewho points out that "praise in honour of any individual in the African context is a mark of honour, self recognition, social acceptance, and general motivation". It promotes good relationship, promotes value, encourages good work, enhances cooperation and builds character. So the object and context of praise in African oral praise poetry is not in dispute. It is usually done or performed by skilled bards em-ployed in the services of the court. And their job is to sing the praise of the king and the court as well.

The bards are rewarded by their lords especially those that are attached to the courts of kings. These rewards could come in the form of cash or money, or it can come in the form of material gifts. Generosity from the lords praised and others whom praises are show-ered upon is a good motivation for the bards. Free lance bards also receive rewards from those they sing their praise. Usually these bards compose, sing, perform at diverse occasions and also preserve the songs for proper transmission to the newer generations. The bards invent images and symbols that suit the context of their performances; they also invent images that portray the character that they have in mind. Below is an example of praise:

Ekele Eze.

Ekele onye eze

Ekele dike mara mma

Nnanyerugo nke mbụ

Igwe ka ala

Oke osisi

Oke mgbọrọgwụ

Omere dike

Omere mba aga mba

Omere onye ukwu mee onye nta

Anụ kpọrọ nkụ na-eju ọnụ

Akịrịka dị na mmadụ

Ọ kaa o mee

Akajiakụ

O mee o kachie

Eze a ma-ama

Dike mara mma ka ịbụ

Translation:

Ekele eze

Greetings, o king

Greetings strong man that is handsome

King that is greater than king

Nnanyerugo the first Heavens that is greater than earth

Great tree

Mighty root

He that makes a town move to another

Benevolent to the big and small

Dry meat that fills the mouth

Strong species of man

He that says and does

Hand that controls wealth

He that decrees and there is no more change

King that is known

Strong man that is handsome you are

(Onuekwusi 94–96)

The above Igbo praise poem is typical of a praise poem in the court of a king and in praise of the king's personality. The singer of this poem employs a lot of words and imageries to eulogize the king and paint him in a good light. It becomes interesting to note that 'the language of praise is usually lofty and exaggerated. No doubt the background to this is that the praisers are doing their best to please their patrons so as to get as much reward as possible' (Okpewho 142).

In Praise of the Farmer

You have weeded your hoe to the soil

You uproot trees with bare hands,

You are the hero who does not care that to fight is to die,

The sun and the rain are the same

To you when the soil must be filled,

Your are the lands that harrow the soil,

The time is come again!

Show us now if you are still the man that you have ever been.

(Mapange and White 15)

The motif of praise runs as a major theme in all African oral praise poetry irrespective of the other issues explored in them. Just as it is illustrated in the two poems above, the first is in praise of a king while the second is in praise of a farmer. The praises are rendered employing words that are exaggerated. Non-humans can also be praised, for example the poem below is in praise of an animal:

Elephant

Elephant, opulent creature, elephant, huge as a hill

Even when kneeling:

Elephant, robed in honour, a demon, flapping fans of war:

Demon who splinters the tree branches, invading the forest farm,

Elephant who disregards 'I have fled to my father for refuge,'

    Let alone 'To my mother':

Mountainous Animal, Huge Beast, who tears a man like a garment

    And hangs him up on a tree:

At sight of him people stamped to hill for safety

My chant is a salute to the elephant. (Nigeria)

                            (Mapanje and White 66–7)

The above praise is a salute and praise to a non-human creature which the persona chooses to eulogize. The persona gives different attributes of praise to an animal in admiration of its physical make-up and appearance; it is also in appreciation of the creation of God. He employs attributes that are used for humans who fear and respond to the praises being rendered. Another illustration is also an oral praise from Nigeria in praise of another animal, an Antelope. It is a poem believed to have originated from a hunter and he sings it in praise of this animal that he admires. To the farmer it is the best game ever hunted and hunting is not complete until the farmer comes upon the Antelope. The poem reads thus:

Your thighs are worth twenty slaves.

Your arms are more precious than thirty servants.

Your neck is glorious like a sacred carving

I cannot be happy when I kill you.

Until I have found your body in the bush.

Your teeth are whiter than bone.

The pregnant woman demands your skin;

Lying on your beautiful skin will bear a beautiful child. (Nigeria)

(Mapange and White 63)

The speaker in the poem just like in the first one appreciates the antelope as an animal worth catching in a hunting game. The antelope has many features which the speaker admires. The farmer from whom the poem originated adores the antelope. The object of admiration in traditional African oral praise does not degrade the poem or make it worthless. The poet personae in both poems employ hyperbole in singing the praise of their object of admiration. Exaggeration is an integral part of African praise poetry. Ngaage explains that "exaggeration is the hyperbolic homogenous quality which is a universal cultural imperative that is an embodiment of most praise songs or poetry—no composer of poet has wings to fly to the sky for a loved one: he presents the image, using hyper-praise words and symbols to buttress realistic occurrences" (176).

WAR, HUNTING AND WORK POEMS

These are the category of oral poetry that Ruth Finnegan calls special purpose poetry while Mapange and White classified them as "Survival Poems" (53). "Poetry about hunting work and war seems to involve the same ideas of romance and glory" (Finnegan 207), and as such would express the dimension of praise. Songs are sung when people are preparing for war and when they gain victory. Likewise hunters render chants with which they eulogize, admire and encourage themselves before and after their hunting expeditions in the traditional African society. Praise as an epithet or device pervades such renditions. This is why Jasper Onuekwusi remarks that "there is above all a fairly rigid form and manner of delivery. War songs celebrate the same ideas of romance and glory associated with praise poetry. It is built primarily on the desire of achievements and heroism" (99). Achievements and heroism are praised, eulogized and highly expected at the instance of going for a war. The singer of such songs encourages the brave by singing their praises, and also builds their pride towards victory. The praise in war songs can also encourage the feeble of heart, and spur them into acts of bravery in war situations.

A look at these oral war poems from the collection of Nketia and p'Bitek as recorded by Okpewho, reveals the presence of the theme of praise in them. Okpewho observes that … "the victorious celebrate their triumph with unlimited arrogance. A song from the Akan-Ashanti of Ghana celebrates such a triumph by Osee—leader of a royal brigade (Apentie)—in the Ashanti wars" (153). The song is recorded by Mapanje as follows:

Osee, man of Apenta

Osee, man of Apenta

We shall fight battles for our nation.

There was a battle brewing, Osee.

But the army of the enemy never arrived

We did not feel their presence.

You are children of ghost, and nocturnal fighters

Night fighters,

You have laid them low,

Osee has laid you low

The night fighter has laid you low,

(Okpewho 152).

The next one is another war song that exhibits praise from the Acholi of Uganda as recorded by Mapange and White.

Cowards, crawl back into your mother's womb

We are sons of the brave

Sons of stubborn people

The coward has blocked my path completely.

Who is calling my name

And arguing stupidly?

We are some of the brave sons of stubborn people. The coward has blocked my path completely, coward, crawl back into your mother's womb (73).

In the two poems above the warriors are praised in various ways. In the first one, appreciating them as warriors who fight at night is a kind of praise which extols their valour and bravery, whereas in the second poem it is sung in honour of warriors, with a special eulogy on Osee who should be the leader of the warriors.

Farmers and other artisans likewise hunters have chants that speak in praise of their profession in order to admire and appreciate their usefulness in society. An example is the following poem from Ethiopia in praise of a farmer:

O cultivator, how great is your merit

O cultivator, how great is your merit!
Wealth flows from your fingers,
The sea gushes in front of your house!
The cripple comes to your door,
You share your produce with him:
The orphan comes to your door
You share your produce with him:
For this you receive blessing.
The ants will not eat your fingers.
When you die, you are destined for paradise.
If you live on, you are destined for blessing.

(Mapange and White 57)

In the above poem, the farmer is praised for his hard work in his profession, which has transformed him into a great man of generosity from whom shards of wealth flow and one who is totally depended on by the people for his generosity.

Is the chief Greater than the Hunter?

Is the chief greater than the hunter?
Arrogance! Hunter! Arrogance!

The pair of beautiful things on your feet,

The sandals that you wear.

How did it all happen?

The sandals are made of the hide of the duiker

Does the chief say he is greater than the hunter?

Arrogance! Hunter? Arrogance

The noisy train that leads you away,

The drums that precede you,

The hunter killed the elephant,

The drum head is the ear of the elephant,

Does the chief say he is greater than the hunter?

Arrogance! Hunter Arrogance! (Ghana)

(Mapanje and White 62)

The above oral hunting poem from Ghana tries to confirm the argument that the hunter is greater than the chief. The song tries to enumerate reasons based on the hunter's exploit to buttress his claim. It is purely of a hunter where the profession produces certain things that service the chief and his subjects in society. The sandals and the drumhead which the chief makes use of in his court are the proofs of the hunter's games.

The singers of these songs pick and project images of prowess, bravery, hardwork and achievement which typify that which is expected. Allusions are made to things that showcase the worth of these artisans. It is also in this vein that C. Ngozi Okezie observes that the war song consists of three parts and she explains that the front part is characterized by praise to the god of war, pinpointing this as "the invocation or prayer of praise soliciting blessing from the gods to the warriors or cursers for the enemies..." (56).

DIRGE/ELEGY

This is the African oral poetry that laments the loss of something and expresses grief. Dirges are usually sung at the occasion of death.

They are sung for the dead; mourners and sympathizers usually express their griefs in diverse ways. Poems of lament also explore the act of praise not to death or loss but in honour of the deceased as the case may be. These are rendered in recognition, admiration or acceptance of a life lived by the deceased, extolling his achievements and the impact of his existence. Finnegan in appreciation of the motif of praise adopts the nomenclature "panegyric" of the dead'. She further acknowledges that "…praise is one of the most frequent motifs" (149). This implies that the dead man or woman could be praised in diverse forms. Though Finnegan makes a particular reference to the Igbo example, the truth of it is that it runs through virtually all the elegiac forms of African oral poetry.

Songs in honour of the merits of the dead at times praise them. Finnegan tries to recall and recapture the kind of lives they lived which the people stand to long for. To her, singing their praise is synonymous with immortalizing them. Below is a dirge in honour of a woman's father-in law:

Where have you gone, father of my husband,

Father of my husband who married me.

Where have you gone, where have you gone.

I am looking for the father of my husband who married me

Has anyone seen my husband's father

Amadioha ozuzu

Did he come to your house?

Umumiri who own the people of Onicha

Did he come to your house?

I am looking for the hand that breaks Irons

Where has he gone? Where has he gone?

He who breaks iron for fire wood.

Father of my husband,

I am calling you.

The root that holds the tree has been broken

The wind that puts off fire that burns in the compound.

The hawk will now fly in to carry the chicks.

The pillar of the house has fallen

The house will now fall with it.

The tree on which birds perch has fallen

The little birds will now fly away.

(Onuekwusi, 128)

In the above poem, the singer appears to be a woman lamenting the death of her father-in-law. It expresses the effect of his death on the living, especially his immediate family. She calls him praise names that typify the roles he played when alive and the facts for which he stood for. Some of the imagery also stand for one who holds the family.

Another illustration of the motif of praise in the African oral elegy or dirge manifests is the example from Nketia, collected from the Akan people of Ghana.

Grandsire Gyima with a slim but generous arm,

Fount of satisfaction,

My friend Adu on whom I depend.

I depend on you for everything, even for drinking water

If I am not dependent on you (i.e. there is any doubt that depend on you), see what has become of me.

Although a man, you are a mother to children

Who builds mighty, but empty houses,

Who is restive until he has fought and won,

Odirikuo, Gyane the short one

Dwentiwaa's husband, and a man of valour

(qtd in Finnegan 153).

The above poem truly laments the loss of a dear one by his friend, but it also exhibits the expression of love, admiration and praise of a man's innate characteristic as felt by his dear one. It confers imagery of strength, love and care. The poet-persona also uses metaphors carefully expressed in very selective words. There is the expression of loss of the good and memorable characteristics and experiences previously shared when the deceased was still alive.

Mapanje and White also record the following poem from the oral lore of the Ethiopians which is a poem lamenting the loss of a king in which the singer expresses the loss of the personality and generosity of the king. The singer, though expressing grief, eulogizes the king in many different ways, using imagery and metaphors to convey the conceptions in the mind. The first stanza of the poem goes thus:

Lamentation

(1)

The Hinnare-tato has become a simple man,

Our magnificent gold has become copper,

O king, how long we long for you!

Our greatness has become simplicity.

We are sorrowful and sad.

O king, how we long for you!

Let me be eaten and thrown for my king,

Let me be buried for my king.

O my king who is like gold,

O my king, a magnificent not a simple man,

O my king, with an excellent aim for a buffalo,

O my king, who can compare with you?

You are like an imposing omo tree,

You are like a calf sucking the udder,

A man who lives a long life.

Live long !!

Be greater than you are !

Feed the people!

O my king, who can compare with you?

You bring back sheep tied in forest vines,

You are wealthy and generous.

Who feeds and satisfies the people with abundant supply?

We bless you saying

Live long!

Be greater than you are!

Feed the people !

What more can I say to praise you ? (29)

Though this poem is a lament intoned for a deceased king, its first stanza is purely in praise of the king, his prowess and personality as though he were still alive. There is the extensive use of words, imagery, metaphors and similes in expressing the admiration and loss of the king. It is the second stanza of the poem that highlights the loss expressed in the first line of the stanza before the eulogies in the sub-segment lines of the first stanza.

(II)

They took the Kafa-tato from his house!

They took the gold from his finger

Since he has gone our land has turned to dust.

Our handsome dark Cinito and our golden Gallito are gone

Our king who was like a wife to us

Was taken from us like a wife from her hearth.

The cup from which he drank,

The saddle upon which he sat

Have decayed on the wall.

We miss our kind prosperous kings, Gallito and Cinito,

Who were as expensive as oceans

Our people are now scattered

No one is present to unify them. (29)

Though the poem is a poem of lament, Mapanje and White classify it as a praise poem because of its nature and the dimension of praise which pervades the poem. The African elegiac oral poem does make extensive use of praise.

RELIGIOUS POETRY

These are oral poems that exhibit certain features that are religious in outlook, that is, they are to God deities, or they may tilt towards people's belief system and interest in god and morality. Finnegan highlights the common features that mark a religion poem. She avers:

> There are three main ways in which poetry can be regarded as being religious. Firstly, the content may be religious, as in verse about mythical actions of gods or direct religious instruction or invocation. Secondly, the poetry may be recited by those who are regarded as religious specialists. Thirdly, it may be performed on occasions which are generally agreed to be religious ones. (168).

Such poems include praise in honour of gods, hymns, oracular poems and possession songs. Within the African oral religious poetry, Onuekwusi identifies two types—divination poetry and libation text'. To him,

> Divination poems are more systematized, more specialized and more complex than other forms of religious poetry. It tends to be highly conventional in form and content and there is very little emphasis on individual creativity or improvisation. (138).

Similarly, he explains that "libation is a high order form of prayers by which man seeks to be at peace with all, gods, spiritual powers in his environment and even man. The libator is a religious functionary especially at the time of libation" (143).But in all these, it is proper to identify and ascertain that the motif of praise is not absent in African oral religious poetry, irrespective of the dimension, whether hymn, praise, divination or even libation when religious poetry is rendered. It is common-place knowledge that the gods to whom much of the poetry are addressed are appreciated and eulogized. A look at the following poem from Tanzania, as recorded by Mapange and White, illustrates this:

Prayer to Ruwa

We know you Ruwa, Chief, Preserver;

He who united the bush and the plain.

You, Ruwa, chief, the elephant indeed.

He who burst forth men that they lived.

We praise you and pray to you and fall before you.

You have sent as this animal which is of your own fashioning,

For you share with no man and none is giver thereof:

Chief, receive this bull of your name,

Heal him to whom you give it and his children,

Sow the seeds of offspring with us that we may beget like bees.

May our clan hold together that it be not cleft in the hand,

May strangers not come to possess our groves.

Now chief, preserver, bless all that is ours (120).

Though the above poem is a prayer to "Ruwa", it is also poetry of praise in honour of the god. It is believed in the African cosmos that even when gods are invoked in prayer for protection and provision, they are also appreciated and praised for their protection and provisions. Divination poems can also embody praises. A Yoruba (of Nigeria) divination poem as recorded by Finnegan typifies this:

Ifa is the master of today,

Ifa is the master of tomorrow

Ifa is the master of the day after tomorrow

To Ifa belongs all the four days

Created by Orisa into this world. (192)

Though the above poem is very short, it is laden with words of praise to Ifa.

Onuekwusi also records a libation text collected from the Ibibio people of Nigeria. An excerpt from the poem is as thus:

God of the heavens, god of all the Earth.

Haume of Eket, Anyang of Nsit,

Hina of iman, Ana of Itam,

Atakpo of uruan, Advang of Ubium

All you gods of the Ibibio people

It is generally said that the giant snake does not strike the ground until it

Has intimated the leavens

It is in that tradition we are now informing you of our wishes

There is drink for all of you. (144).

These religious poems explore the motif of praise in relaying their messages. It is also worthy of note that the other forms like the hymn and what is usually regarded as choruses also contain aspects of praise in diverse forms. African oral epic poetry that occurs in different places of Africa also exhibits the praise dimension. Epics, given their content and context, exhibit diverse forms of praise in honour of the epic hero, his lineage, prowess, personality and achievement.

Conclusion

It is evident that the concept of praise is all-pervading. It pervades virtually all the sub genres of African oral poetic tradition, but it does not invalidate the fact that there could still be forms or versions of poems from the African oral tradition that may not solely or partly exploit the praise dimension. Praise can manifest in diverse ways as long as the motive and intent of expressing admiration, recognition and appreciation are concerned; in other forms of oral poetry like the political songs, satiric songs and other oral songs that are socially inclined. This is because the motif of praise could run in one or two lines of the poem extolling someone, something or a situation. Praise raises the tone of an oral poem, beautifies it and makes it more appreciable. The motif of praise runs through religious, elegiac, praise and other forms of poetry and helps to make these forms significant.

Works Cited

Abrams, M.H. and Geofrey Hapham. *A Glossary of Literary Terms.* 8th ed. Australia: Thomson Wadsworth, 2005. Print.

Finnegan, Ruth. *Oral Literature in Africa.* Nairobi: Oxford University Press, 1970. Print.

Mapanje, Jack and Landeg White. *Oral Poetry from African: An Anthology.* Essex: Longman, 1983. Print

McClure, Ms. <http://msmcclure.com?page id=9329.>

Ngaage, Barine Saana. "Praise Poetry and Globalization in Nigeria" *GOPANLI: Gombe papers on Nigerian Literature: A Journal of the Department of English, Gombe University, Nigeria,* 1: (2010). 176–189. Print.

Okezie, C. Ngozi. *A Hand Book to Oral Literature.* Umuahia: Versatile Publishers Ltd, 2007. Print

Okpewho, Isidore, *African Oral Literature: Background, Character and Continuity.* Indianapolis: Indianapolis University Press, 1992. Print.

Onuekwusi, Jasper Ahaoma. *Fundamentals of African Oral Literature.* Owerri: Alphabet Nigeria Publishers, 2001. Print.

Chapter Five

Of Progress and Distortions:
A Pattern in the Panegyric Ethos
in Igbo Life and Culture

Afam Ebeogu

INTRODUCTION: THE PANEGYRIC FACTOR
IN AFRICAN ORAL LITERATURE

Ruth Finnegan has observed that "panegyrics", "the most special-
ized forms" of praise poetry, are "the most developed and elaborate
poetic genre in Africa" (111). Her subsequent discussion and analysis
of the genre devote considerable attention to these forms of praise
poetry that are formalized and "directed publicly to kings, chiefs,
and leaders, and which are composed and recited by members of a
king's official entourage" (111). Finnegan's orientation thus inevitably leads to her drawing a great deal of the materials which she uses
for her illustration from African societies which are preponderant-
ly monarchial in structure and oligarchical in spirit. Willy-nilly, she
associates the panegyric tradition with feudal institutions, and even
though she does discuss praise names that are forms of praise poetry
which occur in other African societies that are not predominantly
feudalistic, there is no doubt that the thrust of her focus is on these
societies, which, one is tempted to suggest, possess that kind of "high
culture" that easily attracts the rather typically evolutionary spirit of
many students of folklore and social anthropology.

Finnegan's ahistorical scholarship leads to some conclusions
about the value of praise poetry in societies where it dominates: it
validates the status quo of those who control the instruments of leadership and martial coercion; it stresses "accepted values" as perceived

and defined, no doubt, by those whose interests it is to perpetuate such values; it preserves "the accepted versions of history"; records outstanding events; is a medium for transmitting information; shapes the aesthetic perception of the culture along a particular pattern (120–121, 146). This conclusion is as valid in cultures with obvious aristocratic institutions where "panegyric poetry" predominates as it is of other African cultures with less obvious aristocratic tendencies. Panegyric poetry, therefore, like most forms of oral poetry, tends to acquire a pedagogic mission, since it becomes a medium for inculcating in the citizenry the essential factors necessary for the socialization process in that culture.

THE PANEGYRIC ETHOS IN TRADITIONAL IGBO SOCIETY

Ruth Finnegan's conclusion as regards praise poetry in Africa is in many ways valid to the Igbo society of Nigeria, in spite of the predominantly republican nature of the political institutions in that society[1]. Chinyere Nwaozuzu, making commendatory reference to Finnegan, draws a conclusion reflective of hers as to the value of praise poetry (*Ntutuaha*) among the Igbo (61). This society is often described as predominantly achievement-oriented, with the result that the structures of its social organization configurate towards inculcating in its citizenry a competitive spirit in which an individual strives to outdo the other within the framework of an overriding mutual co-existence[2]. The primacy of the individual-achievement ethic apparently characteristic of this society, and which assumed the nature of a socio-economic ideology symbolized in the cult of the *Ikenga* (See 176–195, and Afigbo, *Ikenga: the State of our Knowledge*), is responsible for the penchant for individual-sponsored title-initiations which confer on the initiate a new, higher, status than before. "Titled men in the past virtually monopolized authority in the village group. The making of major political decisions and administration of criminal justice were carried out at public meetings at which all the adult males of the community had a right to express their opinions, and the decisions agreed upon were ratified and virtually imposed by lineage heads" (Forde, Daryll and G.I. Jones 19). It is thus not surprising that title initiations in the society would generate a lion's share of the praise poetry in that culture[3], and it is instructive that some Igbo scholars are tempted to use the expression "Title-Songs" (*Abu Echimechi*), as distinct from the more general "Praise Songs", in the taxonomy of Igbo Oral literature. (See P.A. Ezikeojiaku, 66–83; Chukwuma, 1977 Helen and Ogbalu 137–143).

It becomes evident from our discussion so far that Finnegan's "panegyric poetry" which is characteristic of aristocratic societies is functionally not very different from the "praise poetry" in the more democratic societies of the so-called "acephalous" political institutions. In both societies, praise poetry is a powerful weapon in the hands of those who perpetuate the structures of the status quo. The modality of devolution of power from one set of rulers to another may be, and is indeed, different, among the Igbo; hereditary succession has always been rare, manifesting essentially in sub cultures with marginal propensities (see Onwuejeogwu M.A. "The Igbo Culture Area", 1–10), and class mobility is fairly flexible, but this does not invalidate the fact that those who "succeed" others in positions of leadership tend to retain and perpetuate most of the instruments of socialization and pedagogy. In such circumstances, the panegyric spirit which permeates the feudal and quasi-feudal institutions manifests itself, in such essentially non-feudalistic society as the traditional Igbo, in forms that express a similar urge to project the egocentricism of the privileged subject of praise and canonize the values which his class represents. Any sample Igbo praise poem will serve for illustration:

Ọzọ, fulfilled in the cult of Ọzọ,

Ọzọ, the blower of the Ọzala

Ọzọ, king who is the Sun-tree

Son of "Two Giant Ants" with either feathers.

Son of "One Palm-Nut" which yields oil that fill a pot.

Dried pepper that does not fill the gourd

But is very hot;

Call for me the one who took the Ọzọ title as youth.

The king, who is the Crest of the Hill,

The Chief who is the high priest of Hills and Valleys,

Master of the spiritual craftsmanship

(Egudu and Nwoga, *Poetic Heritage, 79*).

The above is a title praise poem whose aristocratic spirit speaks for itself. The poem could be compared with a different praise poem from a more aristocratic (Southern Sotho) culture:

Nketu (frog) the regiment, companion of

Shakhane and Ramakhwane, Stirring of dust

You came from the centre of the Plateau of

Rathsowanyane,

The child of the chief of Qhwai saw you.

You were seen by Ratjotjose of Mokihethi;

Cloud, gleaner of shields,

When Nketu is not there among the people,

The leaders of the regiment cry aloud and say,

Nketu and Ramakhwane, where are you?

(Finnegan, 125)

The two poems are not "the same"; they reveal evidences of having been generated by different cultures—the notion of hereditary king-ship expressed in the second is unmistakable. But both poems ex-press a similar spirit: the figure in each is towering: metaphors drawn from outstanding phenomena in nature characterize both figures; the reliance of others on these figures for support is echoed in both poems, and both of them are associated with some dimensions of a supernatural stature. Both figures, therefore, represent, in their dif-ferent cultures, that spirit of intimidation which tends to hold the less privileged to ransom. The Igbo praise poem, born as it is out of a spirit of self-achievement, is not niggardly in the expressive rhetoric celebrating that achievement: the object of praise carves a special stature for himself, and one only needs to study the rituals and expenses of initiation into the *Ozọ* title in Igboland, and the perpetual class distinction between the holder and the *Ofeke* (not-titled person), (Onwuejeogwu 1–24), to realize why the Ozọ-title holder in that culture tends to envision himself from Olympian heights. The "kingship"—associated metaphor is a recurrent one in many *Ozọ*-title praise poems in the culture;[4] the *Ozọ*-initiate is normally addressed as *Eze Ozọ* ("*Ozọ* king"). The notion of "king" in Igboland implies more of "the great achiever deserving of a special honour" than "the divine ruler whose word is law", and therefore means that in the culture one could have many "kings", each presiding over his own area of authority or competence. But somewhere in the history of the Igbo people, probably as a result of Nri pan-Igbo ritual influence, (See Onwujeogwu, *An Igbo Civilization; Nri Kingdom and Hegemony*) the Eze *Ozọ* seems to have begun to attract to himself a disturbing aroma of divine kingship, which aroma obviously tended to be bastardized in a culture in which everyman had an untrammelled liberty to constitute himself a mini-king in his own dominance of human activity.

We can say, then, that the traditional Igbo society was, like many other societies, a dynamic one in which the fluxes of change constitute serious strains on the system, resulting in the readjustment of socialization processes in the culture in the light of the pragmatic demands of the moment. As Inyang Eteng puts it:

> Achebe's Umuaro was already collapsing under the grinding strains of its own internal social contradictions arising from class tendencies which had begun to crystallize even before the superimposition of the British colonial administration and its capitalist base which sharpened and reinforced these contradictions. In most communities, two discriminatory systems of Ohu (slavery) and Osu (sacrificial caste) *coexisted with comparatively lower* status accorded the womenfolk, minors, non-titled men, men without material substance, stranger elements, and families and lineages associated with abominable records of stealing, homicide and endemic diseases.

Additionally, the traditional Igbo did sacrifice human beings to deities, buried slaves with their deceased masters, killed children associated superstitiously with "despicable" births (like twins), engaged in fratricidal inter-village warfare or feuds, and even participated effectively in the now calumniated trans-Atlantic slave trade which seriously depopulated several Igbo communities, and ultimately contributed to the subsequent pulverization of Igbo for colonial subjugation. These they did, partly to assuage the emergent acquisitive inclinations of some interest groups, and partly to ensure the ultimate survival of the group (86).

While a good proportion of the praise poetry in that traditional society reflected "the emergent acquisitive inclinations of most interest groups", some revealed less partisan class differentiation, in the sense that the poems extolled values that revealed a diachronic rather than a synchronic view of society. The man who was materially successful at any particular time was not the only object of praise; men and women who manifested aspects of behaviour and achievement which perpetuated abiding, non-material values were also eulogized (See Afigbo, *The Warrant Chiefs*). Hence the orator (*Onye okwu na-adi mma n'onu*), the man of truth (*O kara k'omere*), the jester, who always kept others laughing (*Okpa amu*), the good dancer (*Ogba egwu*), the unequivocator (*Ekwu eme*), the beautiful woman (Apu n'anwu), the striking singer (*Onu okwa/ogene*) etc., were all eulogized either in the form of phrase-based, clause-based or sentenced-based panegyric names, (See Ubahakwe *(Aha Otutu)*, or in the form of more elaborate praise poetry as is evidenced in the following:

Young lady, you are
A mirror that must not go out in the sun
A child that must not be touched by dew
One that is dressed up in hair
A lamp with which people find their way
Moon that shines bright
An eagle feather worn by a husband

A straight line drawn by God.

(Nwoga and Egudu, *Poetic Heritage, 31*)

These praise names and poems which highlighted the non-materialistic values needed for the preservation of those essences of a culture that embody the spiritual, mental and intellectual dimensions of the human being in his society tended to serve as a dialectical, even if unequally weighted, juxtapositional counterpart of the dominant poems that promote the cult of material achievement. This counterbalancing, reflective of the structures of dualistic interaction dominant in the Igbo cultural kinesis, (See Achebe 101) is a requisite for the communalistic ethos of the closed or fairly closed society, and ultimately gives uniqueness to the nature of humanism that is prevalent in any culture. (See Ifemesia). In the typical Igbo village—group, where, as in similar groups:

> all members know each other, are aware of their common membership, share the same values, have a certain structure of relationship which is stable over time, and interact to achieve some purpose (McQuali, qtd in Pickering and Green, 4),

Panegyric poems, like other forms of folk poetry and songs

> arise from within it [the society], from its needs and deficiencies, and subsequently react in a dialectical process on the world of everyday reality. [They] constitute ways of handling the empirically experienced world, as do all imaginative acts and relationships, having either constructive or negative consequences for social action and interaction, and either supporting or challenging 'how things happen', or how they are represented ideologically" (Pickering and Green 3)

When people are praised panegyrically in this society, the praise chanter or singer is painfully aware of the need to perform within the framework of the "truth" of the society, truths that are:

> basically referring to morality rather than to historical facts, or to historical facts of such a general kind that their applications is more likely to be more ethical than documentary. (Tony Green 9)

The object of praise is known by all or almost all in the community; the quality for which he or she is being praised reflects the dominant communalist expectations, values and attitudes in the culture, and there is a dynamic tendency for the collective cumulative perspectives of the songs to discourage iconoclasm and anarchic propensities. Therefore, despite the dominant achievement-oriented praise poems in the traditional Igbo culture, there were also many praise poems in the traditional Igbo culture that were not based on material achievement, and the cleavage between the two instinctively promoted the oppositional dualistic structures of the society which, paradoxically, ensured stability and cohesion in spite of inherent contradictions. The cult of Ikenga was not only a cult of individual achievement; it was also, as some iconographic representations of *Ikenga* show,[5] an ideology in which the drive for material acquisition was tempered by a concern for fairness and justice, symbolized in the *ọfọ n'ogu*. A man's praise name may be *Akụkalịa* ("The-Wealth that-Overflows "), and yet another man's name may be Osinyirioha ("He-who-Satisfactorily-Feeds-The-Masses"), and yet another person's (a woman's, for example) praise name may be *Ugo Agbala* ("The Eagle-Lady). The first suggests immediately only the fact that the object of praise is a very rich man; the second that he is a rich man who likes the community to benefit occasionally from his wealth, and the third suggests a woman of striking quality, not only in physical stature and beauty but also in character since, for the Igbo, the eagle is a symbol of grandeur in terms of physical beauty and purity of character.

THE PANEGYRIC ETHOS FROM THE COLONIAL ERA TO THE PRESENT

The colonial contact involving the Igbo created a kink in the cycle of their cosmological universe, with the result that a barrage of foreign-derived values invaded the culture. While some of these values were foreign only analytically speaking, without implying that the traditional society was, before the contact, insulated from them, others were indeed foreign in the sense of absolute newness. The impact was to lead to new patterns of socialization within the context of a colonial co-existence (See Afigbo, *The Warrant Chiefs;* Ekechi, *Missionary Enterprise,* Isichei, *The Ibo-People and the Europeans,* and Nzimiro, "The Igbo in Modern Setting", 152–174). One of the most obvious changes in the Igbo attitude to life as a result of this contact with an overwhelming outside world is a significant breakdown of the communalist ethos of the village-groups, and the emergence of an easy affinity between clear enterprise and a latent, traditional spirit of cautious capitalism. As Inyan Eteng puts it:

> Most agents of socialization among the modern Igbo are foreign in origin and content. The modern Igbo are not only more exposed to the way of life of other Nigerians, they have even become part and parcel of a world culture. Almost always, most of the new agents and instruments of socialization have developed as a direct consequence of capitalist development in the country. The content, patterns of socialization, and the effects of socialization have, therefore, tended to be capitalist motivated, with serious implications (94).

One of the implications here is the twist in the direction of the panegyric culture. The era of the warrant chiefs, for example, was that in which novel forms of administration were forced on the Igbo culture by perhaps well-meaning but ignorant colonial administrators in pursuit of the dream of "Indirect Rule". Monarchical-oriented political institutions were introduced where they never existed before (See Afigbo, *The Warrant Chiefs).* Novel forms of chiefdoms sprang up overnight throughout the length and breadth of the land, and the new men of status, aware that they did not owe their authority to any traditional institution—with possible checks and balances to the exercise of judicial, administrative and political power—proceeded to carve for themselves a status image that lacked traditional roots and support. People who had not schooled themselves in the toughness, endurance and hardship characteristic of the road to grandeur, which pattern of status achievement the traditional system encouraged, found themselves in intoxicating situations of power control and exercise, and sought to make themselves *Igwes* (meaning, literally, "The Sky") or *Ezes* ("kings"), with the paraphernalia and pomp of power associated with the purely monarchical institutions. The court clerks who had the privilege of a smattering of education under the new dispensation became addressed as *Nna anyi ukwu* (Our-Great-Father") (See Afigbo, *The Warrant Chiefs,* 315). The opposition-al dualism in the culture tended to manifest itself in an extreme form of competitiveness in which the overriding vision of men became that of *"Nwoke n'ibe ya n'azo gini ma obughi nkem g'aka?"*, interpreted by Afigbo as "What else but greed caused trouble between man and man?", (*The Warrant Chiefs, 307),* but which should be interpreted as "The conflict between a man and his fellow is motivated by the urge to become greater". As the author of *The Warrant Chiefs* reports:

> "Asked how the Warrant Chiefs made the money that made them so rich Obiukwu answered, *'Ma ukpara erighi ibe ya o naghi ebu'* ('to grow fat an insect (sic) must feed on fellow insects (sic)')" (309).

The above is very appropriate imagery; it is potentially panegyric and one can imagine the chief joyously accepting the epithet: "The-Grasshopper-That-Feeds-On-Others-To-Grow". It is not that this kind of praise name was really new to the traditional Igbo society; it was that it would be appropriate only under special circumstances. The Igbo praise names that convey the notion of predation were usually borne by such beings as the *Dibia* (Doctor/diviner/Charm Expert) or the masquerade, both of who were in many ways above the ordinary mortals, since the *Dibia* could commune with the oth-er-worldly and the masquerade was a physical manifestation of that other-worldly company, the ancestors. It was proper, then, if such beings had praise names like *Agwoturumbe* ("The-Snake-That Struck-The-Tortoise"), *Eke ji Isi Anya Anwu* ("The-Python-That-Enjoys-The-Sunshine-On-Its-Head"), or

The Shadow that holds Life

The Notorious One

The Dark Sky That Overshadows the Moon

Tiger, That Eats When it bites to Death

The Great Sore.

(Ugonna,42. My own translation)

The imagery of predation in the praise epithets and poems are appropriate to the objects of praise because they indicate the feats which the objects are capable of achieving in the attempt to serve the members of the community whose heroic ethics they resonate.

A good deal of the panegyric spirit in contemporary Igbo society is a continuation of the spirit of predation easily traceable to the era of the colonial incursion. The argument is not that the predatory inclination did not exist in the pre-colonial Igbo society; it was there but only latently, kept in effective check by the counterbalancing ethic of justice and fairness captured adequately in the pervasive Igbo proverb which says that "The kite should perch, and the eagle should perch; whichever denies the other the right to perch should have its wings broken". But in the contemporary situation, emphasis is on the panegyric that evokes the cult of material acquisition rather than on the virtues of honesty, fairness and justice; the magic of the *Ikenga* has become even more fore-grounded, while that of *ọfọ n'ogu* has receded into the background.

It is significant that contemporary Igbo society reflects a striking recreation of the institutional absurdities characteristic of the era of the Indirect Rule System which had to be jettisoned by the colonial authority when these absurdities became very obvious. The current proliferation and official recognition of institutions of oligarchy by post-independent governments of Nigeria is a telling reenactment of the warrant chieftaincy of the colonial predecessors. The *Igwes*, *Ezes* and *Obis* of contemporary Igbo societies are as many as there are autonomous communities, and these are even more in number than the pre-colonial village groups. Each of these mini-monarchies surrounds itself with a team of flamboyant aides—the *Ichies*—representing the various wards in the community. Both the Ichies, whose leader is a kind of traditional "prime minister" to the "king", and their head who is at the apex of this often novel hierarchy of aristocratic grandeur, have appropriated to themselves certain panegyric epithets that smack of the immense egocentricism and conceit characteristic of the values of a large percentage of the Nigerian middle-class oligarchy.

Thus, the whole of Igbo culture area reverberates with such names as *Igwe Ochizue 1* ("The-Igwe-Who-Has-Taken-All-Titles", the First) of Community A; *Obi Ezekibeya 1* ("The-Obi-King-Who-Is-Greater-Than-His-Fellow", the First) of Community B; *Eze Ọkaa Omee 1* ("The-Eze-Who-Does-What-He-Plans", the first) of Community C; *Ichie Akụ Ụbọm 1* ("The-Ichie-Whose-Wealth-Is-Like-Sand", the First); *Ichie Eze Ego 1* ("The-Ichie-Who-Is-King-Of-Money", the First); *Ichie Akụluẹụnọ 1* ("The-Ichie-Whose-Wealth-Has-Got-Home", the First); *Agada Gbachiri Ụzọ I* ("The-Big-Trunk-Blocking-The-Road", the First), etc. Always, the genealogical adjunct, "the First", features along with these names; nobody wants to be anything other than "the First". This mentality goes back to the era of the warrant and paramount chieftaincy when those who first became appointed or recognized as chiefs by the colonial government remained "the First", often because of the discontinuation of the system by the colonial authority.

It cannot be denied that some of these "traditional rulers"—a very convenient nomenclature which enables the governments at the national, state and local government levels to exclude these otherwise influentials from a *de jure* exercise of political power—have panegyric names which are reminders of the diachronically determined values of the pre-colonial Igbo village-groups. Such names include *Igwe Eze Ọranyelụ* ("The-Igwe-So-Declared-By-The-Masses)" of Community D; the *Obi Nwa Chinemelụ* ("The-Obi-Whose-Fortunes-Are-the-Gift-of-Destiny") of Community E; *Eze Anyanwụ Na-Etiri Ọha* ("The Eze, Sun-that-Shines-For-All") of Community F; *Ichie Igwebuike* ("Ichie, the-Group-Is-Strength"), etc. These non-conceited praise names are however few and far between these days, as the dominant ethics of capitalist acquisitiveness and predatory exploitativeness pervade the whole society, and traditional rulers and titled men—who, significantly, increase in leaps and bounds—opt for names that denote distinctiveness in status. It is revealing that only very few of the "traditional rulers" and their team do not control immense wealth.

Reflective too of the spirit of the age is the tendency in contemporary Igbo society by other people who are not part of the institutionalized "traditional" leadership to appropriate for themselves certain praise names by which they are subsequently known and addressed by their friends, business associates and customers. Some of these people, either successful or expecting to be successful, titled or expecting to be titled, assume these ego-boosting names even in defiance of the sociology of traditional onomastics where certain names are only appropriate for certain categories—not necessarily class-determined—of people. This defiance is aided and abetted by the fact that the communities are no longer closed societies, and so the "traditional rulers" cannot adequately impose on their "subjects", whether "at home" or "abroad", any obligation to conform to norms that were in the past only validated by a network of binding social, religious, ritual and cosmological laws and observances. Here, the so called Igbo republicanism manifests itself glaringly: a significant population of the people insists on being recognized, whether or not they are acknowledged as belonging to the group of people who have achieved success. They invade the panegyric repertoire of ancient and contemporary culture, ransack it, and pick for themselves praise names that they fancy, without regard for appropriateness and standard. Thus the woman who chooses for herself the alias, *Madam Odiche* ("The-Madam-Whose-Ways-Are-Always-Different"), forgets the Igbo proverb that *Nkem di iche bu ajọ aha* ("My-Way-Are-Different' is a bad name").

Some of these ego-seekers even pick such names from outside the Igbo culture, and subject them to whimsical morphological permutations, the result being such unique panegyric combinations as *Alhaji Nwata Kpata Akụ* ("The-Alhaji-Chap-Who-Has-Acquired-Wealth"), *Eze Ego the Fabulous* ("The-King-of-Money-the-Fabulous"), *Madam Arụka Akwa* ("The-Madam-Whose-Body-Is-Greater-Than-Clothes"), *Madam Ojemba, Alias America* ("The-Madam-Traveller, Alias America"), etc. As for the panegyric business names which many Igbo traders and businessmen and women all over Nigeria choose for themselves, they would constitute a seminal study in bilingual stylistics, and are therefore better left out of the present discussion. If in their choice of praise names for themselves without discretion the conduct of this new generation of moneyed class borders on the anarchic, an explanation can be sought in the fact that theirs is a society in which continuity is ensured by that complex dialectic of oppositional dualism which had characterized the past, and which continues to inform the present.

Contemporary Igbo discography is replete with the panegyric ethos; many musicians, whether performing within the idiom of traditional music or that of contemporary Highlife, fill up their LPs with all sorts of praise names of men and women of influence and affluence in the society. The financial reward from this practice is immense, for it not only boosts the sales of the discs, but also encourages clubs and individuals to court, by various ways, prominent and promising musicians into making brand new discs in which these persons, groups and clubs are extravagantly praised in the idiom of traditional panegyrics, with a preponderance of praise epithets that reflect the acquisitive, capitalist tendencies in contemporary Nigerian society. As H. Braverman puts it, the ascendancy of capitalist relations is a

> Process that involves economic and social changes on the one side, and profound changes in psychological and affective patterns on the other ... Artistic products and cultural forms also become increasingly turned into a species of commodity ... marketable and inter-changeable 'like an industrial product', to the extent that cultural process and market relations increasingly overlap... (qtd in Pickering and Green 2)

Indeed, this increasing link between market relations and cultural processes has created novel dimensions not only in the dominant textual content of Igbo panegyric repertoire, but, more significantly, in the structure and form of Igbo praised poetry itself. The "well-wrought" praise poems in stanzaic forms, full of rich figurative expressions drawn from Igbo culture and environment, and characteristic of traditional Igbo society, are gradually giving way to the dominance of the solitary clause and phrasal epithets which musicians find quite

catchy and well-suited to the "quick-market-turnover" hustle of contemporary Nigerian ecosystems. These solitary epithetic forms of
praise poetry, eulogizing in extremely hyperbolic terms the singular-
ity of the achievement of the middle-class elite of Igbo society, are
symbolic of the uncohesive and destablished world of present-day
Nigeria—a world in which the predatory instinct greatly overshadows
the communalistic, even if by no means exploitation-free, essences of
pre-colonial cultures.

CONCLUSION

This chapter has attempted to take a historical perspective of
the pattern of growth and manifestation of panegyric poetic forms
among the Igbo of Nigeria. It argues that traditional Igbo society
was suffused by a panegyric spirit, essentially because that society
was an achievement-oriented one in which the economic success of
the individual in the society was almost possessive, and most of the
social and cosmological structures and beliefs in that society were
geared towards the promotion of an extremely competitive spirit.
Bards and laymen sang praises of themselves and of others; this
panegyric ethos was most manifest in the praise poems and names
referring to some individuals in the society. Traditional Igbo Society therefore was latently capitalistic, but this capitalism was greatly
tempered by the mythopoeia and ritual checks which discouraged
corrosive exploitation of human beings by their fellows, and made
it possible for people to co-exist in communalistic harmony in spite
of their differing levels of material status. The popular praise names
in that kind of situation were in conformity with a socio-economic
ethical code in which the cult of economic dynamic was counterbal-
anced by that of fairness and justice.

Praise poetry and names in colonial and contemporary Igbo society, a good deal of which is promoted in the discography of the
people, reveal a trend of continuity which gravitates towards poetic
forms that are reflective of a Nigeria in which the ethic of economic
exploitative and anti-communalist values predominate. The qualitative decline in the nature of these panegyric forms is symptomatic of

a tendency for the quality of oral art in any society to be immensely influenced by the dominant socio-economic system in that society.

NOTES

1. On the various forms of political institutions in traditional Igbo culture, see A.E. Afigbo, "The Indigenous Political System of the Igbo", R.N. Henderson, *The King-In-Every-Man: Evolutionary Trend in the Onitsha Ibo Speaking Society and Culture*; Nzimiro, *Studies in Ibo Political System: Chieftaincy and Politics in Niger States.*

2. See, for instance, T. Uzodinma Nwala, *Igbo Philosophy,* 176–95. Inya Eteng argues that in traditional Igbo society this competitive spirit operated within the context of a communalist welfarism in which the interest of the whole community takes precedence over individual ambition. See Inya Eteng, "Relation of Production and Contemporary Igbo Patterns of Socialization and Development", 70,72–79.

3. See, for illustration, Romanus Egudu and Donatus Nwoga, *Poetic Heritage: Igbo Traditional Verse,* 25–52.

4. See, for instance, the collection of "Abu Echichi" ("Title poems") in Ogbalu, *Abu Na Egwu Igbo,* 137–143.

5. For a discussion of some of these representations, see Chike Aniakor, "Structuralism in Ikenga—An Ethnoaesthetic Approach", 6–28. Aniakor's iconographic collections do not, however, include an *Ikenga* with the *ofo*.

WORKS CITED

Achebe, Chinua. "Chi in Igbo cosmology". *Morning Yet On creation Day.* London: Heinemann Ed. Books, 1975. 175–180. Print.

Afigbo, A.E. *Ikenga: The State of Our Knowledge.* Owerrri: Rada Publishing Company, 1986. Print.

—. "The Indigenous Political System of the Igbo". *Tarikh* 4.2 (1973).13–23. Print.

—. *"The Warrant Chiefs of Eastern Nigeria.* London: Longman, 1972. Print.

Aniakor, Chike, "Structuralism in Ikenga—An Ethnoesthetic Approach". *Ikenga* 11.1 (Jan. 1973). 6–28. Print.

Chukwuma, Obiageli. "Genetic Distinction of Oral Data". Paper presented at the 2nd Ibadan Annual literature Conference. University of

Ibadan, 11–15 July, 1977.

Egudu, Romanus and Donatus Nwoga. *Poetic Heritage: Igbo Traditional Verse.* Enugu: Nwankwo Ifejike, 1971. Print.

Ekechi, F.K. *Missionary Enterprise and Rivalry in Igboland, 1857–1914.* London: Franc Cass, 1972. Print.

Eteng, Inya. "Relations of Production and Contemporary Igbo Patterns of Socialization and Development". *The Igbo Socio Political System.. (Papers presented at the 1985 Ahiajoku* Colloquium). Owerri: Ministry of Information, Culture, Youth and Sports, 1986.27–450. Print.

Ezikeojiaku, P.A. "Classification of Igbo Orature". *Nigeria Magazine* 53.2. (April, 1985). 66–83. Print.

Finnegan, Ruth. *Oral Literature in Africa.* London: Oxford and Cambridge: Clarendon Press and Open Books Publishers, 1970 and 2015. Print.

Forde, Daryll and G.I. Jones. *The Igbo and Ibibio Speaking Peoples of Nigeria.* London: International Institute, 1950. Print.

Green, Tonny. "McCaffery: A Study in the Variation and Functions of a Ballad". *Lore and language* 1,3,4,5 (1970–71). 4–11. Print.

Henderson, R.N. *The King-In-Every-Man: Evolutionary Trend in Onitsha Ibo-Speaking Society and Culture.* New heaven: Yale University Press, 1972. Print.

Ifemesia, Chieke. *Traditional Humane Living Among the Igbo.* Enugu: Fourth Dimension Publishers, n.d. Print.

Isichei, Elizabeth. *The Ibo People and the Europeans: The Genesis of a Relationship-to 1906.* London: Faber and Faber, 1973. Print.

Nwala, Uzodinma. *Igbo Philosophy.* Lagos: Lantern Books, 1985. Print.

Nwaozuzu, Chinyere. "Praise and Satire in Aspects of Igbo Verbal Art". *Anu* 4 (1986).60–72. Print.

Nzimiro, Ikenna. "The Igbo in Modern Setting". *Conch* 111.2 (1971). 152–174. Print.

Ogbalu, F. C. *Mbem Na Egwu Igbo.* Ibadan: Macmillan Nigeria Publishers, 1978. Print.

Onwuejeogwu, M.A. *An Igbo Civilization: Nri Kingdom and Hegemony.* London: Ethnographica, 1981. Print.

—. "The Genesis, Structure and Significance of Ozo Title in Igboland". *Ugo3* (June–Nov, 1976). 1–24. Print.

—. "The Igbo Culture Area". *Igbo Language and Culture.* Ogbalu, F.C. and E.N. Emenanjo. Eds. Ibadan: Oxford University Press, 1975. Print.

Pickering, K and Tony Green, *Every Culture: Popular Song and Vernacular Milieu.* Milton Keynes: Open University Press, 1987. Print.

Ubahakwe, Ebo. *Igbo Names: Their Structure and Their Meaning* Ibadan: Daystar Press, 1981. Print.

Ugonna, N. *Abu Na Egwuregwu Odinala Igbo.* Ibadan: Longman Publishers, 1980. Print.

Chapter Six

The Content, Form and Performance of African Oral Elegies

Chinwendu A. Nwizu

Before the advent of formal literacy and modernity, the African societies in their different locales had always had ways of expressing their
feelings, baring their minds, preserving and exhibiting their norms
and lore orally as the occasion demands. These feelings, invocations
and expressions are articulated and expressed in songs, chants and
tales. This involves every aspect of human existence, association, relationships, exploits and expectations. The African expresses these
issues in diverse forms. At the moments of joy and celebrations, suitable songs are rendered to reflect the mood, at the times of work,
hunting, war and other exploits. There are also renditions to express
the feelings at heart. Likewise, at the moments of grief, loss, disappointment and death, the African also expresses the feelings surging
in the heart. The focus of this essay is to extrapolate the content,
forms and performance of African oral elegies.

The elegy is literally a form of poetry which expresses the loss of
something. It could be the loss of someone or life which is the highest
form of loss. It may express the loss of a fortune, job or relationship.
The most important aspect of the elegy is that it expresses loss. The
bereaved and those who experience loss usually express these losses,
and lament in words rendered in the form of songs, chant and personal expressions. Africans, personally and communally at their very
times of bereavement and loss express their griefs and losses in order
to vent emotion. When these songs, chants and speeches are rendered orally in the African socio-cultural background and context, it
manifests as African oral elegies.

Scholars of African oral literature believe and have expressed views concerning African oral elegies. It is an established fact that Africans at every occasion in the traditional setting find expression in songs and chants which highlight the moods in context. Isidore Okpewho affirms strongly that it is, however, important to bear in mind that:

> ...there is hardly any occasion or activity in traditional African life that is not accompanied by songs and chants.... At the death of the individual, some songs lament the loss of physical life while other songs give consolation for a life well lived and usher the deceased into the glorious company of the ancestors. (138)

Some scholars classify all funeral songs as elegy while some make a distinction between the elegy and the dirge. Ruth Finnegan has the following to say:

> Elegiac poetry is an exceedingly common form of expression in Africa. We hear of it from all areas and in many different forms. The most obvious instances of elegiac poetry are these poems or songs performed at funeral memorial rites. (147)

On another plane, Finnegan notes that "there is also, however a sense in which elegiac poetry also includes poems which take death or sorrow as their general themes without being connected with funerals or actual mourning"(151).

African elegies, just like the literary elegies, include all forms of songs and chants that express loss, including the dirge. Dirges are also poems or songs of lament but are strictly sung for the dead before the dead are buried. Kofi Awoonor explains that dirge poetry "is a very encompassing type ... in the broadest term, the dirges are sung round the corpse (or around the house in which the corpse lies) while it is being prepared for burial" (148). However, to Finnegan, all songs and chants which mourn the death of a person or persons are put together and regarded as elegiac in nature. In the same vein, Okpewho pinpoints that "in Africa as in many other traditional societies elaborate ceremonies surround the occasion of death, and in these a variety of funeral songs and charts or dirges, as they are commonly called—are performed that convey these different sentiments" (156).

Dirges are addressed to dead bodies. It is a very elaborate performance in some African societies. Awoonor points out that

> In the Ewe dirge tradition, the dirge poem has received a tremendous boost through the work of the dirge poet Hesina Akpalu. The Ewe dirge reveals the loneliness and sorrow of death, traditional world views of what the next stage of the journey is, and finally a message or prayer. The dead person is a traveler from the living to the ancestors; he is given intimate messages to deliver to those who had gone ahead. The Ewe dirge is usually performed by women; it is accompanied by any large orchestra to drums but perhaps with a rattle of a gong. Prominence is given to words as in all other chanted poems over the simple melody which serves only as a vehicle to convey the basic notions and ideas of the poem. Repetition of lines or large segments, and of imagery and sounds act to enhance the orality of the lament. This gives it a persistence that tends to relieve the mourners of the burden of their sorrow. (84)

Awoonor sees the dirge as an elaborate oral genre in Ghana among the different tribes that make up the country. He also highlights the Akan dirges; but concerning the dirge among the Illa and the Tonga of Zambia he notes that 'these poems are only composed once, i.e. at the funeral of the person whose death inspires them; these *Zintegulo*, or mourning songs, are short' (84). Similarly, Ezenwa-Ohaeto notes that "in effect, the dominant sentiments and the intrinsic moods of the dirge emanate from the poet's astute use of the previous activities that united poet persona and the departed as the foci of the lament" (125). Analyzing the dirge in another context he avers that 'in the tradition of Igbo dirges death is given the euphemistic name "Chariot of eternal sleep" and the characters are represented in symbols' (113).

Predominantly, African oral elegy mourns the death of somebody. Death is a serious issue and a solemn occasion in the African cosmos. At the event of death the atmosphere changes entirely, a solemn mood descends on the environment and every action, utterance and disposition revolves around the event. Some,on such occasions cry, sing wail, expressing their feelings in songs.

Types/ Forms of African Oral Elegy

Consider the two African oral poems below, one from Sudan and the other from Uganda, recorded by Mapange and White.

The Jilted man

O Ajok !

Ajok whom I chose when she was carried in a sling,

Ajok whom I chose before she could dance,

Ajok whom I chose when she was not yet a clan beauty,

When she grew up, another took her away from me,

What misery! What a way to treat a man!

God has spared me and Marang has spared me.

For the daughter of Kat Atem I have felt miser

I weep and weep for them. (90)

Close to her Husband.

She used to sit

Close to her husband

Touching each other

The beautiful one, sister of Amoo,

She used to boast.

The one loved most by her husband:

He had removed all her worries completely.

Fatie has knelt on her,

Oh mother

Fatie has crushed her completely

She used to sit.

Close by her husband

Touching each other. (95).

The first poem is a lament on the loss of a relationship, where the woman lover disappoints and jilts the man lover. The poet-persona expresses grief and disappointment, and also recounts the experiences of the old on how they started but has been abandoned for someone whom she feels may be better. The poem validates the idea that lament may be expressed over loss and not compulsorily on the death of a person. It is just as we find the Anglo-Saxon elegies of the 11th century which are known to have their origins in preliterate oral culture. Anglo-Saxon elegies mourned the loss of something. Deor's lament of the old English elegies brings to bare the lament of Deor on losing his job as a singer in the court of the king who happens to be his Lord. Deor suffers the situation of being supplanted in position by a more experienced bard and thereby loses the favour of his Lord. Deor believes that many other persons like him had experienced losses in diverse ways and overcame, so would he. On a different note is another old English elegy, "The Wanderer", which laments the loss of Lord. In its context the poet-persona who is the Wanderer mourns the death of his lord and he goes out in search of another lord in replacement of the old lord.

The second poem expresses the loss of a husband. The poet-persona accounts of a woman whose husband died; she recounts the blissful moments the young widow shared with the husband and the love which existed between them when he was alive.

African oral elegies are purely poems, songs or chants that express loss. Certain identifiable types could be located within the elegiac forms. These typologies are purely based on their content, theme and target. The forms identified include: traditional elegies, panegyric elegies, religious elegies, consolatory elegies.

TRADITIONAL ELEGY

This category of oral elegy refers to songs and chants in the African localities sung at funerals and memorials that generally explore

the issue of death. These songs express lament and they are not gender sensitive; it could be sung for a man and it could also be sung for
a woman-usually names are called and attached to them during the
rendition. The song may be a pure lament or it may make references
to issues of existence.

O wutere anyị Wutere anyị	We were sad we were sad
Wutere anyị	when we got the bad
O wutere anyị Mgbe anyị nụrụ	news of death
Ya n'akụkọ	
Ọnwụ eee	Death eee
Anyị na-ajụ ọnwụ	We are asking you and who
Ya na onye ga-ekpe	Will stand to settle issues?

The above Igbo elegies are short and direct. They are usually
sung at the instance of a leader and the generality of sympathizers
responding; once these groups are intoned everybody knows that it is
the solemn occasion of death.

There are some elegies that are sung at the burial of a young one
and there are ones sung at the funeral of an elder one. The death of
a younger person generates a lot of tension emotionally, creates fear
and people are more aroused to cry and wail. Most times such deaths
are believed to have been occasioned by some forces or some enemies
and the elegies sung at such burials depict the idea. The bereaved
rites at such occasions are usually not so elaborate. For example these
songs below give the impression of the sudden death of a young person.

O kuwala o kuwala	It has broken it has broken
Ezigbo ugegbe akụwala ọkụwala	The beautiful mirror has broken
Okuwara n'ike	It broke suddenly by force
Onye mere nwanne anyị o ji nwụ ọ	Who killed our brother/sister
N' ọnụma n'iwe	In annoyance and anger

Nwanne anyị jikwere ya ogu na ọfọ	Our brother/sister is justified
Ala tigbuo ya	Let the earth strike and kill such one.

The same oral elegies portray that the deceased is gradually advancing in age. It goes thus:

Oruo n'ọrụrụ	When it is work time
Udo adịrị	Peace reigns
Ya ruo mbge a ga-eri eri	But when it is time for
Ọnwụ abia	Reaping and eating death comes knocking

Also in the following Igbo elegy, the poet-persona expresses anger towards death.

"Ọnwụ"	"Death"
Ọnwụ anyi mere gịnị?	Death what have we done?
Iwe! Iwe! dị anyị iwe	Anger! We are angry
Ọnwụ anyị mere ole	Death, what do you want with us
Ndị ala aka ndị elu	Those down are bigger than those up
Iwe iwe dị anyị iwe	Anger, anger we are filled with anger
Okorobia ọnwụ atu egwu	The young, death does not fear
Iwe! Iwe dị anyị iwe	Anger, anger we are filled with anger
Agadi ọnwụ atu egwu	The aged, death does not fear
Iwe! Iwe di anyi iwe	Anger, anger we are filled with anger
Ebelebe egbuela	A terrible thing has happened
Iwe! Iwe dị anyị iwe	Anger, anger we are filled with anger
Ọnwụ anyị mere ole?	Death what did we do?

The singer here also highlights the fact that death is no respecter of persons for it does not know rich or poor, young or old. There is also the feeling of pouncing on death and relegating it totally out of existence.

In some of the elegies death is abused and this is one of the reactions towards death. The singer in the following elegy rains abuses
on death:

Onye mere ihe a	Who did this?
Ara gbachiri ọnwụ ntị	Let madness render death deaf
Ọnwụ mere ihe a	It is death who did it.
Ara gbachiri ọnwụ ntị	Let madness render death deaf
Ọnwụ amaghị Okorobia	Death does not know the young
Ara gbachiri ọnwụ ntị	Let madness render death deaf
Ọnwụ amaghị agadi	Death does not know the aged
Ara gbachiri ọnwụ ntị	Let madness render death deaf
Hill…..hooo…..hii…hooo	Hill……….hooo…….hill……

(Ogbalu 20)

It is an established fact that at the instance of the death of someone, while the very close relatives and friends are thrown into mourning, there are cases of those who may put up a *laissez faire* attitude
to the whole situation. There are some elegies that also warn such
people to be mindful of their actions because death awaits all and its
visit is not usually planned, fixed or pre-arranged. The song below
illustrates that:

O nuru olu onwu buru nkata jewe Onitsha mgbere

O zuta ya rewe onwu nokwa nd bed ya.

[He who hears the event of death but carries his/her market wares
to Onitsha for sales should go ahead and enjoy his/her money alone
because death is awaiting him/her in bed.]

I don't care bụ onye ọ bịa bere

[I don't care is for those who have not been hit by death.]

The above is a modern oral elegy in the sense that it code-mixes
the English language and the Igbo language. It reflects the language
of those who do not know death well and the implication of losing a
dear one. It simply means that he whom death has not struck cannot

understand what the experience is like and will usually say "I don't care" in English, or care less in attitude. The sung affirms that it is only when it happens closely that we grieve.

Another dimension of traditional elegy is the attitudinal outlook to death. What is actually meant here is the oral elegies that express grief but convey the state of mind, the mood and attitude of the mourner towards death through tone. Some express anger, annoyance and aggression towards death. This is why C. Ngozi Okezie affirms that "in some funeral songs, death is seen as a snatcher or rogue while in others it is conceived as rest, especially if the deceased attained a ripe age or had been ill for a long time" (64). A good example of an angry attitude towards death is this elegy from Uganda:

The Homestead of Death's Mother

Fire rages at Latima, oh,

Fire rages in the valley of River Cumy,

Everything is utterly destroyed

If I could reach the homestead of Death's mother

My daughter I would take a long grass torch,

If I could reach the homestead of Death's mother

I would destroy everything utterly utterly,

Like the fire that rages in the valley of River Cumy

It rages at Latima oh,

Fire rages in the valley of River Cumy,

Everything is utterly destroyed.

If I could reach the homestead of Death's mother

My clansmen, we would fight ruthlessly,

If I could reach the homestead of Death's mother

I would destroy everything utterly utterly

Like the fire that rages in the valley of River Cumy

(Mapange and White 100)

The singer of this oral elegy expresses rage over death and what were to happen if death's abode can be accessed.

PANEGYRIC ELEGY

Some African oral elegies can also eulogize the dead and this is what Finnegan calls the "panegyric of the dead"; in this context the dead one is praised by his admirers who are mourning him or her. They praise him for his numerous achievements; they also sing of his unquantifiable generosity to the people and society. It becomes more elaborate when the deceased is one who is popular and enjoys a lot of fame among his folk. Instances abound when the deceased happens to be a great wrester, a king, a great farmer or someone whose profession affected the lives of his folk positively. A good example in Nigeria was at the instance of the death of Ikemba Odimegwu Ojukwu who was the Biafran war lord of the Nigerian Biafran Crisis. Many elegies were composed and sung in his honour by different persons and groups as his life affected them now and in the past. These elegies were sung in his honour and they make very close and direct references to him that such may not be sung for another on a similar occasion.

One of such is this recorded by me:

Ọnwụ egbuola Odimegwu Ojukwu	Death has killed Odimegwu Ojukwu
Nwoke ike	A Strong man of valour
Ọzọ Igbo ndụ	Saver of the Igbo
Dike eji eje mba	A warrior for outside war
Nwoke di mma	A good man
Onye Igbo nine lekwasara anya	The whole Igbo nation looked up to him
Odimegwu Ojukwu	Odimegwu Ojukwu
Ikemba Nnewi	Ikemba Nnewi
Eze Igbo gburugburu	The King of the whole Igbo nation

Panegyric elegy becomes more elaborate at the courts of a king at such occasions of bereavement in the court or death of the king, queen, prince or princess. Below is an example of a panegyric elegy from Sam Uzochukwu:

"Okoronkwọ Kalu"	"Okoronkwọ Kalu"
Onyeike "Okoronkwọ Kalu"	Brave man: "Okoronkwo Kalu"
Agụ di ike ma di aju dika agu	Strong lion but gentle like a lion
Ome mgbe ọ dị mkpa	He who takes over when it is expedient
Eleghị 'ike' a na-eme okpogho	He who does not look back in spending money
Omepụrụ onye ọ dịrị	He who does for those who do not have.
Anyị na-akpọ gị oku si gi bilie	We are calling you saying rise
Ma Ị naghị ebili	But you cannot rise

(Uzochukwu 24)

The above elegy in honour of Okoronkwo Kalu may be seen as a dirge because of the nature of address to the deceased but at the same time it sings praises to the deceased for his personality and generosity to mankind.

Panegyric elegy is more elaborate when the court is affected; in this connection let us look at the first stanza of this panegyric elegy of the court from Ethiopia:

Lamentation

(1)

The Hinnare—Tato has become a simple man,

Our magnificent gold has become copper

O king, how we long for you!

We have become simple,

Our greatness has become simplicity,

We are sorrowful and sad.

O king how we long for you!

Let me be eaten and thrown for my king
Let me be buried for my king.
O my king, who is like gold
O my king, a magnificent not a simple man,
O my king, the husband of four wives
O my king, with powerful and accurate throws,
O my king , with an excellent aim for buffalo,
O my king, who can compare with you?
You are like an imposing omo tree
You are like a calf sucking the udder,
A man who lived a long life.
We bless you, saying
Live long!
Be greater than you are!
O my king, who can compare with you?
You bring back sheep feed in the forest vines,
You are wealthy and generous.
Who feeds and satisfies the people with abundant supplying.
We bless you saying
Live long!
Be greater than you are!
Feed the people!
Feed the people!
What more can I say to praise you?

                    (Mapanje and White 28–9)

The above poem is a total praise of a deceased king by his subjects. The king's exit is mourned and his personality praised. There is also the belief in the fact that the king has gone to live in the world beyond; this is why he is still asked to live on by his subjects.

Religious Elegies

These are the types of elegies that have religious undertone. They are usually sung in direct reverence to God who is believed to hold the keys of life and nothing can be done to avert death once God makes the pronouncement. Below is an example of religious elegy which expresses the supremacy of God over man on the issue of death, also from Sam Uzochukwu:

"Ọnwụ"	"Death"
Mmadụ nọ n'ụwa bụ ewu Chukwu	Human beings on earth are god's goat
Mgbe Chukwu chọrọ	When God wants his goat he takes
ewu ya ọ kpụrụ	
Ndị achị ọchi	Some will be laughing
Ndị ebe akwa n'ụwa	Others crying on earth
Ị na-achị ọchị ọbụ gị ka ọkara mma?	Are you laughing, are you better?
Ị na-ebe akwa ọbụ gị ka ọkara njọ	Are you crying, are you the worst hit?

In the above poem human beings are seen as animals—goats belonging to God—who He takes to His heavenly abode anytime he desires, and at such moments no person can resist, differ or reject it.

Some religious elegies also try to establish some biblical facts concerning man in order to remind man that human life and body are not worth the kind of regard and respect man gives it. For example, the elegy below presents the image of God's creation of man with sand and the irony of man's return to mother earth to await the maker of man.

Mmadụ	Man
Mmadụ ntụ ka Ị bụ	Man: dust you are
Na ntụ ka Ị ga alaghachi	And unto dust you shall return
Onyenweanyi ga-ekpe anyi ikpe	Our God shall judge us

| Ma anyị nwụọ | when we die |
| Ya bụ ka anyị kwụsi nfuli elu | so let us not be proud |

Another tries to express the fact that man is a sojourner on planet earth and must one day die lying full back and facing heaven, which is the abode of the most high God, where the soul of man must ascend to await judgment.

"Anyị bịara abịa"	"We are Sojourners"
Eee, anyị bịara abia n'elu uwa?	Eee, we are sojourners upon the earth
Eee, arụ anyị bụkwa aja (2x)	Eee, our bodies are just sand (2x)
Onye nọchanụ o were isi lebe	When life terminates the head lies
Anya n'igwe.	looking up to heaven.

CONSOLATORY ELEGY

This refers to the type of African oral elegy whose major focus is to console, encourage and put the bereaved in a lighter mood and disposition. It tries to bring in the belief that life does not end in death but continues. This is the dimension of elegy that the Elizabethans of the English called "apotheosis"—and elegy of consolation. It can also affirm that man has no right of ownership or claim but it is God who owns everybody and directs their existence. It can also try to console the bereaved to take heart because every other bereaved person endured and overcame the situation. This song below is a kind of consolatory elegy:

Dibe Dibe Dibe	Take heart Take heart
Ndidi ka mma	Patient is the best attitude
Onye o mere ya dibe oo	Anybody who is bereaved should take heart
Ndidi ka mma	For patience is the best attitude.

Lawa na ndokwa ọ ga odịrị gị mma	Go in peace it shall be well with you
Lawa na ndokwa	Go in peace it shall be well with you
Nwanne lawa na ndokwa	Brother/sister go in peace it shall be
Ọ ga odịrị gị mma	Well with you.

PERFORMANCE OF AFRICAN ORAL ELEGY

African oral poetry is occasion-bound. The occasion for the elegy is purely at the moment of loss and grief. It may vary from person to person or community to community. They can be performed at the funeral rites or the memorials. According to Finnegan and Okpewho, some African communities have professional mourners or elegy/dirge singers are invited on the occasion of the death of someone and they gather, mourn, lament, wail and sing elegies at the funeral of the deceased. Upholding the views of J.H.R Nketia, Finnegan opines that:

> On these occasions women are the most frequent singers. Among the Yoruba, women lament at funeral feasts. Akan dirges are chanted by women soloists and the Zitengulo songs of Zambia are sung by women mourners (147).

Also among the Igbo of Nigeria, associates that have close ties with a deceased usually come together during the funeral rites in honour of the deceased and express their grief in songs and chants. Many funeral songs exist traditionally among the Igbo of eastern Nigeria, and these songs are usually sung at burials irrespective of the sex of the deceased. Different groups to which the deceased belonged will usually come and mourn by singing, at times dancing and performing the burials rites due the deceased.

At some point in the performance the group mourners will sing, dance and march out for a mock search of the deceased. They will intone a song which is short and rendered by a leader singing while others respond. It goes as thus:

> Leader: Chọọ ya n'ụlọ ya
>
> Others: Anyị ga achọọ ya anyị ahụghị ya
>
> Leader: Chọọ n'ụlọ ụka ya
>
> Others: Anyị ga chọọ ya anyị ahụghị ya
>
> Leader: Chọọ chọọ chọọ
>
> Others: Anyị ga achọ ya, anyị ahụghị ya (2x)

Translation

> Leader: Search search search
>
> Others: We have searched we did not see him/her (2x)
>
> Leader: Search in the house
>
> Others: We have searched but did not see
>
> Leader: Search in the church
>
> Others: We have searched but did not see

They continue mentioning as many places as possible. Usually, the mourners leave the homestead of the deceased which is usually in the place of interment in a mock search for the deceased within the environment. The mourners return to the homestead singing the above songs in expression of the perpetual exit and vacuum created by the death of the deceased. C. Ngozi Okezie identifies the mock search as a motif prevalent in most funeral songs. She avers " that some death songs have the search motif which is also dramatized by actual search for the person in his market stall, along the paths to the farm, stream and any other place he normally went to" (64). One other important factor to note is that these patterns of elegiac forms cut across the Igbo tribe but there could exist dialect variations as the case may be.

Other occasions of the performance of the elegy are the moments of a person's death, after the mourning period and at memorials, but these are strictly bound by the community or family. Some communities count some weeks after which they come together and observe the month's mind of the deceased and at such times elegies are sung in honour of the deceased. Some other families may from time to time hold memorials in honour of their dead ones, and at such times elegies are sung in honour of the dead ones.

In the rendition of African oral elegies the language is usually emotional. Words are carefully chosen and voiced by the mourners to express grief, loss and bereavement. At times the mourners express moments shared together, deprivations that are established and vacuum created by the death of the person. These words used in expressing the feelings can as well trigger off bumps of cries, drops of tears and feelings of empathy on the sympathizers. Mourners also bring to light the different responsibilities which the deceased have left to go to the world beyond. The words used also heighten the emotion of sympathizers.

CONCLUSION

African oral elegy remains a very important area of oral performance in the African society; its occasion in the African socio-cultural milieu can never be effaced because life begins, traverses through its sweet bitter moments with its diverse expressions and life also ends. As the oral poems are chanted and performed at child birth and other child-birth related ceremonies so will oral poetry for the dead continue to thrive. One important fact is that as the wave of modernity, civilization and advancement in Christianity impedes on the forms, the African oral elegy will gradually adjust to the changes that come upon it but will ever remain. This accounts for the different versions of oral elegies prevalent in the Igbo society today. The content, form and performance of African oral elegy remain an integral aspect of African oral heritage.

WORKS CITED

Awoonor, Kofi, *The Breast of the Earth: A Survey of the History, Culture and Literature of Africa South of Sahara*, New York. Nok Publishers International, 1975. Print.

Ezenwa-Ohaeto. *Contemporary Nigerian Poetry and the Poetics of Orality*. Bayreuth: Bayreuth African Studies 45, 1998. Print.

Finnegan, Ruth. *Oral Literature in African.* Nairobi and Cambridge: Oxford University Press and Open Books Publishers, 1970 and 2012. Print.

Mapanje, Jack and Landveg White. *Oral Poetry from African: An Anthology.* Essex: Longman, 1983. Print.

Okezie, C. Ngozi. *A Hand Book to Oral Literature. Umuahia:* Versatile Publishers Ltd, 2007. Print.

Ogbalu F.C. *Igbo Poems and Songs.* Onitsha: University publishing Co, 1974. Print.

Okpewho, Isidore. *African Oral Literature: Background, Character and Continuity.* Bloomington and Indianapolis: Indianapolis University Press, 1992. Print.

Onuekwusi, Jasper Ahaoma. *Fundamentals of African Oral Literature.* Owerri. Alphabet Nigeria Publishers, 2001. Print.

Uzochukwu, Sam. *Abu Akwamozu.* 2nd ed. Obosi: Pacific Publishers Ltd, 2005. Print.

Chapter Seven

Satire in Traditional African Oral Poetry: The Edda Igbo Example

F.U. Chima

INTRODUCTION

It seems proper and necessary to begin with a brief note on the word, 'satire', which appears in the title of this chapter. The word comes from Latin word, 'satur' and the subsequent phrase 'Lanx satura'. Satur on its own means 'full', but the juxtaposition with 'Lanx' transforms its meaning into 'miscellany or medley'. Yet, the literal expression, 'Lanx satura', means 'a full dish of various kinds of fruits' (Wikipedia). From the authorities of Wikipedia, it is gathered that derivation of satire from 'satura', a Latin word, properly has nothing to do with the Greek mythological figure, 'satyr'. However, to Quintilian, the scholar who used the word satura to denote only Roman verse satire, it was a strict literary form but the term soon escaped from the original definition. Perhaps, it is on this note that Robert Elliott writes:

> As soon as a noun enters the domain of metaphor, as one modern scholar has pointed out, it clamours for extension, and satura (which had no verbal, adverbial or adjectival forms) was immediately broadened by appropriation from the Greek word for 'satyr' (satyros) and its derivatives. The odd result is that the English 'satire' comes from the Latin Satura; but 'satirize', 'satiric' etc, are of Greek origin. By about the 4th century AD the writer of satires came to be known as satyricus. St. Jerome, for example, was called by one of his enemies ' a satirist in prose' (satyicus scriptor in prose). Subsequent orthographic modifications obscured the Latin origin of the word satire. Satire

becomes satyra, and in England, by the 10th century, it was written 'satyre' (qtd in Wikipedia).

From the foregoing, the word satire is a Latin derivative and adaptation into English vocabulary. But for us here, the discourse on what satire means is based on what its contemporary connotations in English suggest. Turning to the *New Webster's Dictionary Of The English Language* (Delox Encyclopedia Edition),

> Satire implies the use of irony, sarcasm, or ridicule in exposing, denouncing, or deriding vice, folly or the like; a literary composition, in versed or prose, in which vices, abuses, or follies are held up to scorn, derision, or ridicule; the literary type constituted by such composition (852–3).

The above premise has only declared the obvious: satire, whatever its maiden connotations were, for example, in Latin of the ancient Romans, or Greek of the ancient Greece or any other language, ancient or modern, apart, is in modern English language, more especially, primarily a literary genre or from that which houses a critique on human demeanour. Also deduced from the foregoing is that if a literary work, be that in poetic, dramatic in prosaic form, is designed to ridicule and laugh at human follies and vices, such a literary work is said to be satirical in nature, and, going by the noun derivatives, the writer is a satirist. Of a truth, this idea of satire in the contemporary English must have informed M.H. Abrams' idea of satire when he says: Satire is the literary art of a dominant subject by making it ridiculous and evoking toward attitudes of amusement, contempt, indignation, or scorn (167).

However, in practice, it should be borne in mind that satire can also be seen in graphic performing arts. Yet, this point being so important and good and needs be mentioned as we have done, are some issues, still, that needing to be ironed out, which surround the meaning of satire. This is very important for us at this juncture, since the obvious has been made that goes contrary to the literary piece which aims at ridiculing the follies and vices of human behaviours that go contrary to the already accepted norms. But what confronts us now is the 'how'? In an attempt to achieve its aim, satire makes use of irony, sarcasm and ridicule among others. Irony involves the kind of speech in which the literary meaning is the opposite of the intended meaning. In other words, irony makes use of ridicule, contempt or humour against its target. Explaining more formerly, the *Webster's Dictionary* states that 'it is a technique often used in writing satire'. For sarcasm and satire, the Webster Dictionary informs us that the words involve the use of a bitter laugh. They involve a bitter, cutting expression, a caustic remark; a jibe; a taunt; the employment of ironical or satirical language and the use of laugh and ridicule. They involve something laughable, a jest, a laugh. They are words or actions, respectively, to excite contemptuous laughter at a person or thing; intended to deride or make fun of. In satire, therefore, the qualities of irony, sarcasm and ridicule are piled on, although the landmark that differentiates one from the other can be deciphered but the gaps are not much. For instance, satire, irony and sarcasm deride or laugh at human follies and vices, yet satire separates itself from the others in conveying a norm whereas irony, for example, urges one to search after an unknown truth (Weisgerber, 1973). However, satire, carrying irony, sarcasm and ridicule derides human follies with the intention to correct.

Because scholarship on satire (just like every other field of study) started from the West, some scholars like Horace and Juvenal had in the early centuries made their marks from their styles of satirical writings. They had also made their names synonymous with this form of literary expression. Yet, no research has been able to establish either the date, day, year or era for the commencement of this genre in the human society. Even at the pre-classical Western era, no proof is established. Obviously, this is an indication that satire as a means of ridiculing and at the same time exposing human follies and vices using humour and lampoon, is an old exercise in every society; that the satirical method of reprimanding human misdemeanor is as old as man in every society.

The traditional African oral setting was not free from such way of life of using satire. In fact, one may not be too far from the truth to say with every mark of sincerity that the West must have copied from the Africans on the use of satirical poems to reprimand the wrongdoers in the society. As it were, as all available evidence has shown, the ancient Greek and Rome influenced the English society alongside other parts of the Western World in almost every field of scholarship. The issue of the satire is a case in point. Without repeating the obvious, satire, a Latin derivative that is applied to a variety of performances, was introduced by Etruscans into English society but was established as a genre by Lucilius. As a movement that started from the ancient Rome, it was introduced by Varro and developed by Horace and Juvenal (Wikipedia, *Encyclopedia Britannica* vol.7).

In traditional Africa, the reverse is the case. In fact, songs and poetry have been part of people's way of life. Existing in traditional Africa are songs and poetry which show the temperament of the singer/poet and the society alike. In his study of the Nigeria Yoruba Ijala, the inspired chant and songs which aim at firing the courage of hunters and warriors before an encounter, Babalola made this known when he says that oral poetry is part of everyday life among the Yoruba (vi). Also from his series of researches on African Oral Literature, Okpewho agrees with Babalola's observation but goes a step further and adds' ... the same can safely be said of the pervasive role of songs and chants in traditional African life generally' (138). For sure, Okpewho here is of the opinion that, as the Yoruba Ijala poetry is meant to spur the hunters about going into hunting expeditions, so are all the oral songs/poetry meant for a purpose in traditional Africa. This is very true because the African songs/poetry or chants are occasion-bound. Every occasion always gives rise to its songs/poetry or chants, which are usually associated with such occasion. For instance, when a pregnant woman is delivered of her baby in traditional Africa, birth songs emerge which accompany such moments of rejoicing and merry-making. This is for good fortune because Africans believe that the issue of child birth is one of life and death. When a child is crying or when the mother or the baby-sitter wishes to make the baby stop crying or to sleep, lullabies are sung. When young boys and girls are to be initiated into, for example in the Edda Igbo area, *egbela, ndagha* or *olo* cults respectively, songs are sung to mark the occasion (Monye, 68). Not only that, when at work, songs are used to relieve the periods in the farm. Even when relaxing, after a long day's work in the field, a variety of songs arises. Such songs could be satirical, historical or praiseworthy. etc. Yet, the themes of these songs or chants are not watertight; by which we mean the functions or the purpose of these songs/poetry in traditional Africa overlap. A given poem or song may have a mixture of many themes. It all depend on the thought of the poet and his or her feeling towards the situation on ground. This idea is summed up by Egudu this way:

> The genesis of any literary piece—written or oral—must therefore be sought in the author's mental response (thought) and his emotional response (Feeling to some events or experience (249).

But it is quite regrettable that right from the outset, since African Oral Literature found its feet among other oral literatures as an independent area of study, rather than a mere appendage to any other oral literature, several of the genres in the traditional African oral literature have suffered some kind of misconceptions in the hands of some Western and African scholars alike. Yet, of all the traditional African oral genres so far explored, as all available facts seem to prove, satire can be said to have been the most affected in that direction. These misleading stock of interpretative analyses of the traditional African oral genres in general and the satiric occasions in Africa in particular, have been popularized by the Western scholars, who actually made the first laudable and bold outing in the study of the African Oral Literature. But, the most unfortunate situation has it that some African intellectuals who later joined in the race with Western scholars, succumbed to the Western ideas and opinions. They discuss, for example, satire in traditional African oral poetry to parallel the Western ideologies and conceptions. Following closely the footsteps of the Western scholars, the African scholars narrowed the concept and scope of satire so that its life-wire, considering its African ideas, seem to be limited to a very restricted area of human

existence and experience. Obviously, as we had said earlier on, this is
to make its meaning parallel to the Western ideas.

A good instance for the above premise is the idea put forward
by the Oxford-trained anthropologist and author, Ruth Finnegan, in
her erudite and epoch-making book, *Oral Literature in Africa*, (1970),
that satire in the traditional African oral setting is nothing but a 'poetry of profound political significance as a means of political propaganda, pressure or communication' (qtd in Agovi, 1). We need not
say much on her idea of satire in traditional African oral setting (as
given to us by Kofi E. Agovi) because the source of her error of judgment is obvious. She used the prescriptive instead of the descriptive
method of data analysis in studying satire in traditional Africa. The
prescriptive method of studying, especially in language or in oral culture, deals with the use of an alien feature or ideas of no relationship
whatsoever with another language or culture to study another language or culture, while the descriptive method involves the use of the
inherent qualities in a given language or culture to study the same
language or culture. This explanation may not be necessary since in
due course the areas of departure from the traditional African oral
sense of satire shall unveil itself. What needs be said, instead, is that it
is based on this idea of satire that many Africa writers in Africa and
the diaspora reasoned along the little they did in their prescriptions
of satire in the traditional African oral poetry. Among the scholars
whom the Western ideas of satire have influenced their sense of satire in the traditional African oral poetry is Kofi E. Agovi. Agovi,
besides being an African, a Ghananian to be precise, is so influenced
by the above cited extract from Finnegan's book, *Oral Literature in
Africa*, that he leaned the weight of his explanation on satire in the
traditional African oral poetry this way:

> According to Ruth Finnegan, the patronage of poetics of poets
> in centralized political systems in the past led to the creation of
> political propaganda, pressure or communication, such poetry
> includes songs of insult, challenge of satirical comment used as
> 'politically effective weapon'(1).

Even before Agovi became a victim of this narrow misconception of satire in traditional African oral poetry in 1991, Dan Izevbaye and Mazisi Kunene had, in twenty and twelve years earlier, respectively, fallen the same victims. So, from similar influence from Finnegan's book, Izevbaye contends that in 'West Africa, at least the earliest important tradition of poetry has its source in political action' (147). Similarly, Mazisi Kunene informs us that during the period of Shaka, Zulu Literature 'changed to become a powerful vehicle of social and political ideas'; and that at that time poets and singers became central

> democratic agents to reaffirm that approval or disapproval of the whole nation. It was through the poet and singer that criticism and evaluation of the heroes and rulers was fully and freely expressed (qtd in Agovi, 1).

From the above comments, a few facts needs be classified. Firstly, for the interest of scholarship, Agovi misquoted Finnegan both in intended meaning and in pagination. It is on pages 272-3 that she makes mention of satire and not on pages 82 and 172 as Agovi would have us believe. On the issue of meaning, Agovi's meaning does not parallel Finnegan's. Yet even from his idea, it needs be said that in Africa, traditional oral satirical songs are not byproducts of political actions. Secondly, satirical songs/poetry do not concern themselves with the activities of the heroes. Again, the satirical poets are not the determinants of the social norms. Theirs is to make sure nobody goes off the already established way of life. We shall return to this issue subsequently.

Returning to where we were, it should be remembered that Finnegan was not the only Western scholar who presents such a narrow and shallow interpretation on some African oral genres to Western standards which some African scholars copy without any reservations. Many European scholars had misinterpreted the traditional African oral setting. C.K. Meek, as Ebeogu informs us, for example, in 1930, made similar mistake on the Igbo, African, people when he was commissioned to study them by the British colonial government of Nigeria. On his misinterpretation of the people's idea of humorous criticism, Meek hastily concludes that

> Mere abuse is not a deadly sin, and one may often see two Ibo
> (sic] reviling each other in the strongest of language for several
> minutes and then bursting into laughter as they walk away (qtd
> in Ebeogu, 29).

But come to think of it, one need not, in the midst of all these misinterpretations of the traditional African oral genres, take amiss. One need to be appreciative of the earlier writers' attempts and contributions to African literary genres, their areas of misconceptions notwithstanding. This is because it is such similar misconceptions, for example, in the area of African epics, that bring a new dawn on its existence and other features about it in Africa. Therefore, through similar means the true nature of most of the African oral genres will be known. Obviously, it is with such discovery spirit in mind that the aim of this research is by no means to condemn or reject outright, [without] any commendation, whatsoever, the attempts of earlier scholars on satire in traditional African oral poetry. More so, and still on the contrary, what we wish to establish is yet not the obvious that satire does actually exist in traditional African oral songs/poetry. Rather, ours is to bring into limelight those characteristic nuances that emanate from its origin, its originator/s, its context and content; its function and life-span, its relevance in the contemporary African society; and in fact, all those features that make its Africanness obvious and unmistakable from the Western sense of satire. However, some of these features may be implied.

As a matter of fact, a discussion of satire in traditional African oral songs/poetry and or setting may be somewhat an area too large and delicate to handle. This is because there is a surfeit of modes— poetic, dramatic and prosaic—by which the Africans satirize and criticize the follies of persons or group in the society. And because Africa is a homogeneous society, we shall use the Edda Igbo area as a microcosm for the study of satire in the traditional African oral poetry. However, considering the enormous ways the Africans verbally attack wrongdoers in the society, satire and its Western connotations may be too little an umbrella to house adequately all the varying means, medium and methods the Africans use is their satirical songs/poetry. D.I. Nwoga seems to have been aware of this fact on satire as an alien nomenclature on the African soil when he says:

> The definition of satire as 'the use of irony, ridicule, sarcasm, or the like, to denounce or deride vice, folly, etc', might be adequate for the dictionary but it leaves much to be explored about its origins, provenance, contexts and complex manifestations (231).

However, before settling for the discussion of satire proper in the traditional African oral poetry, using the Edda Igbo area as a point of reference, it is necessary that some issues are put in place. Such issues if explained can no doubt form the rungs for better understanding of what we shall be talking about concerning satire in traditional African oral songs/poetry. In this paper, we have taken satire in Africa, as it is in the Western World, to be an oral means of flogging wrongdoers in our society. They, the dimensions or modes it has taken in each of these two societies, Africa and the West, are not the same. Besides, a very close examination of satire in Africa and the West will reveal that they do not share a common feature and therefore, there are variations in functions. For example, what brought about satirical songs/ poetry in Africa differ tremendously from what gave rise to the same genre outside Africa. In Africa, the violations of the world-view of the people by an individual or group trigger off satirical songs/poetry. This is not the same in the West where the opinion of an individual poet prompts him or her to satirize the entire and initially accepted way of life of a nation. In a nutshell, what makes the Africanness of the African traditional oral satire unmistakable from any other include its use of direct verbal attack and caricature. Its use of figures of speech, proverbs, anecdotes, etc, drawn from the African culture and environment is another distinguishing factor that marks its Africannes.

Having given these few hints to serve as a precursor for us on what are to come, its high time we turned to satire in the traditional African oral songs/poetry, using Edda Igbo area as a our reference point.

ORIGIN OF SATIRE IN TRADITIONAL AFRICA

The obvious has already been saids in this paper, that satirical songs/poetry abound in Africa and so do their provenance. True-life events or behaviour of people that are contrary to the norms of the society, are normally the mile-stones from which satirical songs/poetry in traditional Africa emerge. As it is in Edda Igbo in particular and other parts of traditional Africa in general, satirical songs/poetry can be traced to the beginning of life itself in Africa when men started interacting among themselves, and man chose to reprimand and expose the abnormal behaviour of his fellow man with the use of lampoon and humorous means. However, some scholars have been giving variant views about the origin. One such variant worth mentioning here, is that from D.I. Nwoga (230–246) who was himself a renowned scholar of African oral poetry. In his view, what brought about satire in traditional Africa was because there were no formalized system for punishing violations of societal norms; that as it were, satire played the role of the judicial systems for punishing offenders of moral norms as there were no prisons. Again, that major crimes were punished with judicial or ritual execution or selling into slavery or being ostracized. What the above idea seems to presuppose is that minor crimes, like unrestrained sexual freedom among young boys and girls, co-wives' rivalry and gossips, theft, the oppressive foster-mother, bad mothers-in-law/daughters-in-law troublemaker, etc, begot satirical songs/poetry in Africa for the simple reasons which include, first, non-formalized mode of doing things in Africa. Second, non-existence of prison; and third, some crimes, which he did not give any example of, attract different punishments considered more grave, as if perhaps, satirical songs/poetry in Africa are only but children's play.

The above submissions as given us by Nwoga are quite on the contrary. Satire in traditional African oral setting was begun not because there were no courts or court-like institutions in Africa: for what reasons or functions were councils of *Umunna* formed or why do all family heads come together? Nwoga even contradicts himself when he says: "Adult males as a class avoid this [i.e satire] since they are the respectable peace keepers who are to arbitrate if problems arise from the practice of satric poetry" (232). In fact, the issue of major or minor crimes as Nwoga would have us believe is ambiguous. In Edda Igbo area, for example, and as in other African societies, there exist traditional courts, prisons and then the satirical songs/poetry. Each of these institutions works independently, yet they are not mutually exclusive in functions. The council of every family head, the council of every adult male members from every community who meet either at the family level, village level or at the clan level, are all akin to the modern-day courts. These traditional judicial strata are evidences that the kind of crime committed determines the level to decide or try such crime. A murder case may be decided or tried at the *ogo* level while the crime that involves a woman beating the village talking drum or the *ikoro*, would only b decided or tried at the clan level, involving every selected adult male members from all the villages. Again, that a person is given a judicial or ritual execution punishment or any other measure of punishment such as selling into slavery or being ostracized does not imply the crime that led to such punishment is greater than the crimes for satirical songs/poetry. At this juncture, it need be made clear that in traditional Africa, every crime is enough and very fit to be the subject for satirical songs/ poetry. And, to be satirized is even worse than any other measure of punishment. This is because if a person is satirized in traditional African oral songs/poetry, the effect is far reaching and all encompassing. The satirical measure does not concern the offender only but goes beyond into the family lineage of the offender.

The issue of lack of prison custody in Africa as one of the reasons for the emergence of satirical song/poetry is a major fault in Nwoga's premise on the origin of satirical songs in traditional Africa. I am a free born of Edda person of a royal family. Therefore, this information as I relate it here as a back-up to my research is as my father gave it to me. According him (my father), his father and his grand-father who were kings before him, had prison custodies called '*mkpuka*', a room without windows. As it was in those days, if any body was caught on the charges of any crime or if any was a suspect for any crime yet failed to tell the truth, the suspect had to be locked up there *(mkpuka)* and an *'ogbo'*, a byproduct of a bunch of a palm fruit, set on fire with a few seeds of pepper on it, would be put and locked up alongside the suspect. After sometime, the person would even call for help with a promise to tell the truth. This was a traditional prison. More so, before the issue of ritual execution or selling into slavery or being ostracized would come in, satirical songs' poetry on the person would have failed to call such a person to order, or when the person's notoriety is a threat to the entire community. Otherwise no punishment surpasses satirizing an individual in a song. Besides, the person's relatives may even wish for any other measure since, as we had said earlier, the song is not always on the person per se but goes beyond into the person's present or future generations.

ORIGINATORS AND OCCASIONS FOR SATIRICAL SONGS IN AFRICA

So far, it had been established that satirical songs/poetry abound in traditional African oral setting; and we have traced its origin to be the mere attempt by man in the early stages to keep his fellow man on track on matters of strict obedience to the societal norms. But, the general statements have had it that the creative genius in African literary tradition is indebted to man's immediate environment or the larger society. Or that it is the society that provides him with the linguistics and literary traditions in terms of a common language or dialect, metaphor, imagery, and proverbs (Ce 78). Perhaps it is from this vantage point that it has been alleged that every artistic work in Africa is communally owned. To refute this, references can still be made to the obvious fact that there has been no time perceptions of people to events have been the same all through. Therefore, satire as a literary genre in traditional African oral literature has been artistically woven by some gifted individuals from the adult males, adult females, young boys and girls as well as some dancing groups of either men or women or young girls. It also originates from masquerades in some parts of Africa. At this juncture, it is appropriate to point out, however, that in Edda Igbo, as in other oral cultures in Africa, the composed satirical song and poetry does not just spring up. There have always been individual originators, those talented creators and performers who stand out in the community as artists and innovators. The satiric song/ poetry is only communally owned after it has been composed and performed by the originators.

As has been iterated by almost all available written evidence, satire in traditional African oral songs/poetry celebrates varying themes in Africa. These themes include sexual promiscuity, stealing, incest, patricide, matricide and murder. Others are womanizing, rape, abortion, etc. In fact, the themes for satirical song/poetry in traditional African oral setting are limitless. Perhaps, the occasional misconception by some scholars that the themes covered by satire in traditional African oral poetry are minor crime or offences only emanates from the mode of satire studied, or due mainly to the arm-chair research of the African oral literature common among present day scholars.

Satirical songs from a lass or a lad-genius, do not go far from themes on, borrowing the term from Nwoga, 'minor crime' (231) such as the theme of abortion, prostitution, womanizing, etc. Yet, although these areas are serious areas of human endeavour, the young teenagers, due to inexperience on philosophy of life, treat their themes on the surface and peripherally. They cannot be blamed because they are not yet mature on the philosophy of human existence and experience. The poem as shown below, which is composed against every young lass who gets impregnated out of wedlock, summarizes our idea about the content of the teenage satire in Africa.

Ụmụ agbọ nọrị ụlọ akwa ọnụma!	Girls are at home weeping!
Melanụrụ agị	What have I done?
Mu menanụrụ woo	I only was to enjoy like others
Mama	Mama
Letukwale efo m	Have a look at my tummy
Sa mụ bu ime	If I'm pregnant
Sa okale aka	If it is due
Ma mụa ya	For me to be delivered of the baby
Ma wo ye m o duo	For me to be impregnated again

Looking at this satirical song, it will seem difficult to establish the obvious that ideally, and most importantly, in the Edda Igbo land, traditional African oral song/poetry, is seriously composed in proverbial statements, poetic in language, philosophical in depth and above all, invocational in its text and tone. However, by the time one gets to the satirical songs/poetry composed by any of the genius-adult members of the society, the conviction of the Africanness of the song/poetry will not in doubt. For lack of space and time, an archetypal example from 'Umu Njoloko', one of the now defunct dancing groups in Edda, can suffice:

Unu afụa	Have you all seen
Elekwa egbu ghu edu	Elekwa who didn't plant arial yam now Has basins full of it
Abụọ eju woo	Basins full of it
Elekwa Ibiam	Elekwa Ibiam
Elekwa egbu ghu edu	Elekwa who didn't plant arial yam now Has basins full of it
Abụọ eju woo	Basins full of it
Agbahe ọsọ nkọkọ	When others are going for a crab hunt
Elekwa agbahe ọsọ egburu	Elekwa will be going to uproot cassava
Agbahe ọsọ nkọkọ	When others are going for a crab hunt
Elekwa agbahe ọsọ egburu	Elekwa will be going to uproot cassava
Ozu nne Elekwa	The corpse of Elekwa's mother
Tọgbọrọ ụzọ Ibiakpani ewenkpgha	Lies carelessly along Ibiakpani road
Imaghị udele egwedulere ozu nne wo taka.	Don't you know the vulture has messed up their mother's corpse.
O nke o di yee ha yaa	It is how it is
Ụmụ Njoloko nọkwanwa yeee	Njoloko are you there?
Ayị jụnu Ụka nwa Nnachi Ụka	We ask Uka the son of Nnachi Uka

Inokwanwa ulo yee ka ibe uja	Are you in the house yet you didn't react
Oko ude Ndukwe	Oko Ude Ndukwe
Ịnọkwanwa ụlọ	Are you in the house?
Kaa Oko Ude ebe ụja	And Oko Ude didn't react
Ụkpaị Ndukwe nọkwanwa ụlọ	Ukpai Ndukwe are you in the house?
Kkaa wondeni ebe ụjaa	And none of you reacted
O nke ọ di yee ha yaa	Is it how it is?
Njokolo nọkwanwa yee ha yaa	Njokoloko are you there?
Gwe gwe yee ụwa mee	Oh! Mine oh! Mine
Ụmụ emea	Its tragic
Ma elenke ọnwa ịkpara ọchị bụ ụtọ	Elekwa, don't you think salutation is love?
Ma elenke ọnwa ịkpara ọchị bụ ụtọ	Elekwa, don't you think salutation is love?
Bianụ leghi goo ụlọ nwaoke anọghu	Have a look at it, where there is no male child
Goo imeri emea woo	It's a tragic event
Goo ọnụma Ude bụnụ ọnụma ite egburu	Of all situations, Ude's can be likened to a pot for fermenting cassava
Ka ọdị mma	And it's not fair
Bunu ọnụma ite egburu	A situation likened to a pot for fermenting cassava
Ka ọdị mma	And it's not fair
O nke ọ di yee ha yaa	Is it how it is?
Njoloko nọkwanwa yee ha yaa	Njoloko are you there?

Ya ọnwa emere Uche eleghi nwa	Why has Uche been treated like an
enwoghu nne	orphan
Elekwa Ibiam	Elekwa Ibiam
Ya ọnwa imere Uche eleghi nwa	Why has Uche been treated like an
enwoghu nne	orphan
Ya ọnwa imere Uche eleghi nwa	Why has Uche been treated like an
enwoghu nne	orphan
Elekwa Ibiam	Elekwa Ibiam
Ya ọnwa imere Uche eleghi nwa	Why has Uche been treated like an
enwoghu nne	orphan
Enya Ukpai zohu okenkwu obi ayi woo	Enya Ukpai the stupid one go away from our compound
Onyue aruru	You wicked man
Dike Akwu buru igwu da akpa ago ayi	Dike Akwu, has been living with lies
Ọdikwaghị mma	And its really not fair
O nke ọ di yee ha yaa	Is it how it is?
Njoloko nọkwanwa yee ha yaa	Njoloko are you there?

Yo ọnwa eme m eleghi nwa enwoghu nne	Why has Uche been treated like an Orphan
Ha e yeee	Haa ee yee
Ya ọnwa emere Uche eleghị nwa	Why has Uche been treated like an
enwoghu nne	Orphan
Ozu nne Elekwa tọgbọrọrị ụzọ	Corpse of Elekwa's mother lies

Ibịakpanị enwenkpogha	carelessly along Ibia akpan road
Oko Ude Ndukwe	Oko Ude Ndukwe
Nọkwanwa ogo akpa asịrị	instead wastes his time at village square gossiping
Ka oju ya aju	And it's not fair
O nke o di yee ha yaa	Is it how it is?
Njoloko nọkwanwa yee ha yaa	Njoloko are you there?
Yo ọnwa eme m eleghị nwa enwoghu nne	Why has Uche been treated like an Orphan
Anyị jụnu	We are asking
Ya ọnwa eme m eleghgi mu bu	Why has Uche been treated like an
atakwa da agaa ogo eee	Orphan
O nke ọdị yee ha yaa	Is it how it is?
Njoloko nọkwanwa yee ha yaa	Njoloko are you there?
Gwe gwe yee uwe meee	Oh! Mine, oh! Mine
Ụwa mee	Oh! Mine
Ma ụlọ nwaoke anoghu goo imeri	So a home without a male child is
emea woo	actually tragic
Ụlọ nwaoke anoghu goo imeri	A home without a male child is
emea woo	actually tragic
Ha eye goo Enya Ukpai	Oh! Enya Ukpai
Zohu Okenkwu obi ayi	Give way from our compound
Goo ọ dịnụghụ mma aa	Your presence is not important
Goo Abalị buru igwu da aga ogo	Abali you have been living with lies

Abalị zohu Okenwku obi ayi	Abali give way from our compound
Goo ọ dịnụghụ mma	Your presence is not needed
O nke ọ di yee ha yaa	Is it how it is?
Njoloko nọkwanwa yee ha yaa	Njoloko are you there?
Imaghi onuma Ude bụ onuma ite egburu	Don't you know Ude's situation is likened to a pot for fermenting cassava
Ka ọ dim ma a	And it's not fair
Onuma Ude bunu onuma ite egburu	Ude's situation is likened to a pot for fermenting cassava
Ọ dịkwaghị mma a	And it's not fair
O nke ọ di yee ha yaa	Is it how it is?
Njoloko nọkwanwa yee ha yaa	Njoloko are you there?
Yo ọnwa emere Uche eleghị nwa	Why has Uche been treated like an
enwoghu nne	Orphan
Elekwa ibiam	Elekwa Ibiam
Yo ọnwa emere Uche eleghị nwa	Why has Uche been treated like an
enwoghu nne	Orphan
Eri nke enyi	The stingy man
Yo ọ bịara alụrụ Orie-agbọ yee oje	He has come to marry Orie, the agbo, let them go
Nna m yee bịara ekuru Nja Nsi yee wo gahe	Oh my father, he has come to take Nja Nsi to go
O nke ọ di yee ha yaa	Is it how it is?
Njoloko nọkwanwa yee ha yaa	Njoloko are you there?

Asiri di Alisi

Rumour has it that Alice's husband

Biara ekuru Ugo-ekpo yee o jee

Came to take Ugo, the ekpo, let them go

Di-Orie-agbo wo biara akporo

Orie's husband, they have come to take

Orie-agbo yee

Orie, the agbo

Wo gahe

Let them go

    O nke o di yee ha yaa

    Is it how it is?

    Njoloko nokwanwa yee ha yaa

    Njoloko are you there?

Uka nwa nnachi Uka o nonwa yee

Uka the son of Nnachi Uka is he there?

Ayi junu itere ofu ese ononwa yee

We are asking the nightingale of many voices is he there?

Uka nwa nnachi Uka ononwa yee

Uka the son of Nnachi Uka is he there?

Ayi ju ma olugbu a okpe nna ononwa

We are asking he that cares more for the father if he is there

Nunu ebu uka ononwa yee

The nightingale of all voices is he there?

Ma mu junu goo itere ofu ese

I wish to ask, nightingale of many voices

ma obikwanwa yee

is he there?

Nunu ebu uka ononwa yee

Nightingale of all voices is he there?

Ma mu juru itere ofu ese ma obikwa yee

I wish to ask, nightingale of many voices is he there?

Ka ebutu uja

yet he didn't react

    O nke o di yee ha yaa

    Is it how it is?

    Njoloko nokwanwa yee ha yaa

    Njoloko are you there?

Ụkpaị Ịbịam egbughu onye aha mini	Ukpai Ibiam didn't kill the rain maker
Oken kugbu a onye odotara ike yo	He killed he that planted as a result of
mayi akụkụ	the rain

> O nke o di yee ha yaa

Is it how it is?

> Njoloko nokwanwa yee ha yaa

Njoloko are you there?

Elerkwa Ibiam egbughu onye hara	Elekwa Ibiam didn't kill the rain maker
Mini mairi akụkụ akụkụ	
Elekwa kugbu a ọdotara ike yo	He killed he that planted as a result of
maiyi akụkụ	the rain

> O nke ọ di yee ha yaa

Is it how it is?

> Njoloko nọkwanwa yee ha yaa

Njoloko are you there?

From the above satirical song, one can see that satire in traditional African oral setting passes its meaning using mostly idioms, proverbs, direct and indirect speech, etc. But the depth of any of those features used, which the oral satire in Africa thrives on, still depends on the ingenuity of the composer or the originator. From this example before us, these features are unmistakable as the composer is not only an adult, but also a genius who is very knowledgeable in African culture and world-view. However, the features that are found wanting, just like it is in every oral satire in written from, are those of tones, those gesticulations, those facial expressions of the performer, etc. More to these are the meanings of words, which lose their significations as they are translated from one African language or dialect—as is the case here, Edda dialect—into the English language. All these notwithstanding, the poem's touch on themes ab initio considered by some European scholars like Ruth Finnegan (1970) and some African schoplars like D.I. Nwoga (1980) as a none-theme for the satirical songs/poetry in traditional Africa, is obvious in the poem. However, more shall be said on this as we progress in our discussion in this essay.

Satire in traditional African oral setting, unlike other African oral genres, is not an inheritance from an earlier generation. It is not passed from one generation to the other. This is because every epoch has its perception about life. Therefore, what serves as a theme for satirical songs in a given generation may not possibly serve same in another generation. The same can pass when it comes to the issue of occasion for the composition and the display of satirical songs/ poetry in Africa. Among young girls and boys, the composition and the display of satirical song, which usually centre on a theme like premarital pregnancy, take place during moonlight night plays at the village square. Or, among the young girls' dancing group, the composition and the rehearsal of their satirical songs take place at any enclosure of their choice and the display of the songs comes up during any festive period such as Christmas day. For the other dancing groups in Edda Igbo, like the 'Umu Njoloko', 'Udo Chia', etc, they have theirs at any enclosure while the display is on invitation. The masquerades in Edda, like 'Okwuu', which stay at their usual enclosure known as 'Eko', display their songs on Orie days. This is the day they are culturally permitted to come out from the 'Eko'. But their performance before any person or group is still based on invitation because after entertaining anybody with their satirical songs/poetry, which goes along with dancing, the man must appreciate them monetarily. Another masquerade that satirizes people's misconduct in Edda (men only like the 'Okwuu' masquerade whose satire is for both men and women) is the 'omaewa'. It is only seen by those men who have been initiated into the *egebela* cult. *Egbela* is one of the deities worshiped by all Edda people in those days before the coming of the white man but today by few. However, as its name implies, 'omaewa' meaning coming at the early hours of the day, it comes on the early morning of the day of 'ukpo' festival in Edda. The *omaewa* masquerade itself does not sing or talk: its bard/s that are seasoned, respected and renowned artist/s in this aspect of the

Edda oral songs sing and in satirical manner too about all those (men only) who had committed one form of atrocity of the other in the society. Because this is in the morning, the sonorous voices of the bard/s penetrate far as all and sundry listen.

However, for some other individuals, the muse for the creation and performance of a satirical song comes to them spontaneously due to the prevalent occasion. Perfect examples for the foregoing are in Edda Igbo birth songs. In Edda, perhaps Africa in general, the composition and performance of birth songs are credited to the women. This is as a result of the state of mind of the women any time a baby is born either to them or to any of their close acquaintance. Perhaps, based on what the news remind them of, these songs are always mixed with joyous, sorrowful and satirical intents. These explain the reason why birth and satirical songs in Edda are said to be developmental activities. The spontaneity of some of the satirical songs emanates from the celebratory situation, which expresses itself in the song.

Let us explain: In some part of Edda where it has been a communal aggrement that if a girl gets impregnated out of wedlock, the girl's parent has to pay a fine of ten thousand naira; the young man responsible receives the same punishment. More to this is that no birth songs are to be heard either on the day of the delivery of the baby or on any other day to mark the arrival of the new baby as culture demands in Africa. But, these sets of communal laws were intact and binding on the people as they were when the news reached a woman whose daughter, in fact the only daughter and child, was involved in such entrapment; she burst into a song which in the strict sense of it is a satirical song against both the law of the land on one hand and the scenario that surround her own efforts to prevent what is now inevitable on the other hand. Lets hear her:

Edda egbebu	Edda indomitable clan
Chinedu amụle nwa oo Atọgbọ bic	Chinedu has given birth to a baby
Wo siri Nedu amụle nwa oo Atọgbọ bic	They said Chinedu has given birth to a baby

Ibe nedu amule nwa	Since Nedu has given birth to a baby
Ma mụ mara ịzụ nwa Atọgbọ bic	I will know how to train a baby
Mamu marari oto esi amụ nwa Atọgbọ	I will know how to beget a bic baby
Mamu mara oto esi ana nwa nri Atọgbọ bi	I will know how to feed a baby
Mamu mara oto esi azu nwa Ekwukwu Atọgbọ bic	I will know how to train a baby at school
Mamụ mara oto esi apa nwa Atọgbọ bic	I will know how to sit a baby
Iko m ndaa onye eyemụ ime eee Atọgbọ bic	Men, who is to impregnate me
Hamu amua nwa oo Atọgbọ bic	For me to give birth to a baby
A mụtale m oto esi amụ nwa oo Atọgbọ bic	I have learnt how to beget a baby
Mu mụtakori oto esi enye nwa nri Atọgbọ bic	I have also learnt how to feed a baby
Mu mutakori oto esi apa nwa apa Atọgbọ bic	I have also learn how to sit a baby
Onye enye ime	Who is to impregnate me
Ha mu mua nwa oo Atọgbọ bic	For me to give birth to a baby?
Enyi nwa Orie-agbo	Orie-agbo, my good friend
Bianu nzu abiale	Come, nzu, the white chalk has come
Atogbo bic	
Wo siri Nedu amule nwa oo Atọgbọ bic	They said Nedu has given birth to a baby
Ife amu amu bunuhu olu	Things to begetting are the same

Ife amu amu buhunu olu oo	Things for begetting are the same
Atogbo bic	
Wo siri nwaq mu amule nwa Atogbo bic	They said my child has given birth to a baby
Kaa wo siri Oko nnachi okoro	Is what they said, Oko Nnachi Okoro
Nwa ghi amule nwa oo Atogbo bic	Your child has given birth to a baby
Oko nnachi nwa ghi amule nwa Atogbo bic	Oko Nnachi your child has given birth to a baby
Ma mu maari izu nwa Atogbo bic	I will learn how to train a baby
Ma mu kaa mara oto esi enye nwa nri Atogbo bic	I will learn how to feed a baby
Ha atogboo bie	Drop bic
Ha eburu mua	Get impregnated and give birth

In the translated version, we deliberately omitted the refrain, 'atogbo bic', ie 'drop bic', which comes almost after every line of the songs as the chorus. This is for two main reasons: first, without the refrain (although it has its contribution to the overall understanding of the birth-satirical song) it can still be understood and second, to shorten the poem.

Another example of satirical song/poetry that comes to the composer spontaneously is those set out and used on 'ebu mbe' day. This is a day in Edda set aside like it is in some parts of Africa, for men, women and children to deride the follies and vices of individuals and groups with the full backing of the communal laws. Unlike the satiric-birth songs discussed earlier, some of the satiric songs used on a day like that are not pre-planned. But the differences between the planned and the pre-planned are unmistakable. The planned are always deep in philosophical matters about life while the spontaneous ones are always shallow on human experience. Yet this rule is not watertight as the reverse may be the case.

CONTEXT AND CONTENT OF SATIRE IN AFRICAN ORAL POETRY

The context and the content of satire in traditional African oral poetry have been referred to in this essay, although the reference was implied. However, the depth of importance of these two areas in an oral genre like satire makes them deserve a more serious attention. Again, it is for better understanding as well as authenticating the points referred in passing, that satire in traditional African oral poetry is occasion bound and performance-oriented. Occasion provides the context which gives rise to satirical songs in Africa. And after the songs have been performed, they exist and live. The satiric al songs/poetry, after the contexts have created room for their creation, begin to live both on the minds and on the lips of every member of the society. Their existence no longer is for the occasions which produced them, rather for the reciting pleasure of the casual singers. It is from this vantage point on satire in traditional African oral setting that Nwoga, perhaps, concludes that 'satire is such a prevalent activity that practically every type of poet or singer is engaged in it' (23). This submission can be summarized as an over-generalization. The truth remains that, in Africa, not every oral poet or singer is a genius in satiric songs or poetry. In an interactive session this researcher had with some oral poets in Edda, his home town, it was discovered that not every oral song is known to every oral singer. There are experts in every song like satiric songs, funeral dirges and historical songs etc.

As it is, the context informs the content of satiric songs/poetry in traditional African oral setting. Again, almost every context produces varying songs that range from praise songs through advisory songs down to satiric songs among others. But, as said before, not every oral poet in Africa prefers and or is a master in each of these songs. Yet, whichever type a poet has mastery of; it is still the context which gives rise to such a song that informs the content. However, the content in turn explores the world-view of the people that radiates through the artistic manipulation by the poet. For instance, when a young lass gets impregnated out of wedlock or is involved in sexual promiscuity, such occasions provide the ideal contexts for satiric songs. And such contexts arouse in the poet some issues, hence providing for him the materials that make the content of the song. Let us illustrate here with this satiric song on a girl who has a promiscuous behaviour:

Nnnenna yee, Nnenna lata	Nnenna, Nnenna come back
Nnenna yee, Nnenna lata	Nnenna, Nnenna come back
Nnenna nwa Kalu lata	Nnenna, the daughter of Nkalu Ugbo
Fua nke imere eme	Have a look at what you've done already
Inem nwa kalu	Inem, the Daughter of Nkalu
Fua nke imere eme	Have a look at what you've done already
Boys riri ụgwọ	Boys who received salary
Wo ritara ya Nnenna a a	Received it for you Nnenna
Boys gbara okwa	Boys who went for a job
Wo gbatara ya Nnenna a a	Went on your sake Nnenna
Tanjela nnenna bu ashawo	Tangela Nnenna is a prostitute
Tanjela Nnenna bu ashawo	Tangela Nnenna is a prostitute
Ekworo mgbe e e	Ekworo of mgbe
Ekworo di uru	Ekworo is wicked
Ekworo mgbe e	Ekworo of mgbe
Ekworo di uru	Ekworo is wicked
Onya amaghi	When not caught
Wa sịrị	As they say
Ekworo gworo ogwu	Ekworo in their fetish life style
Gwo ya ma nwa	Include their generation
Ekworo kpara asịrị	Ekworo who gossiped
Kpaiko ya ma nwa	Include their general
Tanjela Nnenna bụ ashawo	Tangela Nnenna is a prostitute.

Now, as can be seen from the above satiric song, the context of the song centres on the sexual promiscuity of a girl but this context informs the dexterity of the poet in weaving and producing an artistic product whose context reflects a satiric artifact on a girl, not any other person, involved in a misconduct. The content does not reflect any other angle or demeanour but that of sexual promiscuity. Yet, this does not end on satirizing the errant girl only but beyond into her matrilineal life style. In Edda nation, people belong to different matrilineal lineages. Every lineage is known for one thing or the other about their behaviour, either good or bad. In this satiric song, the context gives the poet the material for the content. The girl in question, no doubt, is of Ekworo matrilineal lineage and the song has used the errant girl who is one of them as a take-off point to satirize the life of the entire lineage as well as what the lineage is commonly accused of as their way of life.

Furthermore, for us to understand better the importance of context and content of satire in traditional African oral poetry, let us turn to an example of a satiric song/poem rendered at a child-birth. In Africa when a child is born, the joyful moment is accompanied with birth songs. The context of having delivered a woman of her baby without any record of death triggers off songs. But the content of these songs, in Edda Igbo area more especially,, are not always one of joy. Rather, they retrospectively tell the condition of women in marriages and other issues that surround married life. Viewed from this angle, one may be right to conclude that birth songs in Edda Igbo are mere satiric songs than praise or worship songs on the good omen of childbirth. An example here can prove our point:

Dighi eji	You can't accept them
Dighi agbu	You can't reject them
Ndi iko m a a	These men!

Dịghi eji	You can't accept them
Dịghi agbụ	You can't reject them
Ndị iko m a a	These men!

Dere m gari mụ ria	Prepare garri for me let me eat
Onye Uka	Before your mother comes back
Dịghi eji	You can't accept them
Dịghi agbụ	You can't reject them
Ndị iko m	These men!
Nne ghi jere eleyi?	Your mother! Where has she gone to?
Imata garri	To buy garri
Owutu	At Owutu market?
Dighi eji	You can't accept them
Dighi agbu	You can't reject them
Ndi iko m	These men!

The song satirizes the menfolk behaviour towards their wives. The women performers are invariably and satirically saying but for procreation, the men are good for nothing. The first two stanzas, which are actually a repetition of the other, capture this idea.

However, what is worth noting is that nobody starts deriding anybody else without cause, which is the context; and this cause has an effect, which is the content. It is always the context that provides for the content of the satirical songs in traditional Africa. Therefore, because satire in traditional African oral setting is occasion-bound, the context must be sought for the understanding of the content.

STYLE OF SATIRE IN TRADITIONAL AFRICAN ORAL SATIRIC POETRY

We have said more than once in this essay that the aim of satire in traditional African poetry, in particular, is to ridicule the human behaviour that contrasts with the already accepted norms of the society. But as a literary piece it has stylistic ways of doing it, which help to endorse its Africanness. Let us illustrate with the satire from a woman on a man on the 'Ebu Mbe' day as a reply to earlier rendered satire from the man to the woman-singer and performer.

O da abụnwa gini	What is it
Da abu ọnụma yee	That is seen as a pitiable condition?
O da abunwa gini	What is it
Da abụ anụma yee	That is seen as a pitiable condition?
Homja ụma ya agwule woo	Homja, that is his life-style

Unu siri o gini?	What do they say is it
Da abu onuma yee	That is seen as a pitiable condition?
O kwahi atụghụ ime	Is it barrenness only
Da abu ọnuma yee	That is seen as a pitiable condition?
Homja uma ya agwule woo	Homja, that is his life-style

Oko Ude	Oko Ude
I bunwa atakwa	You are an outcast
Ọbụgh ọnụma yee	Is it not a pitiable condition?
Ibe ibu atakwa	Since you are an outcast
Ọbụgh ọnụma yee	Is it not a pitiable condition?
Homja ụma ya agwụle woo	Homja, that is his life-style

Oko Ude	Oko Ude
I bu enya ani	You are a one-eyed man
Ọbụgh ọnụma yee	Is it not a pitiable condition
Ibe ịbụ enya ani	Since you are a one-eyed man
Ọbụgh ọnụma yee	Is it not a pitiable condition?
Homja uma ya agwule woo	Homja, that is his life-style
Homja uma ya agwule woo	Homja, that is his life-style
Ifụ nwata ikpasituru ya	If you see a child you discuss such with him
Homja	Homja

As stated earlier, this satirical song is a reply to an earlier one. By inference, the song from the man satirizes the barren condition of the woman while the later song before us, as all available evidence shows, is the reply. While she accepts her condition as pitiable, the composer adds that barrenness is not a pitiable condition. Here the poet uses some stylistic modes like repetition, suspense, indirect question, etc, which are common stylistic modes of satire in traditional African oral poetry. In her repetitive style, she tells us what her own problems are in the first two stanzas. On the other hand, she keeps us in suspense about her own attack and reply on the man. This she does at the last two stanzas through indirect questions.

As have been noted by some scholars, Africans are artistic when it comes to the use of their language. This is an event that led to the call for the study of African Oral Literature. But on a careful look at the stylistic modes of some composition, for example, like satirical songs in general and the one before us in particular, one can conclude as right such assertions made many years back. As this satirical song shows, the singer does not start telling us that the butt of her song is an outcast, a one-eyed man etc, rather it is artistically woven with those features into her song. Again, the man in question walks on one leg due to rheumatic disease which deformed him on the left leg. Instead of discussing such deformation in straight language, she pictures same with an onomatopoeic word, 'homja' echoing the way the man walks. As she pronounces the word 'homja' she dramatizes it; 'homja', dramatization accompanies the oral. Besides, most belittling of it all is that the man discusses the issue of barrenness with every child he sees. However, the satiric idea here gets heavier by the time one recollects how he has condescended so low that he discusses with children an issue exclusively meant for the adult ears alone.

We shall look at another example of satire for the revelation of more stylistic modes of satire in traditional African oral poetry. Here we can use the satirical song from 'Umu njoloko' dancing groups already cited earlier on in this chapter, using only the translated version. The first two stanzas of the song, omitting the choruses, can suffice for our emphasis:

Have you all seen
Elekwa who didn't plant arial yam now has basins full of it

Basins full of it

Elekwa Ibiam

Elekwa who didn't plant arial yam now has basins full of it

Basins full of it

When others are going for a crab hunt

Elekwa will be going to uproot cassava

When others are going for a crab hunt

Elekwa will be going to uproot cassava

The corpse of Elekwa's mother

Lies carelessly along Ibiakpani road

Don't you know the vulture has messed up their mother's corpse?

A close look at the style of this satirical song reveals the peculiar manner or style of deriding wrongdoers by elders in Edda: speaking with their tongues in their cheeks. From the song/poem, the butt is a thief. Though it is not mentioned openly, it is there. However, the way this idea is passed is quite remarkable. The target, Elekwa Ibiam, is posed as a nonconformist who never likes doing anything with others at the same time. Perhaps, this is to enable him to carry out his evil intent of stealing from others. More so, that which is revealed, though subtly done, is his carefree attitude towards his mother. In fact, from these two examples, it is enough to prove that poets of satire in traditional African oral poetry make use of varying stylistic modes in their satirical songs. The orality of almost all the styles is unmistakable and this helps to give the satire in traditional Africa its Africanness.

THE RELEVANCE OF TRADITIONAL SATIRE IN CONTEMPORARY AFRICA

In contemporary Africa, African oral satire may be losing its relevance. The source of this could be traced and summed up as due mainly to the influence of modernity and the so-called sense of civility of the modern man. Modernity and man's sense of civilized manner of handling matters came with their attendant evils to the

African's soil. For one thing, the common African ways of evaluation, which include human behaviour, have been shattered on the altar of modernity and civility. The University of Ibadan-trained Literalist and author, Chinua Achebe, in his epoch making novel, *Things Fall Apart*, preferred to fictionalize the entire scenario that because what holds us together is broken, things have fallen apart. Satire in traditional African oral poetry as the collective means of deriding and at the same time correcting any societal misdemeanor, is one of the things that has fallen, if not dead, in the contemporary Africa. Unlike before now people lead an individual life in Africa. Issues like sexual promiscuity, illicit pregnancy, stealing, elopement, loss of virginity, etc, which were seen as wrongdoings in Edda, therefore, served as sources of material for satirical songs, are today seen as a way of life. Moreso, because wrong-doings are relative, there are now no general acceptance of what is good or bad behaviour. To this end, the African oral satires no longer command influence as before.

Besides, there is no unanimity over what is right or wrong behaviour. Satirical songs are seen as barbaric, primitive and uncivilized ways for addressing issues. With such belief at the back of people's mind, the butts in a satirical song can choose to seek redress in the law court where damages could be claimed for character assassination. The worst is seen in the monetary African world where everybody seizes every opportunity to make money. Yet, the worst pitiable scene can also be derived from the rural areas where we have tyrants, money conscious Ezeogos and political office holders. If any oral artist dares satirize any of them (the Ezeogos and the political office holders), including their relatives, in his/her song, the poet would rather curse the day he/she was born.

Again, the influence of Christianity on the Africans is not helping matters either. In the Christian point of view almost every African way of life is revealed as satanic; and the satire in traditional African oral songs is suffering the same fate. In fact, the difficulties I encountered in collecting these satirical songs is a good testimony worth narrating in detail. In one of the days of my fieldworks for this paper, I first called at my elder sister's house as it was close to where I was to record one of my bards. On her enquiry about where I was going, I told her my mission. But her lady visitor whom I met in her house boldly told me: 'my mother was into those songs until she repented and left those evil songs'. On further enquiry why the songs are seen as evil, she answered 'Because they don't glorify God'.

However, and as a way of conclusion, if satire in traditional African oral poetry is pardoned and disallowed on the ground of religious fanaticism, what about African scholars who have failed to collect, let alone study them before they fuzzle into thin air? In fact, some people believe that before the end of this 21st century, if nothing serious is done to record the half-dead satire in traditional African oral poetry, we shall only have them in the nearest future as fossils for study in the oral literature departments in own African universities.

Works Cited

Abrams, M.A. *Glossary of Literary Terms.* New York: Holt, Rhinehart and Winston, 1981. Print.

Agovi, Kofi K. 'A King is Not Above Insult: The Politics of Good Governance in Nzema Avidwene Festival songs'. *The Literary Griot.* 3.1. (1991). 1–18. Print.

Babalola, Adeboye. 'The Art of Composing and Performing Oral Poetry: Ijala Poetry Among the Oyo-Yoruba Communities'. *Oral Poetry in Nigeria.* Ed. Uchegbulam N. Abalaogu et al. Lagos Nigeria Magazine, 1981. Print.

Ce, Chinnenye. "Riddle and Bash: the Creative Wit of Alaa's Children". *Re-imaging African Literature.* Ed. Charles Smith. Enugu: Handel, 2003. 78–107. Print.

Chinweizu, Onwuchekwa Jemie and Ihechukwu Madubuike. *Toward the Decolonization of African Literature.* Enugu: Fourth Dimension, 1980. Print.

Ebeogu, Afam. 'The World of the Lullaby: The Igbo Example' .*Research in African Literature.* 22.2. (1991). 99–117. Print.

—. Njakiri, the Quintessence of the Traditional Igbo Sense of Satire'. *Spoken in Jest.* Ed. Gillian Benneth. Sheffield: Sheffield Academic Press, 1999. 29–46. Print.

Egudu, Romanus N. and Donatus I. Nwoga. *Poetic Heritage: Igbo Traditional verse.* Enugu Nwankwo-Ifejika, 1971. Print.

Egudu, R.N. "The Emotional Elements in Traditional Oral Poetry. The Igbo Example". *Oral Poetry in Nigeria.* Ed. Uchegbulam N. Abalaogu et al. Lagos: Emaconprint. 1981. 247–259. Print

Finnegan, Ruth, *Oral Literature in Africa.* Nairobi: Oxford University Press, 1970. Print.

Nwachukwu-Agbada, J.O.J. 'The Glint in the Ore: Latent Educational values of Igbo Poetic Insult of Similes'. *Lore and Language.* 14 *(*1996*)*.1–14. Print.

Nwoga.D.I. 'The Igbo Poet and Satire'. *Oral Poetry in Nigeria.* Ed. Uchegbulam N. Abalogu et al. Lagos: Emaconprint, 1981. 230–246. Print.

Okpewho, Isidore. *African Oral Literature: Backgrounds, Character and Continuity.* Bloomington: Indiana University Press, 1992.

Ugonna, Nnabuenyi. 'Preservation and Development of Traditional Poetry: The Igbo Example'. *Oral Poetry in Nigeria.* Ed. Uchegbulam N. Abalaogu et al. Lagos: Emaconprint, 1981.283–298. Print.

Chapter Eight

Poetry of Occasion I:
The Feminist Temperament in Igbo Birth Songs

Afam N. Ebeogu

INTRODUCTION

Any discussion of the dominant forms, types or generic categories
of oral poetry among the Igbo of Nigeria which omits the birth (or
maternity) songs would be neglecting a significant aspect of that poetry.[1] For these birth songs are the product of a particular biological
class or group in the society, and, as scholars of the sociology of
literature have recognized, the theme and form of a piece of literary
work may bear witness to" the origin and production" of that literature.[2] It is the intention of this chapter to examine these songs, first
from the point of view of their possible typological classification,
and then to show how, no matter how classified, these birth songs
are an extremely convenient avenue for Igbo women to express their
understanding of the norms and values of the Igbo society, and to
comment on some of these norms and values.

The word "feminism" is not being used here in the rather restricted sense of "female protest" and campaign for "emancipation"
in a situation of male domination and chauvinism in society.[3] Rather
"feminism" is expanded to mean "women's point of view" expressed
in an uncensored medium. The issue is not necessarily whether what
the women say is radically opposed to established conventions, but
that what they say represents their own honest, realistic and constructive perception of order and stability in the society. In handling
our argument, we do not lose sight of the fact that what we are discussing is literature; that the medium of the women's "feminism" is

literary, and that the stylistic demands of the literary genre provide the structural framework for the feminist message.

Igbo birth songs: a typology of situation*

A Typology of a piece of oral literature suggests a generic classification that is based on the performance of the literature. Many an authoritative treatment of oral literature in Africa has been based on this kind of typology, with justification.[4] For it would appear that it is the occasion of performance of a piece of oral literature that determines its form and structure, and even if one insists on a typology of form and structure, as is the tendency when it comes to written literature, one would ultimately be drawn back to considering how relevant the form and structure are to the occasion of performance. Our concern is not to prefer any one typology to the other, but to recognize all possible typologies as they relate to Igbo birth songs.

Birth songs are surely situation-bound, and, in all cases, there is a relevance of the occasion to child-birth. The most common situation is the birth of a child. When the event takes place, other women raise a jubilant alarm called *oro*, which instantly brings every woman to the scene of event. A good example of an *oro* runs as this:

Igbo	*English*
Hia hia hia e e e e e[5]	*Hia hia hia e e e e e*
Oe Oe Oe e e e e e e	*Oe Oe Oe e e e e e e*
Onye ji ego bia ngaa o.	*Who ever has money let him come here*
Ọ mụrụ nnwa gini o o o?	*Did she give birth to what?*
Ọ mụrụ nnwa nwoke oo.	*She gave birth to a baby boy.*
Ọ mụrụ nnwa nwanyi o o.	*She gave birth to a baby girl.*
Hia hia hia e e e e e	*Hia hia hia e e e e e*
Oe Oe Oe e e e e e e	*Oe Oe Oe e e e e e e*
Chineke I meela ooo	*God, you have done well.*

This initial song, which is half-sung and half-chanted in a high pitched tone by many women, usually has a "magic" effect. Every woman in the community leaves whatever she is doing, no matter what, and runs to the direction of the song.

Immediately, the women form a circular dancing formation, and begin to perform as many birth songs as possible. The duration of the performance differs from occasion to occasion, depending, for instance, on the ability of the man of the house to provide impromptu entertainment for the performers, and on the number of women who have come. It could last for one or two hours, and as the earliest callers leave, they tend to be replaced by new ones.[6]

But there are other occasions for the birth songs. These include all the major landmarks in the chain of rituals of thanksgiving and purification involving childbirth, in which groups outside the nuclear family participate. These occasions include the naming ceremony of the child, which takes place in traditional homes twenty eight days after the birth of the child (in Christian homes, the tendency is for the ritual of baptism to replace this occasion); the first "outing" of the mother since child birth—*i puta n'omugwo*—which takes her to the communal market where she fraternizes and frolics with her fellow women in the open, rubbing camwood and powder on them and receiving gifts in return; the presentation of *nri omugwo* ("maternity meal") to the mother of the woman who has given birth, both before she goes to look after her daughter for the traditional one-month childbirth, and on her return from her "in-law's place" with all the goodies with which her in-laws have expressed their gratitude to "the mother of a wife who has given birth to a baby". In some areas of Igboland, like the Arochukwu area of Abia State, maternity or birth songs, are also performed during puberty rites for girls who are to be initiated into womanhood. The rationale for the performance on this occasion is to be found in the belief that such rites are indeed fertility rites,[7] in which the girls' primary values as "bearers of children" are affirmed.[8]

Our situational typology thus shows that birth songs are women's affair; they are occasioned by a woman's event, the delivery of a child, and other activities ancillary to births, and the performance is almost exclusive to women. There is only one known occasion in which men take part in the actual performance of birth songs, and this is when the women invite the father of the child, through the medium of their songs (but in extreme cases they drag the man out of the house) to come out and demonstrate his own role in the whole affair of "making the baby". The following song illustrates such an occasion, and the reference to mat, or wrapper in most modern versions of the song, echoes the sexual act that gave rise to the pregnancy:[9]

Igbo	English
O lee nwoke mere ihe a?	*Where is the man who has done this?*
O lee nwoke mere ihe a?	*Where is the man who has done this?*
Nwoke mere ihe a?	*The man who has done this?*
Ya were akwa oji aṛu ala	*Should come out with his "sneaky" wrapper*
Bia gbara anyi egwu	*Come and dance for us.*

Even from such a song, it is clear that that performance is a woman's affair, that the women's invitation to the man to dance is a way of ridiculing his tendency to be aloof in the midst of the excitement over a successful childbirth.

A TYPOLOGY OF MEDIUM

We have tried to establish the occasions for the birth songs among the Igbo, and a logical sequence is the medium. "Medium" here implies "the how" of the performances of these songs; the manner in which they are realized. These songs are essentially vocal perfromances[10] accompanied by dance, and—but not always—improvised musical instrumentation. They are mostly "songs" in the actual sense of their being sung, rather than in the rather general, "poetry-as-song" which Preminger (780) talks about. The only occasion in which a birth song acquires some chant-like quality, is in the *oro*, when the few women who are present at the moment of the birth call on the other women in the neighbourhood to join in the celebration.

Usually the women dance in a circular formation as they sing the songs, and the performance is accompanied by abundant histrionics, the degree depending on the content of the song. For example, in the songs in which they make allusions to the sexual act as being a glorious act, since it results in pregnancy and child-birth, the women make very suggestive gestures which some people might consider obscene, indicating the location of the organs, and sometimes providing gestural descriptions of the organs that are involved in the procreative act, and the nature of the physiological movement that has precipitated the occasion. The following song is an example of such a song whose total effect depends greatly on histrionic accompaniment.

Igbo	*English*
Ndoghari ukwu lee e	*The wriggling of the waist, look!*
Ndoghari ukwu	*The wriggling of the waist.*
Ndoghari ukwu lee e	*The wriggling of the west, look!*
Ndoghari ukwu.	*The wriggling of the waist.*
Ebe ndoghari ukwu turu ime	*Where the wriggling of the waist results pregnancy*
Ndoghari ukwu	*The wriggling of the waists*
Obughi ebe ndoghari ukwu	*Is not the place where the wriggling of*
Muru nwa	*the waist results in child-birth*
Ndoghari ukwu	*The wriggling of the waists*
Ihe Ndoghari ukwu emeela o	*A wriggling of the waists events has occurred.*
Ndoghari ukwu	*The wriggling of the waists.*

As the women dance this song in a circular formation, they take measured leaps towards the right, during which they hold their hands on both sides of their waists, wriggle the waists, expand the gap between their legs, and point at the position of their genitals, all in rhythm with the song and the dance. Every woman in the group joins in the demonstration, no matter how reserved or shy she might be considered to be in her private life. The performance is therefore, understood by all to be a special event; an event in which song and

rhythm of dance coordinate with symbolic action in order to max-
imize eloquence. It is a medium that affords the women an opportunity to express group consciousness, for, as Ernst Fischer has observed, "rhythmical movement assists work, co-ordinates effort and
connects the individual with the group" (35).

There is a general air of hilarity during the performance of these
birth songs. Most of the members of the audience are men and children, for even where there are women who, for reasons of old age or
ill health, cannot join in the performance, they throw in occasional
expressions of praise and promptings to the performers, thus affirm-
ing their spiritual identification with the essence and mood of the
performance. Some men could make uncomplimentary and humorous remarks about the "immodesty" of the women, but this kind of
remark is usually made in the spirit of the satiric and overall comic
mode of the performance. For no one ever forgets what has occasioned the performance: somewhere inside the house (or in the maternity ward in modern times) a child is lying in the cradle. Thus this
moment is one of demonstration of divine blessing; an Igbo proper
name says that "there is nothing as valuable as a child" (*Ifeyinwa*),
and any anger or gesture of disapproval would be construed by the
community as ingratitude and wickedness.

A Typology of Form.

Because these birth songs are realized through the medium of
vocal music and dance, there is a heavy reliance on the time-line,
repetition of segments, use of address markers and the lengthening
of vowel sounds. Igbo birth songs confirm John Nketia's conclusion
that "the use of time-line (a recurring rhythmic pattern of fixed duration or time span), which clarifies the regulative beat, is a common
feature of rhythmic organization in some African traditions" (131–
2). It does not matter whether the line contains essentially only one
word or whether there are up to ten words. What is important is that
the duration in time of all the lines in the stanza is the same, even if
the line has only a few words, as a refrain which could be a repetition
of just one word, and the word is lengthened through the use of

significant, ululating, vowel sounds as to make the line have the same length as when many words are used in the same breath-grtoup[11]. While the lengthening process through the use of breath is on, the rhythm of the dance is of course maintained so that, in the end, all the lines have the same number of beats *determined by the rhythm in harmony with one complex rhythm of dance steps.*

In our formal analysis of Igbo birth songs, we identify three categories. The first is that group of songs where the song is made up of only one stanza, and no line of the stanza, possibly other than the last, is a total segmental repeat of the other; the second category is that where the song is again made up only one stanza, but where alternate lines of the stanza are merely repetitions of one syntactical segment; and the third category is where the song is made up of more than one stanza, each stanza having either the form of the first category or that of the second. We will examine these formal categories more closely, with a view to identifying their rhythmic structure.

In the first category, the song is made up of only one stanza, each line of the stanza, possibly other than the last, not exactly the same syntactical unit as any other. The stanza is repeated as often as possible in the course of the performance, until the women decide to move over to another song. All the women in the group sing the song in unison; there is no solo as distinct from the chorus. An illustration of this category of Igbo birth songs goes like this:

Igbo	*English*
Unu no n'ulo eme gini e?	*Are you in the house doing what?*
Ayi no n'ulo amuga nnwa o	*We are in the house bearing children*
Ka mgbe ututu, ka mgbe anyasi.	*Every morning, every night.*
Ayi amuala nnwa o.	*We have delivered a child.*
Obi adila ayi mma o.	*We have become happy*
Ayi no n'ulo amu nnwa.	*We are in the house bearing children.*

In this six-line stanza, the first line is a repeat of the second. It is a significant repeat, because it is an affirmation of the central idea of the song: that the primary value of the woman in that culture is to give birth.

Our study of the songs in our collection shows that there is nothing fixed about the number of lines in the stanza: there are mainly four-line, six-line, seven and eight-line stanzas. The four line and six line stanzas are the most recurrent in that order. Where the number of lines is even, the last may or may not be a repeat of the lines, but where the number is odd, the last line is usually a repeat of one of the lines which embodies the central idea of the song. It is easy to determine what constitutes a line in the stanza, if one is able to listen to the songs *in performance*. This is because the line, in performance, is identified as one syntactical unit constituting a breath-group, and *determined by one complex unit of dance steps*. In other words, the line-meter of the song is determined by the rhythm of the dance accompanying the song. Where therefore there are fewer words or syllables in some line than in others, all the singers do is lengthen either the last vowel sound of the line concerned, or add a vowel sound different from the last but easily assimilable to it.

The second category of form of the birth songs is that in which the song is made up of only one stanza, but the alternate lines of the stanza are repeats and also refrains. The following song illustrates this category of form:

Igbo	English
Onye n'onye kuru ọmụmụ?	*Who and who have carried the child*
Ọmụmụ ka mma o o o.	*The birth of a child is the best.*
Onye n'onye kuru ọmụmụ?	*Who and who have carried the child?*
Ọmụmụ ka mma o o o.	*The birth of a child is the best.*
Ihe no ngaa kuru ọmụmụ.	*Everybody here has carried the child*
Ọmụmụ ka mma o o o.	*The birth of a child is the best.*
I kuru ọmụmụ I mụta ọmụmụ.	*You carried the child, you get a child*
Ọmụmụ ka mma o o o.	*The birth of a child is the best.*

Most often, all the women in the group sing all lines of the song, but at times, there is a solo-and-chorus identification, where only one voice in the group (who usually beats some improvised musical instrument) sings the major lines, while the chorus sing the refrain.

Where this happens, the tendency is for the length of the stanza to be determined at the discretion of the solo performer, who could create more of the major lines.

The third category of Igbo birth songs is that featuring more than one stanza. We find, however, that each stanza is of the form of the first category. What needs to be added is that this category of more than one stanza is not as dominant as the single-stanza forms and that, of the two single-stanza forms, the second which features refrains is the most recurring.

The issue that arises from our discussion of the formal typology of Igbo birth songs is the question of composition. There is no doubt that the nature of the situation of these songs gives them a great communal significance. Like most forms of folklore, the songs are "due to the collective action of the multitude and could not be traced to (any) one individual influence..." (Frazer 58). This conclusion is justified by the fact that the songs do not seem to "rely on fixed texts that performers memorize" (Kellog 57). The songs are communal creations of the women as one group, and the unpredictable nature of pregnancies and births makes it impossible for the womenfolk to have any specific "trial versions" of the songs before they are performed. (Kirk 55)

It is rather the repeated performance of these songs, and the fairly standard typology established by the occasion of their performance, that give the forms and words of the song some degree of fixedness.

This fixedness is, however, fragile. Albert Lord's theory of "themes" and "formula" of oral composition would seem to apply very much to Igbo birth songs (Lord 30–98). To that extent then, the songs have "fixed texts", but there is no doubt that at any single performance, there is evidence of some kind of creation in-performance; a creation-in performance that is aided by the factor of liberties associated with solo performances. It is significant that the many cases of repeats of expressions in the songs are usually associated with a chorus, who cannot take the liberties of textual variation. The songs examined in this chapter come from various parts of Igboland,

and are both very traditional and fairly modern in origin. But there is no doubt that they belong to the same genre of oral poetry. Where there are some differences in two or more versions of the same song from different parts of the culture, and performed by groups with different religious orientations, the differences have been in the nature of dialect and lexical items.

In a popular Igbo birth song, to illustrate this, the women argue that the birth of a child is an opportunity for them to receive all kinds of gifts from their husbands. The gifts listed in some versions of the song include cloth (of unspecified quality), meat (of unspecified nature), yam, rice, and a motor car. But in some other versions of the same song the gifts listed include beef, salad, "Etorika" (a kind of very expensive modern textile material), a hand watch, Mercedes Benz and *ntu oyi* (an air-conditioned car). There is hardly a doubt that the first song must have been performed by women whose values have a traditional orientation, whose demands are modest and congruent with the material circumstances of the community, while the second version must have been performed by the younger wives of the modern generation who are in a position to expect such expensive and modern gifts as enumerated from their husbands or somebody else. But the form of the versions is the same: they are all a one-stanza song of our second category, where the major lines constitute a list of the gifts expected at childbirth, while the repeated lines, in one way or the other, denote "the act of giving". In one of such songs, the "modern" form features "the positive act of giving" *("a gam enwe"* "I will have"), in place of that of "expecting" (" *dim ga-enyem"*, "my husband will give me"). These versions indicate different marital attitudes: the first perceives obligations from a husband as mandatory, whereas the second sees such obligations from the point of view of benevolence.

Our typology of form of Igbo birth songs thus establishes that, even from this classificatory point of view, the songs belong to the women entirely, and afford them as exclusive literary forum to make the comments they want.

A TYPOLOGY OF THEME

The last of our typologies for classifying Igbo birth songs is the thematic typology. This typology seeks to examine the content of the songs and, looking into them in their entirety, to be able to identify the songs as birth songs simply because of this content.

One of the most pervading themes in the songs is the idea of the child being the primary justification for marriage:[12] the women's birth songs emphasize this point unambiguously. The refrain for one of the popular songs says that the beauty of womanhood lies in children (*"mma nwanyị bụ nnwa"*); and another song wants to know whether there is any woman who has any other priority to children:

Igbo	English
A Nam ajụ gi si	*I ask you and say:*
Mkpa gi ọdi ole	*How many are your needs*
Na-abụghi nnwa e?	*Other than children?*

The best way to satisfy a husband is by bearing children for him (*Nwayi mmuo nnwa, obi alo di ya o*), and it is only the child that gives a woman a sense of belonging in her husband's place (*Onye mụrụ nnwa nọdụ na be di ya ribe ngwodongwo*), ("Let whoever has given birth remain in her husband's place and feed lavishly"). Childbirth preserves marriage, for no matter what a women does, she is safe as long as she has children (*Ihe omeme, ihe omene/Gbaghara ya na o muru nnwa ohuru*, "Whatever she does, whatevery she does/Forgive her for she has given birth to a child"). Another song says that a barren woman is a thing of ridicule in the community:

Igbo	English
Dadam I meela mụọ nnwa	*My sister, you have done well to get a child*
Asi n'imutaghi nnwa	*Had it been that you had no child*
Ha gara ime gi ihe ọchị	*They would be ridiculing you.*

Hence a protagonist in a song pleads with her husband not to lose patience with her; she would yet bear him a child (*Ezigbo dim e wela iwe na-agam amutara gi nnwa*), since she recognizes that "when a man's

wife fails to get a child/it appears as if she has married a fellow man"
(*Onye nwuye ya na-mutaghi nnwa/Odi k'olutara nwoke ibe ya n'ulo*).

It is easy to see from these songs that the Igbo woman does not
regard child bearing as a necessary evil, but as a thing of joy; an
obligation. This is to be appreciated in the context of a society that
believes strongly in the cosmological phenomenon of re-incarnation.
In this kind of society, the woman is an important link in this recurrent cycle of human existence in the cosmos (Henderson 219). Not
to bear children is to create a kink in the chain of human regeneration; and this would amount to a disaster for the family, the clan and
the community.

This probably explains the fact that the woman in the society,
as is revealed in these songs, sees her role as a bearer of children as
heroic. The woman really makes the world what it is, as one of the
songs puts it:

Ala mara mma	*If the land is good*
Ala joro njo	*If the land is bad*
Obu nwanyi na-edozi ya	*It is the woman who conditions it so.*

And a similar song, defiantly vulgar, asserts:

O si n'olee?	*Where did he come from?*
O si n'ikpu.	*He comes from the cervix.*
O si n'olee?	*Where did he come from?*
O si n'ikpu.	*He comes from the cervix.*
Ma nwa bekee?	*The white man?*
O si n'ikpu.	*He comes from the cervix.*
Professor?	*The professor?*
O si n'ikpu.	*He comes from the cervix.*
President?	*President*
O si n'ikpu.	*He comes from the cervix.*
Govano?	*Governor?*
O si n'ikpu.	*He comes from the cervix.*
O si n'olee?	*Where did he come from?*
O si n'ikpu.	*He comes from the cervix.*

In a gesture of strong protest and complaint all rolled in one, the women, in another song, accuse the men of indolence. For the women do not only go through the rigours of childbirth, but are also always busy, while the men deliberately subjugate female interests. The rigours of childbirth then become a metaphor for the suffering of the womenfolk.

Igbo	English
Kpuru kpuru mbu.	*Being busy is a primordial thing.*
Kpuru kpuru nnwa.	*The business of child-bearing.*
Umu nwoke na-eje ozi soso	*The men do real work only for*
Otu onwa	*One month*
Ma a muchaa nnwa	*For after the birth of the child,*
Emechaa ha e were anyi dowe n'azu	*Again they relegate us to the background.*

One is not surprised that these songs go to the length of articulating the hazards and heroism of pregnancy and childbirth. The pregnant woman bears the greatest suffering in the world, living on the edge of fear and uncertainty, and yet people think that she is in a period of glory (*Nwayi taga afufu n'uwa/Umu uwa asi na a riwela/Ebe oji obi n'abo agariga*). The many birth songs that plead with death not to "kill a woman in her pregnancy" *(Onwu egbule nwayi n'afo ime)* assert the fact that pregnancy is like a journey to the brink of death. Elsewhere it is described as being similar to climbing to the precarious top of the giant iroko tree:

Igbo	English
Ekene diri chineke	*Thanks be to God*
Onye mere ka o ritue n'udo.	*Who made her climb down safely*
N'ihi na ya bu elu oji	*For that top of the iroko*
Adighi ofere	*Is not a plaything*

Many of these songs present the whole business of pregnancy and child birth as being akin to the uncertainties of investment in the market, in which one stands as much chance of losing terribly as gaining; the songs make constant reference to "the market of the night" (*ahia abali*), and the enviable risky business of the climbing of the hill:

Ugwu nnwa di ebube.	*The hill of the child is glorious*
Onye na-adghi ike	*She who has no strength*
Agaghi ari ugwu nnwa.	*Cannot climb the hill of the child.*

And the songs often throw a jibe at the men for being party to a venture for which only the woman bears all the risk:

Ihe ayi diri abuo mee,.	*The thing which two of us did,*
Ahia mgbaji ukwu	*The market of the breaking of waists*
Emerega a si otu onye	*Later only one person is asked to*
bute ibu ya	*carry the consequent load.*

Perhaps one of the most thematic characteristics of these songs is the unapologetic sexual overtones and innuendos. Ordinarily, these women are uncommonly modest, even to the point of prudishness. But their performance of the birth songs suggests that the songs provide them with an opportunity to exhibit a surprising degree of obscenity both in words and miming. But, constant reference to the sexual act in the songs is not frivolous, for the women seem to be arguing that the sexual act is a creative act which leads to generation and regeneration of the human species.

The sexual "content" of the birth songs includes not only the obscene gestures already described under "typology of medium", but also brazen reference to the female genitals as the proud "road" through which the child emerges into the world from the mysterious recesses of the womb. Thus, the woman is happy that the final point of transition which a child traverses before it becomes human is the cervix (*ikpu*). The sexual organs are therefore very useful organs because they bring out riches into the world. One of the songs can therefore frown at the prostitute, because she is misusing her organs for mere satisfaction of the sexual urge (*iri nwancholonwu*), as the song idiomatically calls it). The sexual dance (*egwu ukwu*) which results in the child, is a glorious dance (*egwu oma*), and the joy of sex is not a frivolous one, but the joy of suffering (*odi uto n'afufu*). The noise of sex as couples tumble on the bed (*the biam biam, biribiri or ngwodongwo* ideophonic sounds) is the best of noises, say many of the songs, because it leads to pregnancy and childbirth. As one of the songs puts it so courageously:

Igbo	English
Shaka Shaka	*Shaka Shaka*
Ihe ayi gbatara n'ute	*The thing we won on the mat.*
Piom piom	*Piom piom*
Ihe ayi mitara n'onu	*The thing we won from kissing*
Kiri kiri	*Kiri kiri*
Ihe ayi chitara n'ochi	*What we gained from laughter*
Uru bedi, uru bedi wu nnwa.	*The benefit of the bed, the benefit of the bed is children.*

The sexual overtones and innuendos, expressed through gestures of the sexual act, through liberal mention of the sexual organs, and through the use of ideophonic expressions that suggest the noise of sexual activity, seem to indicate that the women see the occasion of their performance as a moment of liberty and freedom from societal restrictions. Mircea Eliade discusses this phenomenon of "sexual liberties" on a universal, mythic dimension when he says that

> The secret behind it is the revelation of fecundity.... (They) are not erotic, but of a ritual character: they represent vestige of forgotten mystery and not profane enjoyments. We cannot otherwise explain the fact that in societies where modesty and chastity are obligatory, the girls and the women behave on certain sacred occasions ... in a manner that terribly shocked the observers.... This complete reversal of behaviour—from modesty to exhibitionism—serves a ritual purpose, and is therefore in the interest of the whole community. The orgiastic character of this feminine mystery is explained by the need for a periodic abolition of the norms that govern profane existence, in other words, the necessity of suspending the law that bears like dead

weight upon the customary, and of re-entering into a state of
spontaneity. (212–13)

We cannot improve on Eliade's observation, except to add that we
find it applicable to the performance of Igbo birth songs.

An offshoot of the sexual licence which some of these birth songs
suggest is the occasional affirmation in the songs that the occasion
of child-birth is an opportunity for the expression of solidarity by
the women. A good number of the songs actually make mention of
the community where the event of child-birth has taken place, and
in all cases what follows is a call to all the women to gather, for one
of them is on a maternity outing and therefore needs comradeship.
One song affirms that the event of one child-birth by one woman is
a thing of glory and concern for all womanhood, and each second
line of three of the four stanzas of the song expresses this idea in a
different way (*O churu ndi be ya ụra*—"she has kept all her colleagues
awake"; *O kwara umu nwayi ibe ya oru*, "she has stopped all the other
female colleagues from going to work"; *O kwara ụmụ nwayi ibe ya ahia*,
"she has stopped all the other female colleagues from going to market").

Indeed, a good number of these songs express some degree of
group defiance by the women; as one that calls on all women in the
homes to come out and celebrate the birth, for no matter what they
do in the course of events, nobody can make a case (*Ife anyi mere
n'okwu adiro ya*). A similar song asserts that they, the women, are out
(during the performance) solely for the purpose of exhibiting their
pride and importance, for which reason they would not tolerate any
trouble from any quarter (*Anyi biara ebe a ikpa nganga/Onye enyeanyi
torobulu*).

While the women express their non-conformists views, however,
they never keep their focus for long off the primary value of their
event, the value of the child. It is for this that a good number of these
songs emphasize that it is not enough to have a child; it is equally
important that the child be given that adequate training that would
enable it to be useful in life. The most popular expression in many
of these songs is that whoever gets a child has the responsibility of

training that child (*O muru nnwa zua nnwa ya*), an observation which many early scholars of Igbo studies have made[13]. No amount of suffering is too great in the training of a child, and one of the songs expresses delight in the women collecting fire wood, fetching water, going to the market, all for the joy of making sure not only that the child survives, but also that it is well-trained. Another song talks in the same vein, this time listing inconvenient sources from which the women eke out some livelihood for the benefit of training their children; sources and inconveniences like the picking of palm nuts and palm kernels, having to go without supper, doing all types of odd jobs, keeping sleepless nights, and ignoring their sickness. Another song includes the money spent on school fees, books, uniforms and bags as part of the sacrifices of bringing up the child.

But the women do believe that the effort is worthwhile, because they will eventually reap the fruits of their labour. The child, after all, is being trained so that it can become an adult and begin to look after the mother. No wonder a song says that the joy of having a child is best experienced in old age (*mma nnwa bu na nka*). As one of recurrent phrases in Igbo kola nut prayer puts it, "we bring up our children so that our children will look after us" (*Anyi zua nnwa, nnwa a zua anyi*). It is not surprising that a good number of these groups go to the extent of listing all the imaginable good things of life which the mother expects from her children in future, and the unmistakable impression is that this expectation helps to sustain all her expectations in life.

While these songs emphasize the need to give a child an adequate training, some of them do not fail to mention that, after all is said and done, the child belongs to the community as a whole, for which reason the business of training him or her is a communal responsibility. Thus many of the songs insist that whoever hears the cry of a child should respond immediately, for it is not one person alone who owns the child (*O nuru akwa nnwa gbata/Na a bughi otu onye nwe nnwa*). Some of the songs take pains to mention and praise the name of the community "which owns the child". Another song says specifically that whoever undertakes the training of a child alone will never recover from the fatigue (*Onye naani ya na-azu nnwa/Ike gwuru ya).* It is the community (*Oha*) that owns the child. After all, as the last line of the first stanza of a three-stanza birth song in answer to a question as to "who owns the child" emphasizes, it is the Ama Ala, the highest legislative authority in the traditional community, which "owns the child" (*Ama ala nwe nnwa!*)

Conclusion

In this chapter, we have tried to use four classificatory typologies, of situation, medium, form and theme, to establish that Igbo birth songs qualify as good folk poetry with its own generic distinctions. We have tried to show how this poetry is an all-women affair, and that this fact makes it a convenient medium for the women to express certain views and attitudes without inhibition. This lends this repertoire of songs to some feminist possibilities, and the kind of degree of feminism expressed in the songs would depend entirely on the women's sense of responsibility and obligation to the community.

It is generally agreed that the Igbo society, like most other African societies, reveals a large degree of male chauvinism. As Ada Mere aptly put it, "because she, traditionally, is involved in patri-local marriage and does not perpetuate the family name, [the woman's] status in traditional Igbo society is low" (3).[14] But it is also known that, even in the past, Igbo women had some fairly well-organized social mechanism to let their feelings or concerns for society become known. Leith-Ross found these women "possessing startling energy, [great] powers of organization and leadership..., practical common sense and quick apprehension of reality", (337) and that "Igbo women are in theory dependent upon men but in practice independent of him" (20). Francis Arinze, substantiating this view, believes that among the Igbo

> Women have more power than was generally recognized by earlier authors. They can hold their own not only by means of public demonstrations, group strikes, ridicule, and refusal to cook for their husbands but also by their inherent vitality, courage, s

elf reliance and uncommon organizational ability. In this connection the Aba riots of 1929 were an eye-opener (4)[15]

It would therefore appear as if the feminist tendencies in Igbo birth songs are in pattern, rather than out of pattern, with the activities of Igbo women in other spheres of life. What indeed is surprising on the surface is that these women do not use the occasion of these songs, as they well might have done, for protesting in a way that would resemble modern-day patterns of feminist emancipation. Rather, what these women songs reveal is a kind of mature, positive and constructive feminism that could fearlessly ask relevant questions, and make significant comments about the nature of the society, without seeking to capsize cherished values.

One possible explanation for the low-keyed feminism in these songs is to be found in the nature of the occasion of their performance. It is an occasion that is, all told, linked with marriage and, as Jordan has observed, "marriage was an excellent sign of the fundamental sanity of Ibo (sic) view of life, for nothing reflects the sanity or insanity of any society than its attitude toward marriage" (221). But a more appealing explanation of the nature of the feminism in these songs is the fact that the medium of the feminist view-point is literary, for which reason a great deal of subtlety is demanded. These women performers of Igbo birth songs seem to realize not only this need for literary subtlety, but also the fact that the occasion for their performance is joyful and comic. In other words, they are operating within the framework of art, and, as George Deereux puts it, "art ... prescribes polite ways of saying impolite things; it provides ways of expressing the inexpressible". (193)

NOTES

*The Typology schema used in this chapter is modelled after a similar scheme used by Professor Nwoga in his "Forms of Igb o verse: Towards a Formal Typology of Igbo Poetry" *Ikenga* 6. 1 & 2 (1984). 117–130

1. It is revealing that two relevant collections of Igbo oral poetry devote considerable space to birth songs. See Ogbalu 19–62 and Ugonna 105–17.

See also Nwoga who undertook a non-ideological study of the "poetic images of childbirth" in some of these songs, in *"Mma Nwạyi Wu Nwa: Poetic Images of Childbirth among the Igbo"* (142–56).

2. This has been the persistent argument of Marxist literary critics, as is illustrated in Eagleton's *Marxism and Literary Criticism* (1976). In Nigeria, any sample reference will do, like G.G. Darah's "Igho Sh'emu Sua: A Note on Capitalist Ideology in Urhobo Oral Literature", (187–207). But non-Marxists, like Richard Dorson, also recognize this fact, particularly in the area of folk literature, the study of which, Dorson argues, was originally class-motivated. The sociology of literature is the focus of Rene Wellek and Austin Warren in chapter nine (Literature and Society") of their book, *Theory of Literature* (94–109), in which the issue is treated from the point of view of an apparently ideological non-partnership, though theirs is not much of a departure from the conventional "sociological approach" to literacy criticism. Ruth Finnegan's *Oral Poetry* (244–71) is a painstaking study of the dependence of oral art on the society that produces it.

3. For a contemporary study of the ramification of feminism in modern literature, the following sample references are quite useful: Bell Hooks, *Feminist Theory: From Margin to Culture* (1984); Maggie Humn, *Feminist criticism* 1986); E.D. Jones, ed., *Women in African Literature Today 16 (1987)*, and Henrietta Otukunefor and O. Nwodo, ed., *Nigerian Female Writers: A Critical Perspective,* (1989).

4. See Ruth Finnegan, (170). It is not surprising that three major collections of oral poetry of the Igbo are faithful to Finnegan's approach. See Ogbalu (1978) and D.I. Nwoga & R. Egudu, 91971).

5. The forty or so birth songs studied for the purpose of this paper were mainly collected by my 1983/84 students of African Oral Literature. The advantage of preferring their collection to mine is that, whereas my collection was from one local council areas of Anambra State of Nigeria, those of my students were from various area of Imo and Anambra States of Nigeria before the creation of more states in Nigeria in 1991. The similarity in the songs is, however, very obvious, so much so that, in most cases, the words used are the same, barring dialectal differences. There are, however, cases of modifications of songs-in-perfromance, as we shall illustrate later.

6. "One mystical trait of the Ibo (sic) woman", says Sylvia Leith-Ross, "is the connection between the fertility of the soil and the fertility of their bodies". (234). Nina Emma Mba echoes the above when she says that "in most

Igbo land, women were concerned with fertility rites and child rituals,…"
(32).

7. In modern times, women's dancing groups usually include well known birth songs in their choral repertoire. These songs are, however, usually restructured so as to fit into either contemporary forms of hymn-based songs or traditionally-based, carefully composed, rehearsed and adapted choral formats. Because of this restructuring, we hesitate to consider the miscellaneous occasions of their performance in our situational typology.

8. An Igbo proverb says that "you do not get a wife for a man and at the same time provide him with a mat" (*a naghi alunye nwoke nwayi, zutara ya ute*). This is usually used to remind a man that there is a limit to which he can rely on the benevolence of other people. Even if the dowry for his wife had been provided by another, he is at least expected to perform the sexual act himself.

9. Some scholars of oral literature would use vocal performance of poetry as a yard-stick for a modal classification of oral poetry. See O. Olatunji, *Features of Yoruba oral poetry* (1990).

10. O.R. Dathorne (63) uses the "breath-pause" as the criterion for determining the constituents of a line in African oral poetry. And Babalola's treatment of the forms of Yoruba Ijala admits the validity of such an approach. See Adeboye Babalola, "The characteristic features of Outer Form of Yoruba Ijala chants", 34.

11. This is an allusion to the general belief in Igbo culture that women who are desirous of bearing children should always use any opportunity to carry babies and play with them.

12. For an anthropological discussion of this view, See R.N. Henderson, *The King-in-Every man:* (214); C.K. *Meek, Law and Authority in a Nigerian tribe (70–71)*; A.E. Afigbo, "Culture and Fertility Among the Igbo of Nigeria" n.d. Arinze couches his view on the value of the woman in Igbo society as a bearer of children in biblical language when he says that "the Ibo [*sic*] woman could well say with Rachel: 'Thou must need give me children, or it will be my death; Genesis 30:1'" 940).

13. See Leith-Ross 181 & Basden, 189–190.

14. For similar views, see Monsignor Ezeanya 106, and Phoebe Ottenberg 237.

15. For similar views, see, Ottenberg iii, D. Forde & G.I Jones. (14)

Works Cited

Afigbo, A.E. "Culture and Fertility Among the Igbo of Nigeria: A Histori-cal Investigation" *Igbo Standardization Seminars 1974–75,* n.d.

Arinze, Francis. *Sacrifice in Ibo Religion.* Ibadan University Press, 1970. Print.

Babalola, A. "The Characteristic Features of Outer Form of Yoruba Ijala Chants". *Odu* 2 (July 1964).26–45. Print.

Basden, G.T. *Nigeria Ibos:* London; Franc Cass, 1966. Print.

Darah, G.G. "Igho Sh'emu Sua: A Note on Capitalist Ideology in Urhobo Oral Literature". *Theory and Practice (Journal of Nigerian Academy Arts, Science and Technology)* 2 (1977). 187–207. Print.

Dathorne, O.R. *The Mind of Africa: A History of African Literature.* Chicago: The University of Chicago Press, 1962. Print.

Devereux, George. "Art and Mythology: A General Theory". *Art and Aesthetics in Primitive Societies.* Carol Joplin. Ed. New York; E.P. Dutton & Co., 1971. 193–221). Print.

Dorson, Richard. "Africa and The Folklorist". *African Folklore.* Richard Dorson ed. Bloomington: Indiana University Press, 1972. Print.

Eagleton, Terry. *Marxism and Literary Criticism.* London: Methuen, 1976. Print.

Eliade, Mircea. *Myths, Dreams and Mysteries. New York:* Colophon Books, 1957. Print.

Ezeanya, Monsignor. "Women in Traditional Religion". *Orita* x/2 (Dec. 1976): 105–121. Print.

Finnegan, Ruth. *Oral Literature in Africa.* Oxford and Cambridge: Clarendon Press and Open University Booksd Publishers, 1970 and 2015. Print.

Finnegan, Ruth. *Oral Poetry.* Cambridge: Cambridge University Press, 1977. Print.

Fischer, Ernst. *The Necessity of Art.* Harmondsworth: Penguin Books, 1963. Print.

Forde, D and G.I. Jones. *Ibo and Ibibio Speaking Peoples of South Eastern Nigerian.* London: International African Institute, 1950. Print.

Frazer, J.G. *Folklore in the Old Testament.* Vol. 1 London: Macmillan, 1919. Print.

Green, M.M. *Igbo Village Affairs.* London: Franc Cass, 1964. Print.

Henderson, R.N. *The King-In-Everyman: Evolutionary Trend in Onitsha-Ibo-Speaking Society and Culture.* New haven: Yale University Press, 1972. Print.

Hooks, Bell. *Feminist Theory: From Margin to Culture.* Boston: South End Press, 1984. Print.

Humn, Maggie. *Feminist Criticism.* Sussex: The Harvest Press, 1986. Print.

Jones, E.D. ed. *Women in African Literature Today* 15. London: Heinemann, 1987. Print. Print.

Jordan, John. *Bishop Shanaham of South Nigeria.* Dublin: Colonmore & Reynold Ltd., 1949. Print.

Kellog, Robert, Oral Literature". *New Literary History* I. I (1973). 24–36. Print.

Kirk, G.S. *The Songs of Homer.* Cambridge University Press, 1962. Print.

Leith-Ross, Sylvia. *African Women.* London: Faber & Faber, 1939. Print.

Lord, Albert: *The Singer of Tales.* Cambridge Mass: Harvard University Press, 1960. Print

Mba, Nina Emma. *Nigerian Women Mobilized: Women's Political Activities in Southern Nigeria, 1900–1965.* Berkeley: Institute of international studies, University of California, 1982. Print.

Meek, C.K. *Law and Authority in a Nigerian Tribe.* Oxford: Oxford University Press, 1937. Print.

Mere, Ada. "Social Values Heritage of the Igbo". *Ikenga* 2.1 (Jan. 1972). 72–99. Print.

Nwoga, D.I. "Mma Nwayi bụ Nwa: Poetic Images of Childbirth Among the Igbo". *Folklore* 84 (1973). 142–56. Print.

Nwoga, D.I. and R. Egudu Ed. *Poetic Heritage: Igbo Traditional Verse.* Enugu. Nwankwo-Ifejika & Co, 1971. Print.

Ogbalu, F.C. *Mbem Na Egwuregwu Igbo.* Ibadan: Macmillan Nigeria Publishers, 1978. Print.

— and Nolue Emenanjo Ed. Igbo Language and Culture. Ibadan: Oxford University Press, 1975. Print.

Olatunji, O. *Features of Yoruba Oral Poetry.* Ibadan: Ibadan University Press, 1990. Print.

Ottenberg, Phoebe. "Marriage Relationship in Double Descent System of Afikpo of South Eastern Nigeria". University Microfilm Inc, North-Western University. Ph.D Dissertation, 1958. Print.

Otukunefor, Henrietta and O. Nwobodo. ed. *Nigerian Female Writes: A Critical Perspective.* Lagos: Malthouse, 1989. Print.

Preminger, Alex, ed. *Princeton Encyclopedia of Poetry and Poetics.* London: Macmillan, 1974. Print.

Ugonna, Nnabuenyi. *Abu Na Egwuruegwu Odinala Igbo.* Ibadan: Longman Nigeria, 1980. Print.

Wellek, Rene and Austin Warren. *Theory of Literature.* Harmondsworth: Peregrine Books, 1976. Print.

Chapter Nine

Poetry of Occasion II:
The World of the Lullaby (The Igbo Example)

Afam N. Ebeogu

Theresa Brakeley defines a lullaby as "a type of song by mothers and nurses the world over to coax babies to sleep; a cradle song" (Leach 653). This definition could be considered representative in the sense that it takes care of the various conceptual possibilities which the word "lullaby" evokes. Brakeley's subsequent survey of lullabic practices all over the world gives the impression that both in its structure and content the lullaby is a fairly widespread oral genre, with a degree of universalism that underscores the fact that some forms of oral literature are as vibrant in pre-literate societies as they are in literate ones. As Brakeley has shown, the names of lullabies in many cultures are overtly or covertly descriptive, thus emphasizing the function of the genre as an instrument for lulling babies to sleep. Among the Igbo, a popular terminology for the lullaby is *egwu okuku nnwa* ["song for baby-sitting"] or *egwu igugu nnwa* ["song for pacifying a crying baby"], both of which may be translated broadly as "cradle song". Lullabies are therefore a form of baby-talk (Johnson and Waugh 70) insofar as adults or persons much older than the baby compose them, but in such a way as to identify emotionally with the baby whose language is often mirrored in the song. They are then used as a medium for filtering into the baby's consciousness patterns of language and implied world views characteristic of the culture to which both the baby and the singer of the lullaby belong.[1]

The implication of the above definition is that the lullaby is, on the surface, function-oriented rather than the meaning-oriented; in other words, it courts the rhetorical resources of a language more than its semantic resources. However, the genre itself is always flirting along the corridors of semantics (a practice that undermines its so-called universalism) and relying on the code restrictions of the language of a particular culture. We can imagine a repertoire of lullabies from a particular culture as containing a diversity of key-holes through which a student can glance at certain aspects of that culture's world view. This chapter will comment about the Igbo world view on the basis of revelations contained in lullabies collected from various parts of the Igbo world in Nigeria.[2]

FORM, CHARACTERISTICS AND CONTENT OF IGBO LULLABIES

As already observed, many definitions of the lullaby incorporate the specific occasion for as well as the purpose of its performance: when a crying baby is being lulled to sleep. The occasion is therefore extremely informal and unpredictable. For this reason, not all students of folklore will be in a position to collect lullabies during their most authentic performance. The lullaby is indeed one of those oral literary genres which resist a stage-managed and conditioned occasion for performance, with the result that a good number of lullaby "texts" are not collected in an appropriate "context".[3]

A close look at these lullabies reveals two major types, delineated from the point of view of form and style on the one hand, and from the point of view of content on the other. We will refer to these as "overt" and "covert" types. The "overt" type, which forms the greater percentage of performances in the repertoire, identifies the song unambiguously as a lullaby, as is evident in the following:

Nwa na-eku nnwa	Baby-sitter
Awanje	A wanje
Nwa na-eku Nnwa	Baby-sitter
Awanje	A wanje
Kute Ukonwa	Bring Ukonwa
Awanje	A wanje
M gaghi ekute ya	I will not bring him/her

Awanje	A wanje
Ukonwa na-ebe akwa	Ukonwa is crying
Awanje	A wanje
Aguu na-agu ya	He/She is hungry
Awanje	A wanje
Nne ya jere ahia	His/Her mother has gone to market
Izuta akara nnwa	To buy baby's bean cakes
Awanje	A wanje
Nna ya jere ugbo	His/Her father has gone to farm
Awanje	A wanje
I ghota oka mkpo	To harvest dry corn
Awanje	A wanje
A ga-enye Ukonwa	To be given to Ukonwa
Awanje	A wanje
Yan a nwa na-eku nnwa	And the baby-sitter
Awanje	A wanje
Ha ga-ata ata	That they will chew
Awanje	A wanje
Ukonwa ghara akwa	Ukonwa leave off crying
Awanje	A wanje
Nne gi ga-alọ ngwa	Your mother will come back soon
Awanje	A wanje
Nye gi akara nnwa	And give you baby's bean-cakes
Awanje	A wanje
Nna gi ga-alo ngwa	Your father will come back soon
Awanje	A wanje
Nye gi ọka mkpo	And give you dry corn
Awanje	A wanje
Biko rahuo ụra	Please sleep
Awanje	A wanje

The lullabic quality of the above is probably most pronounced in its rhythmic structure, a structure in which there is a strict timing that governs each phrase-line and its "*awanje*" refrain.[4] This timing consists of four hand-claps to each phrase-line and its refrain, each hand clap consisting of two fast pulses.[5]

We would designate this rhythmic structure as the "fast-rocking rhythm, " in contradistinction to the "slow-rocking rhythm" to be discussed shortly. This fast-rocking rhythm, characterized by a heightened tempo in both song and body movement, is typical of most of the lullabies, like the one cited above. The semantic content of such a lullaby easily identifies the genre for what it is; hence, we refer to such a lullaby as "overt". This self-identification is to be found in the fact that the lullaby talks about (1) a crying baby, (2) the baby-sitter, (3) an absent mother gone to the market, (4) the abscent father gone to the farm, (5) the absent mother expected to bring home a delicacy—in this case the bean-cake, (6) the absent father expected to also bring home a delicacy—in this case dry corn, and (7) the expectation of the delicacy being instrumental in coaxing the baby to sleep. These seven semantic indicators are recurrent motifs in this type of lullaby, although the motifs may be more or less than seven.

Our second category of lullabies, the "covert" type, is illustrated in the following song collected from the Idemili Local Government Area of Anambra State:

Nwa ada nne ndoo biko e bena
Benekwe
Nwa ada nne ndoo biko e bena
Na Nne m si ya nwụrụ ọnwụ gi e bena
Benekwe
Na nna m si ya nwụrụ ọnwụ gi e bena
Benekwe
Mu weta agbo kua n'ini nne moo
Benekwe

Mụ solu agbọ gaa be ada nnem oo

Awanje

E e ọbụ ife ọnwụ kpatalụ

Benekwe

[Child of my eldest sister, please don't cry

Benekwe

Child of my eldest sister, please don't cry

Benekwe

For my mother said if she died let's not cry

Benekwe

For my father said if he died let's not cry

Benekwe

That I should plant a gourd (seed) on her grave

Benekwe

That I should follow the gourd (plant) to her daughter's place

Benekwe

E e it is what death has caused

Benekwe.]

This piece, lullabic in form and style insofar as its rhythmic structure is suitably "rocking", is reminiscent of many others. The number of hand-claps is four, but each is made up of three rather than two pulses; consequently the melodic movement is slower, and for this reason we can refer to it as a "slow-rocking rhythm".

But if the song is rhythmically lullabic, its semantic content is not overtly so. Indeed as often happens, the song has been extracted from a folktale and then used as lullaby because of its rhythmic structure. At times such songs echo the recurrent motifs found in the overt lullaby, but this is not always the case. In the song above, there is such an echo, especially in the undisguised presence of a crying baby, a baby-sitter who happens to be the baby's aunt, an absent mother, and the pleading, mournful mood of the song.

However, the song is really an extract from a folktale. In the tale, a widow and her little daughter live with a slave girl who is the little daughter's nurse. The woman suddenly gets ill and is about to die. She tells her daughter that she (the girl) has an elder sister who is married and lives in a land too distant for the little girl to trace. When she dies, says the widow, the daughter should plant and *agbo* (gourd) seed on her grave. This seed will sprout and the creeping plant will begin to move towards the house of this elder daughter. The little girl is to follow the creeper, and wherever the plant stops its growth, that will be the house of the little girl's sister and therefore the end of her search.

Unfortunately, the slave-girl has been eavesdropping on this conversation. When the widow dies, the slave-girl, who is much bigger and older than the widow's daughter, shaves the little girl's hair and dresses her in tattered clothes. She tidies herself up so well that she looks decent while the little girl looks like a slave girl. She plants the *agbo* seed, which sprouts immediately and leads the two to the widow's older daughter's house, where the "ex-slave" girl introduces herself as the sister to this lady and the little girl (the actual sister) as a slave-girl. Thereafter she is affectionately treated as a sister, while the real sister becomes a baby-sitter to the lady's baby.

Each time the woman and the ex-slave girl are away and the baby cries, her nurse (in reality her aunt) rocks and tries to lull her to sleep with the above song. One day a neighbor listens to her song and later arranges for the lady to eavesdrop on it from a convenient hideout. In this way, the lady discovers the calculated injustice perpetrated on her sister and reverses the roles previously played by her sister and the cheating slave-girl.

Because the motif of the underprivileged baby-sitter is a recurrent one in Igbo lullabies, we can understand how this song became so semantically relevant to the lullaby as to qualify as a "covert lullaby". Indeed, it would qualify as an "overt" lullaby if it were independently extant rather than being structurally embedded in the frame work of a folktale. Many such songs abound in the Igbo repertoire of lullabies, although they are not generally as close to the "overt" lullaby as in this particular song.

Both the overt and covert lullabies are bound by greater formal than semantic affinity. The formal qualities of these songs enable them to perform their specific function as lullabies. They are usually single-stanza pieces, and most of the stanzas, especially in the overt lullaby, are short; however, a covert lullaby could be a cumulative tale which theoretically has no terminal point, its end depending on the whims of the performer. These short pieces are repeated by the performer for as long as she wishes, even when she is on the verge of boredom. In fact, the lullaby is one oral genre where boring repetition is functionally effective, since monotony produces a deadening of the child's consciousness and a crippling of its alertness, thereby facilitating the approach of sleep.[6] But other than the formal qualities of the lullaby, there are certain characteristics—some, stylistic, some semantic—which give this oral genre its distinctive quality. The rest of this chapter will identify and discuss these characteristics.

THE SONG PROTAGONIST

By song protagonist we mean the character who, by the evidence embodied within the lullaby itself, is at the center of the song. The song protagonist is not necessarily the actual histrionic performer of the song, but the character identified in the song as the singer of the lullaby. From our examination of the repertoire at our disposal, there are five possible song protagonists: the "regular" baby-sitter,[7] the baby's sibling, the baby's mother, the baby itself, or some other outsider who does not belong to any of the preceding four categories. In most of the songs, the protagonist is the "regular" baby-sitter; in some, she identifies herself as the baby's friend, but in others she presents herself as an alienated character, often an orphan, who is being maltreated by the baby's mother or parents. A good illustration of a lullaby whose protagonist is a "regular" baby-sitter is the following overt lullaby collected from Owerri Local Government Area of Imo State:

Nwanne m nwanne m ebemana o

Hichaa anya mmiri

Nwanne m nwanne m ebemana o

Hichaa anya mmiri

Ebemena o di nga nne gi akugbue moo

Hichaa anya mmiri

Nne gi ga-aku me ihe ma I bema

Hichaa anya mmiri

Ekuela m umu asato ma I mara

Hichaa anya mmiri

O dighi nke ma-ebere m akwa ma I mara

Hichaa anya mmiri

Ebemana o ebemana o ebemana o

Hichaa anya mmiri

[Mother's child,[8] stop crying

Wipe your tears

Mother's child , stop crying

Wipe your tears

Do not cry or else you mother will pummel me

Wipe your tears

Your mother will whip me if you continue crying

Wipe your tears

Your mother will scold me if you continue crying

Wipe your tears

I have baby-sat eight children, for your information

Wipe your tears

None cried to discomfit me, for your information

Wipe your tears

Only you cry to discredit me, for your information

Wipe your tears

Do not cry, do not cry, do not cry

Wipe your tears]

In the song, the "regular" status of the baby-sitter is revealed in the information that she has done the job for eight children, during which none of them alienated her. She is however, in danger of being alienated, and in most of such lullabies the alienated baby-sitter refers to the baby's mother as "your mother", even though in Igbo society, her normal onomastic reference to the baby's mother is "Nne" ("Mother"), a reference which would establish a putative sibling relationship between the baby-sitter and the baby. Hence, in lullabies where the baby-sitter does not feel alienated, she refers to the baby's mother as "Our Mother".

The motif of the alienated baby-sitter is a prevalent one in Igbo lullabies and, even more so, in Igbo folktales. It is a reflection of the underprivileged status of the poor, *ndi ogbenye*, in a society that places a high premium on achieved status and is prone to brusque impatience with the poor. In this society, children of very poor parentage, or orphans, are forced by material deprivation to serve the well-to-do in a society where most wives treat them with minimum tenderness. The society's rejection of such enslavement manifests itself in folktales that depict such underprivledged children in situations where their fortunes are reversed, usually through the agency of the supernatural. It is therefore not surprising that many Igbo covert lullabies are drawn from folktales in which the motif of the alienated poor is foregrounded. A good illustration is the following from Oji in Owerri local Government Area of Imo State:

Nwa ogbenye e nwehu nne na nna

Nwa ogbenye ndo o o o

Onye ihe onwere

Nye nwa obgenye rie o o o

Were din du u u u

Ndu ahuhu u u u

Ndu enwehu ego o o o

[Child of the poor who has no parents

Child of the poor, sorry

Give a little to the child of the poor

So as to remain alive

The life of suffering

The life of poverty

Child of the poor, sorry]

The protagonist of this kind of lullaby is always the baby-sitter herself, and the song shows clear indications of her alienation in the household where she baby-sits.

In the lullabies where the protagonists are not the baby-sitters but either the mother of the baby, the baby itself impersonated, the baby's sibling, or an outsider, the motif of the baby-sitter is absent. Instead, what dominates are the other motifs, that are also prominent in the baby-sitter's lullabies, like the cause of the baby's discomfiture (which is usually hunger), the absence of the baby's parents, the expectation that the mother—who in most cases has gone to the market—will buy the baby certain delicacies, the pleading with the baby to cease crying and to sleep because the mother will breast-feed it on her return while the father will give it palm-wine, the motif of possible maleveolent spirits and animals which could prey on the baby if it continues crying, and the evocation of romantic associations that aid in luring the baby's consciousness into the romantic world of the dream associated with sleep. Also revealed in many of these lullabic songs are significant items of Igbo cuisine (which form part of the stock of dfelicacies promised to the baby), certain values of moral and ethical nature which a growing child is expected to imbibe in the igbo culture, some proper names of persons and places which make certain revelations about Igbo onomastics, the immense significance of the maternal essence in Igbo culture, and certain revelations of the nature of the Igbo language and how growing children grapple with some of its codes in an unconscious learning process. We will discuss some of these as the "content" of Igbo lullabies.

CONTENT

Igbo lullabies provide a great deal of insight into some significant ingredients of Igbo cuisine. In many of the overt lullabies, the performer intones a number of traditional Igbo delicacies with which the baby would be rewarded if it stopped crying, or which the parents, usually the mother, are expected to bring with them when they return. Part of one such lullaby goes thus:

I bee were ji

Na a ga m ta enye gi ya

I bee were ede

Na a ga m ta enye gi ya

I bee were ngwugwu ogiri

Ọ din a ngiga

Ihe ka ngwugwu ukpaka

Di na be nne gi

Ihe ka ngwugwu ogiri

Di na be nna gi.

[If you cry for yam

I will give it to you

If you cry for cocoyam

I will give it to you

If you cry for castor oil

It is in the chimney-basket

Something worth more than the oil bean

Is in your mother's house

Something more than the castor oil

Is in your father's house.]

Such other items of Igbo cuisine in these songs include vegetable soup with *akanwu* (potassium carbonate), coconut (described in the lullaby as "very sweet"), *akara* (bean cakes) *azu gbam gbam* (Canned fish), *aku ukukoro* (Unripe palm kernels), *ugboguru* (pumpkin), *oka mkpo* (dry maize), *mmai* (palm wine), *okpa ada ukwu* (crab), *elele* (*moi moi* made with beans), and *akwa* (egg).

The list reveals delicacies that are associated with the tastes of various age brackets in the culture. For example, while *ukpana nte* (cricket, often dug out during the cultivation of crops) is a delicacy for teenagers, *aku ukukoro* (unripe palm kernels, often cut down prematurely by wine-tappers so as to create enough tapping surface), are usually enjoyed by both teenagers and adolescents. Such items of Igbo cuisine as *akara* (bean cakes) and *elele* (made from bean paste) are usually eaten by people of all ages, but the practice is for mothers to buy them for children each time they return from the market. Children are for-bidden to eat eggs in traditional Igbo society, since such a habit would encourage the development of a taste that could deplete livestock, but occasionally parents treat their children with "stray" eggs. *Azu gbam gbam* (canned fish or sardine), was introduced into Igbo culture by the colonial contact, and it is an item which children who have relations in cities occasionally have the opportunity to taste, whereas such delicacies as coconuts, pumkin, dry maize, breadfruit, etc. are usually not restricted to any age bracket. *Ji* (yam) and *ede* (cocoyam) feature in the majority of the lullabies, and they are of course staple food items, but more than that, they represent the male and female principles respectively in the Igbo culture, as Chinua Achebe indicates in *Things fall Apart (21)*. Their invocation in lullabies is therefore of immense symbolic significance—the two items not only represent the Igbo mind's habit of perceiving things from the perspective of an oppositional duality (which will be discussed later), they also re-echo the cultural vision of the family or home as an institution in which man and woman play complementary roles—an institution towards which a crying baby looks in seeking the protection of parents who, to the baby, are only temporarily absent.

These food items in the lullabies reveal, in some ways, how the Igbo apprehend their universe against the background of certain experiences. The crying child can be said to be living in a world of fear and uncertainty, a world in which it not only lacks the warmth and comfort of its parents (symbols of the child's security in a largely be-wildering universe) but also the food that would enable it to ward off the energy-sapping and latently tragic experience of hunger. As the child cries, its lone companion rocks it, and as she sings, she draws untiringly from a dense repertoire of lullabies. These lullabies, re-plete with concrete images and items of Igbo cuisine, evoke for the child an emotion that counterbalances and attempts to obliterate the child's sense of insecurity. The emotion evoked by expectations of delicacies that will enliven the appetite, and endow material exis-tence with a nobler purpose, is hope, which represents an optimism that will cushion the child's growth into an unknown future. These concrete images and items of cuisine physically prepare the child for the essential struggles in the human passage through the world; they represent the reality of the material universe in which the child will soon be attempting to cope with the opposing demands of man's existence in the material world.

The burden of the lullaby in foregrounding the material world in the consciousness of the baby is exemplified by the dominant pres-ence of proper names—of persons, things, and places—in many of these lullabies. Very often, the personal name is that of the crying baby, as in the following extract:

Onye na-ebe akwa ee

Nkechi na-ebe akwa eee

[Who is crying, I ask

Nkechi is crying, I answer].

The name "Nkechi" is an abbreviation for "Nkechinyere", meaning "That given by chi". It is a very popular female name in Igbo on-omastics, and its constant repetition in the lullaby underscores the place of *chi* in Igbo cosmology; it refers not only to the "personal god" in every individual person, but also to the creative, divine es-sence in every human being (Echeruo, 1979, 20 and Nwoga 24).

A second illustration of the significance of personal names in Igbo lullabies can be drawn from our first song in this paper. In that song, the name of the crying baby is "Ukonwa", meaning "The Scarcity of [a] Child". It is a name usually given to a baby who is born after a fairly anxious period following the consummation of a marriage. The name implies that having a child is not an easy affair, and the fact that this name recurs in many Igbo lullabies is a reminder of the care that must be given to a child; indeed, Ukonwa becomes and Everyman child around which the lullaby weaves its significance.

At other times, the lullaby mentions the names of the baby's siblings and the place names of markets or farms to which the baby's parents have gone, as in the following example:

Nne m gaga Orie, gara Orie

Nne m gara Nkwo Nkwere

Ga I zuta okuko ocha

Mụ n'onye ga-ata isi ya?

Mụ na Ngozi nwa nne m

Mụ n'Obioha nwa nne m

Mụ na Chidi nwa nne m

Mụ na enyi m nile.

[My mother has gone to Orie (market),

Has gone to Orie

My mother has gone to Nkwo (market) at Nkwere

To buy a white fowl

I and who will share the head?

I and Ngozi my sister

I and Obioha my brother

I and Chidi my brother

I and all my friends.]

In the above extract, the singer impersonates the crying baby, thereby singing, as it were, through the child's own voice. This lullaby reveals not only the names of the baby's siblings but also the place-name of the market to which the mother has gone. Two of the Igbo

market names, Nkwo and Orie, are mentioned, but in other lullabies, all four market names—Eke, Orie, Afo, Nkwo—are featured.
These markets constitute the four-day Igbo week (*izu*) and form the
primary basis for computing the Igbo calendar. In the mythology
of most Igbo communities, they are deified forces—often imaged as
women—which comprise the four pillars of the Igbo universe and
whose mystical manifestations ensure the economic prosperity of the
communities (Onwujeogwu 66; Thomas 138).

Where both or either of the parents of the baby have not gone
to market, they have usually gone to the farm, to harvest a crop or, in
this case, to gather firewood. The lullaby therefore persistently confronts the child with a world in which human experience is related
to particular persons, particular places and particular activities, all
of which are associated with providing for the material needs of life.
Because the child grows up with a consciousness that relates life's
discomforts to the absence of these material needs, it is physically
prepared for a future in which many of life's battles consist of grap-
pling with such needs.

One can therefore appreciate why the metaphor of predation
and malevolence is dominant in Igbo lullabies. The weeping baby is
often threatened with the possibility of being harassed by malevolent
beings, usually animals and spirits, if it does not cease weeping. One
of the most popular Igbo lullabies is the following:

Onye tiri nnwa na-ebe akwa?

Egbe tiri nnwa na-ebe akwa?

Weta uziza weta ose

Weta amangororo ofe

K'ụmụ nnụnụ rachaa ha

K'okpo tum kpogbue ha

Egbe oo egbe oo.

[Who beat the crying child?

The hawk beat the crying-child

Bring *uziza* (vegetable), bring pepper
Bring pepery soup
So that the birds will lick it
So that they will die of hiccups
O hawk! O hawk!]

The hawk, in this and other lullabies, is the most frequently mentioned source of the child's discomfort. Significantly, it is also an ideal metaphor for predation. Even as the singer appeals to the baby to stop crying, she is at the same time threatening it with a horrifying experience if it does not oblige. In the same breath, however, the baby is often indirectly told that there is a solution for dealing with malevolent forces: in this case *uziza* and pepper, significant items in Igbo cuisine, are the ingredients with which an irritating soup, usually quite hot even though medicinal for human beings, can be prepared and used to scare away the birds of prey. The lullaby thus draws its validity from a world of human experiences in which living is the product of a perpetual battle between the forces of survival and those of malevolence.

Indeed, as already suggested earlier, lullabies often become a medium of social protest for the performer. Since most of the protagonists are underprivileged nurses who are forced into their position by circumstances of penury, there is a tendency for them to regard their "employers" as predators. The crying child becomes an epitome of a spirit of oppression—a burden thrust on the nurse by the child's parents. For much of the time that the nurse is living in the child's household, she is unhappy, but she does not have the courage or the means to rebel openly against her situation. She may be tempted to maltreat the child, but she cannot always do so without betraying her feelings and subjecting herself to the possibility of being severly punished. Consequently, she often bottles up her anger, and the lullaby becomes a subconscious avenue for venting her protest against a system that oppresses her. The forces of malevolence which her songs evoke are not only instruments for cowing the crying baby; they are also a metaphor for the baby's parents, who themselves are seen as evil agents who are stifling the nurse's aspirations to freedom.

But the reality of the experiential world on which the lullabies are based is occasionally undermined by the songs' sustained evocation of a romantic mood. In this mood, the baby is bombarded with images of a rather bizarre, mythological world in which the flighty spirits of birds and the joyous capering of other animals dominate, creating a carefree and jocular impression. Such a mood is apparent in the following piece:

Nwa enwe I gba n'elu na-eso m gi

Nwa enwe I gba n'ala na-eso m gi

 Nwa enwe nyem ola nyem ngbarimgba

Ka m gbanye nnwa na-ebe akwa

Nwa enwe ndoo nwa enwe ndo!

[Monkey if you run up I will follow you

Monkey if you run down I will follow you

Monkey give me a bangle give me a bell

Let me place them on the crying baby

Monkey sorry monkey sorry]

In this lullaby, as in others, images of music and dance are evoked through the listing of playful musical instruments and the vocalic emphasis placed on refrains and ideophones. For example, the fluttering gaiety of birds is captured in the following onomatopoeic melody:

Chori chori chori

Cho chooriii!

It can also be seen in the alliterative labio-velar combinations and the/e/ vowel clusters of the following snappy, rocking, and rhythmic verse:

Nwa nnụnụ were isi kwemu ekene

Nwa nnụnụ kwe nke m na-ekwe

Nwa nnụnụ olee ebe I na-eje

Nwa nnụnụ nyem ihe di n'akpa gi

Nwa nnụnụ kwe kwe kwe

Nwa nnụnụ kwe m!

[Infant bird, nod a response to my salute

Infant bird, agree to what I am saying

Infant bird, where are you going?

Infant bird, give me what is in your bag

Infant bird, respond respond respond

Infant bird, respond to me!]

The evoked mood of romance thrills the crying baby, who intermittently stops crying to listen in mystification, open-mouthed, and gazing wonderingly into the distance as the melodious rendering permeates its sub-consciousness. This romantic universe provides the infant with a welcome relief from a dominant mood of deprivation and sadness, emphasizing the delicate interplay between the realistic and fanciful imagination upon which the greatness of poetry is often anchored. Art may be an evocation of reality, but it is also a momentary escape from it, and the oscillation between the two moods—the tragic and the comic—affirms an inescapable tension in the human experience.

Even though the lullaby among the Igbo exhibits some qualities of doggerel, it thus also reflects a serious view of life that is firmly anchored in Igbo culture. As other traditional forms of poetry, lullabies are heuristic and may assume a pedagogic quality. For example, one lullaby seems to aim at inculcating in the child the knowledge of Igbo numerals up to ten, and others encourage the baby to stand on its first walking steps. One covert lullaby reveals a number of ecological features of the Igbo environment, while another lists not only major Igbo staple foods but also some of the farming tools with which these foods are cultivated.

One of the most striking heuristic components of these songs is the emphasis they place on the maternal values in Igbo culture. As we have argued elsewhere ("The Female Essence in Igbo Culture..."; "Feminism in Igbo Birth Songs"), the culture, despite the dominance of male-oriented ethics, derives a great deal of its dynamism from an over-riding maternal spirit symbolized by Ala, the great Igbo Earth goddess of morality and ancestral continuity. In virtually all the lullabies, the image of the mother as the great protector is constantly evoked: she is the towering character whose eventual presence will provide breast-milk and other delicacies for the baby. She is the one who will obliterate all the sources of fear and insecurity. One such song goes thus:

> Nne na abia ka o nye gi ara
>
> Nna na abia ka o onye gi nkwu
>
> Zụtara m ite mara mma
>
> Ji ya siere nwoke ofe
>
> Nwoke a si n'ofe amaka
>
> Nwoke e buru tufue
>
> Nwanyi a gbara ụsọ tụtụta
>
> O o o egbe ozo!

> [Mother is coming to breast-feed you
>
> Father is coming to give you palm-wine
>
> Buy me a beautiful pot
>
> Use it to cook soup for the man
>
> The man detested the soup
>
> The woman liked the soup
>
> The man threw it away
>
> The woman ran to pick up
>
> O o o another hawk!]

Here, the woman is associated with restorative action whereas the man is linked with the destructive, and it may not be irrelevant to suggest that the last line links the ever malevolent hawk with the man!

The most prominent lullabic evidence of the dominance of the maternal ethic in Igbo culture is so be found in the pervasive use of the sibling term, "*Nwanne m*", which literally translates as "My Mother's Child". Among the Igbo, this generic term applies to all warm relationships (Amadiume 62), and it is indifferent to gender. A biological sister is "*nwanne m*", so is a biological brother; but even beyond that, any relation, both on the mother's or father's side, is affectionately referred to as "*nwanne m*". Indeed, when two Igbo people find themselves outside their cultural environment and become friends, they tend to introduce one another to others as being "*umu nne*" ("mother's children"). In many lullabies, the performer, whether a baby-sitter, or a sibling to the baby, an outsider, or even the baby's mother, tends to refer to the baby affectionately as "*nwanne m*". Igbo overt lullabies that do not feature the expression are very few indeed. The lullabies thus provide telling evidence of the dominant but subterranean feature of the female essence in Igbo culture.

Other pedagogic tendencies found in these lullabies are in the area of language acquisition. When the performer of the lullaby persistently intones certain functional sounds, phonemic clusters, and lexical associations, the baby is unconsciously initiated into the intricacies of language use in the culture. As Jakobson and Waugh (164) have observed, melody occupies a priority in a child's language, since the child tends to reproduce easily the intonation contours which he or she has heard in the prersence of elders and maids. For example, the Igbo tendency to associate certain duplicated nominals with some verb roots is prominently featured in these lullabies, and the baby obviously would be initiated to this linguistic habit as it listens to the songs. For example, one lullaby has the following text:

Gi na-ebe obube obube!
Gin na-eti otiti otiti!

[You cry cry cry!
You shout shout shout!]

The meaning in this song is that the baby cries and shouts a great deal. When another lullaby asks that the hawk be shot *kpu kpü kpu*, the child instinctively absorbs the fact that the onomatopoeia expresses the sound of a shooting gun. Yet another lullaby explores the intonational pun and implied tongue twister between *egbe* (gun) and *égbé* (hawk) in *"Lèkwá egbè na-egbu egbe"* (Look at the gun that kills the hawk"). Puns and tongue twisters are very effective ways of semantic discrimination and it is significant that many of these structures are featured in Igbo lullabies.

A word that recurs in many lullabies is *ndo* ("sorry"), with which the performer unceasingly pleads with the crying baby. In the Igbo language, *ndo* is used in various situations where the idea of sympathy is being conveyed, and it can thus be argued that the lullabies gradually initiate the baby into the culture's imploratory expressions. But even more striking a phenomenon in semantics is the revealation, in the lullabies, of the Igbo tendency to use patterns of verbal collocations described by Malkiel as "irreversible binomials" ("Studies in Irreversible Binomials", 30–36; *Essays in Linguistic Themes*, 311–55). These are binary word formations in which two otherwise independent words, with meanings tending to be opposite in nature, are used together in a context which suggests a single signification. In the words of M.J.C Echeruo, "Igbo has a pattern of compounds which link related but unidentical institutions to form a third composite name ... [with] a single signification but [whose] elements have their own independent meaning" ("The Future of Igbo Studies" 3–4).

Whenever these binomials are used, they appear in a fixed preferential order, which suggests some kind of systematic hierarchy in the linguistic psyche of the people. Thus, the Igbo always use the expression, *ikwu n'ibe* ("blood relations and colleagues"), which appears in one of the lullabies examined in this essay, and *not ibe n'ikwu*, to refer to that loosely determined body of people with whom a man has socially interacted (as a relation, a friend, or an acquaintance) and who are expected to be among the participants in any significant event (like marriage of death) involving the man (See Nsugbe 22–78 and Uchendu 64–70).

Irreversible binomials abound in the Igbo language, and various forms of them are featured in the lullabies. Fro example, the singer of one lullaby asks:

> Onye na-eme ọkụkọ ahu?
> Ọbụ egbe ka ọbụ ugo?

> [Who has provoked that chick?
> Is it the hawk or the eagle?]

In doing so, he is drawing from the irreversible binomials, *egbe n'ugo*, ("the hawk and the eagle"), which is a metaphoric signification for "friend and foe". Again, the previously discussed expression *ji na ede* ("yam and cocoyam"), is endemic in the lullabies, as is the expression, *nne na nna* ("mother and father"), meaning "parents". In this connection, it is significant that *nne* ("mother") comes first, as it always does in other contexts where this binomial occurs. Evidence of such preferences can be used to buttress our argument about the dominance of maternal values in the Igbo culture, although a systematic analysis of the criteria for establishing semantic hierarchy in Igbo irreversible binomials would obviously be necessary to establish the empirical validity of this contention.

Other significant irreversible binomials in the lullabies include *elu n'ala* ("the sky and the earth"), which expresses the spatial and geometaphysical limits of the Igbo universe beyond which, in a lullaby, the malevolent but flirtatious monkey cannot escape; *ukwu n'anta* (the great and small) in a lullaby where the orphaned baby-sitter laments the injustices she has received from "all and sundry"; *akwa n'ochi* (crying and laughter") which describes the frequent polarized moods of the crying baby. Others include *anwu na mmiri* ("sunshine and rain")[9] which is the metaphor for the scope and suffering to which the absent mother in a lullaby could be subjected; *okoro n'agbogho* ("young man and young woman") to whom a lullaby assigns *ji na ede* ("yam and cocoyam) respectively; *aka n'ọkpa* ("the hand and the leg") which specifies the physical fitness of a protagonist of the lullaby; *isi n'ọdụ* ("the head and the tail"), symbolizing *"meaninglessness"*;

mmuo na mmadu ("spirits and humans") who constitute the "social beings" of the Igbo universe, and *anu n'azu* ("meat and fish"), which embodies all the delicacies a crying baby could expect to receive from an absent mother.

It has been suggested that the dominance of irreversible binomials in the Igbo language reflects the culture's perception of the universe in terms of dualistic structures. As Chinua Achebe declares in his "Chi in Igbo Cosmology" (94), "Wherever Something stands, Something Else will stand beside it". This notion of duality is central to Igbo thought.[10] If language embodies the philosophy of any people, the lullabies discussed above, spanning a large spectrum of Igbo linguistic traits, can be understood as expressing significant notions in Igbo philosophy. The crying baby gradually imbibes not only the strategies of Igbo preferences in the language's semantic hierarchies, but also the philosophical basis for making choices. Significantly, as we have argued, the child's psyche develops within the context of a vision of the universe in which nothing is absolute—a universe in which laws of dualistic opposition and juxtaposition, underpinning the irreversible binomials, exert themselves indomitably. Subtly, the child is being prepared for a life in which all facets of experience reflect fundamental oppositions and ambiguities, a life in which synthesis is an easy mediation of thesis and antithesis, a life in which the individual's intelligence must be brought to bear on the conflicting configurations of meaning that constantly impinge on him or her.

CONCLUSION

Beginning with a definition of the lullaby as a genre of folk poetry, this chapter argues that, although the occasion for the performance of lullabies and the mode of their rendering may suggest a qualitatively low grade of poetry, they actually constitute a serious oral repertoire and deserve serious scholarly attention. On the basis of motif-content, I have distinguished between two types of lullabies: the overt and the covert. These two types are governed by two forms of rhythmic format: the fast-rocking rhythmic lullaby and the slow-rocking type. Both rhythmic formats are related to the function of the lullaby as a melodious form of poetry that lulls the baby to sleep. The paper then proceeds to discuss the standard motifs, the characteristic images, and the philosophical or cosmological content of the lullabies in relation to the Igbo world, its heuristic and peda-gogic values, and certain attributes of the Igbo language, especially insofar as these attributes reflect the philosophy of the Igbo people. Some of the issues raised in relation to these linguistic characteristics of the lullabies call for further research and analysis by linguists, but it should by now be clear that these lullabies constitute a linguistic repertoire that offers an enlightening test case for the study of many aspects of the Igbo language.

NOTES

1. An essential psycholinguistic issue is raised here, and elsewhere in the chapter, as to what extent it can be affirmed that a baby is positively affect-ed by the singing of the lullaby. We do not possess the psycholinguistic com-petence and data to *prove* a case, but we rest our argument on the fact that since the baby *cannot* tell us whether or not it is affected by a lullaby, we can only use other measures, which are essentially literary, to make inferences and draw conclusions.

2. The lullabies discussed in this essay were collected by myself and fifty students of Oral Literature at the old Imo State University in 1987. The various areas of Igboland covered by the collection include Imo, Anambra, Bendel, and Rivers States of Nigeria. The simple stratagem used was to ask mothers and baby-sitters to sing into tape-recorders as many lullabies as they could recollect. These were later transcribed. I would like to take this opportunity to express my indebtedness to these students, whose col-lections—copies of which I was allowed to keep—supplemented my own repertoire, thus enlarging my data base.

3. See the introduction to Ruth Finnegan (1–28), especially the brief dis-cussion on "Performance and Text" (28–29). Isidore Okpewho (135–201) explores the contextual imperative of oral poetry (the epic) elaborately, as does Albert Lord (3–140) and a number of contributors to Okpewho's ed-ited book, *The Oral Performance in Africa* (137–248).

4. For a discussion of rhythmic structures in African vocalic music, see Nke-tia (1968–76). A satisfying rhythmic analysis of the lullabies discussed in

this essay would need some musicological notation. In the absence of that, one can only fall back on a knowledge of the tone for each lullabic song. Only this knowledge, mutually shared by two persons attempting disparately to determine the rhythmic pattern of the song, can ensure that such persons are not working at cross-purposes.

5. Even though Nketia uses hand-claps for the metric determination of the African vocalic song, it should be pointed out that performers of lullabies do not as a rule clap their hands. Very often, the baby is tied on the back of the singer who moves slowly in a circular formation, tapping her legs softy on the floor. It is the tapping of the legs, each often doing a consecutive double-tap before the other takes over, that replaces the clapping of hands. The following lullaby shows that the song is performed while the baby is being rocked on the back of the singer:

> Ori ji nyekwa nnwa m
> Ori ede nyekwa nnwa m
> Nwoke ocha gata enye m
> I nyere m nyekwa nnwa muo
> Nnwa m nkwo n'azu o.

> [Yam-eater give some to my baby
> Cocoyam-eater give my baby some
> The white-complexioned man will give me
> You give me, you also give my baby
> The baby I am carrying on my back.]

6. Scholars often discuss boredom in oral poetry as it if is always undesirable. This tendency explains why Okpewho (*The Epic in Africa 32–79; 135–39*) nearly strains himself in an attempt to demonstrate that the bard of the oral epic can call upon illimitable resources that obviate a boring performance due to frequent repetitions.

7. Most "regular" baby-sitters among the Igbo are girls roughly between the ages of eight and fifteen. They usually come from very poor families and their baby-sitting often provides the means of subsistence for their families.

8. "*Nwanne m*", translated as "Mother's child", is the Igbo cognate term for very close relations including siblings. It is unisexual; its significance will be discussed later in this essay.

9. The English would of course talk of "rain and sunshine". It is tempting to speculate that the preference for *rain* over sunshine in their semantic

188 Ethnosensitive Dimensions of African Oral Literature

hierarchy reflects the temperate climate in which rain influences the biome-teorology of the citizens more than the sun does. The reverse would hold true for the tropical Igbo.

10. This binary vision of the universe is hardly peculiar to the Igbo. As Jonathan Culler has pointed out, "Structuralists have generally ... taken the binary opposition as a fundamental operation of the human mind basic to the production of meaning: 'this elementary logic which is the smallest common denominator of all thought" (15).

WORKS CITED

Achebe, Chinua. *Things Fall Apart.* London: Heinemann, 1965. Print.

—. "Chi in Igbo Cosmology". *Morning Yet on Creation day.* London: Heine-mann, 1975. 160–180. Print.

Amadiume, Ifi. *Male Daughters, Female Husbands: Gender and Sex in an African Society*: London: Zed Books, 1986. Print.

Culler, Jonathan. *Structuralist Poetics.* London: Routledge and Kegan Paul, 1976. Print.

Ebeogu, Afam "The Feminist Temperament in Igbo Songs." *Power and Pow-erlessness of Women in West African Orality.* Granquist, R & Nnadozie Inyama Eds. Umea Papers in English No. 15, (1992). 43–62. Print.

—. "The Female Essence in Igbo Culture: Glimpses from Literature". Un-published Paper.

Echeruo, M.J.C. A *Matter of Identity.* Owerri: Ministry of Information, Cul-ture, Youth and Sports, 1979. Print.

—. The Future of Igbo Studies: A Very Modest Proposal". *Igbo Standardiza-tion Seminars* 1974–75. N.d. Print.

Finnegan, Ruth. *Oral Poetry.* Cambridge: Cambridge UP, 1977.

Jakobson, Roman, and Linda Waugh. *The Shape of Language.* Bloomington and London: Indiana UP, 1979. Print

Leach, Maria, ed. *Standard Dictionary of Folklore, Mythology and Legend.* Lon-don: Harper and Row, 1984. Print.

Lord, Albert. *The Singer of Tales.* Cambridge, MA: Harvard UP, 1960. Print.

Malkiel, Y. "Studies in Irreversible Binomials". *Lingua* 8 (1959): 13–60. Rpt. In *Essays in Linguistic Themes.* Oxford; Blackwell, 1968. 311–55. Print.

Nketia, John. *The Music of Africa.* London: Gollancz, 1986. Print.

Nsugbe, P.O. *Ohafia: A Matrilineal Igbo people.* Oxford: Clarendon Press, 1974.

Nwoga, D. *The Supreme God as Stranger in Igbo Religious Thought.* Ekwereazu: Hawk Press, 1984. Print.

Okpewho, Isidore. *The Epic in Africa.* New York: Columbia UP, 1976. Print.

Okpewho, Isidore. Ed. *The Oral Performance in Africa.* Ibadan. Spectrum Books Ltd, 1990. Print.

Onwujeogwu, M.A. *An Igbo Civilization: Nri Kingdom and Hegemony.* Benin: Ethiope Press, 1981. Print.

Thomas, Northcote. "Law and Custom of the Ibo of the Awka Neighborhood, Southern Nigeria." *Anthropological Report on Ibo-Speaking Peoples of Nigeria.* Vol. 1. London: Harrison and Sons, 1913. 6 vols. 1913–1914. Print.

Uchendu, Victor. *The Igbo of Southeast Nigeria.* New York: Holt, 1965. Print.

PART THREE: THE PROSE GENRES

Chapter Ten

The African Oral Narratives: The Folktales

F.U. Chima

INTRODUCTION

When Ruth Finnegan in the preface to one of her books on African Oral Literature titled *The Oral and Beyond: Doing Things With Words in Africa,* avers that "Africa is commonly known as the oral continent", little, perhaps, did she realize that she was not saying anything less than the obvious about the only black continent of the world-Africa. Africa is truly an oral continent whose live-wire, modes of existence and of course the actual and general means of recording depend mainly on orality. On the literary angle, and as an oral continent, therefore, her wealth of literary corpus seems not to exist for the simple reason that it is not written and has to be realized and based on the examination of the structure and the working of human memory. What the foregoing suggests is that all the cultural lore and mores of the people are verbally recorded and stored in their oral societies' store, which are the peoples' varying forms of oral literature and or oral narratives (Akporobaro, 45; Okpewho, 180–183; Chukwuma, 47). Again, what the foregoing implies is that Africa, being literarily an oral continent, her oral literary genres exist as unique avenues and store-house that serve the people as oral narrative text library, whence any of the narrative texts could be called from in times of need either to refute or uphold an ongoing argument.

At this juncture, one may conclude reasonably that the aesthetic merits of African oral narratives are not meant to stand alone, but, rather, to enhance public functions. Perhaps, this idea is what So-wayan tries to point out when he says:

A poem composed by a Bedouin is not a poem. It would be considered frivolous and unbecoming for a respectable chief to compose a poem just for its sake. It has to have a dignified purpose and serious intent—to defend a case, lay claim, exhort to action, declare war, celebrate a victory, sue for peace, and so forth. Oral literature is, in a sense, like crude oil in that there are so many derivatives you can extract from it, but only if you have good refineries, in the present instances this means sound methodology and a sophisticated theoretical orientation. (134)

From the immediate foregoing, it therefore means that the varying forms of oral literature and or narratives existent in the African oral storehouse can take the aforementioned forms, serve as oral constitution and 'a book of like' for determining and fortifying the people's past, present and future ways of life and world view. Again, a people's oral narratives are used to remind them and make evergreen in memory their generally accepted ways of valuing things and, should the need arise, be a means of determining their genealogy and origin. It was in the light of this that Obiechina says "that oral tradition relies largely on human memory for the preservation and transmission of the cultural repertoire…" (35). Perhaps, it is the same idea that Sowayan tries to portray in his attempt to disclose the importance of oral narratives in the study of tradition when he says:

> Specialist such as Havelock and Ong keep alluding constantly to the encyclopaedic nature of oral literature, a fact realized by the ancient Arab philologist who called Pre-Islamic poetry "The register of the Arabs", meaning that it contains information on their history, genealogy, worldview, cultural values, and entire way of life. (133)

On a look at the title of this chapter: "The Oral Narratives: The Folktale", one particular problem noticeable is that oral narratives and folktales could refer to the same thing. As researches have shown, both words may refer to those stories in Africa that are rendered in prosaic mode. The business of this chapter is to discuss the African oral narrative with an eye on the folktale, and the problem here, which is one of nomenclature, is an age-long one. As it is, scholars have argued that both words talk about the same form of the African oral Literature, and we have chosen "oral narratives" because of the derogatory use of 'folk' by the earlier generations of scholars ofAfrican Oral Literature who were mostly European to refer to the varying forms of African oral narratives. Okpewho, writing on 'Oral Narratives' observed as follows:

> In this chapter we are going to discuss what are generally re-ferred to as folktales. So long as we disabuse our minds of the sort of prejudice which earlier generations of scholars had about the concept of folk as the 'uneducated' and therefore irrational and unimaginative dwellers of communities, then there may be situations in which we can excuse the use of the term folktales for purposes of convenience. The term oral narrative is, howev-er, preferred not only because it leaves little room for that preju-dice but also because—perhaps like the term oral literature—it gives primary emphasis to the medium of expression of this art, which is word of mouth. (163)

What the foregoing aims at clarifying is that the African oral narratives are those oral literary texts that exist in prosaic narrative modes. Even from our emphasis above, folktales are inclusive. We understand the folktale here as such stories in purpose of addressing social vices, and the mirroring of the people's worldview. And it is on this terrain in relation to the functions of the African oral narratives that Obiechina (35) fervently agrees that the oral artist in Africa, amidst other functions with his/her performance, serves as a teacher and social reformer; for he/she uses her art to explore the problems of society.

AFRICAN FOLKTALES: THE TEXT

In Africa, the sources of the varying forms of folktale texts are of two kinds. The first are real-life events that took place sometime ago in the society. Any conscious effort by anybody to narrate how an event happened to a person or group of persons, is a folktale already in existence. It is in the light of this idea that Kofi Awoonor avers that "Among every African people there are stories over migrations and

legends of their movement in vast numbers across great expanses of
land over long periods. These waves of migration took place at periods of great intervals and over many centuries. They also would explain the various historical stories and stresses" (4). What this means
is that, with time, the real events find themselves into the narrative
modes of the people's oral culture and then become texts in the people's oral narrative corpus to be referred to. As texts of reference,
therefore, they can be called for to support or oppose a given point
of view. Within the first group of folktales divide are such narratives
as myths, contest stories, didactic stories and numerous other kinds,
which in each case an attempt is made to explain some issues in
the society that are meant to serve as eye-opener to people on why,
for example, certain things happen in certain ways and why a given
punishment is meted out for violation of community's set custom,
tradition and culture. A good example here is "akuko-ala", tales of
the land, a story involving the experience of entry, possession, and
settlement on the land (Azuonye, 195).

> The narratives become a complex of myths or ideological men-
> tifacts reminding the people of the struggles of their ancestors
> in securing the land and of the responsibility of successive gen-
> erations to defend the land against potential encroachment.
> (195)

In Edda-Igbo of South-eastern Nigeria, such stories involving
not only land possession and entries but also how certain events happened; how a particular thing at a given place came to be; how a
particular lineage (Ikwu) behaving in a particular way, among others,
came to be, etc, are better referred to as "aka" and then "akuko-ala"
the practice of the tales or narratives. Below is an example of an
"aka" or "akuko-ala", tale of the land from the Edda-Igbo narrating how the tradition of the people changed from the patrilineal to
matrilineal—the story, and other narratives in this paper, were collected and translated into English by me.

> Before now, the people of Edda were known as a patrilineal
> nation. Wealth was normally passed from father to children.

At a time everything changed into the other way round. The changing was as a result of the incident which occurred between Oboni Ukwu Eze and his seven wives.

Oboni Ukwu Eze was a man of valour who was from Ekworo lineage. He had seven wives and they had born him many children. The first wife had seven children; the second six; the third five; the fourth four; the fifth four; the sixth three and the seventh two, bringing the total number of his children to thirty-one. He loved and cared for each of his wives and children almost equally but for the extra love he had for the last wife and her children.

One day, as he was coming back from the farm after a long day—work therein, he carried along with him a log of firewood for the last and favourite wife. On reaching home, he saw one of his children (born for him by the favourite wife) groaning under the weight of another child in a fight over a mere plaything. On attempt to separate the two children at the same time in a hurry to drop the firewood on his head, Oboni Ukwu Eze mistakenly dfropped it on another boy-child who had been at the scene to watch the two children fight. The boy dropped dead instantly. Oh! That was how Oboni Ukwu Eze, the child of Ekworo lineage, a man of valour, a man who had been to too many wars and returned home unhurt and with many heads, committed murder.

As a sign or remorse for what he had done and to give room for negotiations, he ran to one of his friends, the king of Ukwuni Akpan in present-day Cross River State. After narrating his story and his reasons for running to him for safety, the king accepted Oboni Ukwu Eze, but with a condition. And, that was that Uboni Ukwu Eze should on no account make use of his toilet, lest people will see and trace him to the king's house. Though the idea meant well for Oboni Ukwu Eze, it was a condition impossible to keep. As if to prove this, Oboni Ukwu Eze became seriously pressed just few minutes after this was said to him. Having no option, he went ahead and made use of the king's toilet. Coincidentally and unfortunately too, when he was about to leave the toilet, the king met with him on his way going to make use of the toilet. The king of Ukwuni Akpa reminded Uboni Ukwu Eze of his order that he should on no condition make use of his toilet. For the punishment, the king asked Uboni Ukwu Eze to pack the faeces with anything he could. Uboni Ukwu Eze then packed his own faeces, wrapped it with a cocoyam leaf and hung it on a bamboo-rafter inside the hut of his asylum and home. This he kept doing as any further attempt to do things the normal way would incur the wrath of his protector: the king. Amidst all this, negotiations were going on at home on a way out. At the end, it was recommended that the family of the child, his lineage and the entire Edda clan be appeased for the act of the committed sacrilege. The appease-ment required that Uboni Ukwu Eze be killed. But because of his position in Edda as a man of valour and uprightness, and above all had committed the act unknowingly, he was given the chance of giving another male child to stand in for his place. Or in the absence of anybody, himself must be given. Uboni Ukwu Eze heaved a sigh of relief when the decisions reached at the negotiation table were made known to him. He felt that there was no problem since he had lots of children in his household.

But he received the greatest shock of his life when one day, one of his wives, of course the favoured and the one whose child he was in the process of saving when he got himself into the problem he was into, went to Ukwu Akpa to see him. While going, she went with her a well-prepared meal for her husband. But the husband refused the food with the reason that should he eat, he would have to use the toilet, which he had no access to. However, he demanded that one of the woman's children be released for him to be used as an appeasement for the person he killed mistakenly. The woman there and then asked her hus-band how was it possible to him that she would release any of her children to be killed for the person the husband had killed. That her husband knew she had only two children and should she release one for him, then she would be left with only one child. Well, if to her husband that was the only way for her to show him that she loved him, then that she was going and would never come to see him again since coming to see him would warrant being told some other rubbish. And she actually left and never went to see him again.

On different occasions the other wives of the man went to see their husband individually. And on each of such visits Uboni Ukwu Eze discussed the same issue with each of them. None of them agreed to release any of their children for the sacrifice. The basis of their refusal was on the ground that the favoured wife had her own children who should be used for the atonement. After all it was her child who caused the problem, yet her children were left out of what they lured him into. That certainly it was because she was mostly loved by their husband that he wanted to leave her children out of this and would want to involve those loved less and their children. For this reason, they all refused him such offer, preferring that he be killed for his act, which to them, whether he committed it knowingly or not, was not their problem. What they were saying by this was that it was not their business whether or not he committed the act knowingly.

Uboni Ukwu Eze, seeing that none of his wives was ready to solve his problem, resigned to his fate. He sent a message across to Afor Ukwu Eze inviting her (who was his only blood sister, but hitherto a mere relation, for she now belonged to the lineage of the man she was married to, according to the tradition; yet, ever since the case started, she had been coming to see him), if for nothing else, to inform her condition of things with him. He never hoped to ask for Uboni Ukwu Eze Junior, her only son named after him for many reasons. Firstly, the namesake is the only child of his sister's. Secondly, the lad in question by Edda tradition and culture was not of his lineage and as such he had no authority over him.

Afor Ukwu Eze honoured the invitation. As she was going, she went with a well-prepared meal for Uboni Ukwu Eze. However, he appreciated the food the sister brought but still insisted that he was not going to eat the food for the same reason he had severally told her. He said to her that this time he had just invited her to let her know the outcome of the negotiation his relations had with the relations of the child he mistakenly killed. That they had accepted it was a mistake but he too must be killed. Or alternatively, another lad had to be provided to be killed in revenge. That as it stood, none of his wives has accepted to provide for him any of their children for this purpose, which meant he would be going in for this.

Having heard this, she bled in her heart and got up from her seat, said to her brother that this would never happen; if at all, only when she was no more, and only when she had no male child for a situation like this. She therefore agreed to release her only child and so on, Oboni Ukwu Ezenta, to him for the purpose. When Oboni Ukwu Eze made to protest against this idea and reminded Afor Ukwu Eze that Oboni Ukwu Ezenta, the child in question, was not his relation, rather her husband's, Afor Ukwu Eze insisted that what bound them was much more than what tradition could divide. That it was better her son died than him to die. This was because she still had a chance of producing another child but could not have another brother after him since their parents had died long ago.

When Afor Ukwu Eze went back home that day, she narrated every bit of the conversation between her and her brother to her husband. The man disagreed with the wife on the decision to give his only son and child for whatever purpose to a man who had many children. She pleaded with him, giving reasons upon reasons. At the end, the man got convinced and both husband and wife agreed that their child be used. This idea was not made known to the child. On the appointed day for the revenge, he was sent to go and see his namesake Ukwuni Akpa and give him food. The unsuspecting Oboni Ukwu Ezenta did not know agreements had been concluded by all for him to be killed as a sacrificial lamb. According to the agreement, the lad would be killed while coming back from seeing his namesake at Ukwuni

Akpa. The young man went and returned safely: a surprise to the parents, but the namesake knew the reason. So when asked by Afor Ukwu Eze the lad's mother, it was explained to her that it was due to the way the lad was dressed on *ukara* cloth, *anugwe*, a cap of tiger brand, and all those that signified the human being in Edda culture and tradition. Seeing all those things the lad wore, the team of avengers refused to touch him. This was because they knew the implication should they.

On second arrangement, amendments were made that the lad's mode of dressing be the accepted one. So after giving the namesake the food and having had a brief discussion with the namesake, the man saw him off. Oboni Ukwu Eze knew that the lad would not survive it on this second time so he spoke to him in proverbs, which the lad did not understand. However, the child took off. On the way, the team of avengers camped themselves in seven groups waiting: should the lad cross this group unhurt, he would never cross the other. The lad kept going home, these plans unknown to him.

At a stage on the way, the lad began noticing some strange movements around the nearby bushes and then had to quicken his pace. He started trotting and before long started running because by now he was completely afraid of the bushes though he could not say for what reason in particular. By then he had crossed some of the revenge groups. At a time the groups began to execute their mission. They pursued and he ran for his life towards the direction he was coming, shouting: "Namesake! Namesake! Namesake!" They only succeeded in giving him several machete cuts. With those cuts, he managed to run to his namesake who with his fake protection came out bragging before his namesake, asking who it was.

As he ran back to his namesake panting, his namesake rushed out, pretending not to know what was going on as he asked: "Ogbo onye, Ogbo onye? Namesake who is it? Namesake who is it?" And those around, who were quite unaware of what was going on, helped the boy, alongside namesake, get treated of his cuts. Thank God the lad survived the wounds. Yet, the avengers insisted the revenge mission was not yet achieved since the boy did not die. Oboni Ukwu Eze saw it from a different light and maintained that the revenge was done for blood had been shed the first time and could not be done the second time. It was at Osisi Oma, the Edda high court of appeal, that the case was decided in favour of Oboni Ukwu Eze.

Oboni Ukwu Eze returned to his house. Eight days after his return, he called his wives together in his *ulonta*, his palour. When all had gathered, he instructed each of them to get her relations informed that he said they should gather at Osisi Oma for he had few words for both them: his wives and children, and Edda clan as a whole. His wives did as he instructed them. On the appointed day all and sundry gathered at Osisi Oma.

Having seen all had gathered, Oboni Ukwu Eze stood from his seat, walked right to the middle of the circled crowd and stood before them. Looking this way and that he began with a greeting to the Edda men and women gathered:

Chee yi! Chee yi! Edda kwen—u

The people responded to the greeting:
Hoa!
Chee yi! Chee yi! Edda kwen—u
Hoa!
Chee yi! Chee yi! Edda kwen—u
Hoa!

This he did for a number of times, turning to the different sides of the group. When he was through with the greeting proper he cleared his voice before he began. He narrated the story of how he killed a lad of his son's age to all those gathered. He also told the people how it all boiled down to giving somebody in place of himself and how all his wives had refused him of his request to them. And that at the end it was his own sister already married to another man, which by Edda tradition and culture was no longer his relation, who offered him her only son and child just for him to be saved. He added in conclusion therefore that now he was back he had called together everybody to hear his will because he could not tell when he would meet his ancestors. So, should he die, his wealth would not belong to his children according to the Edda culture and tradition; rather to the child of his younger sister, Oboni Ukwu Ezenta. Having said this he greeted them once again:

Chee yi! Edda kwen—u
Ho............................a!
Chee yi! Edda kwen—u
Ho............................a!

In this kind of folktale or narrative text, no changing of the names or the scenes and or setting are accepted. In fact, there is no form of fictionalizing of any kind. All remain as they are. However, because these are oral texts that rely on the ability of the human memory, a text may slightly differ from one narrator to another.

The second kinds of narratives are still on real events but fictionalized into a verbal construct. At the initial periods of human settlement, as reiterated earlier on, the main source of folktale texts were based on the challenges arising from situations surrounding places of settlement. Then, as time went on, the complexities arising from human interactions gave rise to yet another form of folktale narrative texts different from those already discussed. Azuonye succinctly captures this idea thus:

> in the environment of more entrenched social systems, the stability of the fundamental myths has been constantly reinforced and extended by other important structures of the imagination communicated through language, namely akuko-ifo (tales of the imagination), ilu (similitude), and okwu-nka (artistic speech). (195)

There is no point doubting what forms the folktale narrative texts because they are real-life situations resulting from human interactions. The fieldwork of Kofi Awoonor attests to this point. Let us hear him:

> This writer was informed by storytellers in the Ewe tradition that the animal stories are sometimes real events which might have occurred in the life of the people. But in order to avoid embarrassing the participants in the events or their offspring

and to keep solidarity intact, animals become the characters. It is the spider man who once said, 'Because I tell stories and never mentioned people by their names, I have been a defender in a court of libel'. (75)

Having identified the means African folktales texts could come to be, we would, therefore, narrow it a bit to the very folktale text this chapter is talking about. And that is, as Igbo oral literature scholars would put it, 'akuko-ifo', tales of the imagination (Azunonye, 195). In this African oral narrative text, different animals form characters to address varying aspects of human follies: animals like lions, tigers, cocks, spiders, tortoise, birds and many others are used. In such narrative texts—'akuko-ifo'—all creations are personified to perform any role the narrator wants them to. However, in various parts of Africa, different animals are used in their folktale texts. The spider, for example, is used as the major character in some parts while in some others it is the tortoise. But, it needs be pointed out still that the issue of text in African oral literature centres mainly on language use, which Sowayan had referred to as having 'sound methodology and a sophisticated theoretical orientation' (134). The method of language use defines the type of folktale narrative text in question: 'akụkọ ala', a tale of the land, or 'akụkọ-ifo', a tale of the imagination, ilu, similitude or 'okwu-nka', artistic speech.

AFRICAN FOLKTALES: THE STRUCTURE

In African oral narrative text, there are generally an accepted manner which every storyteller must follow when telling any folktale. These accepted ways and manners are what are referred to as structure of the folktales in Africa. For one thing, these structuring patterns are not the same all through the regions in Africa. Every region has its own pattern of structuring its folktales, which when talking about the structure of that part of Africa's folktale, such manners or ways may be referred to. However, this does not imply there are no general patterns of structuring the African folktale. Every of the African folktale has at least a formal structuring of the beginning, the body and the conclusion. These pattening cut across all folktales in Africa, with slight differences. Beside the slight differences, the generally accepted formal pattern of beginning folktales in Africa can be exemplified with a folktale session in the Yoruba areas of South-Western Nigeria. In those parts of Nigeria and or Africa, there are already established words by tradition meant for beginning a folktale, which every story-teller about to tell a tale must use. These are:

Story: Alo-o
Listeners: Alo-o

Taiwo (1985) tells us that the storyteller's 'Alo-o' means 'Get ready for what is coming' and the listeners' replied word, 'Alo-o', means 'We are ready'. In other parts of Africa, the same expressions occur but are done in their different dialects and or languages. In Kenya, for example, among the Pokomo, as Okpewho tells us, similar expressions are used during the opening session of their storytelling:

Generations came and went (repeated a few time)
A chief was born in the north
A chief was born in the Central
A chief was born in the South. (Nandwa and Bukenya, 1983:82.
qtd in Okpewho, 223).

In Oku, a tribe in Cameroon, Mbunda informs us that 'tale telling begins with riddles. These riddles serve as a sort of warming up before the actual narrative session begins' (27). Each narrator begins his story with the exclamation such as :'Fengennen oh' meaning 'story oh!' And the audience responds to it this way: 'Fengennen oh!', meaning 'story oh!' In essence therefore, it will go like this:

Storyteller: Fengennen oh!
Audience: Fengennen oh!

Among the Edda-Igbo of South Eastern Nigeria, the opening session of a folktale takes this shape:

Storyteller: Oti-i

Listeners: Oyo-o

Storyteller: Oti-i
listeners: Oyo-o
Storyteller: O nworo otu mgbe
Listeners: Mgbe eruala

After such brief conversation drama, as it is in some parts including Edda, jokes, riddles, among other word games, follow before the story proper, as is the case in Oku, an ethic group in Cameroon. Okpe-who seems to be in agreement with this idea when he says:

> …In the traditional setting storytelling is only one of the entertainments provided on an evening of relaxation … and may come only after other forms of activity, e.g., hide and seek games by children, reminiscences of the day's event by the adults, and perhaps a few songs. Then tales begin. Even the tales themselves are frequently prefaced with a few riddles and sayings. (222)

The body or the folktales proper in Africa is naturally structured in varying forms. This is, were it a written literature, what can be called the plot. What is called plot in written literature is what Vladmir Propp has called 'the moves' (95) in oral stories. In fact, in African folktale studies, this is an area where much still needs be done as it is the nucleus. The distance-study approaches to the African folktales, over the years, have hidden the obvious that folktales in Africa are systematically organized. The reason is that they are literary artefacts with (as is the case of every form of literature: oral or written) tripartite functions of entertaining, educating and instructing the readers and or listeners. With these in mind, therefore, one will understand that the structuring aims at meeting these goals. It has been the erroneous views of most scholars of African oral literature that African folktales' … are narrated usually for children' (Akporobaro, 107) and as such short and precise. The word 'erroneous' is used due to some scholars' general lack of proper understanding of the structure of the African folktales (see Chinweizu, et al, 1980; Chukwuma, 1994, for fuller understanding of structure in African folktales).

The fact remains that the length and or structure of any folktale in Africa depends on the setting (setting here refers to where the story is told as against where the story is situated in time or location) and the audience involved. More so, the audience and dramatic personae help to determine the structure of most African folktales. What the foregoing tempts to suggest is that within the folktale of 'akuko-ifo', exist two kinds: those for children and those for adults.

Those meant for children ideally utilize animals such as the tortoise, birds, elephants and sheep as dramatic personae. They are, no doubt, short and precise due to the instant impact they are expected to have on the children. Romanus Egudu's *A Calabash of Wisdom*, Friday Menka Mbunda's *Wonder Tale of Oku (Camerron) The Aesthetics Of Storytelling* house perfect examples of the folktales for children. However, the use of animals, as has been said earlier on, in African folktales as major and minor characters is for the obvious reason of avoiding mentioning real peoples' names. But because different animals are used in the tales, the storyteller mimics every of the mood and tone of every animal-character. That is not only to make the story interesting but also to make clear the mood and tone of every animal-character. That is where the conclusion that the African folktales assume dramatic mode in performance comes from. Based on this backdrop, therefore, if it is said that folktale narration in Africa is more of acting, one will not be far from the truth. This is because in the course of rendering a folktale to the children, the storyteller impersonates the varying animals in the story, using mimes as well as dialogues.

For the adult or mature minds, their tales are normally different. This is because they contain more than one episode or 'moves'. Among the Edda-Igbo, the foklktales are well differentiated with the words: 'ilu' (folktales for children) and 'ụbụbọ' (folktales for the adults). In the area (Edda), 'ilu' are the folktales already discussed above, which, we said, make use of varying animals as their dramatic personae. Let us have a look at this story of Tortoise and the Birds:

Storyteller: Oti-i
Listeners: Oyo-o
Storyteller: Oti-i
Listeners: Oyo-o

Storyteller: O nworo otu mgbe
Listeners: Mgbe eruala

   Once upon a time, there existed a time when the tortoise and
the other birds of the air were very good friends. One day they
all agree to pay somebody who lives in the heavens a visit. They
are very happy at this decision; but thinking twice they become
sad as the idea strikes them that their friend the tortoise has no
wings and as a result cannot fly. The tortoise himself is also sad
at the idea of his not going to be among his friends on such
august visit.

   Suddenly an idea comes over the birds and that is the idea
of lending their friend, Tortoise, a feather from each of them.
At this wonderful idea, they all rejoice and their lost happiness
comes back to them. On the appointed day they all gather and
as agreed they all lend the tortoise each a feather. He is very
happy and so thanks his friends. He tells them that as they are
embarking on this journey that it is good they take names other than their usual names, which each will bear as the place
they are visiting is a special place. The unsuspecting birds each
quickly choose names. At the end the tortoise tells them that his
name as they are going is 'All of You'. Having each taken these
names, they take off.

   In heaven, their host receives them well and offers them
seats. And having done that, he brings in for them a keg-full of
water. He drops it before them and says 'please my visitors this
is for all of you; excuse me I will be right back'and he leaves.
When he had left the tortoise says to his friends, 'please my
friends you have heard it all that it is for me. I know you all
heard him say 'this is for All Of You', which means it is for me.
Perhaps yours is on the way'. He collects the keg of water and
drinks it all. Again their host comes in with food of different
kinds, well-prepared and the same thing happens. When some
kegs of palm wine are brought to them, the tortoise in the same
manner tricks them out of the drinking.

After eating all these, the tortoise becomes weak and tipsy but the birds are angry at him; so they consult and agree to pay him in his own coin. They agree to collect their feathers from him there and then. They do as they go to him one after the other to whisper in his ear: 'It is time for us to go Mr. Tortoise'. At the end he is left with no feather. Kite is the last to go to him to collect his; and it is the time he seems to have realised what his friends mean to do to him. So he calls kite, reminding him how Kite's father and his had been friends and never offended each other until death separated them; how Kite's mother and his were friends in their younger days and that it is only the want of daily bread that separated them. He goes on and on in that manner. But seeing he cannot convince the kite into helping him, he says to Kite: well you can go like others and I will manage; just do me this favour. If you reach home go to my wife and tell her she should bring out mattresses and even collect some from our neighbours. She should keep them outside because the children have been wetting them of late and there will be great sunshine today".

The Kite with the annoyance over what the tortoise did to them gave the tortoise's wife the reverse of the message. 'Mrs. Tortoise, your husband asked me to tell you to bring outside irons, big stones and all those that can wound someone easily for he wants to use them for something'. Immediately Mrs. Tortoise starts doing as she is instructed. So when the tortoise looks from the heavens and sees his wife busy with something, he thinks Kite has given the right message and he is very happy. When he looks and sees his wife is now standing, he feels the arena is ready for him to land; he leaves his hands and falls from the heavens and lands on the stone and irons and shatters into piece. It is the crabs and snails who take pity on him and mend him and that is why the tortoise's shell is full of cracks.

As can be seen from the example above, such stories are usually precise and straight to the point. Because their aims are to strengthen the moral life of the children-listeners, they are structured like the modern-day Tom and Jerry cartoon where every character talks and behaves like a human being.

But 'ụbụbọ', unlike 'ilu', are not meant for the children. It is not only that children would not understand them due to the content and structure, but also can be terrified by them. A good example here is the experience this writer had as a child. That was many years ago when on one particular evening my parents in one of their 'ụbụbọ'-telling sessions had asked me in to sleep on an 'ụgbọ', a mud bed in our one-room hut. But, I, pretending to have fallen asleep, listened to the adult folktale (ụbụbọ). The story was on a character they named 'Agu-ugo', a being I did not understand what sort of animal it was. The structuring of the story, coupled with the fact that I was alone in the hut, scared me; and when I could not bear it any more I shouted; it was then that my stubbornness found me out.[1] However, folktales in Africa have formal ways of concluding, whether it is those meant for children or adults. For example, in Edda-Igbo areas the storyteller falls back on yet another brief conversation with his/her listeners that runs thus:

Storyteller: Oti-i
Listeners: Oyo-o
Storyteller: Oti-i
Listeners: Oyo-o
Storyteller: O ibe osoro

AFRICAN FOLKTALES: THE SETTING

Every literary work of art, be it written or orally rendered, is certainly set in time (historical setting) and space (geographical location). In Africa, folktales which are literary works rendered orally before a live audience, are normally set in like manners. Folktales in Africa are set in the distant past as shown by the opening formula: "Once upon a time" or "Onworo otu mgbe" in the case of the Edda-Igbo of South-eastern Nigeria. This opening statement that always precedes every folktale in Africa is an ideal indication that what is to come took place not in the contemporary society but in the remote past, as folktale performers in Edda will always put it:

'when branches of trees where still home of the fox'
'when the kite made use of the ground as their homes'

These statements that precede folktales in Africa and Edda-Igbo in particular show that the setting in time-frame is when things were actually different from what they are presently, in the words of Mbunda, "when events impossible today were possible, when human beings, animals and objects interacted and understood each other" (13). For example, the incident in this folktale clarifies our point here:

Narrator::   Oti-i
Audience: Oyo-o
Narrator: Oti-i
Audience: Oyo-o
Narrator: Once upon a time, there lived one woman's only daughter in one particular village. The young lass was the only thing the woman had got after she lost her husband who fell from a palm tree a few years previously. They had their hut just by the road that led to the market place. The woman could not think of anything happening to her only child-daughter as she could not send her on any errand. She did virtually everything for her daughter except eating and easing of self. Even other domestic chores meant for young girls of her age, like washing her cloths, cooking, fetching firewood, and fetching water from the stream among other things, were done for her by the mother who would not let her for the simple reason that she might injure herself. The love was so much so that even when the girl was sleeping, the mother, feeling she had over-slept, would go to open her eyelids to be sure of her daughter's safety.

The girl on her part loved her mother the same way and she always tried to do all that would please the mother. For her, if fetching firewood or water or any other domestic chores seemed to her mother that she was going to die of it; she would never do them as the mother directed. To her, even the ancestors knew that it is not out of laziness or being a weakling on her side that she did not do anything in the house, but only if that would pacify her mother. She was a quintessence of obedience. She cherished all that would make her mother happy. She understood that she herself was the only hope and reason her mother lived. Oh!, the only child that was more than so many!

One day, an Afor day, a day the people of the village had their market—it was on such market days that all and sundry, including spirits (*nde manwu*), came from far and near, including from the spirit world, to market among the human beings. In such condition, the eyes of the children could not see the spirit beings of "*nde manwu*". As a result, parents always advised their children to stay indoors to avoid being taken away by the spirits or "*nde manwu*". It was for a similar reason that when the girl's mother was about leaving for the market on that particular Afor day, she called her daughter:

'Erimma!'
'Erimma'

For that was her name. And the girl answered her mother:

'Mama !'

And then ran into the hut where the mother had sat on a mud bed, '*ugbo*', waiting. When she ran into the hut even as she was standing before her mother, the mother yet called again but this time in a lower tone:

'Erimma'
'Erimma'

She always had tears dimming her vision, a wont she put on anytime she wanted to tell Erimma her daughter something if she disobeyed. Because Erimma was used to her mother's lifestyle and would never afford to have her do it his time, she called out to her mother: 'Mama !' she said. 'I think am here for you, say whatever you wish me to do and I promise you consider it done'. And the mother looked at her daughter and wept aloud because what she saw was not just her daughter but also her dead husband. Summoning courage, she said to her:

'You know you are all I have Erimma?'

Erimma swallowed hard before she replied:

'I know Mama'

'Today is Afor market day of our people', the mother continued. 'As usual the spirits from the spirit world would be coming
to have their marketing activity in the market. You have to keep
off from them by staying indoors as usual for a day like today'.
For Erimma, this was like stating the obvious because she knew,
without being told, she was not to go out.

The time came and the mother left for the market. Erimma
was inside their hut, however still watching people from inside
as they passed by to the market. For her to be engaged with
something while at home alone, in the absence of the mother,
the mother gave her two cups of egusi, (melon) to peel. As an
obedient child, she started the peeling immediately the mother left for the market. She was peeling the egusi, singing and
looking outside through the window intermittently. At a time
she said to herself: 'if I open the door without going out, does it
mean I have disobeyed my mother? No I've not' , she said, then
stood up, went and opened the door and went back to her work.
At a time again she said to herself: 'if I go out to the corridor
and stay and do this peeling, does it mean I've disobeyed my
mother? No I've not' she said, then stood up, gathered her egusi
and went and stayed at the corridor and continued. As usual
she looked up intermittently. All of a sudden a voice called her
by name:

'Erimma !'

She looked up to see who it was that called her name. And a
handsome young man was standing right some distance away
from where she was sitting. But this was a stranger and Erimma
would not answer to such calls. So she did not give the man
attention but rather continued with what she was doing. Then
the young man smiled to himself and persistently kept calling
the unsuspecting young girl:

'Erimma' Erimma'

'Erimma Erimma'

He kept calling her. At a time she could not contend with the young man's disturbance. She looked up and half-shouting at the man said:

'What is it now? Won't you let me alone?'

And the man smiled mischievously at Erimma and said to her:

'Come lady, I've some message to give you'

'But you are only a stranger and I don't need your message', Erimma said.

'Yes I am but if you come nearer, you won't regret you did', the man insisted.

Erimma did not like even having a discussion with the man and wished he could go and let her alone. In order to dismiss him she decided to give him audience.

'Well, what is it? If you think your message is that important to me, you can come nearer and give it to me, Erimma went on.

Moving a bit nearer to Erimma, the young man stopped abruptly and said to her: 'Now I've walked nearer to you, why can't you reciprocate by coming nearer too?'

Looking up, Erimma saw it was true he had moved closer. She dropped her trayful of egusi seeds aside, stood up and started walking towards the young man that was in front of her. However, she kept walking and walking and walking, yet without getting to the man. Then she stopped and said to herself that she had been walking all these while to meet this man in front of her without success, that, she asked herself if it was not better she went back and continued with her chore. As soon as she thought of that idea, she stopped, turned to go back but could not see her way home again. She got lost. That is the end of the story because that is how Erimma got lost.

A look at the world of the folktale above reveals it can be affirmed as true, as pointed out by Mbunda, that African folktales are set in Africa and in the time when events impossible today were possible.

In the example of folktale rendered, common sense shows it is rather impossible in our present-day world for somebody to be looking at a person standing before him; then would keep walking towards the person without meeting him. When she thought of going back and stopped to do so, she only discovered she had wandered away from home. The questions to be asked include: was she walking with both eyes closed that she could not see? Or was she insane? In all totality, this is impossible to be believed by anybody in our present-day world, i.e. in real life. Yet these impossibilities for the present world were possible in the olden days, the time this story is set.

However, it is not only that "this remote setting makes the stories more interesting and gives the narrator license to say anything and behave in any way since nobody will venture to take him to court for libel", as Mbunda would want us to believe, but also it helps the listeners to take a leave of their immediate personal troubles and listen with rapt attention to the story. Above all, the African folktales, as set in the remote past, are not so done for the sake of it or just to make the audience take a temporary leave of their immediate problems. Rather, it is meant to point, paint and draw our attention to the nature of the traditional African society and its philosophy. Every human society has what it believes in. Perhaps, it is in line with this fact that Awoonor avers that "the traditional African society existed and was organized upon certain basic concepts and ideas of the universe and man" (49). The African man has his personal view and opinion about the world he lives in. Among other things, he believes that in the universe every man is a stranger who is on an errand sent him by his 'chi'. And at the agreed time, he will go back to him at the spirit world; the real home. To this end, whatever a man does here on earth must be in line with the earlier arrangement with his chi before coming into the world, or more appropriately, reincarnating into the human world. The African man therefore believes in life-after-life and while he lives, he still communes with those in the other world where he comes from and will retire at the expiration of time. There is no other way the African man reflects his worldview other than through his oral literary corpus like the folktales. As has been the way in every literary epoch, literary artists showcase the worldview of their age with their literary works; the African oral artists have not been left out of this function. Therefore, the setting of the African folktale in the remote past by the narrators has not been by chance.

Besides being set in time past, which helps to reveal the tradition and philosophy of the Africans, the stories are also set in space. These spaces are such that could be inhabited either by humans, animals or spirits. Besides, the stories could also be set in places outside the aforementioned, to places like the heavens and the seas. No matter the places the stories are set, however, the main aim is geared towards reflecting man's love, hatred, cleverness and stupidity. They reflect the actions and the inactions of man which he should or should not have done that bring to him an untold hardship or serve as sources of regret to him at the end of the day; yet, for the purposes of educating him about life intricacies. The story as narrated above clarifies our point here. This is because from the story, it can be seen and understood that the girl Erimma should not have answered the stranger who turned out to be a spirit. In the first place, she gave room for what had happened to her when she disobeyed her mother by coming out of the house to the veranda. Perhaps, if she had stayed indoors, as she herself quite knew what was at stake, she would not have fallen victim to what happened.

That apart, the names of places where the African stories are set are often times mentioned but in most cases are not. Part of the reason names of places are left out is, perhaps, because African folktales are human-centered, by which is meant that their concerns are mainly on the activities of human beings. For this reason, phrases such as "Once upon a time, there lived a man in one village" or "Once upon a time, there lived a woman in one village" or "Once upon a time, a man or woman settled in one village" etc, are often heard as can be seen in the story above.

In stories set in the animal world, the animals live, talk and act like human beings. However, for stories set in this world, the narrators try very much to reflect lives there which certainly differ from those in the human world. In the words of Mbunda, "the opposite of what is done in the human world is practiced where people split wood with their teeth, walk and climb with their heads and turn into bones in the night" (14). The folktale below is a good example of what is being talked about. Lets us have a look at it:

Narrator: Oti-i
Audience: Oyo-o
narrator: Oti-i
Audience: Oyo-o

Narrator: Once upon a time, there lived a family in one village with their two children: one younger and the other older. The two children were all girl-children. One day as their parents were about going to the farm, they dropped for the children a seed-yam and a snail to be used as lunch. They advised their children to first roast the yam before the snail as roasting the snail first will, with its fluid which snails normally contain, quench the fire. The children's parents also asked them not to leave their house for anywhere for that was the day spirits or *nde manwu* carry their fire wood from the human world to the spirit world.

No sooner had the children's parents left the house for the farm than they became artificially hungry and would want to prepare their lunch. They made fire straightaway but contrary to their parent's advice started instead to roast their snail and the fluid from the snail did quench the fire. Neither yam nor snail was therefore roasted and ready for eating: the yam or the snail. Before noon, the children became really hungry. They had disobeyed their parents the first time and had seen the outcome. Because they did not want a repeat of this disobedience, they stayed indoors as the parents had advised.

When they could not endure hunger any longer, they decided to go to their backyard for some firewood to make another fire. This was a suggestion from the older of the two children. But the younger one reminded her elder sister of their parent's injunctions that they should not go out because the spirits were carrying their firewood on that day. But the elder sister would not let her finish as she shouted her to be still, saying to the younger in addition: "Who will let Mama and Papa know we went out, you or me?" The younger sister did not reply to that. They went to the backyard to fetch firewood. It was at the backyard that the children received the greatest shock of their lives. They saw in the first place the spirits as they were carrying their firewood on their buttock while they walked on their heads. The spirits caught them and gave them a log of the firewood to carry to the spiritland for them. Having no option, they complied and carried the firewood. They carried the fire-wood on the instructions of the spirits to the land of the spirits. But on reaching the spiritworld, what they saw again surprised them the more. Everything there was actually going on oppo-site direction compared to what it was in the human world. The spirits walked on their head and backwards too; they had no flesh on their bodies, only bone; they were walking skeletons. The children were very terrified and sad as a result of what they had seen.

However, the spirits were very happy because, for them, the children were game got for the evening meal. So having reached the spirit world, the spirits took them to their house and kept them. The spirits cooked food and asked the children to eat. The older of the children settled immediately for the food while the younger reluctantly joined her sister. But the younger of the children purposely sat nearer the door. So that after roll-ing the fofo into a ball; she deeped it into the soup before them but would not put it in her mouth; rather she dropped it behind the door. Neither the spirits nor her sister who was busy eating and licking every corner of her fingers knew what the smaller girl was doing.

When they finished eating, the mother spirit took away the bowls and asked them to relax themselves. For the mother spir-its, that was the last meal for the human children. The younger of the two children was very keen for an opportunity to leave the spirit world. So after the mother spirit had come and given them her fiendish entertainment and left them alone, she advised her sister that it was time for them to go. And immediately they took off. But unknown to the elder sister, the younger sister took a flute that was fastened at the front roof of the spirits' hut.

By the time the mother spirit came back, the children had left. She alerted others and they searched for the children at every nook and cranny but did not find them. She remembered a solution to their problem and took up her fiendish flute and played out a spell-bound message against the children, thus:

Opi mu gbatete gbatete
Gbagbuara mu nwa ema no uzo
Udara kpekpe
Udara kpekpe
Utara ema
Ọ ya riduru ya
Saaa
Ukporoko ema
Ọ ya taduru ya
Saaa
Anu ema
Ọ ya tara ya
Saaa
O we yegheye
Oweyeghe yeghe ha wo-o

[My flute run and run
Kill for me child of spirit on the road
Udara kpekpe
Udara kpekpe
Spirit's fofo
It is she who ate them all
Saaa
Spirit's Stockfish
It is she who ate them all
Saaa
Spirit's meat
It is she who ate them

Saaa
Owe yegheye
oweyeghe yeghe ha wo-o]

Immediately this was said the older of the children right there
on the road as they were running back home fell down and
died. The younger one could not be caught by the spirit's spell
because unlike her sister she did not eat the food belonging to
the spirits. Having seen her elder sister drop dead, she brought
her own flute which she had collected from spiritland and started unbinding the spell on her sister:

Opi mu gbatete gbatete
Gbgaterea mu nwanne mu uzo
Ụdara kpekpe
Ụdara kpekpe
Ụtara ema
Ọbụkwaghi ya riduru ya
Saaa
Ukporoko ema
Ọbukwaghi ya taduru ya
Saaa
Anụ ema
Ọ bụghụ ya tara ya
Saaa
O we yegheye
Oweyegheye yeghe ha wo-o
Saaa
Nwanne bia ayi la wo
Owe yegheyeghe-e
Yeghe yeghe ha wo-o

[My flute run and run
Wake up my sister on the road
Udara kpekpe
Udara kpekpe
Spirit's fofo
It is not her who ate them all

Saaa
Spirit's Stockfish
It is not her who ate them all
Saaa
Spirit's meat
It is not her who ate them
Saaa

[Sisiter come let us go home
Owe yegheyeghe-e
Yeghe yeghe ha wo-o]

At the end of that song the elder sister stood up and they started running again. However, within a short space of time the mother spirit with her flute understood her victim was up again and re-blasted her evil flute against her victim. The girl wherever she had reached in running for her life would fall dead. Like before, the younger sister would revives her. This kept happening till the children got home safely.

At home their parents were very happy but did not care to know how they got home. As things went on everybody forgot about the children's missing and returning-home euphoria. Then one festive period came. The children's parents, thinking the older of the two children must have been the one that master-mined their coming home safe, went and bought lots of things for her without any for the younger one. Though the little girl was annoyed, she did not show it and her parents did not care about her feelings either. On the day proper the elder sister wore one of the clothes their parents bought for her. The festive event was one of wrestling among men and men. When the arena was set for the wrestling, all trooped to the village square to see whom the real man among men was. As the elder of the two children went among others to the village square, she created a scene and became the centre of attraction in her new clothes and beads worn round her hips. Her younger sister wept bitterly in her heart because she knew the role she played to save themselves but now the glory had been given to her elder sister. For this she went back home to where she hid the flute she

had used to revive her sister each time the mother spirit cast her
evil spell on her, and picked it. This time she blasted the spell on
her sister herself, thus:

Opi mu gbatete gbatete
Gbagbuara mu nwa ema no uzo
Ụdara kpekpe
Ụdara kpekpe
Utara ema
Ọ ya riduru ya
Saaa
Ukporoko ema
Ọ ya taduru ya
Saaa
Anu ema
Ọ ya tara ya
Saaa
O we yegheye
Oweyeghe yeghe ha wo-o

[My flute run and run
Kill for me child of spirit on the road
Udara kpekpe
Udara kpekpe
Spirit's fofo
It is she who ate them all
Saaa
Spirit's stockfish
It is she who ate them all
Saaa
Spirit's meat
It is she who ate them
Saaa
Owe yegheye
Oweyeghe yeghe ha wo-o]

    And right there at the village square the sister dropped dead.
Everybody was running helter-skelter in a noisy uproar and utmost confusion. Yet, in the midst of this, one person was still

careful enough to discover that the younger one of the girls was not within reach. She had hidden herself away. But in their thinking what use was the presence of a little girl of that age in a situation such as this. 'To hell with her!', they concluded in their thinking.

In search of a solution for the immediate situation, a native doctor was consulted and they were told the only remedy was to look for the younger sister. At once they started looking for the little girl, shouting on top of their voices at any direction they took their search saying: 'please come out. We will give you all you want! Please come for your sister sake'. At a time she took pity on her sister and came out of hiding. When she came out, they pleaded with her and she narrated to them how she and her sister got saved from the sprits and now how her parents had treated her. They apologized to her and promised to make amends if only she would again revive her sister. Out of pity for her sister and not necessarily based on the promises made to her, she went to where she hid the flute and brought it out. She blasted out:

Opi mu gbatete gbatete
Gbgaterea mu nwanne mu uzo
Ụdara kpekpe
Ụdara kpekpe
Ụtara ema
Ọbụkwaghi ya riduru ya
Saaa
Ukporoko ema
Ọbukwaghi ya taduru ya
Saaa
Anụ ema
Ọ bụghụ ya tara ya
Saaa
O we yegheye
Oweyegheye yeghe ha wo-o
Saaa
Nwanne bia ayi la wo
Owe yegheyeghe-e
Yeghe yeghe ha wo-o

[My flute run and run
Wake up my sister on the road
Udara kpekpe
Udara kpekpe
Spirit's fofo
It is not her who ate them all
Saaa
Spirit's Stockfish
It is not her who ate them all
Saaa
Spirit's meat
It is not her who ate them
Saaa

Sister come let us go home
Owe yegheyeghe-e
Yeghe yeghe ha wo-o]

At the end of this flute-blast the dead sister jumped up. Their parents were very happy. At once they took the little girl, bathed her and dressed her in very nice clothes. But cunningly they seized the flute from the little girl and threw it away in the bid to avoid a repeat of the incident. The flute metamorphosed into a cocoyam and that is the cocoyam flute we find on the cocoyam growing on African bin. That is the end of the story.

One thing to note about the setting in African folktales is that no story is completely set in the spirit world. Actions move starting from the human world to either spirit world or animal world or from the animal world to the spirit world. These settings act as the background to the actions in the stories. The settings perform a series of functions to the stories and narrators. For the stories, they make them interesting and then arouse the curiosity of the listeners of the stories. For one thing, obstacles or problems the major characters in the stories encounter are determined by the setting of the stories. Therefore, settings in folktales are very important to the function they perform..

AFRICAN FOLKTALES: THE THEME

In Africa, because the folktales address different levels of human relationships in the society, they are structured to house varying themes. This is very much so because of the obvious reason that there are no other major means the people's mores and lore can be passed to the younger generation if not through the folktales. Again, there is no genre of the oral literature that is as down-to-earth as the folktales in touching every area of human relationships. Perhaps it is to this end that the African folktales have been found to have varying themes through their focus on such "anti-social traits as cunning, selfishness, greed, jealous, and craftiness" (Akporobaro 107).

In African folktales, there are lots of themes. In fact, every folktale is meant to pass on one message or the other to the listeners. For this reason, after each tale, the story teller, before engaging the children in another story, pauses to ask them some questions: what lesson were you able to learn from this story? Or, if the children did not get the theme of the story well, the story teller might restructure the question this way: Is it good the way character A or B behaved? And the story teller can bring the theme closer to the children's understanding if, for example, the theme is on disobedience or lying as is the case in this folktale:

> Once upon a time, there lived a man in one village. The man had seven wives. However, out of these seven wives, the man loved one of them most. One day, after the women had finished cooking their supper, they each brought the man his share of the food in his 'ulo nta' or obi. As he is wont to do each time his wives brought his share of the household food, he poured them together, in one of the earthen bowls or 'nja ofo'. Having poured them together he stirred it with one of his fingers and tasted it for salt. But instead he discovered one of the bowls of soup has 'ahuruji', or 'sent-leaf' as its vegetable. This annoyed the man. And out of annoyance he summoned his wives: 'Who cooked a soup for me with an ahuruji?' he shouted. None of the women could accept this mistake as hers. So the man repeated himself: 'Who cooked a soup for me with an ahuruji?' Yet,

none ever volunteered to own the deed. This annoyed the man the more. As none agreed to accept and apologize for this, he decided to get to the root of the matter and bring the culprit to book. 'Ok! Since none of you accepts this mistake', the man started, "I shall take all of you to Ngele Wawa the stream of the deities'. He concluded, 'each of you go and inform your relatives that in four days time we shall go to the stream of Ngele Wawa for each of you women to prove her innocence'. The women agreed, left and did as were instructed. On the appointed day they all gathered at Ngele Wawa stream of deities. The most senior wife was called upon to come forward and prove her innocence of the deed before, not only her husband this time but also her relatives and, most importantly, Ngele Wawa the stream of deities. She stepped forward. Standing before all and sundry, she began:

'Ngele Wawa Ngele Wawa
Yo bụrụ mụ ji ahuruji teara dim ofo
Ngele Wawa bụrụ mụ lahe Oko yara nna ya ma anoyi
Ngele Wawa Ngele Wawa wo-o

[Ngele Wawa Ngele Wawa
If I am the one who cooked a soup for my husband with ahụrụji
Ngele Wawa carry me away. Oko and his father will stay
Ngele Wawa Ngele Wawa wo-o]

Then she fell into the stream, 'toyi-i'. But instead of carrying her away, the stream of deity gently carried her over to the other bank of the stream unhurt. Then her innocence was proved. She was not the person; her relatives rejoiced. Guns were shot; drums were beaten in merriment to this success. After a while, all settled down to see who the victim was.

The second most senior wife was called to go forward to prove her innocence of the act. Like the first wife, she stepped forward. Standing before everybody she began:

'Ngele Wawa Ngele Wawa
Yo bụrụ mụ ji ahuruji teara dim ofo
Ngele Wawa bụrụ mụ lahe Oko yara nna ya ma anoyi
Ngele Wawa Ngele Wawa wo-o

[Ngele Wawa Ngele Wawa
If I am the one who cooked a soup for my husband with ahuruji
Ngele Wawa carry me away. Oko and his father will stay
Ngele Wawa Ngele Wawa wo-o]

As she was going through her song, her relatives present held their breath, not too sure what would be the end result. Had their relative lied to them? And if that was the case, this would be the end of her and they would not see her anymore. As she was about falling into the stream of the deities, their fast-beating hearts missed a bit. But there she was in the air and landed as she did—toyi-i. The stream of the deities did for her what it had done for the first person because she too was innocent of the act. The relatives again rejoiced. Guns were shot and drums of joy beaten and all settled downs again after a while.

When the third, fourth, fifth and the sixth wives were asked, in the manner as the first and second wives, their own innocence was also proved and their relatives rejoiced, amidst shooting of guns and beating of drums of joy. The last and the most loved of the man's wives was called to step forward and, like others, prove her innocence. She did. Standing before the people, she began but in an unusual low tone:

'Ngele Wawa Ngele Wawa
Yo buru mu ji ahuruji teara dim ofo
Ngele Wawa buru mu lahe Oko yara nna ya ma anoyi
Ngele Wawa Ngele Wawa wo-o
Oko yara nna ya ma anoyi

[Ngele Wawa Ngele Wawa
If I am the one who cooked a soup for my husband with ahuruji
Ngele Wawa carry me away. Oko and his father will stay
Ngele Wawa Ngele Wawa wo-o]

The crowd shouted at her to sing it aloud: "Sing it loud!" Seeing she has no way of escape she sang it normally:
Ngele Wawa Ngele Wawa
Yo buru mu ji ahuruji teara dim ofo

Ngele Wawa burụ mụ lahe Oko yara nna ya ma anoyi
Ngele Wawa Ngele Wawa wo-o
Oko yara nna ya ma noyi

[Ngele Wawa Ngele Wawa
If I am the one who cooked a soup for my husband with ahụrụji
Ngele Wawa carry me away. Oko and his father will stay
Ngele Wawa Ngele Wawa wo-o]

At the end of the song she fell into the Ngele Wawa, the stream of deities and it carried her away as instructed because she was the one who prepared a soup for their husband with ahuruji. That is the end of the story.

A question can be framed this way: Is it good to lie? And if the replies are satisfactory, the storyteller moves over to another story.

Themes in African folktales should not be confused with the subject matters thereof. The subject matters are the subject of discourse. For example, in the corpus of African folktale, we have stories discussing the friendship between the tortoise and the lion; the fowl as the most used domestic animal for food, among others, as subject matter. The messages or lessons we learn from the stories are the themes. As such, one folktale may house a series of themes for the consumption of the listeners.

CONCLUSION

In concluding this discussion, it is proper some ideas are put straight concerning the African folktales, foremost among which is that folktales are part of the narrative tales in African oral literary corpus. And there are two kinds: 'akụkọ ala', a tale of the land and 'akụkọ-ifo', a tale of imagination. Yet, within the 'akụkọ-ifo' exists two kinds as exemplified with the Edda-Igbo of South-Eastern Nigerian folktales as 'ụbụbọ', an adult version of the African folktales with complex structure involving animals, spirits, human beings portrayed in horrible manners, and 'ilu', the children's version of the imaginative folktales, which involves animals, spirits, human beings and, in fact, every creature, all at the same time. However, it is the 'akụkọ-ifo', a tale of imagination, which formed our subject of research. And we looked at its text, structure, setting and theme and, with particular reference to the Edda/Igbo Culture. We conclude with a kind of modest proposal: that future scholars of the African folktale should begin to lay emphasis on the individual who ius narrating the folktale: his rendering of the folktale narrative as an oral performance guided by the interplay between communal demands of art and the individual (narrator's) aesthetic sensibilities.

NOTE

1. The adult folktales in Africa contain a series of episodes, and as a result they are not usually short and precise like children's. At this level, they need adult minds to be understood.

WORKS CITED

Akporobaro, F.B. *Introduction to African Oral Literature*. Lagos: Princeton, 2005. Print.

Awoonor, Kofi. *The Breast of the Earth*. New York: NOK Publishers, 1975. Print.

Azuonye, Chukwuma. "Power, Marginality and Womanbeing in Igbo Oral Narrative" *Power, Marginality and African Oral Literature*. G. Furniss and L. Gunner Ed. Cambridge: Cambridge University Press, 1995. Print.

Chinweizu, Onwuchekwa Jemie and Ihechukwu Madubuike. *Toward the Decolonization of African Literature*. Enugu: Fourth Dimension, 1980. Print.

Chukwuma, Hellen. *Igbo Oral Literature: Theory and Tradition*. Uyo: Belpot, 1994. Print.

Egudu, R.N. 'Igbo Tradition of Poetry and Family Relationships'. *Literature and Modern West African Culture*. D.I. Nwoga (ed). Lagos: Academy Press, 1979. Print.

Finnegan, Ruth. *Oral Literature in Africa*. Cambridge: Open Books Publishers, 2012. Print.

—. *The Oral and Beyond: Doing Things With Words in Africa*. Chicago: The University Press, 2007. Print

Mbunda, Frida Menkan. *Wonder Tales of Oku (Cameroon) and the Aesthetic of Storytelling*. Enugu: Keny & Bros, 2002. Print.

230 Ethnosensitive Dimensions of African Oral Literature

Obiechina, Emmanuel. *Culture, Tradition and Society in The West African Novel.* Cambridge: Cambridge University Press, 1975. Print.

Okoh, Nkem. *Preface to Oral Literature.* Onitsha: Africana, 2008. Print.

Okpewho, Isidore. *African Oral Literature: Backgrounds, Character and Continuity.* Bloomington: Indiana University Press, 1992. print.

Propp, V. *Morphology of the Folktale.* Texas: University of Texas Press, 1968.

Sowayan, Saad A. "A Plea for Interdisciplinary Approach to the Study of Arab Oral Tradition". *Oral Tradition.* 18/1(2003). 123–133. Print.

Taiwo, Oladele. *An Introduction to West African Literature.* Lagos: Nigerprint, 1985. Print.

Chapter Eleven

The Dead Can Bite:
Continuity in the Legend of the Visiting Dead in a Nigerian Igbo Community.

Afam Ebeogu

Ghost stories are a pervasive form of legendary narratives among the Igbo of Nigeria. These narratives are as popular in the rural areas as they are in the cities, and there is a continuity of tradition between the village-grown and urban-generated forms, with the essential difference lying in the dominant items of material culture which in themselves become markers of either how recent or otherwise a tale is. An examination of a number of ghost stories in a typical Igbo village since the last forty years or so, against the background of Igbo and Christian cosmological beliefs, reveals that, in the folk imagination, ghost stories reflect varying levels of reality in the daily experiences of the people.

This chapter does not intend to be assertive: at best it is a prolegomenon. In legend scholarship, especially in Europe where a phenomenon like "the vanishing hitchhiker" has been the topic of considerable discussion, as is evidenced by Harold Brunvand's *The Vanishing Hitchhiker: American Urban Legends and Their Meaning* (1981) and Gillian Bennett's *Traditions of Belief: Women, Folklore and the Supernatural Today* (1987), the essay stands the risk of sounding hackneyed. The definitions of "ghost " and "revenant" in Leach (933–34) adopt a stance that immediately suggests the universality of this phenomenon of the supernatural, and the legitimacy of this stance is not being questioned here. What, however, has struck me as worthy of serious reflection is that since 1980 when the Nigerian Folklore Society was formed and the society started organizing its annual folklore conferences, no topic of this nature has ever featured on its programme.

One may easily be tempted to explain this away by arguing that the Nigerian Folklore Society has been preoccupied with the application of folklore scholarship to the urgent problems of national development and integration facing the country. Another explanation that could be offered for the rarity of ghost scholarship in a developing country like Nigeria is that in most communities in the country, whether urban or rural, ghost stories are taken rather seriously; they are regarded with considerable awe, and consequently the student of folklore would find himself or herself in serious difficulties trying to gather field data on such stories. That, at least, has been my experience.

I started hearing about ghost stories similar to the phantom hitchhiker, not necessarily in material details, but in structure and recurrent motifs, right from early childhood. The folk imagination in most Nigeria communities would seem to regard the stories as, in the words of Gillian Bennett, "neither modern (nor) urban" ("The Vanishing Hitchhiker" 45). As to whether, in the African context, they can be called legend, the answer is in the affirmative, and we can use David Buncha's definitions of legend as "stories told (as true) which circulate by word of mouth in contemporary society and exhibit traditional variation" (2) to support our case. In terms of the autonomy of legends, F.H. Nicolaisen's observation, with respect to the European tradition, is appropriate to the African situation:

> Because of their nature, it would seem plausible that legends
> are less likely to be included as items of lengthy narrative sessions or discrete settings like those in which folklore and jokes
> are told by design and association, but are rather offered single
> or perhaps in small cluster, as extraordinary, eccentric, perhaps
> even bizarre narratives of brief entertainment because they
> shape the unusual to provoke laughter or ready belief, followed,
> in all probability, by a little meditative reflection and personal
> reaction. If they are didactic, they never do any crude, explicit,
> public finger wagging; but their moral injunctions and axhorta-

tions though heavily disguised, are too amusing or too poignant to be ignored. (74)

The Igbo of Nigeria do have a term, *ita,* for what approximates to the European notion of "legend". *Ita* is a body of tales which are told as true, and are definitely distinguished from the folktale, *akuko ifo,* which, in the traditional imagination, incorporates the Màrchen, animal tales and fairy tales. Whereas Igbo folktales are obviously regarded as stories of fantasy overtly meant to entertain and covertly to instruct morals, *ita* (legend and/or myth, depending on context and content of narrative, and proportion of the imaginative interplay between the religious and historical consciousness) is meant to be taken seriously. Even if they task credulity, they are not to be rejected as irrelevant because they raise the imagination to certain levels of reality that are quite uncommon. With respect to ghost lore, the issues raised in the narratives tend to emphasize the metaphysical dimensions of human existence.

Ghost stories have, thus, always been traditional in the sense of their timelessness, and their rootedness on a rather small community with common culture, sense of ancestry and tutelage, and in the consumption (cf. Williams 220). But they have also adapted to the sensibilities of the modern society, a society in which, very often, the line between the city and the rural environment is more distinguishable geographically than sociologically—it is easier to identify the city folk in the European world than it is in the Igbo world where most city inhabitants are more of "dwellers" than "citizens". In other words, most ghost stories in the Igbo world can as easily grow in the city as they can in the villages, and are highly fluid with respect to the ease with which they gain acceptability, as legendary narratives, in both environments. People's reaction to these stories is not that of outright disbelief, but of wonder and only occasional skepticism occasioned by the nature of the environment. Large-scale urbanization is not a new phenomenon in Nigerian history, especially in the North and West with their long history of ancient kingdoms and empires. But in the East, among the Igbo specifically, as G.I Nwaka has explained (47–63), urbanization is a twentieth century phenomenon,

and the converging of different and hitherto socio-politically autonomous village-groups into one human organization called the city has
always appeared to the traditional Igbo as implying some degree of
nervous cosmic re-arrangement in the ontological state of things, for
the traditional Igbo mind had for long learnt to relate the cosmology
of his universe to his immediate environment, the village-group (see
Nwala 26-56), even though "there are a number of cultural factors
which are common to all Igbo areas..." (M.M. Green 5).

The city thus became, as Chinua Achebe describes it in relation
to Onitsha, a town that

> ...sits at the crossroads of the world, [that] can be opposite thing
> at once. It was both a cradle of Christianity ... and veritable for-
> tress of "pagan revanchism"... it was always the market-place
> of the world where the riverine folk and the dwellers of the
> hinterland forest met in guarded, somewhat uneasy commerce;
> old-time farmers met new, urban retail traders of known out-
> landish wares ... it was the original site of evangelical dialogue
> between proselytizing Christianity and Igbo religion: between
> strange-looking toeless harbingers of white rule and (at first) an
> amused indulgent black population that assembled in their hun-
> dreds to enjoy the alien spectacle. It was finally the occult no-
> man's land between river-spirits and mundane humans. (40-41)

In that atmosphere of an "occult no-man's land" one cannot be
certain that one's immediate neighbor is a human being: when we
were children we were told that if one stood astride in the city, and
then bent down and took a careful long perspective of all the human
beings about, one was bound to notice those who walked with their
heads! They were part of the many "spirits" that added to the human being to create that overwhelming population. The city is thus
a veritable nursery for breeding ghost stories in which such motifs
as sleekly cars, stores, buildings, ladies dressed in pure overflowing
white, young men dressed in beautiful suits, mermaid-like women
who brought wealth but no children to their lovers, electric light and
hotels tend to recur. As the traditional Igbo would put it, the city is
the place where spirit and man (*mmuo na mmadu*) congregate.

An illustration of a typical ghost story nurtured in an Igbo city is called for. On the 10th of May 1988, I recorded the following characteristic ghost story which allegedly "happened" in Owerri, the capital of Imo State of Nigeria.

Story One

The Owerri urban council had decided to create a new layout for its modern market. Accordingly, it acquired a large tract of land at the outskirts of the city, advertised for tenants, mapped out the plots, and shared them out by ballot. Winners were expected to proceed to develop their own plots. A well-to-do businesswoman who had won a plot she thought was very strategic began immediately to clear the land. On the second day of work, a very handsome young man dressed in a blue suit and wearing eyeglasses walked up to her and inquired why she was working on a plot of land that belonged to someone else.

The woman explained that it was hers; she had won it by ballot, and she had her papers to prove it. But the young man said that the plot of land was his. If she doubted it, she could check with Mr. X (name supplied) of x address (an address given). Whereupon the perplexed woman taxied to the said address, asked for the man whose name the young man had given her, and was introduced to a pensioner in his late sixties. She told her story, after which the pensioner asked her to described the young man. She did, and he said that the description fitted his son who had died five years previously in a ghastly motor accident, and he wore glasses while he lived, liked to dress in a blue suits, and was in fact buried in one. The plot of land which the woman had been allocated, in his reckoning, was where his son was buried. The woman, terribly frightened, immediately abandoned the plot of land. The story was all over the township.

Ghost-Lore And Igbo Cosmology

The way my narrator told the story indicated that she obviously believed it to be true; in any case she said that she had no reason to doubt the story since she knew the woman in question and had heard the story directly from her. But even if the narrator had doubted "the truth" of the story, the folk of Owerri city, where this 1988 legend grew, apparently believed that it was true: real names and status of people are given, a specific event is mentioned which makes it possible to fix the exact date of the event, and real places and exact locations are mentioned. It is a modern tale which features a ghost who looks very human and whose non-materiality is discovered only afterwards. In terms of structure, the story, with its introductory remarks, description of the key human characters involved and of the ghost-characters itself, the circumstances of the encounter between the human and the non-human, the discovery and identification of the "ghost" and the concluding remark about the woman's feeling after the event, is very reminiscent of the basic structure of "The Vanishing Hitchiker" (Benneth 51–52).

This is only one of the very many ghost stories associated with urban areas in Igbo land, but is it therefore an urban legend? The theoretical problems involved in taking a decision on this question have adequately bee covered in Gillian Bennett's essay cited above; what the rest of this paper intends to do is examine the traditional Igbo view of "the ghost" as a supernatural phenomenon, and then discuss some older and cotemporary stories from one Igbo rural community, at the end of which it may be possible to make a few tentative concluding remarks on these legends.

In traditional Igbo thought, death is classified into three types: (1) Ọnwụ Ekwensu ("The Devil's Death") which is usually of a violent nature; (2) Ọnwụ Ọjọọ ("Bad Death") which describes any form of death, other than that covered by the first category, which is unnatural and consequently humiliating, like suicide or death by certain diseases like dropsy, and (3) Ọnwụ Chi ("predestined Death") which then is the natural (see Metuh 135–55). When death is natural, the spirit of the dead "remains in this world for some time, wandering restlessly in the vicinity of his life time" (Leonard 141), until the proper funeral rites have been performed, after which the spirit goes to Chineke, the supreme deity, for judgment before descending to the abode of the ancestors (*Ala Ndichie*) believed to be under the metaphysical earth (See Metuh 142–143; Jordan 126). Only such spirits can reincarnate as human beings, and their fate in that incarnation would depend on the outcome of the judgment by the Supreme deity.

If, for any other reason, the necessary funeral rites, as different from ordinary burials rites, are not performed after death, or are improperly performed, then the spirits of the dead will continue to wander indefinitely as ghost. For those whose deaths belong to the "unnatural deaths", the proper funeral rites are never performed before at least a year of "ghostly existence" has passed. When a person dies the "devil's death", no funeral rites whatsoever can reconcile his or her spirit with the ancestors who are custodians of the purity of cultural norms and the continuity of tradition. The spirits that emanate from such deaths become permanent occupants of *Ala ndi mmuo na mmadu,* the occult zone located between the land of the living and the dead, from where these spirit continue to harass the living—those who were children join a cult of vampires (*Ogbanje*) who play tricks on their parents by continually being born and dying soon after. The only way human beings can check the capricious activities of these "ghosts" is through annual rites of dissociation. Igbo cosmology therefore makes a clear-cut allowance for the ghosts, and the element of disbelief in ghost-lore in the culture is therefore minimal.

It is against the background of such a belief system as above that one can appreciate the nature of certain ghost stories in the culture. In Ideani, a rural Igbo community of about three thousand habitants, there has been continuity in the growth of ghost legends, and the fact that virtually every member of the community now professes one kind of Christian faith or the other, and has ostensibly therefore rejected the traditional cosmology[1], seems not to have affected the proliferation of ghost legends. This writer was born in this community, and spent his twelve years of childhood before secondary school education in the community to which he remains ancestrally attuned. This has made it possible for me to keep abreast of virtually all forms of folklore in the community, including all new ghost events that take place there. As if reacting to the issue raised by Bill Ellia in his "Why Are verbatim Transcripts of Legends Necessary?" (331–60), I suggest that it is the affinity between the scholar and his object of investigation which, to a reasonable extent, provides the proof of authenticity of some of the texts used here for illustration, especially where it has not been practicable to provide a "verbatim text" as conventionally defined. This intimacy may also tend to give the ghost stories the status of rumour, a relationship examined in Paul Smith's "On the Receiving End: when Legend Become Rumour" (197:215), but one takes consolation in the fact that such a status would not invalidate the legitimacy of regarding these stories as legends, as recognized by Noel Williams in his "Problems in Defining Contemporary Legend" (216–28). This is because the moment a particular ghost event takes place in the community, it generates the associated story, a literary piece, that becomes public property and which anybody in the community has the right to narrate in differing circumstances. These stories by their nature have a shock-effect: most people are awed by them and find it difficult to doubt them. The stories confirm some aspects of the other-worldliness of the human experience, and when they are told, the characters whose names are mentioned, or people who are related to them, do not take offence; "the truth" of the event is beyond dispute. Indeed, these people, it has occasionally occurred to me, seem to derive some vague satisfaction from being at the centre of the rare experience. It is therefore as a legitimate member of this community, and thus a carrier of its narrative "virus" that I present the "summaries" of three of the older ghost legends in the community:

Story Two

Mr. T. (name supplied) was a very energetic man in his middle forties known for temperamental ways, for which reason some people regarded him as a wicked man, especially since he had the tendency to beat up his wife severely. He was a professional wine-tapper, and one day he fell down from a palm-tree and sustained serious injuries. He was taken to a traditional healer but never recovered. Because of the nature of his death, he needed special funeral rites which could not be performed immediately. From the moment of his burial he had the habit of going to his wife and beating her up, and she always saw him and pleaded to no avail as he beat her. He would continue beating her until he got satisfied. He continued doing this until his corpse had to exhumed and special rites performed before reburial. After that he never appeared again to beat up his wife.

Story Three

In the Roman Catholic cemetery there is one prominent grave with an elaborate tombstone. For a very long time this grave was fenced with barbed wire, which made people to ask questions as to who was buried there. The story was that the grave belonged to one Mr. O (name supplied), the father of so and so (names of two successful citizens of the community who live in the coal city of Enugu supplied). He was a very prominent member of the Roman Catholic Church. He was one of those who opposed the idea of allowing heathen masquerades to enter the Roman Catholic play ground during festivals, as these masquerades chased some people in order to whip them. One day Mr. O intercepted a masquerade, which had again broken into playground, and beat up the "spirit" mercilessly, in the process unmasking him. The heathens were furious at the abomination, and they invaded Mr. O's house the next night and performed certain rituals, and by day-break all the fruits-trees in the compound had dried up. Four days later Mr. O himself died. He is buried in the cemetery, but was said to have the habit of harassing people who passed by the cemetery road after midnight. At first people were not sure whether the story was true, until one day he furiously chased after Mr. S (name supplied) who was reputed for his youthful energy and hard drinking. That night he was half drunk, and as he went down the cemetery road he was singing songs of palm-wine. The ghost of Mr. O began to pursue him, and did not stop until Mr. S, in spite of his strength, fell down and fainted. He lay where he had fallen, until morning when he was discovered. He was not dead, but obviously much frightened. He told his story, and said that he saw Mr. O very clearly "with his naked eyes", and that the ghost was dressed all in white. After that the Catholic authorities sent for the parish priest at Abatete (a neighbouring community). They performed some special Catholic rites at the grave, after which the tomb was fenced round with barbed wire. Since then he never appeared again to harass anybody.

STORY FOUR

Mrs. N (name supplied) was a widow with four children, and she was quite known in the community for her hard work. One Friday she told her two sons not to go to school because she wanted them to accompany her to the farm. When they asked her why the work could not wait until Saturday she said that it was because she did not have much time left. They did not understand her then. They went to work with her and worked in the farm that day from morning till twilight. As they cleared the shrubs, they also made mounds immediately and sowed the coco-yams, contrary to the practice of leaving the cleared shrubs to dry up before the mounds are made. When they got home that evening, she lay on the bed and said that she had a headache. She died the following day.

While the burial ceremony was in progress, Mr. I (name supplied) came in; he had just returned from Onitsha. He was a cousin-in-law to Mrs. N and had been very kind to her and children: he always gave them food items each time he came back from Onitsha. He was asked who had informed him, but he said that nobody did, but that he knew because she appeared to him under a mysterious circumstance. She was dressed in spotted wrapper over a white blouse—the same, as it turned out, in which the corpse was dressed while lying in state. Mr. I said that she was carrying a large pan on her head when he saw her pass by his stall in Onitsha. He had thought that she had apparently visited Onitsha to sell some food items, and had decided to visit his stall. He had shouted her name, telling her that she had missed her way. But she had not turned back. So he had run towards her and suddenly he no longer saw her. He concluded immediately that something was wrong; that Mrs. N must be dead. So he decided to go back home; he arrived in good time to see her corpse before she was buried.

ANALYSES OF STORIES TWO TO FOUR

The three ghost stories reproduced above, as much possible in the tone the "rumours" circulated in the village, were believed to have "happened" between the 1940s and 1950s, and Story 2 has never been associated with any particular date, but the wife whom the ghost had the habit of beating up is in her sixties, and if one assumes that she would not have married ` before the age of twenty then one can conclude that the event took place about forty years ago.

When I explored the possibility of finding out the details from the woman, and if possible to get her own version of the story, an uncle dissuaded me on the ground that it would amount to insensitivity and insult: there was nothing, he said, our generation would not do in the name of scholarship. Story 3 apparently "happened" in the mid-forties. An informant told me that he was in primary two then, and that soon after the event the Second World War ended. One of the sons referred to in Story 4, who is at the moment a civil servant, felt free to discuss the story with me, which he confirmed as true, and as having happened in 1958 when he was in standard three. If the 1940s and 50s would be regarded as "contemporary", then date would be the only contemporary thing about these legends. Otherwise the three stories belong entirely to traditional imagination from the manner they were told and at times explained. Mr. T. of Story 2 was not a Christian: he performed a traditional occupation which occasionally results in accidental death that a traditional person would regard as unnatural and at times "evil". Wine-tapping, among the Igbo, is supposed to be a profession needing occult initiation because of its hazards. In the case of Mr. T, the story describes him as a wicked person and a wife-beater, and most Ideani folk who tell this story believe that it was because of Mr. T's wickedness that he continued even after death to harass his innocent wife. The ghost of Mr. T, in the traditional imagination, would be manifesting obviously because he had not received the proper funeral rites—which must wait until at least one year after his death because of the nature of that death—and so his spirit must still be in *ala mmuo na mmadu*, the zone of transition between the living and the dead.

As for Mr. O, it was obviously the nature of his "abomination", and the consequent premature death, that made it possible for his spirit to continue to be manifesting in the mundane world. That he would chase people who passed by after midnight was characteristic of this man who was an extreme Christian zealot and moralist, and who would regard anybody still walking about after midnight as a criminal-one of the Igbo derogatory praise names for a thief is *Abani di egwu* ("The Night is Dangerous"). The cosmological explanation of Mr. O's manifestation is complex. Catholics would see his spirit as being in purgatory from where, in Catholic theology, it is possible for the spirits of the dead to manifest themselves amongst humans—the fact that a priest of that church was prepared to perform certain rituals in order to confine his spirit means that the Catholics did not doubt the truth of his wandering ghost-while traditionalist would see him living in *Ala ndi mmuo na mmadu* where he must stay for at least one year before he would go to the supreme Deity for judgment. The explanation of Mr. N's appearance presents no problem to the traditional folk. He was just doing what any dead person, good or bad, old or young, could decide to do before the completion of the funeral rites: manifest himself before a friend or lover as a gesture of farewell.

As to the style of these narratives, one notices that they are particularly detailed. Names of places and persons involved are given; so are the family and social circumstance of the deceased. There is also a tendency for the narrative to explain why the ghost event occurred, and to reveal an underlying moral tone. On the whole, one perceives a sense of anxiety that can only be the result of a hidden suspicion that the story could be doubted because of its ethereal quality.

To a large extent, then, it can be said that these ghost stories are "traditional". Let us compare them with other ghost stories whose events took place in the 1980s in the same community, and which were recorded by me (in Igbo) in June 1987 from narrators who were close to me enough to consent to be recorded, as long as I would not mention their names in my write-up. Since the narrative situations were induced, it was possible for me to ask some questions for clarification in the middle of a narrative. The translations of the stories are as much as necessary, transliteral.

STORY FIVE

Interviewer: There is this fascinating story about a ghost who was working in Mr. S's (name supplied) bread factory. As one who lives in this community, could you narrate it to me as you heard it?

Narrator: My brother, that story, it disarms. But I think that it is true because it happened before the eyes of everybody in this village. Was it not in 1984? Yes, in 1984. Do you know that Mr. S (a business name supplied) wound up his bread business after the incident? That bakery is no longer in operation. Because the man himself was so frightened. You see, the ghost in question was the bread-mixer. They say he was from Awka area, and was interested in the girl; in fact they were lovers. Rumour has it that the girl was pregnant, and that it was this bread-mixer who was responsible. Mm, imagine being made pregnant by a ghost. I don't know whether it is true, but that is what they say. What I know is that the man decided he wanted to marry M. Later they prepared to go to know his place before any-thing would be done; I mean M's people decided to do this. That is how the whole thing got exposed. They wanted to find out the actual town and about the reputation of the family, and so on, as our people do. They even hired a car for the trip, and the man was willing to lead the group to his place. As they got near the place, the man said that he should be excused for a moment. He pointed out the building and said that was their family house. He said they could go ahead while he went into one or two neighbours' houses to intimate them of the event. So the people proceeded to drive towards the house without the man. When they got to the house they met the man's father. He was surprised to see them: M's father was among those went. There were three other men, and then the girl herself. They introduced themselves ... said they were from Ideani and so on, and they sat down and waited for the man himself to join the group. But he did not appear. So they began to tell the man's father the reason for their journey. The man asked them the name of the person whom they said was interested in their daughter. They called the young man's name. The father said that couldn't be true because the person they were talking about was his son and that he died some time ago. He pointed out the remains of a grave right in front of the house and said that was where he was buried, and that he died during the civil war (about twenty years before the incident) but that he was among the lucky few whose corpses were sent to their homes for burial.

The people were dumbfounded and M began to cry. She was shaking all over. Later they came back and told their story. My brother, Mr. S. was very frightened. The loaves turned out that week from the factory, nobody touched them. Because, you see, the man who was M's lover and the bread-mixer had disappeared and never showed up again. When they got to the house where he rented a room, none of his belongings was there any more; everything in the room had disappeared. That surprised people, you see, so Mr. S wound up the bread business, because nobody was buying his bread any more now that they had become aware that the bread they had been eating was mixed by a spirit. Before then the business was thriving: no matter what quantity was baked in a day they were all sold off. But after the incident people began to say that the reason the bread sold like hot cake was because it was mixed by a spirit. I heard that S sold off everything he used for baking the bread including the oven.

Interviewer: What happened to the girl?

Narrator: I don't know. Oh yes. They say that she later got married. A lucky girl, isn't she? She later got married. I now remember, to a certain man from Abatete.

Story Six

Interviewer: How true is it that the ghost of your uncle who died over twenty years ago was harassing his senior wife?

Narrator: When my uncle died … My uncle died in 1972 and after the full traditional funeral—you known, he was an Ọzọ titled man and therefore reputable—he did not disturb anybody. He was a very hard-working man; he farmed extensively at Oze, and you known that only real professional farmers went that far to farm. The wife whom he came to disturb was the senior wife. He did not disturb her between 1972 and 1983. In fact, when the story started to spread my father did not believe it and was annoyed with the woman. My father did not believe it partly because he knew the kind of brother he had, and partly because he is a staunch Catholic. But he later changed his mind.

Interviewer: Are you saying that even though your father is a strong Catholic, he does believe that a dead person could come back after so many years to harass the living?

Narrator: Mm.. (Hesitates) I think so. Why I say I think so is that he (my father) called my uncle's wife to ask her the nature of the harassment which my late uncle was giving to her ... So, on one of the occasions the woman came to our house next door and called my father and both of them heard ... for, you see, when my uncle was alive, he had a way of walking, with the walking stick, always noisy on the ground. He had a peculiar way of striking that walking stick on the ground. Not because of age, for he was a very strong man. But whenever we heard the sound of the walking stick on the ground we would know that he was the person coming in. So when my uncle's wife discerned that his ghost was on his way again to the house to disturb her, she came and called my father. Both of them remained in her house, conversing. My father knew the steps of my uncle; so he knew when the man came into the room striking his walking stick in the usual manner. The wife began as usual to scream. And she shouted: "Look at him! He has come in!" But my father did not see anybody; it was only the woman who saw him.

Interviewer: Do you mean the woman saw him with her naked eyes?

Narrator: Yes, she said that she always saw him with her eyes. She said that sometimes he was accompanied by some people, and one day the ghost came in and invited his companion to come into the house and sit down. She said that she did not know the person; that she did not know if he came from our community. She said that the companion said to her husband, "Lets go, leave the woman alone. There is nothing she has done to you". But my uncle's wife did not see the other man but saw only the late husband. Then the husband came in and began to beat her. She started screaming and calling for help. Later her husband left with the companion. So on this occasion when she started to scream that the man was coming to beat her, there was nothing my father could do because he did not see any-body. How can one fight against a ghost empty-handed? So in spite of my father's presence he still beat her, after which he left.

Some period passed. And the woman's people came to our house and accused my father of neglect. They said Papa was indifferent to the whole matter because it did not concern him personally; if it was his wife, they asked, wouldn't he have started seeking for ways of solving the problem? They said it was because the woman had no male children, for if she had a son the son would have begun to look for the meaning for it all.

The next time my uncle visited again, the woman again called my father. Papa started rebuking his brother, even though he did not see him. He asked him: "What is it? What has the woman done to you? If there's anything you want from her, tell me and I will see that you have it. But stop disgracing me. The way people are gossiping with my name, do you like it? Please refrain, I am begging you. I am prostrating before you (and my father prostrated). I am kneeling be-fore you (and my father knelt). Please go away and leave this woman alone. Do you want me, your brother, your only brother remaining in the world, to also die like you, before my time? And the whole compound would be without an adult to protect the family name?" After this incident my uncle's ghost stooped beating his wife. He nev-er came again since then.

Story Seven

Interviewer: What is this story about the ghost of your brother?

Narrator: You known the story of C and J (real names mentioned) ... the two were very closed. Most of the time C was ill it was J who looked after him in the hospital, and because J stays at home more than any of us, she was always in the company of C. I guess that was why they were as close even unto death, so to say. Because if J had not gone to Nsukka (University) for her Sandwich programme, she would have been at his bedside the day he died.

Well, the day C died J saw him … J said that she saw him, that he visited her at Nsukka. But the way he went to her, he was very shady; his figure was blurred. J said that she was going to the university library, that she was moving from one of the classrooms to the university library. She was going to see her girlfriend with whom she usually studied. It was drizzling that evening, and the light along the pathway to the library was not very bright. When she was walking along this lonely path, somebody was following her closely as if the person wanted to walk right on her footsteps. Each time she turned to see the person, the person would turn away his face, but the first thought that came to her mind was: "Look, this person resembles my brother C very much". As they walked, it would appear as if the person was trying to overtake her and, you know, each time she tried to take a close look at him, his face would becomes very indistinct. He would pass her and she would pass him, and the feeling was persistent in her mind that this person was very much like C. At a stage she was determined to see his face properly but it was always the side view that she saw and that side view looked very much like C's face. As this happened, she suddenly became overcome by a feeling of gooseflesh. So she started to run towards the direction of clear lighting and when she glanced backwards the person had disappeared. She ran into the library. When she got into the library she discovered that she was shaking terribly and her girlfriend began to ask her what was wrong. She told her that she had seen something: somebody looking like her brother and who later disappeared. She told her that she was afraid that her brother C was no longer alive. The girlfriend dismissed her experience and told her she was merely being superstitious. So she tried to dismiss it from her mind, until she received the message the following morning that C was dead.

Even while he was being mourned at home—I think it was on the fourth or fifth day, round 2a.m. when most people had slept—there was one boy who was very friendly with C at home. This boy suddenly shot up from where he was lying and began to shout: "Look at C! Look at C! Hold him! Hold him!" The boy rushed out of the building in pursuit of something and said it was C and that he must hold him. You know, people got up and started running about in panic. After some time the pandemonium subsided. People went and held the boy and tried to calm him down. My mother started to cry again.

Interviewer: Is it true that there is an item in his belongings that suddenly disappeared and was never found?

Narrator: Well, after the bed where he would lie in state had been prepared, we started looking for his album. You know, he had very many photographs. They went to his room and ransacked it, but it was not there. None of his photographs whether black and white or coloured would be found. And he had many of them, up to a hundred. In fact the photograph that was displayed eventually was the one from B's collection: the one he had given to B (a brother to the deceased). Even till today his album has not been found, or any of the photographs he kept. People say that he took them away, that having suffered for much of his life and yet dying young, he did not want to leave behind any image of him in a world he had found so unfulfilling.

STORY EIGHT

Interviewer: Madam, could you narrate to me the story going around this town last year of a dead man's ghost who beat his widow to death.

Narrator: What happened was that the woman was the lastborn of Chief U … you know Chief U, don't you? This sister of his was married at Umuru village. The husband was a night watchman in our secondary school. The family was somewhat impoverished, but this woman was very pretty. There was one man, his name was J (real name supplied), who befriended her and they became lovers. He too was from Umuru village and he was wealthy by our standards. He traded in clothing materials in Onitsha. The man was in the habit of giving the woman everything she wanted, and the husband just kept quiet. He knew that what the wife brought enabled them to support the family; at least they could eat properly and pay school fees for their children.

Interviewer: When did this happen?

Narrator: I think it was in 1985 or so. As it turned out, some people in the man's extended family were jealous of the man's progress. The man was an only son and he had ten children, and the wife died while giving birth to the tenth child. But that's by the way. As I said he was this other woman's lover and he gave the woman whatever she wanted. But there was somebody in the man's family who was envious of his success, and this man went and paid the woman to poison J. They say that he gave the woman Three Thousand (Naira) and she used it to buy bundles of zinc with which to roof the house where she and her husband and children lived. She also used the money to help in other commitments in the family, pending when she would kill her boyfriend and receive the rest of the money. So she gave J the poison and he became very ill. He was taken to many hospitals but nothing could be diagnosed, though everyone could see that this man was dying. Eventually he died. After his death he was buried at home. It was of course a Christian ceremony. On the third night the church women were going to keep a vigil. They assembled at the agreed place from where they proceeded to the man's house. When they called on this woman who was the dead man's lover, she asked them to wait for her, saying she was on her way. Meanwhile the others had proceeded to move. When the woman finished what she was doing in her house she set out for the vigil. She started to run so as to meet up the other women. Then as she ran the dead man's ghost attacked her. He struck her and struck her and struck until she fell on the ground crying: "J, leave me alone! Leave me alone! Please, forgive me!" and, you know, she continued crying in this manner …, so people, the women going to the vigil and everybody, all started running, everyone at their fastest speed. The story is that people ran away from the spot, and even neighbours took refuge inside their houses and bolted their doors. The woman continued to cry and call on the dead boyfriend to leave her alone and to forgive her for having been bought by his own relation to give him poison. After the man (ghost) has stopped beating her, somehow she managed to get to her house; you know, the husband was a night watchman and had gone on duty. She became very ill and people started trooping to her house as the story spread. She became so ill that she could no longer talk. It wasn't the kind of illness for which one goes to the normal hospital. So they sent her to *Dibia* N.O., that traditional healer in you village. He treated her and said that she would recover. But after three days, she died.

ANALYSES OF STORIES FIVE TO EIGHT

Now, all these are contemporary in terms of date: the four events took place between 1982 and 1987. Most of the key materials in the legends are of contemporary culture—photographs, car, bread, money, electric light, library, university, etc. But they are not urban legends in so far as the events took place in a rural community. From the tone of the narrations, and from obvious rhetorical evidence, it is clear that all the narrators believe the stories, some in spite of themselves. In any case, the stories are believable the way they are told—the mention of real names, dates and places, the elaboration of circumstances and the emphasis on collaborative evidence. All the narrators are Christian, three of them well-educated. The narrator of Story 5 is a female teacher in a local secondary school, that of Story 6 a university undergraduate with occasional fanatical Christian views, while that of Story 8, though not educated, is quite enlightened and a strong member of the Christian Mother's Union.

The stories themselves cannot easily be pigeonholed the way the earlier more traditional ones were. But the continuity between the "traditional" imagination and the "cotemporary" mind as revealed in the stories is evident. Both Stories 7 and 8 can be explained from the point of view of traditional Igbo cosmology. Story 7 is about the ghost of a very young man of eighteen who dies a natural but premature death—he suffered from hereditary diabetes and in that condition had an attack of hepatitis—and, as in Story 4, the ghost appeared before a loved one just after the death. He was a very well mannered boy, and obviously bound for heaven, as people commented during the funeral. For some reason, he did not want his personal photographs to be displayed beside his corpse, and so took them away—the narrator's explanation at the end of the story as regards the photographs sounds like the gist of comments which many in the community must have made, and bears the stamp of traditional thinking.

Story 8 is a typical "revenge" ghost story, and there are many of such in the traditional repertoire of ghost-lore. The mere fact that the main events took place within the context of a Christian activity—funeral vigil—is significant of how a very traditional theme can grow in a contemporary environment.

Story 6 is somewhat more complex to analyze. The ghost belonged to a man who was not a bad character, and who had died twenty years previously, since which time he never manifested as a ghost. From the point of view of traditional cosmology, such a spirit would long since have become an ancestor in which metaphysical state he must remain until reincarnation. The man was not a Christian, and so he would not have gone to purgatory; in any case, twenty years would seem to be too long a time for a soul in purgatory! Could it then be that, for some reason known only to Chineke, the Supreme Deity, the spirit of this man was permanently confined in that zone meant for only people who had died the "devil's death" and did not qualify for reincarnation?

Finally, Story 5 is every inch a contemporary ghost legend, quite reminiscent of our first "urban" legend which we showed is almost like a version of the vanishing hitchhiker, the only striking difference being that its setting is rural, though it is a rural community that is becoming sophisticated in some ways: where most people are literate, and a man can set up a thriving bakery and workers rent houses as people do in cities. However, that this quintessential urban legend can take place in a rural community shows how invalid the demarcation between the "contemporary" and "non-urban" legend can be.

CONCLUSION

This essay began by showing Igbo cities as being such a contemporary, uncanny phenomenon that they are a very conducive breeding ground for ghost legends. It shows too that the "urban" legend has many thematic and structural similarities with "the vanishing hitchhiker" repertoire of contemporary legends popular in Europe. But the essay examines ghost legends that were nurtured in a typical traditional Igbo society, relating these legends to Igbo cosmological beliefs which thus render the legends "traditional" in content as well as in setting and style. There are, however, other legends that sprang up in the same community which have characteristics of the "urban" legends, though they also retain qualities of the traditional ones; this thus makes the link between the "traditional" and the 'contemporary " a graph of continuity rather that of disjuncture. We are therefore to mention that the ghost phenomenon *per se* transcends time, theology and science even though these do affect the credibility quotient of the stories and their narrative details, especially in terms of material instruments of narrative embellishment. Ghostlore must therefore have motifs that are fundamentally universal and primordial. As Sandy Hobbs tentatively argues (140–146), and for a more satisfying explanation of the ghost phenomenon, it may well be necessary to focus scholarly attention on a synthesizing analysis of a representative repertoire of ghost-lore from all parts of the world.

NOTE

1. Edmund Ilogu (1974) has argued that the extensive Christianization of the Igbo does not imply a displacement of traditional cosmological beliefs; instead certain fundamental aspects of that cosmology have been adapted to fit into the christain theology. Rev. Canon Illogu, however, like many other Igbo Christian priests of his generation who are also anthropologists, has shown great enthusiasm in proving how Christian the Igbo have become, and is reluctant to accept the possibility that it is Christianity that is under pressure to adapt the Igbo cosmological beliefs, and not the other way round.

WORKS CITED

Achebe, Chinua. *Morning Yet on Creation Day.* London: Heinemann, 1975. Print.

Bennett, Gillian. "The Vanishing Hitchhiker: Neither Modern, Urban nor Legend". *Perspectives on Contemporary Legend.* CECTAL Conference Series No. 4 Paul Smith, Ed.Sheffield: Centre for English Cultural Tradition and Language, 1984. 45–63. Print.

—. *Traditions of Belief: Women, Folklore and Supernatural Today.* Harmondsworth, Middlesex: Penguin, 1985. Print.

Bennett, Gillian, Paul Smith and J.D. A. Widdowson, ed.*Perspectives On Contemporary Legend* 11 Sheffield: Sheffield Academic Press, 1987. Print.

Brunvand, Harold. *The Vanishing Hitchhiker: American Urban Legends and their Meaning.* New York: W.W Norton, 1981. Print.

Buchan, David, "The Modern Legend". *Language, Culture and Tradition.* Eds. A.E. Green and J.D.A. Widdowson. CECTAL Conference Series No..2. Leeds & Sheffield: Institute of Dialect And Folklore Life Studies and Centre For English Cultural Tradition and Language, 1981. 201–220. Print.

Ellia, Bill. "Why Are Verbatim Transcripts of Legends Necessary?" *Perspectives on Contemporary Legend* 11 Ed. Gillian Benneth, Paul Smith and J.D.A. Widdowson. Sheffield: Sheffield Academic Press, 1987. 31–60. Print.

Green, A .E and J.D.A. Widdowson eds. *Language, Culture and Tradition,* CECTAL Conference Series No..2. Leeds & Sheffield: Institute of Dialect and Folk Life Studies and Centre for English Cultural Tradition And Language, 1981. Print.

Green, M.M. *Igbo Village Affairs.* London: Frank Cass & Co, 1964. Print.

Hoobs, Sandy. "The Psychology of A Good Story". *Perspectives on Contemporary Legend* 11. Ed. Gillians Bennett, Paul Smith and J.D.A Widdowson. Sheffield: Sheffield Academic Press, 1987. 140–46. Print.

Ilogu, Edmund. *Christianity and Ibo Culture.* Leidein: G.T. Bill, 1974. Print.

Jordan, J.P. *Bishop Shanaham of Southern Nigeria.* Dublin: Colonmore & Reynolds, 1945. Print.

Leach, Maria, ed. *Standard Dictionary of Folklore, Mythology and Legend.* London: Harper and Row, 1984. Print.

Leonard, A.C. *The Lower Niger and Its Tribes.* London: Frank Cass & Co., 1968. Print.

Metuh, Ikenga. *God and Man in African Religion: A Case Study of the Igbo of*

Nigeria. London: Geoffrey Chapman, 1981. Print.

Nicolaisen, F.H. "The Linguistic Structure of the Legend". *Perspectives on Contemporary Legend* vol. 11. Ed. Gillian Bennett, Paul Smith and J.D.A. Widdowson. Sheffield: Sheffield Academic Press, 1987. 61–78. Print.

Nwaka, G.I. "Urban and Industrial Culture in Igboland: The Crisis of Adaptation". *The Igbo Socio-Cultural System.* Owerri: Ministry of Information, Culture, Youth and Sports, 1967. 47–63. Print.

Nwala, T.U. *Igbo Philosophy:* Lagos: Lantern Books, 1985. Print.

Smith, Paul, "On The Receiving End: When Legend Becomes Rumour". *Perspective on Contemporary Legend. Ed. Paul Smith. CECTAL Conference Series No. 4.* Sheffield, Centre for English cultural Tradition and Language, 1984. 197–215. Print.

—, Ed. *Perspectives on Contemporary Legend.* CECTAL Conference Series Sheffield: Centre for English Cultural Tradition and Language, 1984. Print.

Williams, Noel. "Problems of Defining Contemporary Legends". *Perspective on Contemporary Legend.* CECTAL Conference Series No. 4. Sheffield: Centre for English Cultural Tradition and Language, 1984. 216–228. Print.

PART FOUR: THE DRAMA GENRES

Chapter Twelve

Negotiating the Hegemonic:
Ritual and Mythological Recuperation
in Irobi's Drama and the Soyinka Model

Isidore Diala

M.J.C. Echeruo's sober appraisal of the dramatic limits of Igbo ritual in 1971 generated quite some spirited critical debate on the nature of Igbo/African theatre. Pointing to the distinctive Eurocentrism of the Greek model privileged by Echeruo as the viable universal paradigm for the evolution of ritual into drama, several other Igbo scholars sternly rebuked him for the failure to recognize cultural distinctions in the dramatic form and consequently for the failure to advocate a culture-authenticating notion of drama. Esiaba Irobi's drama since the 1990s has-reopened this debate, and, moreover, virtually constitutes a demonstration-piece of Echeruo's postulations. Advancing insights deriving from Soyinka's postulations rooted in Yoruba theatre, Irobi makes the theatrical basis of his truly challenging corpus the dramaturgy of demonstrable Igbo ritual performances. In his iconoclastic recuperation of Igbo myths and expansion of ritual to facilitate secular projects in a contemporary postcolonial society, Irobi constantly sets in relief a specifically Igbo theatre/tragedy as well as foregrounds his audacious innovativeness.

Noting the dramatic potentials of Igbo ritual in 971 at a seminar on Igbo studies at the University of Nigeria in Nsuka, M.J.C Echeruo in a seminal paper had contended that those potentials were severely inhibited by the liturgical form of ritual, ritual being "A representation in action of a faith or a dream, like communion or baptism" (138). Seeing as a basic condition for drama to flourish the satisfactory transformation of ritual into a celebration and the conversation of the mythic structure of action from the religious and priestly to the secular (138), Echeruo had discerned in the evolution of Greek drama a paradigm for the Igbo to emulate.

> What is needed then, it seems to me, is to force that ritual to yield its story, to cut through the overlay of ceremony to the primary events of the *mythos*. Ritual is, and has always been, a dead end, it cannot grow. It only shrinks steadily into inevitably inaccessible (though powerful) symbolism. The Igbo should do what the Greeks did; expand ritual into life and give that life a secular base. (147)

In their separate interrogations of Echeruo's argument and basic assumptions, two other Igbo scholars, Emanuel Obiechina and Ossie Enekwe, extended the debate on the nature of Igbo theatre. Contending that Africa had a culture and a history different from the Greek, Obiechina refutes as illogical the consideration of the Greek paradigm as a universal model. His submission is that Igbo/African ritual festivals are in no further need of evolution, being already authentic drama though understandably differentiated from classical Greek drama. Interrogating the assumption that the conventions of the European theatre are universally applicable, he wonders:

> Is there any particular reason except that of meeting the specifically practical pressures of the present age, why an enactment should last only two or three hours instead of six months? Is the sense of organic unity which we assume in the modern theatre and its conventions not possible on an extended scale among a people whose sensibilities are trained to absorb more diffused ritual and symbolic significance of action? Is a broad command canvas not more suitable for painting more inclusive social and emotional action than the mere mouse-tongue platform called the modern stage? (300)

On the other hand, Enekwe argues, contrary to Echeruo's opinion, that drama does not even have to evolve from myth since history or any other form of activity could equally offer material and structure for drama (158). Observing that theatre is anchored in impersonation and interactive activity, he argues further that myth can only play a subordinate role there and notes that elements of myth when found in drama function in social restructuring, in other words, to establish an ideological position (150). Contending that function determines the nature of drama in every culture, Enekwe notes that poetry was central to the drama of 5th century BC Greece because poetry was regarded by the Greeks as "the most desirable and perfect art form" and that the order of events in Greek tragedy reflected the moral order given the crucial emphasis on moral rhetoric (152). On the other hand, "because of its importance in Africa, ritual is an integral part of the African theatre. Consequently, African traditional dramas are participative and celebrative. It is also total, because it combines many art forms, music, poetry, dance, acting, miming, mask, painting, singing, dialogue, etc, hence, speech is not dominant as in the mainstream European theatre" .(154)

Unlike Echeruo, however, neither Obiechina nor Enekwe is concerned with the practicalities of African playwright's appropriation of the dramatic potentials of ritual in staging postcolonial African experience (or, by the way, with the creation of more rituals on the model of the communal paradigms they enthusiastically claim as intrinsic and full fledged drama). The traditions of various cultures re-authenticate themselves not by the possession of eternal signal value but by adaptation and conscious appropriation by their artists with the inspiration occasionally deriving from culture contact. Irobi's attitude to tradition, like Soyinka's, illustrates this.

In a 2003 interview with Nnorom Azuonye the Nigerian poet, dramatist and literary theorist, Esiaba Irobi appraises his work as counter hegemonic in its response to the canons of Western art. *Nwokedi*, Irobi contends, illustrates "the possibility of dramatizing the Igbo tragic folk drama in such an elevated accepted dramatic texts" (49). Regarding orature as "the most valid and most accessible and most universal as well as relevant form of human poetry", Irobi discerns "continuities of African ontology, teleology, semiology and narratology" extending even to the new World:

Concepts and notions of creativity and performance, ritual and festive models were translocated to the new world during slavery and these elements helped our people to negotiate new identities and create new syncretic cultures. We see some of these elements of African orality in the work of Toni Morrison, Ralph Ellison, the music of blues and jazz musicians and most vividly in the African-American gospel music and worshipping style—a direct echo of our indigenous ritual performance, invocations, chants, ululations, yodeling etc. (49)

In his exaltation and bitter indictment of Africans in the continent for their failure to appropriate fully that rich resource, Irobi draws attention to the root of his own drama in Igbo ritual. His theatrical practice in fact re-opens and complicates the criticism started in the early 1970s about the nature of Igbo theatre.

Irobi's exaltation of folk literature and beliefs makes them the compelling background of his art. He ascribes preeminence to orature: "Orature in what is used to regulate the world from Gregorian chants through Ohafia war songs to Rap"; and discerns in poetry (as opposed to "verse") a magic and occult force that regenerates and propels life. And by further locating the source of authentic poetry in the realm of nature's mysteries and in the oracular voice of the god, Irobi illuminates the convictions that account for his fixation with Igbo myths and rituals as well as their mode of performance.

Ake Hulkrantz considers ritual as a "fixed usually solemn behaviour that is repeated in certain situations. Anthropologists like to call the latter 'crisis situations', but there is not always any crisis involved. It would be better to speak of sacred situations in Durkheim's spirit" (136). In Irobi's drama contemporary society is mired in "crisis situations" that recreate the primordial ones in which ritual had evolved and helped a promise of resolution. Thus, claiming for ritual an efficacy and a timeless sacred origin going back to ancestral memory, Irobi demonstrably makes the basis of his drama the dramaturgy of identifiable Igbo ritual performances—propitiatory, divinatory, funerary, regenerative rites. In traditional society motivated primarily by the dream of life and plentitude—multiple births, bountiful harvest,, a general renewal or rebirth of society—these ritual events, employing impressive stylized performances and poetic invocations,

had equally provided an avenue for spectacle, dancing and conviviality. Rooted in all the tensions of a contemporary post-colonial society, and demonstrating an awareness of the dramatic conventions
of the West, Irobi's drama invariably tends to the climactic ritual
of communion, expiation or celebration inscribed as a validation of
ancient wisdom.

Enekwe contends that a "ritual becomes entertainment once it
is outside its original context or when the belief that sustains it has
lost its potency" (155). On the other hand, in transforming ritual
into drama, that is a secular performance with a deep infusion of religious implication, Irobi aims indeed to highlight its sacredness and
efficacy, to revive and revalidate the faith that nurtured and sustained
ritual. Recuperating Igbo myths and occasionally recreating them
to endorse his preferred ideological position, Irobi transforms the
chief participant in the ritual event into towering symbolic figures in
his drama of elemental forces. His inclination is always to formulate
an alternative literacy tradition and worldview by transforming Igbo
cultural experience into paradigms potentially applicable to a wider
humanity. Irobi's drama, therefore, recurrently recalls Soyinka's.

Soyinka's undoubted iconic status in the development of African
drama derives mainly from his providing crucial models for interrogating the universality Europe had arrogated to its artistic paradigms as well as for deploying traditional African motifs. Soyinka's
articulation of a post-colonial tragic vision in *Myth, Literature and the
African World* sets this in full relief. Noting the persistent efforts to
re-define tragedy in terms of cultural or private experience, Soyinka
considers this man's recognition as inadequate attempts to explain
certain areas of depth-experience satisfactorily by general aesthetic
theories. Soyinka regards this insight as having particular relevance
to tragedy considering its centrality in the effort to understand the
human paradox.

Writing then from a Yoruba perspective, Soyinka accounts for
tragedy basically in terms of the pains and glory of the pilgrimage
through the abyss of dissolution in a striving towards a reintegration
of self with essence. However, by repeatedly summoning Hellenistic

tragic paradigms and Nietsche's ideas, Soyinka apparently valorizes them as points of departure and as classical models against which he must measure his revelations. In his recognition as a basic delight the purgation of the hero's ego through suffering, and the hero's unusually enhanced powers of spiritual perception, Soyinka attempts to establish the truly universal character of tragedy.

> Suffering cancels the opaque pleasure of human existence : suffering, the truly overwhelming suffering of Sango, of Lear, of Oedipus, this suffering hones the psyche to a finely self-annihilating perceptiveness and renders further action futile and above all, lacking in dignity. And what has the struggle of the tragic hero been, after all, but an effort to maintain that innate concept of dignity which impels to action only to that degree in which the hero possesses a true nobility of spirit? At such moments he is close to the acceptance and wisdom of Obatala in which faith is rested, not on the self, but on a universal selfhood to which individual contributions are fundamentally meaningless. (134)

In reality, then, Soyinka does not quite repudiate the idea of universal paradigms (to which individual contributions are meaningless) as the idea of European hegemony inherent in its closely guarded idea of a universalist concept of tragedy and of an essential human nature. He summons European models—but only to subvert them. Soyinka writes: "the function and nature of music in Yoruba tragedy is peculiarly revealing of the shortcomings of long accepted conclusions of European intuition" (147). After some initial precaution taken to acknowledge his theory as specifically Yoruba, Soyinka's assertions increasingly become all-embracing: "Tragic music is…" (145); "tragic fate is…" (156), "powerful tragic drama follows…" (156). Of course, Soyinka's ambition is to displace European tragic paradigms by this post-colonial model. Ogun is Dionysos, Apollo, and Prometheus all in one. To this unapologetic exaltation of Ogun may well be traced the vital source of the inspiration and model firing the zeal of generations of American writers to search the African pantheon, myths and legends for deity-heroes capable of stimulating the creative imagination and dramatic action or of illuminating the human situation. Irobi's career is in this regard revealing.

Commenting specifically on the creative use of ritual, Adebayo Williams remarks on the contrasted apprehension of ritual in Western societies beginning with the Enlightenment and in the emergent post-colonial cultures of the Third World. Williams contends that the Eurocentric pejorative conception of ritual as a meaningless exercise is imperialistic and forcibly evacuates the space of the Other. Positing that such emptied spaces must be recontested to set in relief this subtle hegemonic assault, he draws attention to African writers whose recourse to ritual is refutation of Western assumption of cultural superiority (67-68). Of all such writers, Williams considers Soyinka exemplary in his enlistment of ritual for ideological purposes as well as an organizing principle (68-69). Similarly, Eni Jones Umuko writes: "The ritual icon in theatre may be one of the most enduring, indispensable keynotes to understanding of African indigenous theatre practice" (1). He attributes this conviction to his experience of directing Soyinka's *Death and the Kings Horseman* which Umuko contends can only be presented authentically and faithfully as "a ritual for the stage" (17). Regarding Soyinka's pervasive influence on younger Nigerian dramatists as the consummate use of culture, Ezenwa Ohaeto notes the exploitation of this cultural imperative in the work of Ken Saro-Wiwa, Emeka Nwabueze and Esiaba Irobi. He identifies as its unique virtue the appropriation of "nuggets of experience with wider implications for humanity" (219).

With about six plays to his credit (but receiving less critical attention than he deserves) Irobi has been preoccupied with the frustration and dispossession of the Nigerian youth by the country's leadership, military and civilian alike, and by the passionate espousal of a violent ethic as a resolution to the corruption of Nigerian politics. Yet Irobi's political theme (especially since the publication of *Nwokedi* in 1991) is explored against the backdrop of a ritual symbolism that evokes the atmosphere of much of Soyinka's drama even though earlier on his career, with an iconoclast's passion to demolish existing structures in the bid to create new artistic forms,

Irobi had denounced Soyinka's style. For example, representing Soyinka as Ogun in one of his earliest and most controversial plays, *Gold, Frankincense and Myrrh*, Irobi characterizes him as obscurantist. Ogun's self-defense is in itself incriminating: "Obscurantism is the creative symptoms of a deep running inspiration. It is the distinguishing characteristic between a great writer and middle-of-the-road writers. It is the volcanic effluvium of literary ingenuity" (*Gold* 25). Through parody and mimicry, as in Ogun's appropriation of Soyinka's famed dismissal of Negritude, Irobi constantly identifies Ogun as Soyinka and presents what he regards as Soyinka's distinctive style for ridicule and censure: "A tiger does not preach his tigritude. Neither does a gorilla preach his gorrilatude. Only buffoons preach their buffoonery and nycompoops their nycompoop-ery" (*Gold* 29).

In reality, however, Irobi's attitude to Soyinka is far from rejection. Speaking to Nengi Ilagha in 1989 on his ambition as a writer, Irobi has said: "I would as a writer want to do for any generation what Soyinka, Achebe and Okigbo have done for their generation. In fact, I would like to write three of them out of literature if that will be possible" (11). Seeking in his own Igbo cultural background enabling myths to comprehend contemporary society as well as life's abiding mysteries, Irobi's work often indicates appropriations of Soyinka's insights in stagecraft as well as in his subjection of his material to a demonstrable Soyinka interpretation. Fascinated by Ogun's revolutionary attributes, Irobi, perhaps understandably, is drawn to the myth of the Igbo god of thunder, lightning and justice, *Amadioha*, whom he often re-creates partly in the image of Ogun. But Amadioha's spectacular cleansing flames prove equally irresistible to an artist devoted to the ritual purgation and re-creation of society. Yet, perhaps, it is inevitable, even for a writer committed to the ideological transformation of society, that given his abiding fascination with Igbo propitiatory rituals and with the myth of the scapegoat whose suffering and death expiate the guilt of an entire society that Irobi should often illuminate the Igbo vision of tragedy anchored in the complex and mysterious relationship between the individual and his/her *Chi*.

Privileging the role of Chi, Chinua Achebe, whose *Arrow of God* pays crucial attention to deities in Igboland, in *Home and Exile* refers to Chi as "Chukwu's agent, assigned exclusively to [an] individual through his or her life. This Chi, this presence of God, in attendance on every human being, is more powerful in the affairs of that person than any local deity or the conspiracy of any number of such deities against that person" (14). Echeruo comments further that this particularly complex Igbo theological concept explains both the universe and individual fortune: "It is a concept which both accounts for the universe, explains Good and Evil, tragedy and good fortune, order and conflict, character and destiny, free will and metaphysical order" (*Ahamefule* 20). For the Igbo tragedy is rooted in the concept of "Chi ọjọọ", "bad Chi".

Igbo discourse is in this regard replete with the people's chastened awareness, even horrified apprehension of the working out of tragic fate. *Onye Chi ọjọọ chọrọ imapu ime mapu mkpuru anya ya, chọọ ituta mkpuruanya ya, sojie aka.* (A person with a bad Chi wanted to blow his nose but blew out his eyes, tried to pick his eyes but broke his (arm) and *Onye Chi ọjọọ wua nkwuru amu ya akpafara* If a man with a bad Chi jumps a fence his genitals get stuck) are among many sayings on the plight of the tragic. However, in noting that a good Chi brings prosperity and that a bad Chi is a source of tragedy, Echeruo observes that a bad Chi is not necessarily absolute nor is it necessarily a consequence of sin. Prayer is thus an exhortation of Chi to action just as sacrifice aims to appease the spirit forces that interfere with that fulfillment (*Ahamefule* 21)

Writing more recently, Echeruo identifies two separate worlds in Igbo religious thought, the world of the spirits and that of humans. Where the beings of the former world-gods, spirits and similar entities—have power to influence humans, humans too are invested with a power of their own which the gods respect. Human power, however, is extremely precarious, given the influence of malevolent spirits and evil men capable of collaborating with them (18). Sacrifice, therefore, is the obligatory human gesture of recognition of and homage to the gods, the tariff par-excellence for human existence.

Thus Echeruo discerns in the Igbo conception of sacrifice a revelation of the Igbo notion of divinity: "Igbo sacrifice is the offering
made to the gods and the ancestors to buy peace. It may call for the
sacrifice of a hen or a goat; even of a human being, in the most dire
circumstances. But it will be done. With "*aja*" [sacrifice] a general
premium is paid, and not necessarily to powers we love or admire,
but often to those we fear and even hate. It is the price we pay for
being mortal/human; for not being spirit" ("Religion" 19). Citing
Rev. Fr. Dr. Metuh, Echeruo remarks that Igbo sacrifice is not only
primarily an act of duty but often a joyless one and notes that the
saying "*Aja agwu ike* summarizes Igbo frustration as well as acceptance of the gods and the necessarily of obedience to them. Humans
can never be tired of offering sacrifice. The offering of sacrifices
is the price we pay to remain human" (Religion" 18). However, as
the gods are not obliged to participate in the negotiation of destiny
which sacrifice ritually initiates, Igbo tragedy could be appreciated
as human's presumptuous persistence in spite of the antithesis between the human will and the disinclination or disability of Chi to
affirm. The Igbo saying "*Onye kwe Chi ya ekwe*" (If a man affirms, his
Chi affirms too) is itself a prayer, an exhortation, not an affirmation.
Irobi's work, like Soyinka's, raises fundamental questions about the
role of ritual-often in its extreme form of human/self sacrifice—to
ameliorate both individual and communal destiny as well as the tragic dimensions of such ritual.

The paradigm for the *Ekpe* festival in *Nwokedi* is the communal
expiation of guilt and sacrifice held annually in many African societies, especially at transitional moments (for example the eve of the
new year) to placate the gods and renew the lease of life. In the past,
as indicated by the play, among the Ngwa-Igbo the setting of the
play, as among many other African people, the preferred sacrifice
was a human, usually the village idiot or the stranded and unwary
stranger. However, in a pioneering effort in 1966 to establish the authentic background of African literature, Ben Obumselu cites Frazer to acknowledge that the sacrificial victim was a common fact of
African life, but notes the lack of the imaginative exploitation of the

theme in African folk literature. Obumselu suggests as a possible explanation for this the fact that the ritual proceedings were probably so hedged round by irrational fears that they proved infertile soil for new literary invention. He seeks, therefore, in the imaginative world of *The Golden Bough* or even the gospels and the intellectual milieu of the twentieth century the background of Wole Soyinka's *The Strong Breed* (56). There are significant verbal echoes that suggest that in writing *Nwokedi* Esiaba Irobi himself may have sought for suggestions in Soyinka's work in his daring attempt to find relevance for a traditional festival, the Ekpe, in contemporary Nigerian society.

Irobi actually points to the heart of a central belief in Igbo traditional religious faith the idea that communal deities are human creations instituted to perform certain function for society. The implication of such a pragmatic concept of divinity is that only that the gods survived that could demonstrate an ability to carry out the responsibilities assigned to them, the others were replaced. Commenting on this, M.J.C. Echeruo acknowledges that the Igbo

> are a thoroughly iconoclastic people, that we keep our gods in our hearts and have only an appropriately respectful attitude to the circumstances that surround them. We respect the gods, but as the proverb says, we also expect the gods to respect us humans. We acknowledge the power of the gods, and cultivate that power, but when these gods consistently fail to prove themselves powerful, we reserve the right to discard them and seek out new gods. (18-19)

Echeruo identified *Ala*, the earth goddess, as the only divinity beyond the capriciousness of Igbo people, noting that if the Igbo ever recognised a supreme divinity it certainly was Ala (18). Irobi adds to this picture in *Nwokedi* the insight that the medium who mediates between the people and the communal deity is himself the god-incarnate. Thus the Ufo-bearer who articulates the mystical relevance of the Ekpe festival notes:

> When a people decided to create a god, they create a god in the image of the trade that sustains their lives ... when a people mould a god, they also make a man the spirit of the god.

And whenever the god is summoned, the spirit appears in the
wake of the god ... Nwokedi Nwa Nwokedi: you are a spirit.
We made you a spirit. But at this hour, as you cross that spill of
blood, you will become a god. And like a god you will walk the
earth. With your naked feet you will stomp the barren soil until
it stirs with the greenness of a new life. (91)

But by narrowing down the frontiers between the divine and the
human, Irobi creates the tragic situation in which the human easily
overreaches the limits of his kind. The Igbo concept of hubris is
indeed epitomized in the plight of the proverbial gazelle which after over-feeding challenged his Chi to a wrestling bout.[1] Nwokedi's
self-appraisal as superhuman accounts for his (mis) conception of
heroism and his role in the scheme of ritual purgation in his community. However, the dialogue which establishes the hereditary burden
of the expiration of communal guilt as the lot of the Nwokedi family
vividly recalls Soyinka's earlier work.

The expository exchange between Nwokedi and Habiba runs
thus:

NWOKEDI: I am the one empowered by the land to slaughter
the sacrificial animal at the shrine of the gods and renew the
strength of the earth with its blood

HABIBA: Can't someone else do that...

NWOKEDI: Nobody else can. The courage that act requires
reposes in our family. That is why we are called *Nwokedi*. (37)

Eman's father's revelation to the son in Soyinka's *The Strong Breed* of
the family's hereditary election to a far more demanding redemptive
vocation is similarly phrased:

Ours is a strong breed my son. It is only strong Breed that can
take this boat to the river year after year and wax stronger on it.
I have taken down each year's evil for over twenty years. (*Short
Plays* 103)

He notes further, "Other men would rot and die doing this task
year after year. It is strong medicine which only we can take. Our

blood is strong like no other" *(Short Plays* 104-5). Where Soyinka chooses the title of his work from the first passage, IROBI finds his in the corresponding passage in *Nwokedi*. Indeed, the very expression, "Nwokedi", an affirmation of masculine strength, is virtually an Igbo translation of "The Strong Breed". Moreover, Eman's reverie of his final encounter with the father is the conceivable immediate predecessor of Nwokedi's reverie of his encounter with Dafinone and the flash back on his experience as a buccaneer.

Again, the rhetorical stance of mediating on drumbeats from the fringe of a trance, and using them as a cue to reveal and comment on the significance of a rite which Nwokedi admires must be a legacy which Irobi inherited from his experience of acting Eleisin in Soyinka's *Death and the Kings Horseman*. Soyinka, for instance, writes as Elesin approaches the moment of sacrifice:

> (They listen to the drums). They have begun to seek out the heart of the king's horse. Soon it will ride in its bolt of raffia with the dog at his feet. Together they will ride on the shoulders of the King's grooms through the pulse centers of the town. They know it is here I shall await them. I have told them. (His eyes appear to cloud. He passes his hand over them as if to clear his sight. He gives a faint smile) (*Death* 40-41)

At the corresponding moment of Nwokedi's own experience, Irobi writes,

> *(The drums are almost at the door steps. Nwokedi drapes the wrappers around his shoulder and with the matchet in his right hand to dance, intoning)* ... They have brought out the mask from the rafters of the shrine. The priest has shown it of root and dirt *(displays)* I have brought out the ancient matchet. It has shaken hands with the whetting stone. The earth is panting like a tired dog. The world is waiting for a new life. The land awaits its spill of blood ... *(The drums are louder. His dance more violent...).* (75)

Yet the younger dramatist's vision (in spite of his apparent admiration of Soyinka's stagecraft) differs so greatly from Soyinka's. While Soyinka is interested in the legend of the sacrificial victim as the

savior, Irobi is fascinated by the myth of the saviour as the execu-
tioner of the guilty. Where then in both *The Strong Breed and Death and
the King's Horseman* Soyinka's protagonists are sacrificial victims, in
Nwokedi Irobi's protagonist wields a sharp knife. Soyinka foregrounds
the modesty of our human nature which inhibits our assumption
of responsibilities for our communities, especially when the penalty
for the expiation of communal guilt is the sacrifice of life itself. Irobi's hero, on the other hand, boasts of having worn out a whetstone
sharpening his matchet. His world is the opposite of the victim's and,
predictably, his enthusiasm mounts where Emman and Elesin found-
er. If, however Irobi finds Soyinka instructive in the interpretation
of ritual symbolism and action, the theatrical basis of his work remains the dramaturgy of Igbo ritual. In this regard, J.N. Amankulor's documentations of the contemporary form of the Ekpe festival
in Umuode-Nsulu in Ngwa Igboland (a people who "have retained
the traditional and original attributes of *ekpe*") (129) are invaluable.

Remarking on the potentials of the Ekpe festival *as dance-drama*,
Amankulor has described it as action packed, full of song and dance.
He comments that the Ekpe itself is the seventh—the culmination
and the climax—in a cycle of activities spanning religious—ritual
year of the people (114). Identifying the three dance movements of
the Ekpe as the vehicles of plot advancement, and recognizing the
second as the climax, Amankulor comments on the role of the chief
actor as a communal representative and provides the myth behind
the ritual of goat decapitation, a potent symbolic gesture meant to
re-enact an ancient sacrifice. "When the actor takes the knife, he
moves round and round the sacrificial goat tied to a peg on the sacrificial spot trying to make a decision. As in all traditional dance-drama and ritual the goings-on in his mind are those of the village. That
he is re-enacting an ancient sacrifice by which the people recall an
adventure by their forbearers during which a human being was sacrificial to appease the gods, is known by all" (122).

Irobi significantly divides *Nwokedi* into Cycles (rather than acts)
and retains the essential structure of the Ekpe as a dance-drama.
The first Cycle begins with villagers chanting *"with festive verve and*

passion" (1); at the outset of the second, "*A parade is going on at a nearby field. From there, a song bursts above the thunder of martial music*" (23); and the initial stage direction at the beginning of the third Cycle is: "*Festive music in the distance*" (51). Singing and dancing go on throughout the entire drama in their colourful and multiple varieties—traditional chants and drumming martial music, the buccarneers' boisterous songs, the light satirical pieces of corps members—only occasionally receding to the background before rising once more to the fore. In Irobi's drama as in traditional festival performances, music is at the centre of communal participation. The metaphor of dance, however, assumes its most ominous dimension as the sacrifice approaches, in Nwokedi's final dialogue with his father and Arikpo:

NWOKEDI: *(dancing)* father, we shall dance again.

NWOKEDI SNR: *(dancing)* Yes, son. We shall dance again.

NWOKEDI: At the festival...

NWOKEDI SNR: *(Still dancing)* Yes, at the festival. *(pause)* But we shall dance in a wider circle.

NWOKEDI: And it will be a wider dance

NWOKEDI: Arikpo, we shall dance again.

ARIKPO: *(pause)* Nwokedi, haven't we danced enough to know each other's dance steps? (85)

Nwokedi's next contact with them is at the moment of their decapitation.

Amankulor identifies the mythical primal sacrifice as a friend of the village who had to be immolated as a demonstration of loyalty to the village deity, *Alumerechi* (123). He discerns intense tragic moments in the entire experience and points to the "strange contradiction of pleasure through pain which is the basic element in tragic pleasure" (116). Amankulor's inclination in fact is to account for the comic elements in the contemporary Ekpe festival experience (seeking to de-emphasize the element of sacrifice and tragedy) in terms of the impact of Christianity (128). The post-sacrifice dance movement known as the *Okoro-Oji* (very probably borrowed from another part of Igboland) is the embodiment of this trend. This movement of self-accusation and pathos, rooted no doubt in guilt consciousness arising from the ancient human sacrifice, re-enacts the drama of the sacrifice just over. Amankulor notes that in the dance movement, the chorus leader intones:

I mere enyi—e [you betrayed a friend]

I mere enyi—e [you betrayed a friend]

To this the group replies:

I mere enyi [you betrayed a friend]

L'enyi mere enyi ya [Behold the friend who betrayed his friend]

I mere enyi (123) [You betrayed a friend]

Translating the songs as "You did a friend/ A friend did a friend" (123), Amankulor comments that "did" stands "for a bad turn meted to that unfortunate victim-friend when the village was confronted with a choice of loyalty. Singing and dancing here assume an ominously suppressed atmosphere" (123). This is an unlikely context to inspire the revival of human sacrifice.

The *Okoro-Oji* is the dance movement missing in *Nwokedi*. The sacrifice of the goat, rather than awakening remorse for the primal human sacrifice becomes indeed only a foreshadowing of the climactic decapitation of Nwokedi Snr. and Arikpo, a two-fold regression to the primordial act, especially as the victims are also bound to the village by blood. It is in the translation of a ritual festival that marks the renewal of life in traditional society to contemporary Nigeria as an agent of purgation that *Nwokedi* seeks function and relevance. Recognizing political corruption as the ailment that threatens the contemporary Nigerian society, Nwokedi and his age grade, the *Ekumeku*, charged with the responsibility of renewing the face of the earth through the ritual sacrifice of a ram, regard the elimination of the corrupt politicians themselves as the proper purgation. If in the past they only participated in the symbolic cleansing of society, they assume in the present the practical responsibility of the immolation of those whose actions pollute the land. Nwokedi's physical brawls with the military at the National Youth Service Corps orientation camp Bakalori, his grim-quarrels with both his father and his brother-in-law, Senator Arikpo, and his eventual beheading of them as representatives of the corrupt political class apparently demonstrate his commitment to revolutionary change.

However, A.B.C. Duruaku has noted that but for the infusion of the ritual idiom, *Nwokedi* would have been mere propaganda (91). He contends that though presented "as a necessarily ruthless crusader rather than a blood thirsty villain" (90), Nwokedi in reality "is a warped personality with a mission that cannot possibly solve anything" (91). Duruaku's conclusion is that Irobi exploits the grey edges of artistic freedom to rekindle the atavism in man, and moreover paints it as glorious, and that by shielding the protagonist's mindless bloodletting by rural faith through a suspect return to traditional values and primeval rites, Irobi, rather than absolving Nwokedi of guilt or diminishing the heinousness of his crime, indeed exalts anarchy and survival of the strongest (92).

Irobi's exploration of Nwokedi's obsession with violence is indeed sustained. Nwokedi threatens to smash his mother's "head against the walls and watch [her] illiterate brains surge out like congeal milk" (68). He threatens his brother-in-law, Arikpo, in similar terms: "Soon, your skull will bounce on the surface of the earth like a coconut blown down by the wind ... and your cunning brains will gush out on the ground like congealed milk" (72). Nwokedi recalls to his father with relish a dream in which he had beheaded the latter instead of the sacrificial ram:

> They brought out the ram. I peered at the ram. I could not see the ram I only saw you there bleating like a ram ... But my knife was already in the air. Its glinting edge descended on your neck. Your head, severed with that single stroke, fell off that way. Your body this way. And, blood! Blood drizzled from your body liker rain. It drizzled on and on until the contour of the earth was covered with a garment of blood. (83)

274 Ethnosensitive Dimensions of African Oral Literature

For this feat, he notes further, his age-grade, the Ekumeku, "came in here, their eyes on fire. The hot-blood roiling in their veins. They came and carried me shoulder high, a symbol of triumph. They bore me like from myth to myth-centre of the village" (83-84).

Irobi dedicates *Nwokedi* to "all the members of the Umuaku Progressive Union/who not only initiated me into the metaphysics /and ecstasies of th*e EKPE* festival/but have also stubbornly sustained a dying Igbo tradition" (iii). *Nwokedi* is apparently Irobi's contribution to the revival and sustenance of the EKPE: "this annual ritual of the Ngwa people; a renewal of their agricultural season, a cosmic prayer for plenty; a cry for change!" (iii). Aware of the intrinsic limitations of all translations, Irobi refers to his translation of the Igbo songs used in *Nwokedi* as "detergent versions" of the original ones which he identifies as "extremely mythical" (*Nwokedi* 94). He adds that the "translations do not in any way render the full meaning, or contrapuntal lyrical power of these songs, so evocative in performance" (94). Consistent with the central ritual idiom of the play, these songs, mainly ritual propitiatory, and war chants serve to evoke an enchanted and heroic atmosphere in which the valiant of heart lived and acted heroically, unencumbered by the taboos of everyday life. Thus, the ritual with its music tends to disguise Nwokedi's lust for blood as heroism. However, the flashback on Nwokedi's cultic activities as an undergraduate foregrounds his thirst for the macabre and the violent. Even among fellow cultists, with a reputation for gangsterism, Nwokedi's murder of Dafinone in what others regard as a game causes consternation and even condemnation. Significantly too, Irobi in a stage direction describes Nwokedi's grimaces as he circles round Arikpo as "cannibalistic" (75) and has the play end at a moment of choric appraisal of ritual human sacrifice as tragic, an image of the apocalypse. The point indeed is that Irobi depicts self-indulgence in uncoordinated incidents of violence as tragic, that is merely cathartic. In the September 2003 *Sunday Vanguard* interview, Irobi had noted: "What is needed is methodical and strategic insurrections. Insurrections aimed at change. Permanent change. What the Irgun Stem gang did in Israel to the British. What the Mau Mau did in Kenya" (49). *Nwokedi* makes its greatest impact read as the tragedy of the overzealous reformer.

In his (1999) *Odenigbo* lecture, "Echi Di Ime: Taa Bu Gboo", Chinua Achebe has drawn attention to the anchorage of the Igbo concept of tragic pride partly in the self-esteem that manifests in the exaltation of excessive physical prowess because the ego desires to subject all to its will. Commenting on two different but related misunderstandings of the character of Okonkwo and his conception of that character in *Things Fall Apart,* (one by an Igbo, the other by a German), Achebe had noted that where the former had assumed that Okonkwo's unmindful adulation of chauvinism and excessive physical strength was the Igbo ideal, the latter considered Okonkwo the representative Igbo man. Achebe remarked that not only did both of them err but that the greatest irony was that Okonkwo too fails to recognise his position in the Igbo scheme of things! Achebe then points to the Igbo ideal as a complex balance of masculine and feminine attributes:

> Okonkwo sili ike, di uchu, an-agba mbo, na-ekwu eziokwu, kpata aku, chie echichi. Fa nine bu ife Igbo kwulu ka ana-eme. Oburo sooso na-okwulu etua, okwulu ya n'onu uda. Okonkwo we nu, wee mebe. Mana onwelu ife ozo Igbo takwunyelu ayi n anti. Osi na ife kwulu, ife akwudebe ya; ayi wenata aka na egbe na mma, ayi akotona oja na ogene na aja-mbene na izu umun-wanyi na ndi obi nlo. Okonkwo anuro ozia ezili na obele onu. Umuofia wee gbakuta ya azu mbosi otijili ukwu minye n'oku. (31)

> [Okonkwo is strong, devoted, hard-working, honest, wealthy, and has taken titles. All these are ideals affirmed by the Igbo. And not only that he affirmed these, he affirmed them clamorously. Okonkwo heard and heeded. But there was another thing that the Igbo whispered into our ears. He said that if something stands, another stands beside it to hold it firm, that we should de-emphasise the gun and the matchet; that we should not despise the flute and the iron gong and cock-and-bull stories and

the frivolity of women's talk and the soft-hearted. Okonkwo did not hear this message delivered in a mellow voice. Umuofia abandoned him the day he broke his waist and dived into the fire. (My translation)

The insight of the Igbo story of the proverbial gazelle which overfed and challenged his Chi to a mortal combat (which by the way, Achebe highlights in *Things Fall Apart)* is worked out in greater length in the folk narrative, "Ojaadili". A matchless wrestler in Igbo folklore, Ojaadili conquers all the earth, human and animal kingdoms alike, and takes his awesome challenge to the land of sprits. There also he is equally victorious. But to be all-triumphant, he accepts the mortal challenge of his Chi with predictable tragic consequences. An archetypal story of the human individual who aspires beyond the sane limits of mortality, Ojadili also illustrates the Igbo belief that tragic pride is consistent with delusion, even with madness. The Igbo cult of individual achievement through adventure or daring is eminently expressed in the concept of the *Ikenga* usually represented in a wood carving. Cardinal Francis Arinze refers to it as "The personification of a man's strength of arm [which] has everything to do with his good fortune. It is a man's 'right hand' that leads him through thick and thin. This sword that *Ikanga* is represented as holding shows intruders what they can expect. *Ikenga* is personal to a man and its symbol is split at the person's funeral" (16). But the veneration of the individual will does not blind the Igbo to the superior divine role of Chi in determining an individual's fortunes. This belief is expressed in the proverb "Onye bute Chi ya uzo, O gbagbuo onwe ya n-oso" (The one who places himself/herself before his/her Chi runs himself/herself to death) and in the common Igbo name "Chibuzo" (Chi precedes). The inversion of the hierarchical Igbo binaries, "Chukwu na-mmadu" (God and humans) and "muo na mmadu" (spirit and humans), sets the limits of human presumptuousness. Irobi's protagonists are significantly variations on this paradigm: gifted but deluded, indeed neurotic characters, contemplating themselves in the divine and invariably over-reaching themselves with tragic consequences. Significantly, accused of madness, Nwokedi's response exalts that state of mind: "The madness of every moment makes history". (*Nwokedi* 29)

• • •

Irobi's next two plays, *The Other Side of the Mask* and *The Fronded Circle* were both published in 1999. The plays, unlike *Nwokedi*, to adapt Brian Macaskil's words, are not staged against any specific Soyinka's anterior hypotext with which they exist in a critical relationship. But all through Soyinka's pattern of exploring the cultural thickets of the Yoruba remains an instructive point of departure. For both plays through different art forms-the former sculpture and the latter ritual music-attempt an illumination of the Igbo traditional mystical life as well as tragic view of life. *The Other Side of the Mask,* very probably Irobi's finest play to date, is a sustained meditation on art, its motivations and delights, its nature and demands, the tribulations and travails as well as the triumphs of the artist. Like *Nwokedi*, a first class graduate of Mass Communication, Irobi's sculptor-protagonist of the *Other Side Of The Mask,* Jamike, is an intellectual, a university lecturer of Fine Arts. Through the elder brother, Kamuche's rapturous recollection of Jamike's exceptional career, Irobi draws attention to his unusual academic brilliance. Irobi's thesis in most of his plays is the inevitable culmination in violence of the frustrated creative energy of even the most gifted individual; Nwokedi, Jamike, and members of the Suicide Squad in *Hangmen Also Die* are, of course, his demonstration pieces: "…when the creative juice is neglected it percolates and ferments. And when it ferments, it evaporates into the vehicle of violence" (*Other Side 61*). Irobi's contention is that this fate is the singular lot of the talented Nigerian youth frustrated by "our contemporary epileptic political situation" (*Nwokedi* 94).

Irobi's many indications of Jamike's neurosis range from the simple and obvious to the oblique and subtle. References are made to his going "to lectures in a pair of shoes with different colours" (*Other Side 12*); to his sleeping "with his key outside, forgotten in

the lock, the door wide open" (13), and to his talking to himself"
"punching the air and slashing the wind ... Muttering wicked im-
precations at some bearded sentinel ... Shouting and screaming
at them ... to give him his laurels" (14). Attention is also drawn
to his vehement self-acclamation as a master (the name, "Jamike"
itself means "Exalt my greatness!") as well as his equation of dedication to art with religious worship and the winning of laurels
with the attainment of salvation. There are also his anguished
flights from ecstasy to suicidal despair. He declares to Professor
Njemanze: "I am a genius. A neglected genius. Look at my work.
Every piece of sculpture here is an ultimate masterpiece" (66).
Yet in the next breath, Jamike is inconsolable: "I am neither a genius nor a great artist. I am neither acclaimed nor accepted. Only
neglected" (67). Yet typically, his hysteria finds an issue yet again
in arrogant self-celebration: "I am the next! The next! The very
next! I am a genius. Everything I touch turns to gold. Everything
I create is an ultimate masterpiece" (67). And then there are outright lunatic ravings such as Jamike's eccentric explanation of his
murder of Dr. Animalu as a gesture towards transcendence:

> I want to transcend life. As an artist, I must transcend life by
> creating life. But if the world will neither let me create life nor
> appreciate it even when I have created life, then I must destroy
> life. To destroy life also makes me transcend life. (55)

It is probably only to be expected, given that most of his central characters are academics, that in attempting to explore the suspected ancient kinship between inspiration and lunacy, Irobi should
make knowledgeable allusions to European art history and artists.
If Jamike suggests that the denial of recognition drives artists mad,
Njemanze explains:

> Artists ... whether poet or painters or sculptors or m-usicians....
> often go mad because they work very close to dream and intu-
> ition and impulse ... That's why they go mad or have mental
> breakdowns more often than other people. Their work is ex-
> tremely hazardous both to the body and the sprit.
>   Remember van Gogh....(89)

Jamike himself is constrained recurrently to appeal to Goya, Picasso, Camus, Nietzsche, Ted Hughes, Carl Jung etc to account for his temperament or his art. Of course, in his self-appraisal as a master artist, he locates himself in the ranks of acclaimed European artists: "Michelangelo. Leonard da Vinci. Van Gogh. Pablo Picasso" (13). Similarly, the contemplation on the role of art in society is rooted in the European tradition. Yet the kinship between genius and madness is an ancient one in Igbo thought and both are indeed in the domain of the same deity, *Agwu*.

As the repository of all arcane and esoteric knowledge, Agwu is associated with divination and inspiration; but as Agwu is equally linked with lunacy and aberrant behaviour, lunatics, deviants, heretics are considered to be under the influence of this deity. Regarded also as a primary cause of misfortunes, Agwu apparently is central in the Igbo conception of tragedy. If Irobi does not refer to this deity, he makes constant knowledgeable but oblique allusions to the influence. Considered rascally and mischievous, Agwu, like Ekwensu, the spirit of evil, is an interfering spirit force capable of frustrating the fulfillment of human ambitions. Jamike's anguished consternation at the source of the relentless futility that haunts his life is Irobi's poignant allusion to the malevolent forces capable of interfering with human destiny.

> Why is it that every work I carve becomes a knife that laughs into the flesh of my life. Every song I sing becomes an arrow that turns back in flight to find the eternal target of my heart. What unforgivable evil is it I chose a chisel as the instrument with which I will reshape the face of the world and leave it more beautiful than I found it? (*Other Side* 53)

The Other Side of the Mask offers a profound interpretation of Igbo traditional conceptions of the relationship between the plastic arts, religion and the mystical life, between art and society; it also attempts to account for the travails of the artist by attempting to illuminate the mystical source of inspiration.

Irobi conceives of Jamike as the embodiment of the Igbo conception of the visionary artist as a priest and prophet[2]. Thus he necessarily also inherits the sacred responsibility of tending the family realm. "An artist is a vortex of the forces and vibrations swirling all around his world. He digests life at both an empirical and metaphysical level"(49). His devotion to his calling is absolute and is hallowed with religious zeal. He fasts for days to carve Ziphora, his muse and the incarnation of the obsessive, single-minded artistic spirit, explains: "When he has fasted for about three days, without food and water mind you, his reflexes become sharper. His intuition deeper. His consciousness more visceral and his vision more urgent … yes, that is when his spirit takes flight and soars above the mundane. Beyond the profane, into the profound, the sublime, into the realms of the sacred" *(Other Side 11)*. Jamike himself locates his essential aspiration as an artist in the spiritual: "I am interested in the formation of souls. I am interested in the creation of a new world. I believe I am a spirit, my father's spirit, that is why I carve out of a spiritual reserve" (76). Jamike's account to Professor Njemanze of his travails in his painstaking gestures towards perfection indicates that his aspiration is clearly the attainment of the ideal forms:

> O Prof.; if I could tell you what it costs the body and the mind to wade the swamp towards the anus of the Sea just to scoop the clay for the moulding of these master-pieces. (*hysterically*) if only I could tell you what the skin endures as my palms and fingers delve into the clayey soil to redeem from the worms what belongs to man. If I could show you the blisters from the shells of the periwinkle, the conch, the hermit crab, the oyster, the mudskipper and the electric fish as I defy the crocodile to harvest from the earth what belongs, to me. Prof., if I could present to you once again the tribulations of the true artist. (*Other Side* 63)

Jamike is perhaps justifiably mortified that such devotion fails to win him recognition and laurels. But then Irobi also draws attention to the distinction between the self-image and the reality, between self-torture and sacrifice. Moreover, he aims to reaffirm the ancient insight that a mortal's claims to the grandeur of the go-ahead are not only invariably tragic delusions but are often also indicative of lunacy. He, however, brings to this theme a peculiarly Igbo perspective.

Jamike's god, Amadioha, the Igbo god of thunder and lightning, epitomizes divine inscrutability. Writing on this thunder-throwing god of the sky usually invoked as a deity of justice, Cardinal Arinze notes:

> The spirit of thunder has widespread influence in Igboland and has such different local names as *Igwe*, *Kamalu* and *Ofufe*. Those struck by thunder are not mourned, a most serious censure among the social Ibos. Such people are believed to have received the just reward of their atrocities. The corpse is not carried into the house and sacrifices must be offered at the fatal spot. The most notorious thing about *Amadioha* is his grim policy of seizing all the possessions of its victim. (16)

N.S.S. Iwe concurs, noting that Amadioha "is regarded in Igboland as a divinity of vengeance against the wicked and evildoers. Victims of *Amadioha* are as a rule not given a normal burial, and their possessions, especially movable property and personal effects, are either ritually alienated or publicly cast away as refuse. Some call *Amadioha* "God's Minister of Justice" (14). As Amadioha may, however, be invoked by only the morally upright, caution and painstaking introspection are sine qua non in the worship of the god since even delusions of innocence invariably prove fatal. Given the chasm between the limitations of the mortal condition and the disincarnate purity of the divine, the invocation of Amadioha remains danger-fraught. Pointing to this in his review of Isidore Diala's *The Pyre*, a play in which Amadioha is an abiding presence, Afam Ebeogu observes: "In Igbo cosmology, anyone who is a victim of Amadioha's flaming thunder must have committed some form of abomination which must have attracted the wrath of this deity of contradictions who is adored but also dreaded by its worshipers; the most ardent worshiper of Amadioha could offend the god even by the very act of a blissful adoration" (1).

Represented in *The Other Side of the Mask* as "a small carving made of wood and copper" (20) with a "grisly face" (77) carved by Jamike's father as in *Nwokedi* where Nwokedi Snr. makes his political associates take an oath on "an evil-looking juju effigy" (1) *of Amadioha*, Amadioha is invoked in Irobi's drama as the god of justice. Kamuche, who is reassured of Jamike's sanity on discovering that Jamike still tends the god, notes: "The god of justice. Amdioha! If solicited it can send thunder and lightning to one's enemies" (*Other Side* 20). Of Amadioha Jamike himself notes that "It settles disputes and dispenses justice" through lightning (78). Expectedly, this is the god Jamike invokes to mediate between him and the judges who for six years deny him the National Award for Sculpture. He tells Njemanze:

> Prof., I mentioned your name, the names of the other judges and my own name before the incantations. So if I am wrong in my assertions about the quality of my works, I will die tonight. But if I am right, if the judges have used my genitals as a rope to tie me to the tether of failure, the judges will die tonight. Including you Prof! (80)

Although Jamike acknowledges that being under possession he could not affirm with any certainly if he mentioned Njemanze's name before the god, he remarks nonetheless that the state of possession is the most likely for a deep-seated grievance to find expression in. That Jamike dies on the night in question and in his dying breath identifies himself as a victim of Amadioha would seem to indicate that he is wrong and the judges right. But then the self-indulgent Marxist, Dr. Animalu, dies the same night even if Jamike is behind the Amadioha mask that murders him. Jamike notes significantly that the black and yellow mask also carved by his father is for "tending Amadioha and doing his will" (18). Again, that Jamike wins a major international award where he has failed for six years to win the National Award for Sculpture seems to vindicate his claims to greatness and allegations of foul play on the part of the judges. Yet, significantly, Njemanze acknowledges as a masterpiece the award-winning sculpture Jamike enters for the international competition. Irobi presumably through these paradoxes reaffirms the enigmatic, inscrutable nature traditionally ascribed to Amadioha. Yet *The Other Side of the Mask* actually enlarges and modifies the traditional Amadioha myth.

If the acclaim won by European master artists constitutes Jamike's measure of greatness in the artistic vocation, the Igbo veneration of the artist of religious artifacts is his paradigm of the artist's ultimate possible relevance to society: "a time there was when a sculptor had his place in society. When he was venerated. When he moulded the images of the god of his clan. When he, a mere artist, held captive, for one whole year, the garment of wood for the naked spirit of the festival of life. When he stood out among his fellow men and was revered" (*Other Side* 84). By the creation of a god, the artist presumably transcends the limitations of the mortal condition. Irobi also alludes to the distinction of the master artist's special privilege to participate in the highest form of art as sacrifice in Igboland: the creation of *Mbari* houses. Writing on this distinctive form of sacrifice among the Igbo, Cardinal Arinze notes: "These are peculiar buildings set up to avert an imminent disaster from an angry spirit … A dibia (diviner) is consulted. The elders make plans and communal labour is employed. Special people are selected and these dedicate about a year to the building. They live together under strict laws. Famous artists are invited. The *Mbari* house when finished looks like a place of worship. It is dedicated, but after this, the aim is achieved and it is totally neglected and allowed to go to rack and ruin" (87). Yet hounded persistently by the full terrors of an evil fate, (and unlike Demoke in Soyinka's *A Dance of the Forest*, protégé of a protective deity), avatar of an enigmatic god whom he is to hold responsible for his death, Jamike is to apprehend self-immolation itself as both the perfection of his artistic vocation and the final sacrifice. But if suicide is to the person with a bad Chi the ultimate temptation, holding the promise of a radical re-negotiation of destiny, among the Igbo it is indeed the ultimate abomination, irredeemably tragic. When the Igbo say that instead of accepting a situation, they would rather hang, the aim is not to delineate suicide as a viable opinion: it is to evoke it as the unthinkable horror.

The intensity of the ending of *The Other Side of the Mask* arises in part from the fact that Jamike's dual but related roles as priest and artist coalesce and that resolutions coincide. The expectation of Amadioha's verdict, of the outcome of the international art competition, and of the resolution of the firm battle between Elesie (and her promise of a normal life of conviviality) and Ziphora, all on the night of the ritual propitiatory sacrifice to Amadioha in which Jamike's role is again central: all these stretch the anxieties of the audience to the fullest. The point is that in the process Irobi recreates the myth and the god, annexing the roles of Ala (the patroness of the arts) and *Ahiajoku* (the god of fertility) in Igbo cosmology.

In the tradition of Soyinka's interpretation of the Ogun myth, Irobi's inscriptions of the paradoxes of the Amadioha myth set in relief not only the god's destructive fury but also his creativity. Indeed, he brings the arts into the domain of the god. Jamike calls him "the god of carvers" (*Other Side* 77) and indentifies him further as "The god that sends lightning to kill the evil spirits who inhabit the trees from which carvers hew their wood" (77). In a state of possession at the approach of the moment of sacrifice, Jamike, moreover, apprehends the god as a fecundating deity: "it is sunset, and the arena has been swept by the feet of spirits and dancers. Tonight a god must stomp the earth until it is soft like the mud the carver uses to mould his mounds. Yes, the god will stomp the red earth until it bleeds like the throat of a murdered man…" (*Other Side* 82). Mircea Eliade points out that the bull and the thunderbolt were as early as 2400 BC symbols connected with gods of the sky and weather (87). Commenting on the appearance of the Iranian deity, Vrthraghana, to Zarathustra as a bull, a stallion, a ram, a he-goat and a boar, Eliade cites Benveniste-Renou to indicate that these were all symbols of the male and combative spirit and of the elementary forces of the blood (86). The association in Igbo cosmology between Amadioha and the ram is two-fold. Himself imagined as a white man, Amadioha's proper and preferred offering is also a ram. Yet, typically, Irobi's ideal sacrificial victim is a man. Jamike envisions human sacrifice, where the blood of the immolated victim moistens the creation clay of the artist and is also food for him.

> This night, dancing must invade the arena. This night the god
> must dance. He must dance in the center of the circle. (*Lyrically*
> *reminiscing*) yes, silently the village will form a circle for there
> is a magic in circles. (*Pause*) In the center, there will be a man,
> bound hand and feet. The edge of the glinting blade will know

the strength of the flesh! After, his blood will be mingled with the earth and the clay and the yam for the tonsured sculptors. At midnight their hands weighted by the sacred clay, they will sneak into the Mbari hut to mould images in honour of *Ala*: Mother earth. (83)

Yet in Irobi's universe, Ala, the earth goddess, feminine, benign, and attaching the highest premium to the sanctity of human life, cannot be the supreme deity. For a writer committed to violent revolution and the destruction of the (politically) guilty, the myth of Amadioha is indeed a divine boon. The point, however, is that by annexing the realms of other Igbo deities to arrogate supremacy to Amadioha, Irobi engages in a radical re-creation of Igbo cosmology. Noting the historical challenge to the supremacy of the earth goddess, Ala, by the establishment in Umunoha (in present Imo State of Nigeria) of a sky divinity, *Igwe ka ala*, Echeruo comments:

> Igwe ka ala was quite simply not only a devilish sect but a he-retical one. Its very name was daring—a consciously daring—challenge to the supreme deity of the Igbo people. This cult placed *Igwe* above *Ala*, and claimed him as supreme. To propose that was in itself an abomination, that is to say, a defilement of the earth, *imeru ala*. In short, Umunneora and *Igwe ka ala* must be seen in the history of our institutions as a phenomenon which came closest to setting up a god cult above that of *Ala* herself, the ultimate sanction to morals. (19–20)

The artist is, of course not obliged to subscribe to his people's world-view. But for an artist apparently devoted to the resuscitation of folk ways, the boundaries between ascertainable cultural values and icon-oclastic artistic projections should be clearly marked, especially for a people some of whose institutions are mired in a crisis of identity.

• • •

Wole Soyinka's attestation to the validity of the Yoruba worl-dview in *Death and the King's Horseman* receives a special boost in the character of Olunde. If Iyaloja and Praise singer elect for the sustenance and continuity of the only world they know, Olunde consciously chooses that world fully aware of other traditions.

Trained as a medical student to valorize the scientific outlook, he demonstrates nonetheless the authenticity of a mythical worldview; brought up to preserve life, he sacrifices his for the spiritual well being of his community. His experience of Europe and the European value system, rather than causing him to reject his cultural background, serves the primary function of leading him to appreciate the greatness of his own Yoruba culture. Irobi makes similar use of the academic background of his major characters. Nwokedi and Jamike are not illiterate tribesmen with an uncritical allegiance towards tradition. On the contrary, the exposure to Western education clarifies and strengthens each protagonist's appreciation of the significance of ritual and tradition. To Professor Njemanze's claim that Amadioha is a disembodied god-head towards whom his appropriate attitude as an intellectual can only be scepticism, Jamike responds that Amadioha is a virile, potent god who defies intellectuality. By signs and wonders he awakens in Njemanze holy terror. At the heart of the solemnity of divination, in the hands of the true *dibia* an efficacious ritual capable of connecting with the spirit world, the Igbo discern intense drama. All the special effects, costuming, chalk marks on (left) eyebrow, ankle bells ringing, dramatic behaviour, esoteric incantations, when not contributory to the realization of the mystical experience but aimed instead to impress and compel the client/audience to experience awe are referred to as *anwanse*, a show, spectacle. Irobi's Jamike is a true practitioner both of the mysticism of divination and of its dramaturgy. Similarly by his anecdote about four educated young men who abandon at their mortal peril the family god, *Osisiogu*, handed over to them by their illiterate father, Jamike seeks to demonstrate the efficacy of traditional religious ritual. In *The Fronded Circle*, through the character of Dr. Gilbert Onwutuebe, Irobi contends that the educated African's inexcusable alienation from the tradition of his people amounts to *ngahe ukwu*, "a tragic misstep".

If Nwokedi and Jamike even in their failures and in spite of their excesses still retain a measure of the affection of the audience, the reason is that both aspire to worthwhile human ideals,

one an egalitarian society, the other human acclaim, each, moreover, is great though flawed. The Igbo saying. "O mewere ma Chi
ekweghi, onye uta atana ya" (One whose aspiration is frustrated by
his Chi hardly deserves any blame) though it certainly encourages
no presumption beyond the limits of humankind clearly excludes
sympathy for aspirations that are contrast to the value of society.
In *The Fronded Circle*, Onwutuebe's dread of death and futile gestures towards immortality, just like Onwudinulo's acquisitiveness
fall into this latter category. Almost as old as humankind as these
themes may be however, and common as they are, in the literatures of diverse people and generations, the ritual idiom through
which Irobi explores these are rooted in Igbo traditional beliefs.
Okwu's revelation to Uka in the expository scene is the working of
the ritual through which Onwutuebe attempts to insulate himself
against death: "...A man buries his head as a protective charm
against death. It is a powerful medicine. It lets the man swop his
age (sic) life with the lives of other men especially ... his kith and
kin" (*Fronded* 3) Nwannediya's account of the uncanny circumstances of the drowning of her youngest son, Ndubuisi, and the
even more mysterious disappearances of his four elder brothers
reaffirms Okwu's view: "four of them disappear when their father
is ill. Whenever he is on his sick bed they disappear. He calls them
to his bed and later they disappear" (14). Anguished, archetypal mother of bereavement and sorrows, Nwannediya, referred to
several times simply as "mother" or "mother of men" and also lik-
ened to the bereaved and inconsolable Rachael of the Bible, loses
five sons, has a daughter, Kelechi, in the pangs of childbirth who
cannot bring forth her baby (boy) unless Onwutuebe breathes his
last, and is equally on the brink of losing another young man, Gilbert, who used to call her mother. She is thus uniquely placed to
articulate the course of the natural cycle and the cultural norms
that Onwutuebe violates.

> Our people say ... when a man has made his will ... after a man
> has shared out his farms among his wives and his yams among
> his sons ... after a man has boasted his life and has seen the

end of his road … if Death refuses to come, the man goes out in search of Death … But Onwutuebe will not! (*The drums as if in sympathy, pound somberly*) Our people say … when a vain and wanton moon dances out late into arena of the sky, it shines its brightest before the twilight hour and then disappears just to rid her face of shame. But Onwutuebe has no shame. *(The drums punctuate her painful singsong).* (15)

With an eye on the family inheritance, Onwudinulo, by secretly un-earthing the pot of charms which has to be neutralized to release Onwutuebe's spirit from his disintegrating body, exploits Gilbert's ignorance and lures him to his death on the *Ese* drum.

Irobi's fascination with drum language, masking and the state of possession, which they induce, is consistent with his abiding interest in the idiom of religious ritual. Andrew Hom contends that a fundamental disparity between ritual and drama lies in the conception and status of the "actor" in both performances: "In ritual the actor is seen either as a representative (a priest) or as another being entirely (a spirit) … As a medium, he is presumed to become another entity, to cease entirely being himself. Whatever the degree of his dissociation, whatever the depth or duration of his trance, he is perceived by the audience, if not always by himself, as the spirit incarnate" (96–7). Irobi's protagonists attain the state of possession through drumming, dancing and masking. As the moment of sacrifice approaches and the drums rent the air, Nwokedi, gradually entranced, becomes even more confrontational towards his father. The stage direction and the dialogue that follows immediately after account for this in terms of the influence of the drums.

[*They face each other, poised in fear and murderous anger. The drums are progressively louder and thunderous. Nwokedi is in the throes of a trance possession*]

ARIKPO: What is wrong with him?

NWOKEDI SNR: It is the drums.

ARIKPO: The drums?

NWOKEDI SNR: Yes, the drums. They get into the head. In my youth, I used to do what he will do this evening on behalf of the entire village. (*Nwokedi* 79)

In *The Other Side of the Mask*, the suggestion of the differences between the identities of the protagonist and the masker is even more dramatically realized. Jamike masked and Jamike unmasked are different beings: the former mentioned Njemanze's name before Amadioha, the later did not.

Jamike: (*as he puts off the mask*) Prof., I never mentioned your name. I was only joking

Njemanze: Thank you.

Jamike: (*he puts on the mask*) Prof, I did. I mentioned your name. And the god heard your name.

Njemanze: Jamike, why? Why?

Jamike: (*he removes the mask, smiles*) Anyway, I did not.

Njemanze: Thank you.

Jamike: (*the mask in front of him*) Prof., to be candid, I cannot remember if I mentioned your name or not. You know I was possessed. And under possession, grievances borne in the mind often leap out of the sub-conscious like tadpoles in a boiling pond. (80–81)

If, however, there is at least some measure of consistency between Jamike's and Nwokedi's convictions in their sober moments and in their states of possession, in *The Fronded Circle*, at the peak of his experience of possession, Gilbert ceases completely to be himself and assumes the identity of Onwutuebe, confessing the latter's crimes with fatal consequences for both: "I tied up my head. I hid it in a pot and buried it in my yam barn. I sacrificed my five sons in exchange for my life" (*Fronded 72*). Entranced, and oblivious of Onwutuebe's repeatedly shouted warnings he draws attention to consanguinity as the mortal link but remains blind to the implications of his words:

The tiger is a feline. The lion is a feline. The hyena is nothing but a forest dog. The monkey is an ape like the gorilla. The little chick becomes the hen, and the puppy the bitch. It is the same string and the same blood. The same umbilical cord and same womb. It is the same Erim. Onwutuebe we are one. (*Fronded* 68–69)

Married to a black American medical doctor, and with a doctorate in musicology, Gilbert retains only a scholarly ethnographic interest in his indigenous culture. This is treated as the tragic arrogance that seals his fate as Onwudinulo indicates. "He is an outsider. A total outsider. He lived in America for twenty years. He knows no tradition and no customs. He understands no proverbs. He cannot interpret the message of the drums" (*Fronded* 50). Later, with Gilbert already in a state of trance, Onwudinulo highlights the comparative shallowness of Gilbert's great Western knowledge, considering the moment of his self-estrangement from his roots the symbolic moment of his death. "When a man wanders away from his roots he becomes a ghost. The blind bat that flies into a witch's pot has sealed its fate. The tortoise carries a world of wisdom in its shell yet it does not know how to climb a tree. Afonne Onwutuebe, the crab may wade the mighty ocean but it ends up in the soup pot of a woman". (65)

The *ese* drum is described as "an old, weather beaten short form drum disfigured with dirty eggshells and age" (*Fronded 61*). Danced to only by the accomplished who in the process declare their achievements to the acclamation of the audience, the *ese* music is death to the desecrating feet of the unaccomplished. The dialogue between Nwannediya and Diegwu (when the latter and Onwudinulo seek to use Nwannediya to lure Gilbert to the dance) clearly indicates this:

Diegwu. We just want to dance.

Nwannediya: Dance? Don't you know what it means when a man steps on that male Ese drum to say what he never achieved.

Diegwu. You don't understand. He will be saying it for his elder brother—Onwutuebe.

Nwannediya: Does it matter who he says it for. What matters is that as far as he has stepped on that drum, as unaccomplished as he is, he is doomed to die. (*Fronded* 51).

Writing on this funeral performance among the Igbo, Helen Chukwuma enunciates its dramaturgy:

> The audience assembles in the front compound space of the deceased's house. They are seated in two blocks at one end forming a semicircle with the assembly. The drummers start the music and the actors, four men dance out into the centre of the semicircle towards the drummers. Music ceases and the first actor steps forward and salutes the audience. He addressed first, the audience on the right, and then the audience on the left. (317)

Remarking that the audience on the right is greeted as "humans" and that on the left as "spirits", and that the latter unlike the former do not respond to the greeting, Chukwuma notes that ceremony is not a tribute to the living and the dead but equally "rehearses the meaning and significance of death" (317). In this solemn convocation of humans and spirits, the accomplished are presumably folk-heroes exorcising the fear of death in a symbolic ritual dance which reclaims life as an experience of value by *staging* human achievements. Society thus revivifies its values by ritually foregrounding its privileged cultural accomplishments in the face and in defiance of death.

Consequently, by denigrating his people as "superstitious" and their rituals as "primitive" (52), Gilbert breaks a taboo that has to do with life and death by dancing to the *ese*: in symbolic terms, he too is like the proverbial gazelle challenging his Chi to a mortal battle. In both Ọnwụtuebe and Gilbert, Ọnwụdinulọ identifies self-destructive and tragic arrogance. "Our people say, when a drum sounds too loud we tell it what wood it is made of, we tell who carved it, what implements were used, we also tell the drum what its end will be, whether it will rot away or blaze to embers in an inferno of flames" (71). (Interestingly, a variant of the proverb substitutes a "proud god" for a "loud drum"!)

In his trance, Gilbert envisions the natural regenerative cycle:

> The seed is the seedling, the seedling is the plant. The plant
> is the tree, the tree is its branches. Its branches are its leaves
> and its leaves bear the flowers, the flowers bear the fruits, the
> fruits ripen and fall. They fall and become seeds, the seeds
> grow into seedlings and seedlings into trees. This is the spiral
> of life. This is the cycle of life. This is the journey of our soul;
> the road from life to death and from death to life again. This
> is the mystery of the world—It is the rhythm of our souls.
> (*Fronded* 69)

But his tabooed self-exclusion from his roots and consequent self-el-
evation above his people and the mores he enunciates make him a
threat to that cycle. Gilbert approaches a ritual of transition as a
"mock-funeral" dance, that is as drama, while Irobi aims to re-create
ritual in its primordial religious state. Thus words become incantatory and re-establish their kinship with magic and gestures, charged
with the deepest conceivable consequence, become primal forces.
Therefore, if the splitting of the Ikenga is symbolic of the death of its
owner, its fall from Gilbert's hand coincides with his and Ownutue-
be's death. The point is that underlying Irobi's appropriation of traditional Igbo rituals as drama is an obvious attempt at a validation
of folk ways and the religious truths of rituals. That the schemes of
Onwutuebe on the one hand and those of Onwudinulo and Diegwu
his collaborator on the other are frustrated, is therefore, also only to
be expected, their actions are aberrations of societal norms. But if
the three illustrate the self-defeating processes of the abuse of ritual,
Gilbert's own experience equally reveals the grim dangers of treating
rituals as inefficacious.

However, given that Irobi's central preoccupation has been
with the ritual expiation of communal guilt for the regeneration
of society, the Gilbert/Onwutuebe ritual passage is also presented
in part as propitiatory. By the act of the Gilbert/Onwutuebe con-
fession paid for with life itself, the curse of an era is expiated and
the future made possible. Thus in the wake of the deaths, that future embodied in Kelechi's baby is born: the stage direction reads:

"*Suddenly a baby's cry pierces the tragic air*"*(Fronded 72)*. Irobi's abiding theme is the role of ritual in the rebirth of society.

• • •

Appraising the dramatic potentials of the Ekpe festival in 1981, Amankulor had enthused:

> From the drama—theatre development point of view, *Ekpe* contains the same germs which housed the plays of Aeschylus, Sophocles and Euripides. What remains to raise it to the Aeschylean level of drama is a reconstruction of its dialogue to provide for greater communication between the chorus and the chief actor. The idea of the chorus is present in *Ekpe* and it does the same function of communal representation. (127)

Similarly, commenting on the fourth ceremony of the Ekpe cycle, *Ogbom,* Amankulor notes its possession of basic dramatic elements—good music, song, dancing, gorgeous costuming, mimetic action—but remarks that "*Ogbom* has not passed through the transition necessary for it to become drama because dialogue and word sequence remain merely repetitive and unelevated beyond the sphere of traditional ritual" (114). Amankulor appreciates the fact that, given cultural distinctions, the evolution of ritual into drama among the Igbo may well have to differ from the Greek model but proclaims the enormous dramatic potentials of religion and ritual though they had been originally designed to solve practical problems by initiating a state of rapport between the creator and the created. The Ekpe is especially dear in this regard to Amankulor's heart: "Through its media of song and dance, great drama could be forged" (128). A decade after in 1991, *Nwokedi* was published.

Esiaba Irobi, like Amankulor himself, from Ngwa in Igboland[3], in writing *Nwokedi* demonstrates his apprehension of the dramatic potentials of Ekpe as dance-drama as well as its dramatic limits. The traditional festival was an inspiration to him not only in terms of structure and dramaturgy but also in characterization and costuming. Writing on the *ufo*-bearer in the Ekpe festival, Amankulor notes: "The *Ufo*-bearer carries a magical concoction belived to destroy the power of charms. He guards against any foul deeds or intentions by any member of the audience. His costume consists of tattered rags and he smears his body with charcoal. A real devil-incarnate!" (126). Irobi's character, Ufo-bearer, in *Nwokedi* is virtually indistinguishable: *"He is smeared all over with charcoal. In his hands is a smoking pot"* (38). But working also in full awareness of the dramatic traditions of the West in which dialogue rather than incidental speech is crucial to the theatrical experience, Irobi creates new roles for the Ufo-bearer beyond mere provision of splendid spectacle by giving him a pivotal role in the scheme of the enunciation of the symbolism and significance of ritual action. Keeping an appropriately open creative relationship with the Western dramatic tradition as in his creation of an evocative and poetic, if occasionally bombastic, dialogue in the worldview it projects and the dramaturgy it advances, Irobi's drama nonetheless contests the European hegemonic.

Conclusion

In a recent passionate defence of Echeruo's postulations on Igbo ritual, Ogbonna Agu contends that in privileging Western dramatic paradigms, Echeruo disregards a strong call for a culture-authenticating status for African drama and advocates instead a culturally dynamic attitude towards myth as a source for drama. Highlighting the implication of Echeruo's proposition for contemporary Igbo drama, Agu indeed illuminates Irobi's imaginative procedures:

> It means, therefore, that in adopting it as a method of obtaining materials, creative thinkers and artists can use it to develop new myths based on their own peculiar circumstances. It may even be possible for these writers to reinterpret the cosmological outlook of the people, expand it, and give it a historical or secular base. (5)

Irobi clearly exemplifies this trend. His plays do not dramatise specific changeless myths subsumed in Igbo ritual, and alleged finished artistic product in its own right. His inclination is rather to appropriate Igbo rural ritual as basic source material for enunciating a secular vision of contemporary society, as Echeruo would suggest.

Recreating in terms of contemporary experience situations in which ritual had cogency, and treating myths as malleable narratives capable of authorizing an ideological position, his attempt at the expansion of Igbo ritual into contemporary (Nigerian) life are significantly marked by a deep belief in the religious efficacy of ritual. Irobi's theatre is still a house of faith in which the ceremony of drama does not only provide spectacle and entertainment but is also aimed at resolving practical problems in society: an ideological resolution of the political impasse that has characterized the post-colonial state. Thus, the bond between the sacred and the secular is still very strong. Thus the state direction that dwells on Jamike's invocation of Amadioha in *The Other Side of Mask* reveals on the part of the playwright himself dread before the sacred:

> He roots out an egg from a corner, swings it round his head seven times, and over the wooden effigy. Dons his former mask and begins to mutter incantations which the playwright cannot put down here for fear of the repercussions of sacrilege (sic). (78)

In *The Fronded Circle*, also, Reverend Akwarandu and his congregation are mocked and their prayers prove ineffectual before Onwutuebe's spell. Irobi ascribes primacy as well as supremacy to ritual over institutionalized or at any rate the self-delusions to spiritual power of a later day Christian sect. Irobi's work of the preponderant appropriation and validation of ritual exists in a polemical opposition to the authorized European worldview. Yet, remarkably, Irobi strives to sustain the traditional ritual purity and dread associated with the invocation of the gods and even incantations sacred to them while *daring* to recreate the deities themselves as well as the cosmological framework that guaranteed faith in their worship. In reality, he cultivates and harnesses the ancient potency ascribed to ritual to authenticate a new secular vision. His expansion of ritual into life and giving of a secular base to that life is indeed marked by an iconoclastic projection of traditional Igbo paradigms to facilitate secular projects.

Irobi is obsessed by the possibility of the regeneration of a society laboring under the burden of guilt. The actions of *Nwokedi, The Other Side of a Mask and The Fronded Circle* typically, therefore, take place at a moment of transition, December 31. Like Soyinka, Irobi envisages a pattern of ritual purgation of communal guilt for the rebirth of society which demands suffering and sacrifice. If Soyinka, however, exalts the ideal of martyrdom, Irobi is preoccupied with the efficacy of ritual human sacrifice for the atonement of communal guilt. In transforming ritual into drama, he retains its full religious associations but naturally subjects his material to a pattern of interpretation that suits his temperament and his aesthetic convictions. Yet in the changed circumstances of Nigerian life, Irobi's passionate espousal of the political relevance of ritual sacrifice would seem increasingly atavistic and criminalized even when the victim is guilty except, of course, when appropriately accepted as *symbolic* thinking. The attempt to seek the origins of and possibly justification for (revolutionary) violence in primordial ritual human sacrifice and ancient myths about the gods can hardly avoid implication in mystification. His true achievement consists in his reclamation of a much maligned African heritage as an emblematic motif. He moreover, like Soyinka, takes us back to the origins of drama in ritual.

Tracing the origin of Greek tragedy to the rituals that marked the Dionysian festival, Luyster dwells in detail on the rites performed by the female worshipers of the deity, the Maenads and remarks: "Finally, at the height of their frenzy, the maenads converged upon a calf or kid, tearing it apart bare-handed and devouring the raw flesh. It was whispered that in the days gone by the victims had been human" (44). Indicating though that Dionysos was paradoxically both the slayer and the slain in the ritual, Luyster discerns in the god's experience of being rejected and despised "the paradigm of all tragic history", explaining that this "is the stuff of which Greek tragedy came to be compounded: the inevitable suffering and death of a noble being in the interests of a greater life" (48). In his recent study of tragedy, Eagleton equally inscribes the idea of suffering at the heart of the tragic experience:

> Where tragedy is concerned, the question of universality cannot be side-stepped by a glib particularism. In one sense, to be sure, all tragedies are specific: there are tragedies of particular

peoples and genders, of nations and social groups … And none
of these experiences is abstractly exchangeable with the others.
They have no shared essence, other than the fact of suffering.
But suffering is a mighty powerful language to share in common, one in which many diverse life-forms can strike up a dialogue. It is a communality of meaning. (xvi)

Yet it is conceivable that the cultural symbols through which we attempt to express this experience could enhance or diminish the urgency of its meaning to varying audiences. In identifying the culturally representative Sango, Lear and Oedipus prototypes of the tragic
experience, Soyinka inscribes that vale of soul-making as a veritable
human thoroughfare. Irobi advances this project.

Irobi's interaction with Soyinka is invariably an appropriation
of a formulation rooted in a specific African culture, the Yoruba, in
terms of his innovative interpretation of his own Igbo background.
He leads us through the enchanted atmosphere of Igbo cosmology
(which he occasionally recreates) to illuminate an authentic vision
of tragedy which, inevitably accounting for typically *human* suffering
and greatness, in essentials often reaffirms other known paradigms.
His work enhances with particular urgency our apprehension of the
often tragic gulf to be negotiated and transversed in the complex dialectic between the individual's will and ambition, on the one hand,
and the mysterious disposition of Chi on the other. Irobi's innovativeness is equally magnificently emonstrated in his making the dramaturgy of traditional Igbo performances the basis of his drama.

Notes

1. It is equally illustrated in an Igbo myth of the origin of death. Offered
the opportunity by *Chukwu Okike*, God the creator, to choose between immortality and mortality, humans had, of course, chosen the former, and
sent two emissaries to God, one with the message of life and the other with
that of death. But the dog, the human messenger for life, so-self-conceited
with his swiftness and physical strength, especially in comparison to the
tortoise, the messenger for death, merely fiddled on the way, hoping to out-
run the tortoise in the final lap of the race to God. He, however, overslept
and the tortoise got to God first with the message that humans had chosen

death which God granted.

A variant of the story has it that the tortoise places his relations on strategic positions on the route, with the result that in spite of the dog's swiftness, a tortoise was always ahead. At any rate, both versions censure the dog's (the human representative's) delusions that led him to believe that in the mother of all races all that was needed was physical prowess and skill.

2. The Nigerian poet of Igbo extraction, Christopher Okigbo, in a 1965 interview with Majority Whitelaw noted about his art:

I am believed to be a reincarnation of my maternal grandfather, who used to be in the priest of the shrine called Ajam, where the Idoto, the river goddess, is worshiped. This goddess is the earth mother, and also the mother of the whole family. My grandfather was the priest of this shrine, and when I was born I was believed to be his reincarnation, that is, I should carry on his duties. And although someone else had to perform his functions, this other person was only, as it were, a regent. And in 1958, when I started taking poetry seriously, it was as though I had felt a sudden call to begin performing my full functions as the chief priest of Idoto (qtd. in Anozie 42)

3. Esiaba Irobi was Amankulor's student at the university of Nigeria, Nsuka, and dedicates *The Fronded Circle* to him: "Whose heavier footsteps/ stamped out a shining, pathway/ into the sacred arena / within the fronded circle / where bow-legged drums / dirge softly; THE MUSIC / OF THE DEAD" (iii)

Works Cited

Achebe, Chinua, *Echi Di Ime: Taa Bu Gboo* (1999 Odenigbo Lecture). Owerri: Catholic Archdiocese of Owerri, 1999. Print.

—. *Home and Exile.* Oxford: Oxford University Press, 2000. Print.

Agu, Ogonna Anagudo. "Echeruo's 'The Dramatic Limits...' and the Search for Igbo Dramaturgy". *Abalabala* 2 (2003). 1–12. Print.

Amankulor, J.N. "Ekpe Festival as Religious Ritual and Dance Drama. " *Drama and Theatre in Nigeria.* Ed. Yemi Ogunbiyi. Lagos: Nigeria Magazine, 1981. 113–129. Print.

Anozie, Sunday O. *Christopher Okigbo: Creative Rhetoric:* Ibadan: Evans, 1992. Print.

Arinze, Francis A. *Sacrifice in Ibo Religion.* Ibadan: Ibadan University Press, 1970. Print.

Azuonye, Nnorom. "My E-conversation with Esiaba Irobi". *Sunday Vanguard* 21 Sept, 2003. 49. Print.

Chukwuma, Helen. *Igbo Oral Literature: Theory and Tradition.* Abak: Belpot, 1994. Print.

Duruaku, Toni. "The Limits of Artistic Freedom: Esiaba Irobi's *Nwokedi*". *Okike An African Journal of New Writing* 34 (1996). 86–93. Print.

Eagleton, Terry. *Sweet Violence: The Idea of the Tragic:* Oxford: Blackwell, 2003. Print.

Ebeogu, Afam. "Isidore Diala's *The Pyre:* A Review". Unpublished Rev. of *The Pyre.* By Isidore Diala. Print.

Echeruo, M.J.C. *Ahamefule: A Matter of Identity* (1979 *Ahiajoku* Lecture). Owerri: Ministry of Information and Culture, 1979. Print.

—. "The Dramatic Limits of Igbo Ritual". *Research in African Literatures.* 4: 1(1973). 21–31. Rpt. *Drama and Theatre in Nigeria.* Ed. Yemu Ogunbiyi. Lagos: Nigeria Magazine, 1981. 139–148. Print.

—. "Religion, Imperialism and the Question of World Order". *Religion in a World of Change: African Ancestral Religion, Islam and Christianity.* Ed. T.I. Okere. Owerri: Assumpta Press, 2003. 14–25. Print.

Eliade, Mircea. *Patterns in Comparative Religion.* Trans. Rosemary Sheed. London: Sheed and Ward, 1993. Print.

Enekwe, Ossie. "Myth, Ritual and Drama in Igboland". *Drama and Theatre in Nigeria.* Ed. Yemi Ogunbiyi. Lagos: Nigeria Magazine, 1981. 149–163. Print.

Eni-Jones, Umuko. "Ritual in Performance: A Stage Director's Interpretation of Soyinka's *Death and the King's Horseman*". *Enyo: Journal of African Theatre and Drama* 1.1 (2000). 1–18. Print.

Ezenwa, Ohaeto. "The Cultural Imperative in Modern Nigerian Drama: A Consolidation in the Plays of Saro-Wiwa, Nwabueze, and Irobi". *Neohelicon* 20.2. (1994). 207–220. Print.

Horn, Andrew: "Ritual, Drama and the Theatrical. The Case of Bori Spirit Mediumship". *Drama and Theatre in Nigeria.* Ed. Yemi Ogunbiyi. Lagos: Nigeria magazine, 1981. 181–202. Print.

Hullkrantz, Ake, "Ritual in Native American Religions. "*Native Religious Tradition.* Ed. E.H. Wlish and K. Printhipaul. Waterloo: Laurier UP, 1979. 24–38. Print.

Irobi, Esiaba. *Gold, Frankincense and Myrrh.* Enugu: Abic, 1989. Print.

—. *The Fronded Circle.* Enugu: Abic, 1999. Print.

—. *Hangmen Also Die*. Enugu: Abic, 1989. Print.

—. Interview: "Irobi Chats with Nengi Ilagha: Call the University a Ministry of Certificates". *Newslink* May 1989: 11–12. Print.

—. *Nwokedi*. Enugu: Abic, 1991. Print.

—. *The Other Side of the Mask*. Enugu: Abic, 1999. Print.

Iwe, S.S.S. "Igbo Deities". *The Igbo Concept of the Sacred: Papers Presented at the 1988 Ahiajoku Lecture (Onugaotu) Colloquium*. Ed. G.M. Umezurike et al. Owerri: Misnitry of Information and Culture, 1989. 1–22. Print.

Luyster, Robert. "Dionysos: The Masks of Madness". *Parabola* 20.4 (1995). 43–48.

Obiechina, Emmanuel. "Literature—Traditional and Modern—in the Nsukka Environment". *The Nsuka Environment*. Ed. G.E.K. Ofomata. Enugu: Fourth Dimension, 1978. 5–38: Rpt. As "Nsukka: Literature in an African Environment". *Language and Theme: Essays on African Literature*. Emmanuel N. Obiechina. Washington: Howard UP, 1990. 182–206. Print.

Obumselu, Ben. "The Background of Modern African Literature". *Ibadan* 22 (1966). 46–59. Print.

Soyinka, Wole. *Death and the King's Horseman*. London: Methuen, 1975. Print.

—. *Myth, Literature and the African World*. Cambridge: Cambridge UP, 1976. Print.

—. *Three Short Plays:* Ibadan: Ibadan University Press, 1980. Print.

Williams, Adebayo. "Ritual and the Political Unconscious: The Case of *Death and the King's Horseman*". *Research in African Literatures* 24.1 (1993): 67–79. Print.

Chapter Thirteen

A Type of Popular Secular Theatre:
The Dramaturgy and Rhetoric of Oral Advertisement
of Medical Products in Nigeria"

Afam Ebeogu

INTRODUCTION

Contemporary scholarship in oral literature studies has been full of
surprises, not the least the pleasant realization that there are forms
of literature which we live and experience every day at virtually no
cost. This realization always compels us to want to revisit established
notions about the discipline of literature, and modern scholars in
the field have had to modify the ancient notions of the subject as
necessarily a written verbal art, so as to accommodate the apparently ambiguous phenomenon of a literature that is "oral" because
"unwritten" (see Lord 1–24 and Finnegan 77–95). This expansion of
the scope of the literary discipline has brought with it new challenges
in definitions: expressions which have become popular in the face of
the new frontiers in the literary scholarship have had to attract the
urgency of definitive restatements.

While some departments of Language and Literature in the universities are satisfied with enlarging the scope of their programme
to accommodate "Oral Literature", some scholars would want this
apparently fertile area of vigorous research wrenched out of the domain of the traditional Department of Literature, and properly instituted within the framework of a burgeoning Folklore scholarship, or
what has became fashionably known as folkloristics, especially in the
United States. This appropriation of "Oral Literature" by "Folklore"
is manifestly reflected in the twenty one definitions of "Folklore" in

the *Standard Dictionary of Folklore, Mythology and Legend. (Leach 398–403)*. Virtually all of these definitions incorporate the unwritten verbal art, as is represented in the brief definition by Jonas Balys:

> Folklore comprises traditional creations of peoples, primitive and civilized. These are achieved by using sounds and words in metric form and prose and include also folk beliefs or superstitions, customs and performances, dances and plays. (Leach 398)

The insistence that oral literature includes both ancient and modern forms of lore is an understandable emphasis, against the background whereby there had been an earlier tendency, as clearly shown in Alan Dundes's book, *The Study of Folklore*, to associate that field of scholarship with an antiquarian sensitivity. Whereas W.J. Thoms, who originated the term *folklore* in 1846, associated the folk with an illiterate peasantry, the contemporary scholar of that field, like Marion Bowman, would insist that "we are all folk". It is necessary to quote her in full:

> It is not now necessary to locate some decrepit, rural, materially-deprived, preferably illiterate ... peasant who has never been tainted by the media or travelled outside his/her community to find the stuff of folklore. City bankers circulate legends about computer fraud; a graduate wears a St Anne medal to discos to help her find a prospective husband; scientific research staffs worry about a hunted lab; nurses know not to put red and white flowers together in a hospital ward. Folklore is all round us, whoever and whatever we are, and we all folk. (quoted in Bennet 10)

It is on this spirit of "we are all folk" that this chapter is based. If we use the expression "Folk Literature" and "Oral Literature" interchangeably, it is because we want to associate the scholarship with all the trappings of modernity it deserves. We share Bowman's view that "folklore is all around us, whoever and whatever were are". No phenomenon can illustrate this point better than the performance of oral advertisement of medical products in Nigeria's buses and motor stations. This literary phenomenon, motivated primarily by commerce, is both rhetorical and dramatic, and it is the intention of this essay to examine these aspects of this form of literature which is recreated every moment in many places in Nigeria. The data for the study is based not only on the many recordings which we have managed to make in buses in recent years, but perhaps more importantly on the very close observation and alertness with which we have monitored this phenomenon of the strategy of oral advertisement of drugs in Nigeria's cities and buses. Because the recordings were made in moving vehicles, more "folkishly" known as "luxurious buses" in Nigeria, it has been quite problematic transcribing some of the tapes, due to poor audibility. However, we found one of the tapes fairly reliable in terms of audibility,and this recording provides the texts which we have used to illustrate the rhetoric of this performance. For the discussion of the dramaturgy of this genre, we can do no better than to rely on our recollections of the on-the-spot critical observation of one of such performances in a motor station in Onitsha. The alternative would have been to use video equipment, which facility we did not have, and even if we had, it would not have been available at that auspicious moment of performance.

ORAL ADVERTISEMENT OF MEDICAL PRODUCTS IN NIGERIA:
A BRIEF SOCIO-ECONOMIC BACKGROUND

Oral advertisement of medical products in Nigeria emerged as a result of colonial contact, and subsequently became a phenomenon in certain parts of Nigeria, especially the urban centres where the development of extensive commercial activity led to the growth of large markets. (See Ukwu and Hodder 1969). Onitsha is such a place and as Emmanuel Obiechina has observed in relation to the growth of the chapbook tradition in this sprawling city,

> Onitsha was the Educational and Commercial centre of the eastern Region of Nigeria. Its importance depended very much on its favourable natural locations. Situated on the left bank of the River Niger ... it is thus well-suited for trade between the areas lying to the east and the west and, because the Niger is navigable north and south, with places up and down the River.

The early European missionaries and traders, realizing the strategic position of the town, made it their first base of operation … From the late nineteenth century, Onitsha became an
important trading missionary centre…. The existence of the
Onitsha Main Market which dissects the town…. [made it] the
commercial hub of Eastern Nigeria. Its market remained for a
long time a sprawling bazaar where people could purchase virtually everything from a "pleasure" car to the teeth of an adder.
In the late 1940s it was re-structured and given a new look. It
became one of the most splendid of its kind in West Africa, if
not in whole Africa. (4–8)

Among the items of trade for which Onitsha has remained known
are medical products of all sorts. Large areas of its multi-localized
markets are associated with medicines of various brands, and the
mode of trading in these incorporates both the exclusively wholesale pattern, the combination of the wholesale and the retail, the
exclusively retail operations and the ubiquitous hawking tradition.
The products are not only imported from all parts of the world and
through the many multinational drug companies in Nigeria, but are
also manufactured in Onitsha and its suburbs. It is generally believed
in Nigeria that if any type of medicine is not available anywhere in
Onitsha, then it is not likely to be found anywhere in the country. A
perverse corollary to this fact is that one cannot always rely on the
currency and genuineness of medical products bought in Onitsha,
especially from the retailers and hawkers.

Because of the rate at which new medical products invade the
Onitsha market, and the novel claims of efficacy often attributable
to some of them, the traders have never lacked sufficient patronisers,
and one often hears Onitsha traders comment that dealers in medical products form a significant percentage of the very wealthy class
of people which the Onitsha market has produced. No amount of
Government legislation has been able to control the activities of the
quacks among these traders, especially because medical treatment in
Nigeria's hospitals, whether public or private, has remained quite expensive, and the dealers and their agents who have permeated even

the remotest of villages, find easy patronage from the unenlightened rich, the enlightened poor, and the unenlightened poor who are easily the most vulnerable of the customers. Over the years, these traders have perfected strategies of oral advertisement with which they persuade their customers into reluctant or willing patronage.[1] In the 1950s and 1960s, as witnessed by this writer as a teenager and adolescent respectively, the dominant strategy was the itinerant use of gramophone records and a couple of highly professionally competent dancers by means of which crowds of prospective buyers were attracted. This strategy has persevered even in modern times, though it is now somewhat less pervasive. But other complementary strategies have emerged, the most current being advertisement in luxury buses that ply between major urban centres in the country. The rest of this essay will examine the dramaturgy and rhetorics of the strategy of medical product advertisement, as studied by the writer, using two differing contexts for analysis. The first context is a scene witnessed on Saturday, 24 February, 1991, in one of Onitsha's motor stations, and the second is a tape-recorded rhetorical performance by a "transcity" itinerant advertiser in a luxury bus travelling from Onitsha, in the eastern part of Nigeria, to Jos in the north, on 3rd June, 1990.

THE ORAL ADVERTISEMENT OF MEDICAL PRODUCTS: A DRAMATURGICAL PERSPECTIVE.

That there is an easily perceived theatrical technique which the oral advertisers of medicines use to attract their audience, from whom they ultimately draw their customers, is not in doubt. We use the word theatre, not in its purist conventional sense of an institutionalized locality for elaborate and carefully stylized dramatic presentation, but in a more general sense. This is articulated appropriately By Bakery Traore when he says:

> We know that among the ancient Greeks, the word "theatre" not only signified the building where entrainments were presented, but every place that is common to actor and spectators. (55)

This vision of the theatre accommodates certain impromptu performances which, by their nature, are not divisible into scenes, nor do they necessarily have a narrative framework. These performances are no doubt mimetic in the sense of "representation of action", but they would not qualify as "conventional theatre", especially modelled after Aristotelian canons of drama. Indeed, they are more in consonance with the concept of the "popular theatre", described by Yemi Ogunbiyi in the following words:

> The term [popular theatre] is used in the finest tradition of a genuinely popular theatre where all that a living popular performance needs is, not necessarily a text or an elaborate stage, but rather, a place, a time, and audience and himself. (11)

The audience of the theatre of the oral advertisers of medicines is very impromptu. Practically all the audience are men, women, children, idlers, busy-people, the educated and illiterate, who are compelled by curiosity to abandon what they are doing by the sheer strategy of advertising which the performers have employed. This is a "folk audience" not only in the sense of their coming from one locality and being associated with a number of activities which, in one way of the other, have spatial affinity with the place of the theatrical performance, but also because there is a bond of "brotherhood" common to them and built around a magic wand of curiosity that impels then to recognize a point of common interest—an emotional pull to which they all subscribe. The actors themselves are practical psychologists who, over the years, have taken time to study and understand their audience, and have therefore come to possess more than an instinctive knowledge of what to do in order to build an immediate audience. They may not have attended any formal classes in advertising, but they are intelligent and experienced enough to recognize that all creative advertising must do more than merely inform and entertain ... It must change or reinforce and attitude or behavior. (Wright 10)

On the day of the particular theatrical event under study, I had taken my wife to the Onitsha market to do some shopping. Then, for reasons of safety, I had parked in one of the motors stations, where lorries to and from the northern part of the country load and unload. It was around eleven in the morning, and I had reclined in the car, determined to keep myself busy with a novel while waiting for the end of my wife's shopping. Then noises that indicated some mild commotion permeated my concentration, and I raised my head to behold a gathering crowd a short distance away. As I watched, the crowd increased, and I noticed that some small-time traders were abandoning their wares to join the crowd. Instinctively, I grabbed my tape recorder, got out of the car and joined the spectators. Then I was able to witness the entertaining spectacle at first hand.

The crowd had formed a ring around somebody who, at first sight, appeared like a lady. But one did not have to look for too long to realize that the character was physically too masculine to be a woman, in spite of the fact that the face was effeminately handsome enough to look like a woman's, and that he was costumed in trendy long skirts and blouse. But the biceps were too muscular for a woman's; his unisexual sandals were too large, the hair was undisguisedly a wig-wig's are obviously out of fashion for the contemporary Nigerian woman—and, even though the face was very handsomely cut, the eyes did not look effeminate, in spite of the heavy eye-shadow. The lipstick he was wearing, however, was expertly applied, and when he spoke, the voice, a smooth and well-practiced falsetto, was moderately effeminate. When he walked, his gait and steps were admirably ladylike, and he carried his rather long hands in such a way that the long, varnished nails would show prominently. I realized immediately that the figure before us was that of a young man who was, however, quite familiar with the strategies of female make-up. Even then it did not take most other members of the audience long to realize that the figure before them was that of a man disguised as a woman.

As his performance progressed, I realized that he was already known by some of the spectators as a man. The character was therefore not so great a novelty as such, and he was ultimately under no illusion that the audience mistook him for a lady. In many ways he reminded one of a Brechtian character. His was not a costuming

meant to convince; it was a comic disguise. His falsetto was not intended to be the voice of a lady; it was a deliberate pretension not
aimed at perfect deception. This became obvious even in his miming
and mimetic acts. He seemed to be saying to the audience: "I am
only pretending to be a woman, and I am aware you know it. On
that score we are agreed, and therefore nobody is deceiving anybody.
I am here to entertain you, and in the process coerce you into patronizing me". His theatricals were therefore reminiscent of a theatre
for a purpose—a functional type of theatre in which acting is mere
pretence and in which, in the same breath as one is entertained,
one is being pressurized not to absorb any notions of a dramatic
illusion demanding a willing suspension of disbelief. The essence of
his disguise and acting was to attract an audience and to keep that
audience long enough to buy what, ultimately, he was selling. And
what he was selling, contained in a plastic basket before him, was a
particular kind of medical product.

This actor in an unelevated, open-air stage, completely sur-
rounded by spectators who, however, kept a respectable distance
between them and their entertainer, had at his command a limitless repository of miming and mimetic intrigues. He would, ladylike, exhibit a number of masterful dance-steps to which he sang
gramophone numbers extracted from current and trendy LPs. He
would occasionally stop, move to a spectator, and whisper audibly
and coquettishly some sweet nothings that set the audience roaring
with laughter. He spoke in English most of the time, even though the
grammar was far from being standard. For example he approached
me, placed his hand on my shoulder and said in coquettish falsetto,
"Hello darling, I like your dress. You are the kind (of) person I like
to move with. What say you to a tete-a-tete at the Metro? It is a nice
hotel you know; no nonsense women there. Decent darling, and I no
cost much money.[2] Just a bottle of *Udeku*[3], and a little naira and then
back for ground"[4]. To this the spectators responded with thunderous
laughter. The actor moved away from me without even waiting for a
reply, after blowing a loud kiss. He immediately moved on to another
person. He had a masterful way of getting the audience involved in

the performance. In no time he had gathered a crowd which he obviously considered adequate, and then proceeded to the main business of the day.

He produced from his basket a tiny bottle which he raised for the audience to see. It contained some liquid substance with heavy sedimentation. He walked round the circle of spectators, displaying the bottler for proper view. Then he said in the lady's voice:[5]

> Ladies and gentlemen, you may wonder why a lady of my repute is exposing herself to the full glare of the market-place, in order to sell some medicine. In reality I have not come to sell but to advertise. This thing in my hand is the product of New Wonders International Pharmaceuticals Limited, based in Geneva, but with a branch at No. 12 Port Harcourt Road Onitsha. I am the Confidential Secretary to the branch managing Director. The Company had intended to announce the arrival of this wonderful new product, called Afro-skin Wonders, on the television, radio and newspapers. We will still do that. But out of respect for the enterprising people of Onitsha, the company decided to first of all introduce the product to you by personal contact, and the fact that they decided to send a lady "of a no mean caliber" like myself is a testimony of the great love and respect which the company has for this great commercial city.

> This great medicine is for all kinds of skin disease, from eczema, acne, skin rashes to pimples. Its ability to cure is instant, and I will demonstrate this fact soon. When the manufacturers were manufacturing it, they had the black skin in mind. You see, the black person has very tough skin, and most of these medicated creams which the white man manufactures—Ambi, Dorot, Clear Tone, Nature Essence, Collagen Elastin, Shirley, Simba, Esoterica, and so on and so on—are all meant for the white skin. My company, realizing this, decided to manufacture something unique for the black skin. What did they do? Can anybody here guess what they did? (The audience shouted a loud "No!"). You cannot. Well my company went into deep meditation, consulted the divinities of the land, asked questions from traditional herbalists, and then went into the black

forests. When they came out of the forests, they came out with a particular kind of root. Ladies and gentlemen I will not waste your time in 'procrastinated talk'. This medicine in my hand is called Afro-skin Wonders, and it is produced from that particular herbal root. It is manufactured by our home branch in Geneva under the best hygienic circumstances, and its cure is instant. To show you that its cure is instant, I want a volunteer from the crowd, somebody who has some skin problem, like pimples. Any volunteers?

The crowd was hesitant; nobody volunteered. The actor said, very coquettishly: "Come on loves, do not embarrass a lady. Any volunteers?". Still there was none. Then the actor moved to a lad standing nearer him, perhaps no more that twelve years old, and gently dragged him to the centre of the stage, saying, "Come on bob[6]. It will do you no harm". He shook the tiny bottle and opened it. Then, using one of his long finger nails he cut open a small pimple on the boy's forehead. He applied a little of the liquid on the cut, and asked the spectators to watch attentively. The waiting was not for more than three minutes, but it seemed like ages. Then something happened. I noticed some whitish substance coming out from the opened pimple; a chemical action of some sort was obviously in progress. Then, with deft movements one would associate with a surgeon, the actor used his nail to scrape the substance off the boy's forehead. The actor asked softly, "Do you feel any pains?". The boy shook his head. The actor straightened up with deliberateness and began to walk the boy round, showing the spectators how the cream had apparently dug into the boy's skin to extract the offending pimple. After the round, the actor went back to the basket, turned to the spectators, and said:

A bottle of Afro-skin Wonders will cost just three naira on the counter. Compare it with the price of any of these skin creams imported from all over the world. The quantity I have here is for promotion sales only, and I will give each to you at one naira; that is the benefit of buying straight from a company's Managing Director's Secretary.

At first there was little hesitation from the audience. Then somebody asked for two bottles, and paid two naira for them. Then the rush began, and within ten minutes or so, the actor had sold out all the bottles in the basket. It was difficult to guess how many they were: perhaps up to a hundred. After the sales, the actor did something quite unexpected: he began to undress in full view of the spectators, some of who had begun to go away. First went the wig, revealing a young man with a Tyson haircut. He brought out a comb and a mirror from a handbag, and tidied up his hair. Then he pulled off the blouse, revealing a yellow American sleeveless polo singlet underneath. The next to go was the long skirt, revealing rolled-up trousers which he proceeded to straighten with deliberateness . After that he turned to the face make-up, and in no time the lipstick and the eye-shadow were gone. Then, with studied patience, he began to pack his things methodically. The last thing to disappear from view was the bundle of naira notes which he arranged neatly and put into an underpants pocket. Then he straightened up, turned to the remaining members of the audience and said, still in his false lady's voice: "Bye-bye for now, my dearies". He picked up his basket and handbag and began to walk away, waving at the audience. One or two voices called out, "Ayoola", and the disappearing actor replied, "Yeah guy, business, men". His voice was no longer falsetto. On inquiry, I learnt that he was fairly-well-known in Onitsha as an oral advertiser of medicines, and that Ayola was his alias.

An examination of the above spectacle reveals a number of significant issues. It is clear that Ayoola, the popular actor who uses his theatrical craft in order to persuade an audience to buy his medical products, does not pretend to be a woman. His make-up is not designed to mask his identity; rather he dresses as a woman in order to achieve a comic effect, which is buttressed by his deliberately acting like a woman while in performance. The comic performance is aimed at a functional purpose: that of attracting an audience, and then persuading that audience to buy. His most effective theatricality is acquired not in any training school but through innate intelligence and repeated performance. It is the Brechtian strategy of destroying dramatic illusion through the agency of mock-illusion: he does not want the audience to believe that he is true, and that a great deal of what he says is true, but his acting and whatever he is saying need to be "accepted" by the audience on the understanding that they are not necessarily accepting a "truth". There is therefore a tacit conspiracy between the actor and the audience, and this conspiracy is revealed even in the long speech which he uses to persuade the audience. For example, he makes several exaggerated claims: that "she" is the Confidential Secretary to the Managing Director of a company with a name that is somewhat suspect; that the company has an international scope of organization; the medical cream, skeptically named Afro-Skin Wonders, is the product of the genius of African herbalism and the best skin cream amongst a host of others which "she" proceeds to list with unquestionable familiarity; "she" sells the medical cream to the audience at a promotional price that is one third of the expected counter price.

It is doubtful if any member of the audience would believe many of the above claims. And yet the same audience proceeded to buy the product, perhaps even if vaguely aware that it might be fake! It is true that the actor has visually illustrated how effective the cream could be, but one wonders if the audience would not be skeptical of a medical product, and a skin cream at that, that is an instant cure. In a different but similar spectacle, a spectator observed that most of these advertisers plant their own people amongst the audience from where such people either volunteer or are "persuaded" to be used for illustrating the instant efficacy of the medicine being advertised. If this is so, it would be further evidence of the Brechtian vision characteristic of this form of popular theatre in which a member of an impromptu audience is transformed immediately into an actor of sorts. It is indeed possible that most of the members of the audience, and potential patronisers of the advertiser, do not, in their heart of hearts, believe in the efficacy of the medicine, but are courteously paying for their thirty minutes or so of entertainment. Perhaps they would not mind very much doing so considering that the "charge" for the performance, which is the price of product, is quite moderate. It is instructive that the prices at which these advertisers sell their judiciously chosen medicines are always moderate.

Lastly, one notes the methodical and deliberate manner in which the actor disrobes after the performance right there in the presence of the audience. It is a most effective method of destroying Aristotelian dramatic illusion. It is made clear to the audience that they had been "deceived", and this revelation does not daunt them. The actor is merely being faithful to the terms of the tacit agreement between him and his audience, and he would not leave the scene without destroying whatever illusions may have remained over the reality of his person and role!

ORAL ADVERTISEMENT OF MEDICAL PRODUCTS: A RHETORICAL PERSPECTIVE

From an open-air context of the performance of the oral advertisement of medicines we move on to that which takes place in buses, known as "luxurious buses", that ply between Nigerian cities. The majority of the owners of luxury buses in the country happen to come from the Igbo ethnic group. This arose perhaps because the earliest transport magnates in the country were Igbo, and their success tended to attract many other Igbo businessmen to the enterprise. Many of these businessmen are based in Onitsha, with the result that though all Igbo and other Nigerian cities have stations and substations for buses, Onitsha has gained the reputation of being the headquarters of the luxury bus business in Nigeria.

Most modern oral advertisers of medicines have seen in the phenomenon of transportation by luxury buses an opportunity for quick turnover sales. By special arrangement with the driver, an advertiser boards a bus bound out of the city, with his wares properly packed in an expensive-looking briefcase. For about one hour of the journey, usually between the city of departure and the next station or substation where there is bound to be a brief stop, the advertiser hawks his medical products to the passengers in the bus. He is most likely to alight at this substation, wait and board another luxury bus returning from any of the Nigerian cities to the headquarters, which is usually, but not always, Onitsha. The practice has assumed such a regular dimension that one can always be sure of encountering one or two such oral advertisements during any major journey by luxury bus. I therefore developed the habit of travelling by such buses whenever I had the need to make a long distance journey in Nigeria. The usual strategy is to choose a seat somewhere about the middle of the bus, preferably by the aisle, with a tape recorder ready. Since an advertiser tends to occupy a position in the aisle about the middle of the bus, the possibility of one being near enough to him for a tolerably clear recording has always been high. The recording made on June 3 1990, part of which is reproduced here, was made in such circumstances as described above.

On that occasion, I traveled by car to Enugu, where I boarded a Jos-bound luxury bus which had started off at Onitsha. The bus obviously had not loaded fully at Onitsha, and so had to stop for some time, as is the usual practice, at the Enugu Ninth Mile corner in order to load fully. When that was done, and just as the bus was about to set off for the long journey to Jos, an advertiser, carrying the usual executive briefcase, leapt into the bus and staggered to the centre of the aisle. After the bus had gathered speed, the advertiser, speaking in Igbo, began to attract the attention of the passengers and to announce that he had an important message for them, but somebody from the back of the bus shouted at him to the effect that he did not understand the Igbo language. Consequently, the advertiser apologized, and switched over to what turned out to be fluent but largely ungrammatical English, punctuated by occasional code-switching involving pidgin English and Igbo, the latter often employed in the form of proverbs, idiomatic witticisms and ideophones. For purposes of easy communication, however, I have chosen to produce the text in fairly Standard English translations, retaining as much as possible the advertiser's own diction.

The advertiser, a young man probably below thirty, first of all started off with a Christian prayer, which he prefaced with a comment to the effect that every traveler by "motor" was solely in the hands of God who alone was "the Almighty Driver who knows not what an accident is". After the prayer he proceeded in a declamatory tone, reminiscent of a church sermoner:

> Ladies and gentlemen, some of you are, I am sure, baffled by the way I prayed. You may be wondering: who is this man who prays like the Bishop of Rome? (Giggles from the audience; the performer clears his throat dramatically). The fact is that though I am not a bishop, I received the proper training that could have made me a bishop if I had continued in the profession. You see, I was to be a reverend gentleman. I attended the Juniorate Seminary at Awomamma.[7] Does anybody know it? (pauses for an answer). You do, you are nodding. Thank you very much: it shows that you are a good Christian. Christ will remember you in the day of paradise (Giggles from audience). After my education at the Juniorate Seminary I proceeded to Ikot Ekpene for my training in "Episcopal Philosophy". At the end of that training I decided to complete my studies as a reverend gentleman in Germany. Unfortunately, when I got to Germany, I defected. (He makes a sign of the cross as if asking for forgiveness). I will not tell you the details of the story, because it pains my heart to think of it. When a church has invested a lot on you so that you can become a priest, it is sinful to decamp from the call. (he makes another sign of the cross). However, I prayed very hard about it, and I know that I have been forgiven. Consequent upon that experience, I decided that I would spend the rest of my life in the service of "the rest human beings". A German Professor of medicine immediately recognized the great talent in me, and offered me a place in the German School of Pharmaceutical Medicine for a study in Pharmacology. I won three German scholarships for the purpose, one from the German Government, another from the German College of Theological Medicine and a third from the German Institute of Advanced Medical Research. I then did my studies at the German School of Pharmaceutical Medicine in the University of Munich, and qualified as a professor of Pharmacology. After that I was employed by a German company which specializes in the manufacture of drugs.

Now, some of you may have guessed who I am. I am no other than Professor Brandt, spelt B–R–A–N–D–T, John Nduka, alias Omeile,[8] the Special Representative of Veksam Medical Complex Limited, a German pharmaceutical company known all over the world for the "most efficacious medicines". My company has just come out with its latest "medical release", which is "an antibiotic of no mean caliber" (He stops, bends down, clicks open his brief case, and brings out a packet of capsules. From the packet he extracts a card, and walks up and down the aisle in order to display the bluish substance). But there is something I want you to realize before I tell you about this wonderful medicine.

You are all travelers, and every traveler is a target of gastrofungal infection, by which I mean a disease that destroys the intestinal tissues, causing wear and tear to the abdominal walls of the stomach. Why do I say so? Because as you travel from one place to another, you buy this and that. (mimicks voice of hawker): "Buy banana, buy banana" (Mimicks the voice of passenger): "Hello banana-seller, come here. How much?" You buy banana, (then mimes ideophonically the act of eating as the banana is rushed down the stomach) (again mimicks the voice of a hawker) "Buy groundnut, buy groundnuts!" (Mimicks the voice of the passenger)" Groundnut, come here! (mimes ideophonically the act eating groundnuts). And the groundnut is rushed down the stomach. In this way you buy and eat everything that a hawker carries about. Rotten biscuits, iwwu[9] (demonstrates the speed with which the food moves down the alimentary canal). Decayed bread, iwuu[10], boiled eggs, iwuu, fried snails, iwuu, roast chicken, iwuu, akara[11] iwuu, moimoi,[12] iwuu, bush meat, iwuu, domestic meat, iwuu, everything, iwuu. Nor is the passenger satisfied with all these. When the bus breaks the journey at any popular stop, you all rush to the hotels. (mimicks voices of passengers in hotels): "Madam,[13] give me this; madam, give me that. I want coke, I want beer, I want garri, I want rice. Madam, this water is dirty, change it". And you rush everything into your stomach as if there will be no other opportunity for you to eat another day. All the hurry because you do not want the bus to leave you behind. "Po poo o, zoo" (mimics the sounding of the horn by the bus driver, and the setting off of the bus), and the journey is resumed.

You know the human system is a machine. Your intestines wait a bit to allow you relax in your position, and then the music begins. (Demonstrates the noise from the stomach as the digestive system goes to work). It is the grinding of all that have been "masticulated" that is in progress. (Demonstrates again). You have given the "machine of your digestive system" a task, and so the commotion goes on. The Igbo say that he who brings ant-ridden firewood to his house invites a dance of the lizards. Before the bus has covered ten kilometers, air bubbles begin to issue from your anus like air leaking from the valve of a tubless tyre. (Mimics the "sighing" sound of a leaking tyre. Prolonged laughter from the passengers). And you shout, "Driver, stop. I have stomach upset; I want to ease myself. Driver stop". Eziokwu[14], "You want to ease yourself" (repeats with mock English intonation). But when you were putting all those *ngwodongwo*[15], into your stomach, you did not realize that you were getting yourself into trouble.

Well, you cannot stop passengers from behaving the way they do. But you can save yourself from gastrofungal infection and other germicidal disease which you have caused yourself. That is where this medicine which I am holding comes into the picture. It is called Epiclomycin. It is the latest invention by Veksam Medical Complex Limited. I know that there are many types of antibiotics in the market, like Tetracycline, Penicillin, Ampicillin, Ampiclox, Terramycin, Septrin, Cocomycin, Metamycin, Yoyomycin, Luxurymycin, and so on and so forth. (general laughter from the passengers). But this invention by my company, Epiclomycin, is the winner. Just take one capsule in the morning before you set out on your journey, provided that you have eaten properly. Take it with a lot of water. Let me warn again, you must eat "pro-per- what?" Properly. And you must drink plenty of water. Only one capsule in the morning, and that will deal with all the *nta nta na ngwo ngwo*[16] which you will eat on your way. When you get home, take another capsule after food, with plenty of water. That will deal severely with whatever stubborn germ that is still "a refugee in your belly" (general laughter from the audience).

Now, how much does the medicine cost? In any medicine store, this costs ten naira per card of ten; in the market, you may get it at eight naira. But for me, just bring five naira. This is because this is promotional sale. There you are; you have your choice. I carried a curative to your house so to say; if you choose to ignore me and die in silence, that is you business. After all, according to the Bible, the Jews asked God for a Messiah, but when He sent Christ to them they killed him (Prolonged laughter). Now, who wants to buy? Going, going _____[17] Do not waste time because I will get out at *Obolo-Afo*.

A passenger asked for a card. It was as if that was all the rest were waiting for. Hands shot into the air, requesting cards of the capsule, and in about ten minutes the advertisers stock of "Epiclomycin" was exhausted. Then he announced that he had other "latest" medical products to introduce to the passengers.

A close examination of the performance of this advertiser gives an insight into his strategy of persuasion. One of these is the proper and non-proper names which he uses. Some of the names, like Awomamma and Ikot Ekpene, are real place names, and the Roman Catholic clerical institutions he attributes to them do exist in these places. His choice of such names would seem to be a deliberate attempt to give some degree of legitimacy to his otherwise fantastic claims. But he seems not really to be attempting to convince the audience that he attended such institutions, because some of the other names which he attributes to himself are obviously fabricated. When he calls himself "Professor", he would not expect to be taken seriously, especially since his first name, "Brandt", is quite exotic and may well have been an obvious attempt to "Germanise" his identity; after all, he claims to have been educated in Germany, and has chosen questionable but seemingly reputable names as belonging to the institutions which he attended there. His Igbo name, "Nduka", translates as "Life is Superior" and may have been deliberately chosen in order to associate his name with his profession as a dealer in medicines with which life is saved. This argument is strengthened by the fact that his alias is "Omeile", which means "That which is Efficacious". Our investigation reveals that the root name of the German pharmaceutical company for which he claims to work, Veksam Medical Complex Limited, also suggests this image of efficacy which he is trying to construct around himself. It is not unlikely that "Veksam", which seems to me the nearest orthographic representation of the word uttered by the advertiser, is the same as the German "Wirksam", which could translate as "very effective". This advertiser may have thus come across the word, or a medical firm that answers that name, in the course of his searching through medical literature, or his interaction with colleagues in the business world of medicine. It would therefore appear as if our advertiser has cultivated a habit of serious homework in the course of his hawking business.[18]

This impression is strengthened by his obvious "mastery" of the medical register. He uses some medical expressions with ease, and even though some of such expressions may have been fabricated by him, he has taken care to make them fall into the morphological pattern of the non-fabricated medical names. For example, he uses freely such terms as *pharmaceutical, pharmacology, efficacious, antibiotic, gastrofungal infection, intestinal tissues, abdominal tissues etc.,* which suggest that he must have been reading medical drug literature studiously. Some of the antibiotics which he lists as available in the market, like Tetracycin, Penicillin, Terramycin, Septrin, Ampicillin, and Ampiclox, are rather familiar and perhaps well known to many, but such other names as Cocomycin, Metamycin, Yoyomycin, and the really satirical "Luxurymycin", are obvious fabrications by the advertiser, perhaps aimed at emphasizing that there are already too many of these antibiotics in the market, and that the latest invention by his company, called "Epiclomycin", is aimed at putting a stop to the proliferation of these antibiotics; "Epiclomycin" is then the ultimate antibiotic! His audience would be impressed by this "formidable" display of medical knowledge, including the fact that capsules must be taken only after meals, and with "plenty of water".

The advertiser's other strategy is the prefacing of his advertisement with a prayer. Here he is courting an emotional empathy with his audience. He realizes that travelling by road is hazardous in the country, and that most travelers resort to prayers to God for a safe journey. Interestingly, many of these luxury buses are fitted with powerful radio cassettes to public address equipment. The drivers play various forms of religious music during their journeys. The advertiser's knowledge and assessment of the psychology of the travelers therefore puts him at a distinct advantage, and so he begins early enough to court their patronage by praying for their safety. And the prayer, the text which has been excised from this essay for reasons of space, was offered in so appropriate a linguistic idiom and style that one might well be tempted to believe the advertiser's claims that he had received some clerical training before going into the business of selling medicines.

Perhaps the most effective advertising strategy used by this oral performer is humour. All through the performance, he is able to create and maintain a comic atmosphere in which many members of his audience keep on either chuckling or laughing uproariously. He achieves this through a number of strategies. One of these is frequent resort to mimicry, as indicated in the text. The mimicry is not only vocal but also histrionic, with the result that his performance is greatly underscored by a combination of visual and auditory demands in the appreciation of the aesthetics of his art. For example, he mimics the calls of hawkers of various kinds of food and snacks at the major stops along the expressway, the calls from the passengers to them to bring their wares, and the breaking of wind that follows the constipation caused by indiscriminate eating of various foods. He also demonstrates the speed with which passengers gulp down the food, and their agony during the pains of constipation. All these transform the drug advertiser into an imaginative folk actor drawing liberally from his repertoire of histrionic competence.

In addition, the advertiser makes very effective use of ideophones, like *iwuu, ngwodongwo* and *ngwongwo*. By their vocal and tonal qualities, they enlarge the lexical resources of the performer, creating dramatic associations in situations where ordinary words would have not been effective, and enforcing a sense of linguistic familiarity between him and many members of the audience with whom he shares a common cultural background. Even more importantly, these ideophones highlight the satiric content of the performance, for there is no doubt that the performer uses the opportunity of his performance to satirize certain attitudes associated with travelers in particular, and the Nigerian public in general.

To illustrate the above, one notices that while the advertiser may be serious over the need for travelers to pray to God, he may also be satirizing the tendency by many to pray fervently only when they are in uncertain situations. While he satirizes the indiscriminate buying tendencies of travelers, he may also be laughing at the culture of scramble and greed which is becoming engraved in our national psyche. From the text, it is obvious that he is also satirizing certain dirty habits which have come to characterize a large percentage of the catering industry in Nigeria. Indeed, whereas it is true that his primary aim is to sell his medicines, there is an air of blatant deceit underlying the whole exercise. Indirectly the advertiser may be laughing at the gullibility of his patrons, and this gullibility provides his resources of livelihood. This may explain why, in his list of antibiotics, he can include fabrications that are quite obvious, without being afraid that this might undermine his trade.

Those who constitute his audience usually cover all spectrums of classes in Nigeria, from the literate to the illiterate, and from the poor to the well-to-do, and most of these end up buying the medical products. I myself have had occasion to buy some of the medicines, with the excuse that I had known about them before, that they are quite efficacious, that their sell-by date had not expired, and that they were cheaper when bought in the buses. Some educated patronizers of the hawkers whom I interviewed admitted that they had bought the advertised medicines on excuses quite similar to mine. Incidentally, the most popular types of medicines involved in this hawking business are antibiotics, analgesics, balms (especially Chinese balms) and multivitamins. These, one may argue, feature prominently in first aid administrations which may not need professional consultation. As long as the sell-by date of the medicine has not expired, some patrons have argued, and as long as one needs them, one might as well buy them from the quick turnover sellers.

Conclusions

It can therefore be concluded that, from the point of view of artist-audience relationship, all the passengers of a luxury bus constitute one folk consciousness during the period of their journey. They share a sense of geography and social culture which is Nigerian; a stage which is restricted in space, and in which there is easy interaction not only between the actor and the audience, but also between some members of the audience; a sense of common fate predicated on the state of uncertainty created by hazards of travelling on Nigerian roads, and a shared knowledge of some of the latest arrivals in the medical market, and the range of diseases which these medicines can cure. The passengers and the advertiser also share a common language, whether it is the Igbo language, or some significant patterns which have come to characterize both "Nigerian English" and Pidgin English in Nigeria. This common folk consciousness which is established in the luxury buses is also reminiscent of that established between the oral advertiser of medicines in the motor station and his willing audience.

In both cases, there is a shared recognition of a popular form of performance for which nobody pays in the technical sense, as one would pay in order to go and watch a play on a proscenium stage. It is true that passengers pay in order to use the buses, but this fee is not for the entertainment which they get from the performance of the advertiser, nor is it for the satisfaction they get from buying the medicines. Some of the patronizers are aware that the hawking of medical products is illegal in Nigeria. Yet nobody, not even law enforcement agents (who themselves are sometimes part of the audience), has cared to get them apprehended. Perhaps this audience is sensitive to the fact that a performer is playing a dual role: that of an entertainer and a bread-winner. As an entertainer, he is providing for audience that which institutionalized structures of entertainment in the country lack: a widely accepted tradition of the popular theatre. As bread winner, he is involved in a business in which nobody is compelled to be a custom-er. Above all, there seems to be a shared understanding between en-tertainer and audience that no moral issue is at stake; what is at stake is an aesthetic demand which the performer seems to satisfy. The oral advertisement of medical products is popular folk entertainment and oral literature in Nigeria, and may remain so until such time that its obvious medical and moral implications compel the relevant authori-ties to severely enforce the law that proclaims the activity illegal. Until then, this form of folk performance remains a transmitter of a rhetor-ical and dramaturgical tradition, and provides telling evidence which shows that forms of folk art or oral literature are a dynamic product of the socio-economic consciousness of an era.

NOTES

1. John Munonye's novel, *A Dancer of Fortune*(1974), is a fictionalized por-trayal of the activities of the dancing drug advertisers.

2. "I no cost money" is Pidgin for "I am not expensive"

3. A Nigerian euphemism for a large bottle of Stout-beer.

4. "Back for ground" is from "Money for hand, back for ground", a com-mon expression in Nigeria, often attributed to women of easy virtue. It means that once the customer paid the required cash, the prostitute would supply his sexual needs without much ado.

5. The taperecorded speech was partly in ungrammatical English and part-ly in Pidgin. For reasons of space, I have chosen to reproduce only the version translated into Standard English, retaining as much of the colloqui-alism of the actor as possible.

6. A term of address generally used "guyishly" by adolescent males to refer to one another.

7. A Roman Catholic Juniorate Seminar does exist at Awomamma in Imo State, Nigeria; so does a senior seminary, essentially for study of philosophy, in Ikot Ekpene in Akwa Ibom State.

8. Meaning "Most efficacious"; in traditional society, the name was mostly borne by herbalists.

9. Ideophone for the act of rushed eating.

10. Some of the passengers subsequently pick up the *iwuu* refrain.

11. Fried Bean cakes.

12. Cooked bean pastes.

13. Refers to the proprietress of the hotel

14. Igbo for "True"?, but uttered with a great deal of skepticism.

15. Ideophone for "hotch-potch".

16. Igbo onomatopoeia and ideophone from *ita*, "to masticate" and *ngwo ngwo* suggesting "hotch-potch".

17. This gives the impression that he is auctioning the medicine.

18. A number of attempts made by me to interview the advertisers proved abortive. On one occasion I approached one of them who was about to begin an advertisement in a bus and requested him to stay near my seat so that I could taperecord his speech audibly. I suggested that I would not mind paying for the favour. The effect of my request was a result quite opposite to what I wanted: he kept as far away from me as possible. It became clear that these advertisers whom I wanted to interview were suspicious of my intentions. They might have suspected me to be a kind of police agent attempting to enforce the law making hawking of medical products illegal.

Works Cited

Bennett, Gillian. *Traditions of Belief.* Harmondworth: Penguin, 1987. Print.

Finnegan, Ruth. *The Oral and Beyond: Doing Things with Words in Africa.* Oxford, Chicago, Scottsville: James Currey, The University of Chicago Press, University of KwaZulu Natal Press, 2007. Print.

Leach, Maria. Ed. *Standard Dictionary of Folklore, Mythology and Legend.* San Francisco: Harper & Row, 1984. Print.

Lord, Albert. "Perspectives on Recent Work on Oral Literature". *Oral Literature (Seven Essays)*. Ed. Duggan. Edinburgh: Scottish Academic Press, 1975. 1–24. Print.

Munonye, John. *A Dancer of Fortune*. London: Heinemann, 1974. Print.

Obiechina, Emmanuel. *Onitsha Market Literature*. London: Heinemann, 1972. Print.

Ogunbiyi, Yemi. "Nigerian Theatre and Drama: A Critical Profile". *Drama and Theatre in Nigeria: A Critical Source Book*. Ed. Yemi Ogunbiyi. Lagos: Nigeria Magazine, 1981. 1–8. Print.

Traore, Bakary. *The Black African Theatre and Its Social Functions*. Trans. Dapo Adelugba, Ibadan: Ibadan University Press, 1972. Print.

Ukwu, U.I. & B.W, Hodder. *Markets in West Africa*. Ibadan: University of Ibadan Press, 1969. Print.

Wright, W *et al*. *Advertising*. New York: McGraw-Hill, 1962. Print.

PART FIVE: THE RHETORICAL GENRES

Chapter Fourteen

Rhetorical Genres of African Oral Literature: The Idiom, Puzzle, Tongue Twister and Pun

Ogbonna Onuoha and Ugochukwu Ogbonnaya

INTRODUCTION

Oral Literature remains an important component of African literature. This can be attributed to the hereditary possession in language, literature and culture, where oral tradition cannot be dispensed with. Thus, Africans cannot alienate their souls from their restless quest for the African essence: identity, consciousness, emancipation and communication.

A genre has a specific stricture and content that defines it. It is a type of text—a coherent stretch of speech involving two or more participants. Genres could be distinguished according to their respective form(s) or function(s). A study of the genre is a study of the form and content of a message as to whether it is appropriate or not to the rhetorical situation. Form and content of a genre reveal much about the speaker, his/her language, audience, the social milieu, norms, values, preferences and constraints.

Rhetoric, from a traditional stand point, is a "discipline that concerned itself with the effective use of language to persuade, to teach, to inform, to give pleasure and so on" (Mathews 2007). Rhetorical genres of African oral literature are those stretches of speech involving participants, and in which there is effective use of language to perform a number of functions. In Africa, although rhetorical genres are indispensable, they are the least studied or referred to in literature. In this essay, we present the idiom, puzzle, tongue twister and pun as genres of elevated rhetorical speech, use of expression in the

African verbal or oral art, using Igbo as the language of expression.

THE IDIOM

This is called *akpaalaokwu* in the Igbo language. The *New International Webster's Collegiate Dictionary* defines an idiom as "an expression not readily analyzable from its grammatical construction or from the meaning of its component parts. It is the part of the distinctive form or construction of a particular language that has a specific form or style present, only in that language". *Oxford Concise Dictionary of Linguistics* sees the idiom as, "a set of expression in which two or more words are syntactically related but with a meaning like that of a single lexical unit". According to Wood (1979), an idiom is a phrase which allows no element therein to be replaced by a synonym or phrase in which the individual parts, if taken separately, do not suggest the meaning of the whole. Wood further describes the idiom as a phrase in which no part can be omitted.

In his own contribution, Clerk (1990) defines idioms as "words or phrases whose meanings cannot be taken literally as they defy logical or grammatical analysis. They are characteristics of a language but because they are illogical, they have not been learned". For instance, "dark horse" and "queer fish" may be used to describe a person, but *dark fish and queer horse* are not idioms in English. *The Random House Dictionary of the English Language* characterizes the idioms as follows:

1. "An expression whose meaning is not predictable from the usual meanings of its constituent elements as "kick the bucket" or "hang one's head" or from the general grammatical rules of a language as in "table round" and that is not a constituent of a large expression of like characteristics.
2. A language or dialect or style peculiar to a people.
3. A construction or expression of one language whose parts correspond to elements in another language but whose total structure or meaning is not matched in the same way to the second language.
4. The peculiar character or genius of a language
5. A distinct style or character in music, art, etc".

We can sieve out salient points from the above definitions that can aid our understanding of idioms:

1. Idioms are to be mastered through learning.
2. Idioms do not accept inter-lingual transfer or comparison as they are language-specific.
3. The meaning of an idiomatic expression is highly unpredictable.
4. No part or item should be omitted or swapped
5. Individual components cannot supply full meaning of the whole. It is the group of words or phrases that supply full meaning.
6. The constituent parts are indivisible as any extraction or substitution produces a different meaning from the intended one.
7. Idioms do not accept synonyms (see also Ogbonnaya 2005).

Idioms are culture-bound. This is why they are not amenable to translation from one language to another. Thus, an idiom is not to be taken literally as its meaning is not predictable from the words that compose it. Furthermore, an idiom is seen as not readily analyzable from its grammatical construction/structure. The following are examples of idioms in the Igbo language:

(1). Ọ na-eme aka abụọ
   He does hand two
   'He does two hands' (literal meaning)
   We cannot derive the meaning of the above idiom by saying that:
   "He uses his two hands to do things"
   Rather, the above (1) idiom simply means:
   Ọ na-ezu ohi—"He is a thief"
(2). Ịchi obi n'aka
   To carry one's heart in one's hands (palms) as in:
   "Njem Ụgbọelu bụ ịchị obi n'aka".
   Journey aeroplane is to carry heart by hand.
   This is however, not the meaning of the above idiom.
   The Idiom (2) means:
   "Journey by air is hazardous (or keeps one on one's toes)"
   (This is due to fear of plane crash)

332 Ethnosensitive Dimensions of African Oral Literature

Fowl season water

"Rain season fowl"

as in:

Ada bụ ọkụkọ udummiri

(Ada is a rainy season fowl)

This idiom has nothing to do with rain season or the fowl, but simply means that:

Ada is a sickler (Ada falls sick always).

(4). Ita akwa ndụ

'to chew egg raw

"to chew raw egg" as in:

Uche na-ata akwa ndụ

'Uche chews raw egg'

This idiom has nothing to do with the chewing of raw eggs.

Idiom (4) simply means that:

Uche is foolish.

(5). Ịgba ụgbọ nwamkpi

'to transport vehicle he-goat

'to transport in the manner of he-goat' as in:

Maazi Oji gbaara nwaodibo ya ụgbọ nwamkpi

Mr. Oji transported his apprentice in the he-goat train".

This idiom simply means that:

'Mr. Oji sent his apprentice packing untimely or prematurely (without the apprentice serving out or being compensated)'

The following are phrasal or infinitival idioms which share the same hidden semantic characteristics with the ones described earlier:

(6). Aka azụ (hand back)—back hand—meaning 'bribery'

(7). Afọ ịta mmiri as in 'Afọ tara ya mmiri', portraying wickedness and not mmiri' (water) and 'afọ' (belly/stomach)

(8). Afọ ọma (belly good)—good belly as in, 'Ada nwere afọ ọma' (Ada has good belly (literally). But the idiom, as usual, neither implies *good* nor *belly*. It means 'Ada is kind'.

(9). Ịtu ndụ mmanụ—a reference to 'enjoyment'

(10). Ịtu ndu ahia as in 'Uche tụrụ ndụ ya ahia'—meaning that Uche takes life-threatening risk (Uche does not value his life).

(11). Ire abụọ as in 'o bu onye ire abụọ'—This refers to Uche as a 'liar'

(12). Ita mma n'ọnụ as in 'Njideka tara mma n'ọnụ' (Njideka chewed beauty in the mouth (lit). This means that Njideka is very beautiful'.

(13). Inwe anya anọ as in: 'Dike nwere anya anọ'—possessing the power or ability to see beyond the physical or ordinary (clairvoyance).

The above few examples of idioms show that for one to understand an idiom, one needs some foundational knowledge or experience in the culture where the idiom is localized. One can rightly argue that idioms are more of "part of the culture, tradition, philosophy and worldview of a people than the grammar of a language" (Ogbonnaya 2005). However, language is a part of culture (non-material culture), hence, the idioms are rightly located in the sphere of language studies. It is very important for us to note that idioms and idiomatic experiences do not obey, and cannot be predicted from, the usual rules of grammar of a language.

There are a group of idioms whose meanings are easily decipherable. They are described and regarded as 'transparent idioms'.

Examples of these are as found in the following (14–17):

(14). Isi ike 'strong head' as in

Ọ na eme isi ike

"He is strong headed". (lit). This is to say that: He is head-strong

Ọkara mmadụ ọkara mmụọ (part of human, part spirit)—
"This idiom is used to depict 'one who communes with both the gods and (his fellow) humans"

Njinji ejiela—This describes a tragic or ghastly event

Ekwu eme as in: Anyị chọrọ ndị gọvanọ bu ekwu eme.

'We want action-oriented governors/leaders' (see Ogbonnaya (2005), Ofomata (2004).

There are also idioms whose meanings cannot easily be deciphered. Such idioms are regarded as 'opaque idioms', (see examples 1–14). Only people who are competent or conversant with the Igbo culture can easily understand such idioms. Therefore, participants

in this rhetorical genre (idiom), should posses common culture references, otherwise, effective or meaningful communication in idiomatic Igbo expression(s) would be impaired, thus defeating the aim of
rhetoric. In other words, the difficulty in understanding idioms lies
in the opaqueness of the words that make them up, in relation to the
actual meaning of the idioms, making idiom not an all-comer affair.

IDIOMATIC APPEALS/PSYCHOLOGY OF IDIOMS

It is interesting to know that idioms appeal to our psyche and
value system whether ascribed or achieved. We shall discuss these
appeals in six headings (also see Ogbonnaya 2005).

(A). Aesthetic Appeals: Idiom in the group touch and appeal to
our sense of beauty and appreciation (see example no. 12)

(B). Humanitarian Appeals: Idioms in this category appeal to our
sense of humanitarianism of philanthropy (see example no.
17). This appeal is acceptable only when it is in the positive direction. If 'ekwu eme' was used to depict a "thief" or "killer",
it automatically loses its humanitarian appeal, and instills fear
and disapproval, even in the most competent speaker of the
Igbo language.

(C). Intellectual Appeals: Idioms in this category appeal to our
love and respect for knowledge/wisdom, as in: 'ụbụrụ ighọ
nkọ'—'uburu na-aghọ nwa gị nko'—(the brain of your child is
very sharp) meaning "Your child is very intelligent".

(D). Materialistic and prestigious Appeals: Idioms in this group appeal to our incurable quest for success in life, for example: Oji
bụ aka ji akụ—'Oji is a very wealthy man". Uche bụ agụ bata
(agụ nwa)—depicting bravery or ebullience.

(E). Sex Appeals: Idioms in this category appeal to our sense of sex
or sexuality as in:

(i). Obi gbaturu nwunye ya afọ gara aga "Obi impregnated his
wife last year"
This idiom has nothing to do with shooting (with gun or arrow)

(ii). Ngozi erijuola afọ—Ngozi is pregnant
A greenhorn in the use of Igbo language may mistake this for
eating (food) to one's satisfaction.

6. Macho-Appeals: Idioms in this category appeal to our sense of macho pride, as in: Akpụ obi. Ude bụ (onye) akpụ obi. 'Ude is a macho man (muscular/muscle-chested man).

Some idioms have some measure of public disapproval while some have overlapping appeals. Yet there are Igbo idioms that appeal to all aspects of our life. In other words, there are numerous idioms in Igbo.

PUZZLE (AGWỤGWA)

The 'puzzle' or 'riddle' as it is also called, is one of the rhetorical stock expressions used in African languages and literatures, to test native-speaker competence and performance. It is used in inculcating oratorical prowess in the speakers, especially children and non-mother tongue learners of languages. It is one of the guarantees for sociolinguistic diligence, culture milieu observance and adaptation. The term puzzle suggests something 'difficult', 'mentally tasking' and psychologically foot-sweeping in solving and interpreting. A puzzle therefore is that fixed verbal formula which in itself is confusing, perplexing, and bewildering. It requires native-speaker skills or ingenuity to solve. It is necessary for us to note that age is not a warranty in understanding and solving a puzzle as a brilliant young child may solve a puzzle better and faster than a bright or dull old man. An Igbo puzzle usually starts as 'tell me why! tell me why!! tell me why!!!—question', that is: gwa m! gwa m!! gwa m!!!…? According to Ofomata (2004), the Igbo use agwụgwa (puzzles) to test the extent of a person's intelligence and familiarity with his or her sociolinguistic and cultural milieu. It does not matter who posits puzzles (agwụgwa). A child could pose a puzzle to an elderly person, and vice versa. Nwadike (2000) rightly categorizes agwụgwa (puzzle) in Igbo, as follows:

(a). Agwụgwa ụdaolu—(Tone puzzle)
(b). Agwụgwa nlefereanya—(unexpected puzzle)
(c). Agwụgwa mpụrụiche—(special puzzle)
(d). Agwụgwa oke uche—(super-intelligent puzzle)

(e). Agwụgwa mgbagharịị—(confused puzzle)

Agwụgwa Ụdaolu (Tone Puzzles)

In the Igbo language, the puzzle is determined by both the tone and onomatopoeic nature of the words used. However, it is not easy to crack through by the respondent. Examples of this category of puzzles include:

1. Gwam! gwa m!! gwa m!!! Gwa m, tụm, gem-gem.
   The puzzle rests on tụm-tụm, gem-gem alliterative phonological pattern whose answer is hardly discernible to the uniformed or incompetent speaker in the language. The too-hard-to-discern answer/response is:

   Ọsọ mgbada bụ n'ugwu (The race of the hare is on the hill)

   As can be seen from the constituent words of the above puzzle, there is no expression suggesting the response to the riddle, either in part or as a whole.
   ('The race of the hare is on the hill')
2. Gwam! gwa m!! gwa m!!! Gwa m,: tụngélè tụngéè
   Tell me ! tell me!! tell me!!! Tell me: tungele tungee
   The response in 2 (above) is:

   ìriéla édè táà?
   'Have you eaten coco-yam today

3. Gwam! gwa m!! gwa m!!! Gwa m, Gwa m: tụngélè tụngélèńgē
   The response in 3 is: ihu bikwa gị na nkume akị
   'May your face hit on the palm-kernel cracking stone!'

In some instances the puzzle and the answer share equal number of syllables as in example 1 and 2. In the Igbo language, Puzzles and their responses/answers are community-based, but may vary from one patois, idiolect or dialect area/community to another.

Agwụgwa Nleferanya (Unexpected Puzzles)

In this type of Igbo puzzle, the answer may share no common relationship with posed puzzle since the puzzle could be animate and the answer inanimate or vice versa. The following examples would suffice.

4. Gwam! Gwa m!! gwa m!!! Gwam: agadi ji ikpere jezuo ubi
   'An old one that went round the entire farm on his/her knees'
   The response/answer is: Ọgụ eji avọ ahihia ('local weeding hoe').
   In Igbo land we use the local hoe to make mounds, dig holes, and weed round the whole farm. Imagery or symbolism here is the wooden extension to which the hoe blade is attached which is shaped as an 'elbow', comparable to the knee of humans.

5. Gwam! Gwa m!! gwa m!!! Gwam: ihe mere onye eze jiri rachaa ntụ?
   '…why a king licked wood-ash?'
   The correct response/answer is ùbé—'pear'
   In Igbo land, we melt the local pear in hot ash, and, no matter how much one cleans the pear, there must be traces of the ash on the pear. And, since the roasted pear is not usually washed before eating, for it not to lose its delicacy, anyone, including the king, must eat the pear together with the traces of ash on them.

6. Gwam! Gwa m!! gwa m!!! Gwam: ihe kuuru mmiri laa n'elu?
   '…what hangs up with water?'
   The answer is: akị oyibo (bekee)
   The coconut seed grows on top of its tree and is encapsulated with a quantity of water (usually sweet), in it.

7. Gwam! Gwa m!! gwa m!!! Gwam: nwaagboghọbia mara mma abụ (avu) na-agba n'isi?
   '…a beautiful girl that emits pus on her head?'
   The response/answer is: 'ụdara' 'the cherry apple'
   The ụdara fruit always has whitish gummy substance like the pus, emitting from the plucked stalk.

Agwụgwa Mpuruiche (Special Puzzles)

This type of puzzle comes in the song mode: In this type of puzzle, one person (the poser of the puzzle) sings it while the audience, which may be an individual or group, responds. The song leader asks questions on creatures or things that share similar features or characteristics. He or she may suddenly suggest or bring in an odd or incompatible answer. Whosoever opts for the incompatible option supplied by the poser of the puzzle, has failed the game and would be laughed at by the audience. The following are examples of puzzles in this category:

Singer (poser)	Audience (respondent)
8. Ole anụ na-efe efe?	Na-efe efe
'Which animal flies'?	'flies'
Egbe na-efe efe	Na-efe efe
The kite flies	'flies
Obu na-efe efe	Na-efe efe
Obu flies	'flies'
Ukpara na-efe efe	Na-efe efe
Grasshopper flies	'flies'
Nkita na-efe efe	(silence as a dog does not fly)
Dog flies	
9. Ole anụ nwere ụkwụ anọ?	Nwere ụkwụ anọ
'Which animal has four legs'	has four legs
Ewu nwere ụkwụ anọ	Nwere ụkwụ anọ
'Goat' has four legs	has four legs
Nkita nwere ụkwụ anọ	Nwere ụkwụ anọ
Dog has four legs	has four legs
Atụrụ nwere ụkwụ anọ	Nwere ụkwụ anọ
'Sheep has four legs'	has four legs
Ọkụkọ nwere ụkwụ anọ	(No response because the respondent knows that the chicken has only two legs)
'Chicken has four legs'	
10. Ole anu nwe mpi?	Nwe mpi
'Which animal has horns'	has horn
Ewu nwe mpi	Nwe mpi
Goat has horns	has horn
Ele nwe mpi	Nwe mpi

Antelope has horns	has horns
Mgbada nwe mpi	Nwe mpi
Deer has horns	has honr
Nkịta nwe mpi	(silence!)
Dog has horns	Because dog has no horns)

Nkịta (dog) in example 14, Ọkụkọ in 15 and nkịta in 16, are odd in the features mentioned about them and under normal circumstances there is no response for them.

AGWỤGWA MGBAGHARỊ (BIZARRE/CONFUSING PUZZLES)

11. A naghị achọpụta nzọukwụ ngwere n'ikpo akị
"No one can trace the footstep of a lizard on a heap of palm kernels".

12. A naghị achọta (ahu) ụkwụ ndanda n'ite mmanị
"No one can trace the footstep of red ants on a pot of palm oil".

13. A naghị achọta ụkwụ ndi mmụọ jiri bịa gbuo mmadụ.
"No one can trace the footsteps of the spirits when they came and killed someone"

14. A naghị achọta ụkwụ di na nwunye jiri lakpuo ụra.
"No one can trace the footstep of husband/wife when they went to sleep'.

The above four puzzles in 11–14 involve ụkwụ—'footsteps'— and confusing or difficult to decode. It is, however, the opinion of the present study that the four 'footstep' puzzles above be classified as proverbial puzzles. They refer to things that lie beyond human comprehension or discernment, and, therefore, literally imply that, whatever one cannot discern, understand or comprehend lies beyond one's ability.

AGWỤGWA OKE UCHE (SUPER-INTELLIGENT/COMPLEX PUZZLE)

This is another type of puzzle that is difficult to solve. It often comes in the form of short story to which the listener is required to eke out answers. It requires super intelligence or extra skill to solve. For example:

15. Ọkụkọ na akwa: olee nke ichere bu ụzọ mụta ibe ya?
'The fowl and the egg: which do you think first produced the other?'
Here, we would proffer Ọkụkọ (chicken) since it is the chicken that lays the egg!

16. Otu nwoke na-aga njem kpụ ewu, kpụrụ agụ ma bụrụkwa ji. Mgbe o rutere n'otu mmiri, Ọ maghi otu ọ ga-esi wefee ha n'otu n'otu ka ewu ghara iri ji na ka agụ ghara iri ewu (see Nwadike 2000:133).

A certain man embarked on a journey, carrying a goat, a lion and yam. When he arrived at a river shore, he could not discern how to take each of the three items across the river, without one item harming the other! Advise him!

Respondent's correct advice: take the lion and the yam over first; then come back for the goat.

Tongue Twister (Okwuntabire, Okwuntụhị)

Meaning, Nature and Uses of Tongue Twisters

The *Oxford Advance Learners Dictionary* defines the tongue twister as "a word or phrase that is difficult to say quickly or correctly". For Dorson (1972), tongue twisters are "words, phrases or statements, pure or derived, designed to test ones skills in rapid speed production". This definition by Dorson (1972), applies more amenably to the present study.

The tongue twisters, in their form, composition, and uses (functions), are a folk genre which Onuoha (2005) has characterized to be significant in the sociolinguistic life of the people. According to him, tongue twisters are associated with "an anticipatory or a phonological license, which does not modify, twist, or scramble the morphology or syntax of the Igbo language". Because of what he considers as "articulatory peculiarity or complexity" and "repeated phonemes" or " convergence of internal alliteration", several names have been given to this figure of rhetoric (tongue twisters) such as tongue tripper and "tongue tangler" (see Finnegan 1970).

In Igbo, we also have such varied names as: okwuntuhi (twisting speech), okwuntabire (tongue biting speech), okwuojuọnụ (mouth-filling speech) or okwumgbawaọnụ (mouth-bursting speech), for tongue twisters. The difficulty to speak fast is because of alliteration or a sequence of nearly similar sounds that occur mostly at the beginning of each word in the sentence, hence the Igbo names for tongue twisters are fitting. For Ofomata (2004), the tongue twister is a rhetorical genre that helps to develop speech skills. It is also used in "speech therapy". The tongue twister is found in every language, and is used for fun, teaching and learning. The faster one can say a tongue twister correctly without slipping up, the stronger one's language skills become. Tongue twisters are meant to be repeated several times and as quickly as possible, without mispronouncing the words. This is also where the fun function lies.

COMPOSITION OF TONGUE TWISTERS

Onuoha (2005) observed that "tongue twisters are composed of physical images that conjure up a picture of significant, exotic, symbolic lessons or concepts, culturally exotic animals, plant, or symbols and other phenomena". He further categorized Igbo tongue twisters into two, namely:

1. Pure tongue twisters
2. Derived tongue twisters

Let us discuss each of the two types of tongue twisters, as follows:

Pure tongue twisters, according to Onuoha (2005), are mostly artificial fabrications which embody effective rhythm alliteration, onomatopoeia and ideophone. He observes that this class of tongue twisters is primarily constructed for their alliterative sound or phonological foregrounding more than their meaning or sense and are also translatable into English, for example:

1. Ụkọchukwu kwuru okwu chukwu n'ụlọ chukwu di n'Arọchukwu (The man of God preached the word of God in the house of God, at Arọchukwu).

2. Ọkụkọ ocha yiri akwa ọcha n'elu akwa ọcha nwaanyị ọcha sawara n'ala ọcha (A white hen laid a white egg on a white cloth which a white woman spread on a white ground).

3. Papa Pita patara pọọpọọ panye papa Pọl (Peter's father carried pawpaw and gave it to Paul's father)

4. Ị na-eme ka mkpi, I puru mpi mkpi puru? (As you behave like a he-goat, do you have horns like a he-goat?)

5. Nwanyị bu ọrụ ele, Ị na-ere ọrụ ele ere ka ị na-eri ọrụ ele eri? (A woman selling the leg of antelope, is the leg of an antelope for sale or for your consumption)

6. Tọrọ ocha chụrụ sịsị ọcha ọsọ (three white pence chased after three six pence)

7. Nwanyi na-akwa akwa na-akwa na ọkụkọ yiri akwa n'elu akwa o kwara akwa
   (A seamstress is crying because a hen laid an egg on top of her sewn clothes).

   Derived tongue twisters are those fixed traditional stock expressions such as riddles, proverbs, idioms or poems (also see Onuoha 2005). This type of tongue twisters exists in the collective memory of the people, and, like their worldview or culture, is transmitted orally from generation to generation. The tongue twisters under reference here are not amenable to translation. Derived tongue twisters bear meanings that transcend the individual or general words(s) that constitute the expression. They may occur or be cited as declarative, conditional or interrogative statements only a literal translation or transliteration is possible, as shown in the following examples:

8. Egbuo ele n'orie, o ruo n'orie ele eree olu
   (An antelope killed on Orie market day decays at its neck on the next Orie market day)
   This is used for privy discussions on issues/matters or communal values/worldview which time has come!

9. Ka odu kwara okpo, o kwakwara okpo kwem?
   (As the rat made its path, did it make the path straight?)
   This is used to ask a person who claims to have performed a duty whether he/she did so in accordance with laid down rules!

10. Were eriri kpunye ewu; were ewu kpunye eriri.

(Take the rope and tie the goat; tie the goat with the rope!)
This is used to express things, issues or matters of sameness.
It should be noted that, unlike the pure tongue twisters which
carry normal or ordinary meanings, derived tongue twisters
bear meanings which are hidden from all or individual words
in the construction. For instance,
The derived tongue twisters group tend to be more dialectal
than general, whereas the pure tongue twisters group tend to
be more general, and as such, are more frequently used and
understood by the Igbo, as we can listen to them in almost all
the state-owned radio houses in Igboland.

11. I na-eme ka mkpi, ipuru mpi mkpi puru?
'Do you behave like a he-goat, do you have horns like a he-goat'

12. Nwaanyi ne-ere ọrụ ele, Ị na-ere ọrụ ele ere ka, I na-eri ọrụ u ele eri?
'Woman selling the leg of an Antelope, is the leg of an antelope for sale or for your consumption?

13. Tọrọ ọcha chụrụ sịsị ọcha ọsọ
'White three pence ran after White six pence'

14. Papa Pita patara pọpọ panye papa Pọọl
Peter's father carried pawpaw and gave it to Paul's father?

15. Nwaanyi na-akwa akwa na-akwa na ọkụkọ yiri akwa n'elu akwa ọ kwara akwa
"A seamstress is crying because a hen laid an egg on top of sewn clothes).

Rhyme and alliteration are important aspects of tongue twisters as can be seen in the above examples. In tone languages, such as Igbo, tone plays a very important role in tongue twisters as in:

mkpìí LH
mpÌ LL
pùrú LH
púrú LL

Tongue twisters are language-specific as the best one could get in its inter-lingual transfer or conversation is transliteration. So the translations given above are mere guides to non-native speakers.

Techniques used in creating tongue twisters

(a). Use of alliteration—use of same phonetic sound repeatedly at the beginning of each word in the sentence as in example (14)

(b). Consonantal alternation or re-ordering as in (11), changing from mkpí to mpì and back to mkpí

(c). Shifting from the one type of sound to another, for example; shifting from front vowels to back vowels and to front vowels again as in (13); or from double sounds to single sounds as in example (11) mkpi and mpi.

(d). Shifting from one tonal type to another in the case of homographs as in (15) where akwa—a homograph means

    i. ákwà—cloth
    ii. àkwà—'cry'
    iii. àkwá—'egg'
    iv. àkwà—'sewing'

Pun

Pun is a rhetorical expressive style that plays on words. It is meant to make people laugh. Some jokes are puns. In puns, words or parts of that which have more than one meaning are usually used. Examples in Igbo include:

1. Ụwa na-chọ ikpu.
   This can mean (i) the world is about to be destroyed, or, (ii) the world is looking for female genitalia. The pun centres around Ikpu. In (i) ikpu is an infinitive meaning—to turn upside down. In (ii) ikpu is a noun meaning vagina.

2. Ọ tụọ ọ tụchaala
   In the pun, ọ is pronominal while tụ is a verb root for decide. The pun is generated by an unusual and ungrammatical combination of the pronoun + the verb, in an articulatory process, to generate Ọtụ (vagina'). This agrees with Wikipedia (the free Encyclopedia), that puns are made or created to make other people laugh, and many jokes are actually puns whose words have more than one meaning whether the spelling is the same of different:

3. Obidiya eriela Ọnụma (in Akoma 1973). Iri ọnụma means (i) anger/vexation. (ii) It can also mean a personal name: In Akoma's Obidiya, Ọnụma is the husband of Obidiya, and when Ọnụma died without a child, the author said that Obidiya (the wife of Ọnụma) eriela ọnụma

4. Onyeiseala tụọ atụmatụ, ọ tụchaala
   Ordinarily, example 4 should mean that whatever the President decides on is final. On the other hand, it could be punned on to mean "Once Mr. President speaks, vagina brightens up!"

5. Ọ na-ala Ụmụaka
   ('He is going to the village called Umuaka) (in Orlu). As pun, it can also be punned in Onitsha dialect that the man in question is in the habit of having sexual intercourse with children who hail from Umuaka.

6. I jee Lagos, a rapụ gi, I ga-alọta?
   Example 6 can mean (i) if you go to Lagos, and you are left stranded, can you find your way back? (Ijee Lagos, arapụ ị, I ga-alota?) or (ii) If you go to Lagos and you become demented, can you find your way back?

7. Ọ nọ n'ụzọagba girls
   The real or normal meaning of the above example is
   (i). She is at Uzoagba girls secondary school
        while the punned meaning is
   (ii). He is on the road having sex with girls (Ọ nọ n'ụzọ agba girls)

CONCLUSION

Rhetorical genres of African Oral literature are an everyday affair in African languages. Perhaps, due to their complexity and largely fixed structure, many scholars and researchers consider them infinitesimal and so do not give them the prominence they (the genres) deserve. As stock expressions, they are largely untranslatable to avoid a muting of their meaning(s). Each genre is different from another and serves different purpose(s) from one another. Rhetorical genres are, generally speaking, entertaining, educative and therapeutic. As sources of early or traditional education, they are used more by the grassroots for whom they constitute sociolinguistic menu in both daylight and moonlight activities.

As rhetorical genres which lie in the centre of the people's linguistic and cultural performance or practices, it is necessary for modern African literary scholarship to delve fully into them, for the good and development of the people, their culture and language.

Works Cited

Akoma, E. *Obidiya*, Ibadan: Oxford University Press, 1973. Print.

Clerk, J.O.E. *English Idioms.* London: Harrap Books Ltd. 1980. Print.

Dorsoh, R. M ed. *African Folklore.* Chicago: Anchor Books, 1972. Print.

Finnegan, R. *Oral Literature in Africa.* Nairobi: Oxford University Press,1970. Print

Mathews. P.H. ed.*Oxford Concise Dictionary of Linguistics.* 2nd edition. London: Oxford University Press, 2007. Print.

Ofomata, C.E. *Ndezu Ụtọasụsụ Igbo Nke Ndi Siniọ Sekọndiri.* Enugu: Formar Publishers (Nig) Ltd., 2004. Print.

Ogbonnaya, U. "Idiomatic Expressions in Igbo". *Nigerian Societies and Cultural Heritage.* Ed. J.O. Onwuka. Okigwe: Fasmen Educational & Research Publishers (FERP). 2005. 177–199Print

Onuoha, O. "A Socio-linguistic Analysis of the Oratorical Coefficient in the Igbo Tradition of Politics" *The Igbo and the Tradition of Politics.* Ed. U.D. Anyanwu & J.C.U. Aguwa. Enugu: Fourth Dimension Publishers,1993. 144–154. Print.

Random House Dictionary of the English Language. Print.

The New International Websters Collegiate Dictionary. Oxford Advanced Learners Dictionary (6th Edition). London: OUP. Print.

Wood, F.T. *Dictionary of English Colloquial Idioms.* London: Macmillan Press Ltd., 1979. Print.

Wikipedia (free Dictionary). www.wikipedia

Chapter Fifteen

Proverbs Yield in the Igbo Field:
Why Are We So Blest?

J.O.J Nwachukwu-Agbada

If what I am about to say regarding the Igbo and their fecundity in proverb yield bespeaks of the proverbial child's claim that his mother's soup is always the most delicious, I should be forgiven, since that is not intended in this essay. It is simply that this is the culture I know a little more about, having been raised in it. Although what I may have to say about the prodigious harvest of proverbs among this hitherto 'primitive tribe of the lower Niger' could be applicable to a few other Nigerian and African groups, I would rather restrict myself to the Igbo whom I am fairly conversant with, I having been born and bred among them.

Like most African cultures, the Igbo entity has flourished on a high tradition of lore which remains essentially verbal. As one writes one is yet to encounter a folklore genre in other lands which has no counterpart in the Igbo gnomic collection. Myths and legends (*ita*), folksongs (*ifo*), riddles (*gwamgwam*), tongue-twisters (*okwu ntabire*), poetic insult of similes (*iko-ọnụ*), proverbs and wellerisms (*ilu or ilulu*), folktales (*ufe or ufere*), puns, name-calling and innuendoes (*atutu ikpe*), abuses (*mkpari*), joking relationships (*njakiri*), anecdotes (*akụkọ imatụ*), funeral dirges (*abụ akwamozu*), curse (*iyi mmụọ*), invocations and incantations (*abụ afa*), work ditties, birthsongs (*egwu ọnụ nwa*), love verses, praise poems, aliases (*aha ntutu*) balladic poetry and bridal chants (*egwu ụlọ di*) are some of the verbal artistic forms in the Igbo milieu (see Ezikeojiaku, "Classification"; Achufusi, "The Main Genres"; Chukwuma, *Igbo Oral Literature* etc.)

The impact of 'modernism' on these forms is quite noticeable, particularly in its desire to completely muffle the people's artistic heritage. Most of these oral artistic modes are virtually 'caged', left only in the memories of those who know about them but are not able to transmit them to their children because the fora for such informal transfer ceased to exist at the advent of a totally new way of life and life-pursuit challenges. Parents who know a few of these oral genres, even if they would like their children to equally know about them, return from their modern workplaces dog-tired while their children are glued to the fun on the television set or may have in fact gone to sleep. Through Western education and religion, and recently rabid Pentecostalism, the Igbo culture as a whole is at the brink of total annihilation, gradually being replaced by a *tertium* quid life-approach which in the end has left it half-dead, left it neither African nor European. The continuous attack and the gradual ebbing away of the Igbo cultural essence came to a head in 1996 when a group of Pentecostal Christians demanded that the name of a pan-Igbo public lecture series be changed because it has something to do with Igbo god of the farmstead in charge of agricultural yield. The group is also alleged to have brought down the big *Ikenga* cast on Library Roundabout in Owerri, capital of Imo State. *Ikenga* was a wooden carving which represented a man's desire to realize in full the strength of his arm, the Igbo being largely farmers in times past. It was to remind him of his potentials to achieve greatness using his God-given strength. Although it is dishonest not to admit that some of the practices of the people in the olden days fall short of the paean and dignity of today's prevalent civilized human and humane ideals, to consider *everything* about a people's past as deserving to be thrown away is in itself dishonest, vicious and reactionary. It is akin to self-betrayal, like publicly denouncing that one's mother's soup is not delicious!

Of all the Igbo cultural artifacts relating to their artistic tradition which has refused to be muzzled up or put on leash is the proverb. Whereas these other forms are either played down or in fact subdued, the proverb remains irrepressible. Instead of going extinct as many of these verbal forms appear to be doing, the Igbo proverb

corpus continues to expand in number and variety. New sayings continue to arrive the arena of Igbo social and aesthetic communication
on a constant basis (Nwachukwu-Agbada. "The Proverb"). Not only
are true proverbs used in the current speech events of the Igbo, there
is now a class of proverbial lore in the 'Engligbo', a variety of sayings in Igbo English code-switch (Nwachukwu-Agbada "The African
Proverb"). In spite of the combined forces of what is now ascribed
as 'modernity' against the Igbo culture, the easy abandonment of
aspects of this heritage and the quick embrace of anything Western
and new, the typical Igbo man or woman is often proud when his
or her 'Igboness" in speech, dressing or action is either recognized
or called to question, particularly by a fellow Igbo. This is precisely
why every articulate Igbo person occasionally invests what he/she
says with some Igbo proverbs and saws, an indication that he/she is
still in touch. As a consequence, new proverb coinages continue to
roll out from the Igbo proverb 'mill', at the instance of the sane, the
insane and the imbecile, yet directed by no one in particular. Where
the fanatical Christian preacher shuns its use in his/her sermons, so
as not to encourage a return to the past, Nollywood movie actors and
actresses of Igbo origin though speaking largely in English or Pidgin
will use it because it registers freshness in what they say or how they
say it. This is in spite of the fact that the medium is often times English. One can then imagine what the beauty of these home videos
and films, nuanced in the Igbo speech pattern, would have been were
they to have been directly rendered in Igbo.

IS THE PROVERB NOW FOREIGN TO WESTERN SPEECH AND WRITING?

No doubt the proverb and its variants have declined as a speech
event in the western communication medium. However, one's perception about proverb use among the whites is that it is no longer a
desired speech model to be invoked as a utility item. This is not to
say that it has absolutely no place in the western speech tradition.
We shall return to that because the preponderant use of proverbs
and proverbial expressions during President Barack Obama's elec-
tioneering campaigns for the American Presidency in much of 2007

and 2008 paints a different but interesting picture from what we have been made to believe.

Be that as it may. The truth is that the proverb was once an important artistic vignette in the Western literature of the 15ᵗʰ and 16ᵗʰ centuries. But with the coming of the Age of Enlightenment, proverb usage in both Western speech and writing waned. Thus as Mac Barrick says, the Western writers today who "rarely use proverbs, receive high critical acclaim, while others who employ proverbial materials as class indicator for the characters they are depicting, are relegated to secondary status" (3–4).

Probably because most mature Igbo speakers still deploy the proverb in what they say, for which they easily attract attention to themselves and imbue value to their utterances, novels written by the first generation Igbo writers such as Chinua Achebe, John Munonye, Flora Nwapa, Nkem Nwankwo and all those who have so far written Igbo literature have considered the proverb a very useful oral tradition material to deploy in their works. Even as one writes, the proverb is still a trusted conversation opener, discourse flavor and dialogue closer, particularly among elderly speakers of the Igbo language. It is still used to smoothen out argument and to strengthen a counter view in the normal daily communicative events. As it shall be emphasized presently, proverb use in Igbo discourse is still associated with wisdom and a deep knowledge of tradition, a rootedness which may not be easy to earn from some other engagements in Igbo life.

Thus when many years ago, an otherwise respected Nigerian writer and critic tried to put Chinua Achebe on the spot for "transliterating obsolete proverbs into English nonsense-rhymes", which in "other societies" should have been the first proof of illiteracy" (Osofisan 21), not a few were taken aback. Achebe was after all a user of a flourishing tradition, even among the critic's Yoruba ethnic group. One suspects that Achebe has remained a monadnock in African writing precisely because of his artistic use of the so-called obsolete proverbs, they being a sure way of evoking an old African life and tradition which is still relevant to the Igbo up until today. Perhaps we here in Africa are yet to get to the development pinnacle which will discourage us from the use of proverbs in speech and writing. It would then appear that the Western ethic of precision, the exactitude of its science and technology, is yet to get to us. Put then in another way, the current place which saws and saying still enjoy in African interpersonal communication awaits its surmounting when Africa attains the Western flare of discourse without its disguises and prevarications which the proverb is known for. More importantly, one awaits a time when technology and its concision would affect our reasoning and action to the extent that we begin to emote like Europeans or begin to take our bearing from life the way the Western people do. This is another way of saying that such a time will take quite a while to materialize.

In any event, the claim that the proverb is no longer a Western imprint can be misleading. One may recall that the animated speeches of Barack Obama during the 2007 American presidential campaigns were largely impactful by their beauty earned from their immersion in the lilt of proverbs and proverbial expressions. He was after all the examples of some past American leaders such as Abraham Lincoln, Franklin Roosevelt and J.F Kennedy. In a publication on Obama's proverbial rhetoric to the presidency', Wolfgang Mieder has had to observe that "what is amazing from a proverbial point of view is that no matter when, where, or about what he speaks, [Obama's] oratory is incredibly consistent in its vocabulary, syntax, and fixed phases". Mieder further states that "formulaic language in the form of traditional proverbs, proverbial phrases, and twin formulas is simply part of his natural speech pattern, and since he is determined to communicate with the people in an authentic fashion, these phraseological units also appear in what must be considered his most eloquent and thoughtful speeches" (107–08), comparable to those of notable American leaders known for their rousing rhetoric. Thus the constant claim that the West no longer cherishes proverb use may have been overstated after all.

WHY ARE WE SO BLEST?

This essay strives to adduce reasons for the imperishability of the proverb and the proverb form in the Igbo social ethos of speech and communication. After all, as it seems, the Igbo are supposed to be a people who quickly embrace change (Ottemberg, "Ibo Receptivity"), and are known to have done so in various aspects of their life. Why is it that in the case of proverb lore, they have not let go? Why is it that they even coin newer sayings and saws, have gone ahead to produce in recent times proverb structured utterances in 'Engligbo'?

The first reason is that the Igbo are a republican people. In such a setting, speech is largely free. In both the Igbo of old and that of the present, it was (is) offensive not to allow a full-fledged man to express himself at the public arena, at the town hall meeting. Such an Igbo would ask: 'Are you in my mind?' 'Do you control my thinking?' 'Are you the one who reasons for me?' 'Do you feed me?' The scenario could even lead to the man who thinks he has been violated by being stopped from speaking to ask his violator to 'break the pot with which you feed me'. This is like drawing a battle line, of declaring war between two antagonists. Their republican nature has enabled the Igbo to constantly engage the Igbo language, to search through it all the time, to strike its expressions with linguistic hammer with the intention of creating new words, new manner of speaking, new sayings and new linguistic nuances. The Igbo who are regularly involved in the formulation of new speech slants language and sayings include, the commercial motor drivers, auto mechanics, motor-park touts and lorry loaders (known in Igbo as *ocho passenger*), long distance traders, commercial motorcyclists (*inaga* riders), traditional musicians and political thugs. They regularly 'confront' the language in order to express out of its words a new meaning, a new significance. These are then passed on to the general circulation of the language, in comparison to the banking system releasing new currency notes into the economy while the old ones remain legal tender. It may be a truism, a clearer way of saying something, a new saying, a new fact or a new but pragmatic attitude. We shall expatiate on this in the course of this essay.

Another reason is the appositeness of the Igbo proverb's philosophical content. The snippet of philosophical poise in it is almost always too intriguing to be neglected. Being the most enduring tenor for the conveyance of the Igbo outlook on life, proverb formulation and reformulation are a constant activity. The fact is that Igbo view of the world continues to be moulded by proverbs, and since no society may live without updating its philosophy, new proverbs and sayings continue to be born as the group is enriched by new experiences. In a way then, in this practical manner that is, there are really no old sayings in the Igbo milieu since all proverbs which still exist and or have the capacity to be deployed in verbal and written discourses are those which do still make sense in the current Igbo social interactive model while those which are no longer applicable, gather mould, slowly fizzle out or will do so sooner than later. Most Igbo proverbs are capsules of philosophical discourse(s), even if of a primordial nature. For sure, it is unscholarly to make too much claim for the proverb as a philosophical data on which to study a people, the same way that nobody may place absolute trust on the proverb as a historical resource. Yet no serious scholar may ignore them where and when they contain useful hints and hunches.

In real life, the Igbo revel in deep meaning; they marvel at philosophical prevarication, and use it quite often. The culture being as yet a largely oral one allows verbal expressions a pride of place in what is said and what is reckoned with. In other words, the power of words is still efficacious. For instance, an ineffective political representative or a corrupt politician deprecated in writing by a concourse of traditional rulers from his constituency may not feel as threatened as he would be if he were verbally cursed for the same offence. Not only would he be afraid that sleeping gods may have been woken up for him, the incident of the voicing of curses and expletives would travel faster, usually from mouth to mouth.

The Igbo culture is still a minimum message culture as distinct from a maximum message matrix usually known for its overt and open communication. As a consequence, a mature communication in Igbo is often remote, faint, almost esoteric. An Igbo anecdote referring to this kind of mute communication is about a man who stole a chicken and was given a hot pursuit by children, and later caught. The hullabaloo attracted a large crowd. Although the stolen chicken was right in the raffia bag hanging over his shoulders, the thief beckoned on the few elderly ones in the throng to look into his bag with 'the eyes of elders' and say if they had seen any chicken in the sack. We are not explicitly told by the anecdote whether or not he got the cooperation of the elders around, but what is important is that he sought their protection using a limited amount of words. In the process the clever thief may have also used eye contact, mouth-pouting and nose-twitching as he invited his select witnesses.

In the Igbo speech matrix, it is not always that words are explicit or that words and expressions with specific meanings maintain such meanings at *all* times. In my part of Igboland (Mbasie), if a moment or occasion demands tact or carefulness, someone may warn others, "Lee kwe ariri' which ordinarily means 'Look at the millipede'. But there is no millipede around! Yet an important piece of advice has been given in very few words. There was an incident in Mbaise too when an illustrious son of the land was being recommended to the traditional rulers' council of the clan to confer a chieftaincy title on him at a future date. It was a gathering of both the native rulers and the ruled. One man who did not want the auspicious son to be given the honour simply told the traditional rulers that he could not touch the wall on both his right hand on his left! This apparent bizarre remark attracted a din both in support of, and in condemnation of the suggestion that the matter on ground be deferred until her could 'touch the wall'. This was his mean way of adjoining the meeting indefinitely and probably killing the initiative in the process.

Among the Igbo, certain uses of words and expressions are rather suggestive while meaning is negotiated out of combination of values, experience, precedents or intent, depending on whose intent it is. In a minimum message context, remarks Nabuhiro Nagashima, "If a communication" fails, the receiver, not the sender, is apt to be accused of lack of comprehension"(96). This is especially true if the receiver is supposed to be a mature member of the speech community and should have been fully acculturated. Thus, it is appropriate to state that a mature user of the Igbo language combines self-intent, philosophy and custom with few and well-chosen words, grunts (*ude*), eye movement, a smirk, a scratching of the eyelid, (*oko iki*) a head slant, each of which could neither indicate a position, a disbelief, a refusal or an acquiescence.

It is equally crucial to observe that nearly every philosophical issue has in one way or the other received some bit of attention in Igbo sayings. Love, truth, courage, attitude, fairness, justice, beauty, caution, generosity, hope, optimism, kindness, duality, prowess, etc. reside in Igbo proverbs (Shelton, "Relativism"; Egudu, "Social Values"; Sofola "Okwu di na Nka"; Nwadike, "The Igbo Proverb"; Nwachukwu-Agbada, "The Old Woman" and Chinua Achebe's "Literary Proverbs"; Opata, "The Nature of Speech" and "Igbo Attitude to Women" etc). Such is the apparency of proverbial truth that the Igbo occasionally equate it with the truth and expect it to be considered as such by their interlocutors. It is for this reason too that they deploy the proverb in their speech activities when they want to confer authority on their view point even though they may also refer to another proverb of equal but opposite force when a different occasion arises. The fact is that each deft deployment of the proverb in Igbo discourse is rated as an index of one's astuteness, one's fertile imagination, the philosophical complexity of a person's mind. Anyone who would want to encounter such a person would be his match in intellectual terms or, as if often happens, goes in the company of another who is better grounded in the art of proverb use than himself.

The truth content of the Igbo proverb needs a little more emphasis. The Igbo believe that the proverb is ordinarily imbued with uncontestable verity. It should be noted that every good proverb is logically self-sufficient, and may not require a proof beyond itself (Cram, "A Note"; Otakpor, "A Note"). This enables the proverb to sound "so right" (Kirshenblatt-Gimblett 821) because its diction and referents are always drawn from the local flora and fauna, from the logic of custom and norms, the propriety of tradition, in short, from the prevalent reality perceivable around. This way its simplicity and earthiness are almost always assured. A well-cited Igbo meta-proverb describes as a fool one to whom a proverb and its meaning are simultaneously explained. What the coiner of such a proverb had in mind is that the truth in a proverbial utterance is often so self-evident that only the foolish is not in a position to realize it. However, just to leave it at this is to imply that there are no proverbs which require some explanation or illustration, at least not when they are historical or culture specific. What cannot be gainsaid is that every proverb is subject to context for its intended meaning to be fully realized. After all the Igbo also say: "Onye tụrụ ilu kọwaa ya, makana ilu bụ ọghọm" (He who cites a proverb should explain it because proverb use is a product of accident). More metamorphically still, they also say "Onye tụrụ ikoro waa ya eze" (He who carves a wooden drum should give it a slit").

Perhaps the most critical basis for the continued yield of the proverb and proverbial expressions in Igbo culture is their functions in the society. Nwoga considers as the two basic functions of the proverb in the Igbo setting those of illumination and correction (198). Whereas Joyce Penfield identifies five functions (4–12), the present writer locates six functions as those of amplification, authoritativeness, education, rhetoricism, image-building and aestheticism (Nwachukwu-Agbada, *The Igbo Proverb* 13–134).

The amplificatory function enables the proverb to broaden perspectives through a correlation between context situation and proverb situation (Seitel, "Proverbs"). By relating these two situations, the point at issue is given the relevant spotlight for better grasping. The authoritative function is an appeal to traditionality where traditionality serves as a timeless arbiter. In that case, both the user and the one appealed to by the proverb have sufficient faith in the social efficacy of tradition. In other words, rather than appeal to specialists or auspicious personalities, the proverb leans on what is largely agreed upon as a truism or axiom of life. This preceding remark is important because even when a proverb is coined by a local or popularized by a never-do-well (*yoghologhom*), its sustenance is derived from social

and collective approval and then passed on to tradition for circulation. Thus, the tendency to introduce an Igbo saying with the matrix
clause, "My father/mother said...', 'As our elders say...' or 'As the
Igbo say...' is an attempt to imbue the ensuing proverb with the
aura of power of influence derived from ancientness. Proverbs serve
as precedents, social anchors and time-tested answers to recurrent
social questions and situations requiring external authentication.

The educative function includes the proverb's didactic, cognitive
and corrective purposes. The Igbo didactic proverbs are socializing
in nature, particularly for the child in his/her early formative years
in life. Proverbs exist which instruct children on the best way to approach issues of living or the best strategy for achieving meaningful
existence (Nwachukwu-Agbada, "An African Oral Literature" 108).
Such proverbs contain issues of morality, equality, justice, co-oper-
ation, obedience, respect, wisdom, hard work etc . Although when
proverbs usually meant for children are directed at an adult target,
it acquires offensive and deeper connotation, becomes an outright
vilification. Apart from serving as didactic and cognitive oral speech
capsules, proverbs posted on satiric occasions elicit appropriate behaviour and initiate a new attitude in a person. These they achieve
through sarcasm, quips, analogy, irony, understatement of image,
and even of fact, all of them found in proverb content.

As it has been hinted at the initial segments of this chapter, the
Igbo relish their freedom and express it through a constant engage-
ment with words, expressions and speech making, and as is well
known, proverbs are handy tools in mature communication. In the
Igbo social setting, eloquence attracts respect and trust. Subsequently, because most speeches aim at persuasion, the proverb is a helpful
rhetorical aid. Proverb in persuasive speech act/aim to bring about
a change in attitude, a conviction, a new estimate of the speaker and
a reinforcement of worthwhile values. An adult speechmaker who
spices his/her speech with local sayings is instantly regarded as being
rooted, firmly tethered to the earth as it were, identified as *nwafọ, diala or nfunala.* A little more elaboration of this view shall be done in the
next paragraph. At any rate, in speeches proverbs amplify a speaker's

view point and give it a stamp of authority by drawing analogies outside of the immediate circumstance. Because proverbs come to us as self-evident truths, they seem to require no further proof. A good speaker exploits this fact first by the appropriate alignment of the interaction situation and the proverb situation. This point has already been made. Secondly, the more copious such relevant proverbs are in relation to the context situation, the more convincing and effective the speech. Moreover, proverbs are akin to charters handed down from generations whose truism on many occasions are apt, reasoned and apparently inviolate.

It is in fact the image function of the proverb that really brings out what had already been said about the Igbo love for an expansive use of saws. By the image function, one is referring to proverb usage as a way of enhancing one's public reckoning not just as a good speaker but also as one versed in tradition. Every adult speaker among the Igbo would like to be seen as a true son or daughter, *nwafo*. Conversely, to make a speech without even an occasional reference to a saying or anecdotal proverb is to sound ordinary, to deny oneself of a mystique. Public-speaking before an Igbo audience demands a spasmodic citing of proverbs as a means of foregrounding ideas or justifying one's impressions and attitudes. Poor speakers in the Igbo milieu are those who cannot utilize proverbs at appropriate speech nodes; they are excluded from representing the community at inter-community negotiations or arbitration processes, and may never be community emissaries either of war or peace or reconciliation.

The aesthetic function of the Igbo proverb seems not to have been appreciated by Igbo scholars until much later (Emenanjo, "Some Notes" and "Phonological Repetition"; Monye, "The Use of Repetition" and *Proverbs in African Orature;* Nwachukwu-Agbada, "Aliases", "The Proverb in the Igbo Milieu", and *The Igbo Proverb*). The initial effort of the foreign and local scholars was to explicate, to show the profoundly of the Igbo proverb, its rich and protean philosophical content and the logic of its discourse properties. There was nothing wrong with this exertion, but to continue to consider the Igbo saying only from those prisms is a disservice to Igbo studies on the proverb and the other forms. The reason is that the Igbo also love rhythm, repetition and rhyme; they love poetry, song and dance. Above all they love pleasure derivable from what is said or heard. Thus the aesthetic function of Igbo proverb is located in its poetic application. It is the conscious use of proverbs in conversation and speech for the purpose of infecting one's audience with pleasure. Akan proverbs, remarks Lawrence Boadi, are popular not necessarily for their "truth value" but for the quality of the imagination or poetry that has gone into them. The same can be said of the Igbo effort at proverb coinage.

It is true that the proverb is a vehicle of ideas, and of traditional currency; however, their survival as speech acts owes more for their "style than for content; they impress, more for their technical appeal than as fossils of a complex world view" (Okpewho, *The Epic* 2). Elsewhere Okpewho was also to insist that

> Proverbs do have an entertainment value to them; whether we are referring to the way they are used in spicing up statements or making them more exciting to listeners or we are referring to their preludial or interludial use in narrative performance or even to songs made up entirely of proverbial lines, there is clearly a sense of beauty attached to them that appeals to the ears and to the imagination of the audience (*African Oral Literature* 235).

No doubt proverbs, nay Igbo proverbs, by their nature embellish speech and invent it with artistic finesse; they equally posses some rudimentary magic, combining luxuriant diction with apt imagery and picture-casting.

Igbo proverbs are equally sources of hurmour in native life, and indeed wherever an aggregation of the Igbo reside, whether in urban Nigeria or overseas. Some proverbs by their nature elicit laughter or a quick smirk when they are uttered, even when they are cited in serious and appropriate contexts. However, such humour proverbs enliven the audience, and their users thus go for them, notwithstanding that there may be alternative proverbs which could serve the same purpose. For instance, rather than say it is when you are close to someone that you can perceive the odour of his mouth, another user may prefer to say, 'You don't bite someone from a distance.' Or rather than remark that it is wrong to provoke another from a close shot, a proverb user may prefer to deploy this smile-inducing one: "A musician doesn't beat 'it is heavy, it is heavy' at the backyard of the man suffering from hydrocele". (Anaghi akụ 'o deberele, odeberele' na azụ-ụlọ onye ibi). In a usage situation, a good user of the Igbo proverb achieves more with 'new' or refurbishes ones. Those that can easily pass for a new are those rendered in 'Engligbo'. An observation about the emergence of Engligbo proverbs has been made earlier, but it should be said as well that their tendency to start off in Igbo and dovetail into English is an itself a source of humour. An example is, "Ozu nwabekee: ebulie ya elu 'no no no'; lower it, 'no no no'). (The white man's corpse; raise it, 'no no no'; lower it, 'no no no'"). In this saying, there are historical hint, code-switch, mimicry, mockery, characterization and invective. The historical information relates to the power enjoyed by the white colonialists borne on a hammock over long distances by able-bodied Africans, more or less his slaves. His corpse' is his body. The local people had to refer to his body as corpse because only corpses were borne that way in Igboland. There then is malediction, more or less a thorough abuse to so describe a living, breathing body. In the saying, the white man is characterized as one who is not easy to please, somewhat a perfectionist. The mockery is the introduced English particles of 'no no no' which would ordinarily be nasalized for effect.

Conclusion

So far in Igbo studies there has not been proverb enumeration to establish its number and variety. Nor would any such exercise yield a dependable figure for a reasonable period. The late D.I Nwoga started a project in that direction, but death did not allow him. His effort was to thematize the Igbo proverb corpus wherein each saying could be pigeonholed under certain themes whenever a new saw is encountered. Even then that could have given only an idea about their extent rather than their size or number. The reason is as already mentioned, namely that proverb production in Igbo is a continuous activity. Otherwise the proverb corpus in Igboland is really a large one. The intent of this paper has not been to hazard a guess as to its number, but to proffer reasons why the Igbo proverb yield may continue to be rich, to found probable reasons why both proverb minting and proverb usage are popular engagements, why proverb production and proverb deployment in utterances are such attractive events both in the Igbo past and in the present. In other words, why is it that Westernization has not been able to discourage proverb coinage and use? As a people who are said to easily abandon their heritage once it cannot serve a material purpose, why are the Igbo still in love with the aesthetic deployment of sayings in their speech and conversational events?

WORKS CITED

Achufusi, G.I. "The Main Genres of African Traditional Literature". *Nigerian Magazine* 53.2 (1985). 66–83. Print.

Barrick, M.E. "Welcome to the Clothes': Changing Proverb Function in the Spanish Renaissance". *Proverbium* 2 (1985). 1–17. Print.

Boadi, L.A. "The Language of the Proverb in Akan". *African Folklore.* Ed. Richard Dorson. Bloomington: Indiana University Press, 1972. 183–91. Print.

Chukwuma, Helen. *Igbo Oral Literature: Theory and Tradition.* Abak: Belpot (Nig.) Co.; 1994. Print.

Cram, David. "A Note on the Logic of Proverbs". *Proverbium* 2 (1985). 271.72. Print.

Egudu, R.N. "Social Values and Thoughts in Traditional Literature: The Case of the Igbo Proverb and Poetry". *Nigerian Libraries* 3.2 (1972). 63–84. Print.

Emenanjo, E.N. "Phonological Repetition in Igbo Proverbs. An Aspect of Traditional African Poetry". *Nigerian Journal of the Humanities* 3.3 (1979). 107–117. Print.

—. "Some Notes on the Use of Repetition and Contrasts in Some Igbo Proverbs". *Ikenga* 1.1 (Jan. 1972). 109–114. Print.

Ezikeojiaku, Ichie. "Classification of Igbo Orature'". *Nigeria Magazine* 53.2 (1985). 66–83. Print.

Kirshenblatt-Gimblett, Barbara. "Towards a Theory of Proverb Meaning". *Proverbium* 22 (1973, Old Series). 821–27. Print.

Mieder, Wolfgang. *Yes We Can: Barack Obama's Proverbial Rhetoric.* New York: Peter Lang, 2009. Print.

Monye, Ambrose. *Proverbs in African Orature: The Aniocha Igbo Example.* Lanham: University Press America, 1996. Print.

—. "The Use of Repetition and Contrasts in Igbo Proverbs: A Comment". *Ikenga* 7.1&2 (1985). 170–71. Print.

Nwachukwu-Agbada, J.O.J. "An African Oral Literature and the Socialization of the Youth: The Case of Igbo Child-Proverbs". *Frankfurter Afrikanistische Blatter* 2 (1990). 107–199. Print.

—. The African Proverb and the Living Present: A Paradigm from Recent Igbo Paremiology". Plenary Speech at the 1st 'Proverb Conference in Nigeria', Obafemi Awolowo University 1st–5th August, 2006 (18pp).

Nwachukwu-Agbada, J.O.J. "Aliases Among the Anambra Igbo: The Proverbial Dimension". *Names* 39.2 (June, 1991). 81–94. Print.

—. "Chinua Achebe's Literary Proverbs as Reflections of Igbo Cultural and Philosophical Tenets". *Proverbium* 10 (1993). 215–35. Print.

—. *The Igbo Proverb: A Study of Its Context, Performance and Functions.* Enugu: John Jacob's Publishers, 2002. Print.

—. "The Old Woman in Igbo Proverbial Lore". *Southern Folklore* (Kentucky) 46.3 (1989). 241–54. Print.

—. "The Proverb in the Igbo Milieu". *Anthropos* (Frankfurt) 89 (1994). 194–200. Print.

Nwadike, I.U. "The Igbo Proverb: A Wilder Perspective". *Nigeria Magazine.* 57.1&2 (Jan-June). 31–37. Print.

Nwoga, D.I. "Appraisal of Igbo Proverbs and Idioms". *Igbo Language and Culture.* Vol. I. Ed. F.C. Ogbalu and E.N. Emenanjo. Ibadan: Oxford University Press, 1975. 186–204. Print.

Okpewho, Isidore. *African Oral Literature: Backgrounds, Character, and Continuity.* Blomington: Idiana University Press, 1992. Print.

—. *The Epic in Africa.* New York: Columbia University Press, 1979. Print.

Opata, D.U. "Igbo Attitude to Women: A Study of a Proverb". *Power and Powerlessness of Women in West African Orality.* Ed. Raoul Granqvist and Nnadozie Inyama. Umea: Umea University, 1992. 95–108. Print

—. "The Nature of Speech in Igbo Proverbs". *Proverbium* 9 (1992). 187–204. Print.

Osofisan, Femi. "Literacy as Suicide". *Afriscope* (January, 1977). 17–23. Print.

Otakpor, Nkeonye. "A Note on the Logic of Proverbs: A Reply". *Proevrbium* 4 (1987). 263–69. Print.

Ottemberg, Simon. "Ibo Receptivity to Change". *Continuity and Change in African Cultures.* Ed. W.R. Bascom and M.J. Herskovits. Chicago: Chicago University press, 1959. 130–43. Print.

Penfield, Joyce. *Communicating with Quotes: The Igbo Case.* Wesport, Connecticut: Greenwood Press, 1983. Print.

Seitel ,Peter. "Proverbs: A Social Use of Metaphor". *Folklore Genres.* Ed. Dan Ben-Amos. Austin, Texas: University of Texas Press, 1976. 125–43. Print.

Shelton, Austin. "Relativism, Pragmatism and Reciprocity in Igbo Proverbs". *The Conch* 111.2 (Sept, 1971). 46–66. Print.

Sofola, Zulu. "Okwu di na nka': The Art of the Word Among Bendel Igbo". *Nigeria Magazine* 54.1 (1986–). 68–75. Print.

Chapter Sixteen

Njakiri, The Quintessence
of the Traditional Igbo Sense of Satire

Afam Ebeogu

THE QUINTESSENTIAL NJAKIRI

C.K. Meek, a British anthropologist commissioned by the British colonial government of Nigeria to study the Igbo in the 1930s, observed of the people's sense of humour:

> Mere abuse is not a deadly sin, and one may often see two Ibo (sic) reviling each other in the strongest of language for several minutes and then bursting into laughter as they walk away. (230)

This is a perceptive observation, though it ignores the contexts in which this apparently inoffensive mutual verbal onslaught can take place. The practice whereby, among the Igbo, two parties revile each other in the strongest of language "with laughter and apparent light-heartedness" (Egudu 77) is called *njakiri*. It has two essential rhetorical ingredients: sarcasm (*ikọ ọnụ*) and curse (*ikpọ iyi*), except that the latter in an *njakiri* situation loses its virulence and cannot be equated with the curse that is associated with supernatural and magical ends.[1] When these two shades of the rhetorical art, in combination with relevant literary instruments, are given informal dramatic situation, then an *njakiri* context emerges.

Let me illustrate this point with a representative *njakiri* contest recorded in June, 1987 at a gathering of a section of my patrilineage, in which I was both an observer and a participant. The occasion was festive: all the available adult males of this section of the patrilineage had assembled in order to slaughter and share a cow given to them by a patrilineal nephew who had bought himself a car.[2]

While the event was in progress, the men chatted, the conversation oscillating between the serious and the comic. The extract from the *njakiri* duel below was recorded, transcribed and translated by me.[3] In the transcription, square brackets surround explanatory comments; round brackets distinguish paralinguistic features.

> Z: Brother [to N]. I did not know that you would be here for this occasion. See you, you have come to eat the meat brought by someone who bought a motor car. And yet when you bought your own 'chassis' [meaning that the car was brand new] nobody heard *pim* [that is, nobody knew]. The day I saw you, you sitting in the car like a woman with a painful waist and drove past *fiam* [that is, with great speed], I called and called and called your name and you stuck out your bald head from the car window and said, "I am coming" (mimics voice). Up to this moment you are still coming, he who enjoys eating only when it is another's.

> K[4]: Don't mind N; just leave him to do whatever he likes. They say he is educated, but I say he has lost his senses.

(General laughter)

> K: If what I have said makes you laugh, you laugh. But I am not amused. It is not a laughing matter. Look at him, see him, this N that I am just looking at, with a head like a vulture's. (Laughter). He thinks that he is wise, but it is the wisdom of a young man who tells his father that he got a son before him [his father]. N bought a new car, drove it past this patrilineage, mark you, he drove it past this square that I am just looking at and went down to his in-laws' place for the car to be blessed. And he has not shown the car to his patrilineal kinsmen. It is an abomination.

> N: Brothers, you know it is not the truth—

> K: What is not the truth: that you bought a car or that you drove it down to your in-laws' to be blessed?

(Laughter)

> N: K is not telling you the truth. As usual he is trying to kill a fly with a mortar. He is like the old man who wastes the soup.[5] I—

> K: (Voice raised) Will you shut up, you kid! Have you presented the car to us, yes or no?

N: Is it too late?

K: Ha! Ha! Ha! Is it too late? You mean that after taking the car first to your in-laws, you will then bring it to us to bless? There is nothing these my ears will not hear in this age.

N: It is not true that I took the car to my in-laws to bless. You are just fabricating that lie[6]. I went to my in-laws in the car, but not for them to bless it.

K: *E ... ei!* (expressing disbelief). You are telling me. Go and tell that to a child born yesterday [that is, a baby] .

Z: I even hear that he spends the night there occasionally. (General laughter) He leaves his house and sleeps in his in-law's.

N: (to Z) Keep quiet, you good-for-nothing. So when others talk you also talk? At least I have a house. Look at you. At you age you are not even thinking of getting married.[7] As for building a house, that will be in your next incarnation. And when other talk you also talk.

E: *Chei!* That was a hard one. Brother Z, are you going to let him go with that?

Z: Won't you keep quiet, you charcoal-complexioned one? If you "venture to talk again" (said in English), I will expose you. I will spread you as a piece of cloth is spread in the sun.

E: Me?

Z: Yes, You bugger.

E: (Roars with laughter) I was only trying to save you from being fried alive by this brother. Was I the person who said that you are playing "bom-boy" while your age-mates are marrying and building houses?

Z: My brothers, you see how E is trying to ignite my anger? Let no one touch the leopard by the tail, whether he is alive or dead.

(General laughter)

E: Where is the leopard, you? What do you think you can say against me, you tout?[8] '

Z: See this "Money-Miss-Road" coming here to open his mouth wide. (general laughter) What is it that makes you proud? Because you built that hut you call a house? That is why we shall

all run whenever you pass? You do not see the two and three-sto-reyed houses that people with whom you left for the city are building? D you mean that if those who have houses are asked to file out, you will join the queue?

(General laughter)

K: (in tears of laughter) The world is really gone berserk. A man who still sleeps in his mother's hut jeers at someone who owns his own house.

Z: (Somewhat animated) I know that I have no money. But you wait. Someday I am going to be rich, And—

E: That is after you must have robbed a bank.

General laughter)

Z: You wait, I tell you. And when the money comes, I will not be the miserly goat that you are. I will show you that I am "The One Whose Wealth never Finishes".

(Prolonged general laughter)

The *njakiri* session of which this is a part lasted throughout the event that brought the group together, with new material for humour replacing exhausted material. When, however, toward the end of the festivity, N wanted to leave, K went back to the original subject-matter and asked him if he was sure that he was actually going back to the city: was he not going to his in-laws? Thunderous laughter followed this remark. N, laughing too, got into his car and as he drove off, he remark: "Z, You're wrong in the head!"

The sense of humour underlying the episode is unmistakable. It is satiric humour, and the satire is not mild, but hard-hitting. In the first place, people are ridiculed in unsparing language for actions which are considered culturally inappropriate: K says N is mad for apparently loving his in-laws more than his patrilineal kinsmen; N calls him a "good-for-nothing" for not having been able to get married and build a house; and Z, in turn, jeers at N for his miserliness, calling him a "Money-Miss Road". Secondly, people make fun of others for defects of nature (though not deformities): K calls N "a vulture" because he is bald; Z lampoons E for his very dark complexion; and E ridicules Z for daring to allude to himself as a leopard.

Like Horatian satire, *Njakiṛi* is "most useful" (Bullit 7) though, in contrast, it does have the potential for giving offence. Its "usefulness" arises from the corrective overtones of the jibes; people use the opportunity afforded by this exchange of verbal missiles to make serious criticism of others. For example, K, the oldest in the group, is quite serious about the "abomination" N has committed in by-passing his patrilineal kinsmen in favour of his in-laws; and it becomes increasingly clear that N is being ridiculed, not just for going to his in-law's first to have his new car blessed, but also for his habit of visiting his in-laws more than his patrilineal kinsmen. To traditionalist, this is a violation of Igbo etiquette and suggests that the wife is the "boss" of the home.

At the start of the *njakiṛi* session, we note that the first speaker has his tongue in his cheek when he tells N that he did not know N would be present at the party. Since the invitation was to all members of that section of the partilineage, morally speaking, attendance was almost mandatory. N's presence would in fact, give some members of the group a good deal of satisfaction, since it would afford an opportunity to tell him, by means of an *Njakiṛi* session, what very few of them would dare discuss with him privately. Ordinarily N's preference for his in-laws would be considered a private matter, but it is apparent that it had become the subject of disturbing rumour in the community and that the men of the patrilineage felt obliged to bring their kinsman to order.

It is obvious that Z, too, is being ridiculed, in this case for not having an enterprising spirit—which is indeed the case, for many people in the community regard him as a good-for-nothing who enjoys basking in the glory of his brothers' achievements. Nevertheless, Z still has the verbal felicity to hit out at E for being a "Money-Miss-Road"—which again is the general opinion and a serious criticism. The Igbo generally work very hard, perhaps too hard, for material success. This success is demonstrated by letting others benefit from it, either by giving festive parties which enable the less-privileged to feed themselves to the full without paying, or (by awarding scholarships for the education of the children of the poor or by building major institutions, schools, medical clinics and civic centres, for the community. Though E is generally regarded as well-to-do, he has not done any of these things, so he is generally regarded as a man "whose wealth has not yet reached home" (that is, whose wealth has not been of benefit to his kinsmen). When, therefore, Z taunts him for his miserliness, this opinion reflects that of the community.

We notice that, toward the end of the duel, Z, ever hopeful, boasts that he expects to be a rich man, and that when this happens the world will know! He has in fact already appropriated to himself an Igbo praise epithet, *Okpata Aku Ericha Ericha*, which literally translates as "He whose wealth never Finishes". Thus, within the context of this particular *Njakiri* session, Z is a kind of foil top E. A man who is a material failure (the Igbo, unfortunately, have no sympathy for failures) becomes a useful instrument for reminding the successful man that his success is not yet culturally valid.

Underlying the *Njakiri* exercise, therefore, is the expectation that attitudes and practices unacceptable to the community can be corrected by members of that community. But what probably gives the *Njakiri* its uniqueness is that, though it is inherently defamatory, no one is expected to take offence at any insult; rather, one is expected, not necessarily to *possess*, but to be able to *muster* the rare discipline to remain felicitous and to deny words their power to hurt. Indeed, what the victim of the verbal onslaught is expected to do is have the presence of mind to initiate a counter-offensive to disarm the opponent.

This point can be illustrated from the transcription. When K uses a number of deflating expression to ridicule N, the latter does not take any obvious offence. Instead, though no doubt he recognizes that he owes K the respect an elderly person is always accorded to in this community, he proceeds to call K "an old man who wastes soup". He can do so because he is aware that, within the *Njakiri* context, K will not take offence at this jibe. Nor does he do so. What K recognizes quickly enough, however, is that N's comment is an attempt to snatch the verbal offensive from him, so he instinctively strives to retain his advantage. First of all, he attempts to intimidate

N by loudly telling him to shut up, then, while the shock of this re-
buke is still registering, he rushes back to the topic of the car-owner
that by-passed his own patrilineage on his way to the in-law's. "Have
you presented the car to us yet? Yes or no", he demands, which
quickly puts N back on the defensive again. Aware of the moral twist
which K has now introduced into the dialogue, N attempts a placa-
tory explanation, "I went to my in-laws in the car, but not for them
to bless it". K. however, merely scoffs: "Tell that to a baby!" and
pursues his advantage. At this point Z hauls up a verbal missile—"I
even hear that he spends the night there occasionally"—and N is
quick to espy an avenue of escape from the masterful grip of K. He
turns on Z, the small fry, and introduces the latently sensitive issue
of the latter's material wretchedness: "At least I have a house!" E,
recognizing the satiric potential of the fresh topic, tries to fuel that
new thrust: "Chei! That was a hard one. Brother Z, are you going
to let him go on with that?" Z, aware of his vulnerability, seeks to
bolt out of a difficult situation with a quick insult—"Won't you keep
quiet, you charcoal-complexioned one?"—and gain the offensive by
fencing with E rather than with N.

A new topic now opens up: Z lampoons E's miserliness and E responds with jibes about Z's material wretchedness. Note that, though
Z is being ridiculed over an issue as sensitive as poverty, he dares not
take overt offence. Instead, he deals his master-thrust: he admits his
poverty, and in the same breath asserts that he has plans to become
the richest and most generous man on earth. His verbal felicity is
disarming and everyone collapses in laughter.

Though participants in a *Njakiri* are not expected to take offence,
some may do, especially if what they have been told makes them
feel humiliated. As A.E Afigbo puts it, "the Igbo are exceptionally
humorous, but there is nothing they hate more than being ridiculed
and humiliated" (22). Nevertheless, to react with violence or ill-will
to what one is told in an *Njakiri* duel is regarded as unmanly: others
will comment disapprovingly that the fellow "is not an *Njakiri* person", which implies that he is too serious and may have something to
hide. What is expected of a person who may feel hurt by an *Njakiri*

satiric comment is that he will correct the fault that makes him or her vulnerable. In any case, everyone has the opportunity to hit back at their opponent.

A story is told of a well-known rich man who was once quite poor until, in an *njakiri* spirit, he was denied an opportunity to speak in a community gathering on the ground that a titled man was on his feet. Whereupon this man swore that he was going to devote the rest of his life, even if he died in the attempt, to try to become wealthy enough to initiate himself and fourteen members of his extended family into the *Ozo*-titled class! For the *ozo*-titled praise epithet he chose *Ezekwesiri Eruchalu*, "The one Worthy to be a King, Whose Wealth is the Big Flood that Collects the Rest". It is an obviously hyperbolic choice, as most Igbo praise epithets are, but one appreciates the psychology behind it: it is the product of an *njakiri* episode.

Would any topic, therefore, be suitable for *njakiri*? In theory, every Igbo community expects its individual members to exercise some measure of discretion, not only in choosing what topic to use as a subject for *njakiri*, but also in the way a verbal onslaught is framed. Certain topics and events, either because of their sensitivity or because they are issues for which no human being can really be held responsible, are considered unfit for *njakiri*. For example, in the *njakiri* duel we have discussed in this essay, participants carefully avoid ridiculing N's in-laws, and to restrict the attacks to N himself. A covert resentment against the people who have hi-jacked the attention of a member of the patrilineage is discernible, but the participants are careful not to drag the absent in-laws directly into the duel. The in-law relationship is highly revered among the Igbo. The people have a saying to the effect that "one's in-law is his personal god" (*ogo bu chi onye*). The participants in this verbal art would not want to undermine their sense of propriety by disparaging N's in-laws. Ultimately, the choice of materials for the verbal duel lies at the discretion of the individuals, although a tactless choice might lead to unpleasantness.

So far, this essay has concentrated on *njakiri* in its quintessential form: an informal verbal event possessing its own atmosphere and dramaturgy and relying on a dynamic interplay between event, occasion, character and timing. As a satiric art, *njakiri*

1. attacks without animosity, both the individual and his "fault";
2. perceives that "fault" essentially from the perspective of its community dimensions, its spiritual or moral aspects assuming only secondary importance;
3. deploys all available verbal resources of ridicule with intent to humiliate the object of the assault;
4. relies on wit and humour for effect;
5. expects the victim of the attack to absorb the wound without reacting violently, no matter how indignant he may feel;
6. implies that the attacker is in turn prepared to receive and absorb any form of response from his victim;
7. allows that, outside the *njakiri* context, no party in the duel is expected to be held accountable for whatever might have been said during the contest.

NJAKIRI IN ITS LITERARY CONTEXT

The literary and rhetorical devices employed in an *njakiri* duel usually include true narrative and fictionalized experiences, anecdotes, folk tales, proverbs, idioms and other forms of oratory. The participants in this verbal fencing may also employ:

> Invectives, sarcasm, burlesque, irony, mockery, raillery, parody, exaggeration, understatement, wit in any of its forms-anything to make the object of attack abhorrent or ridiculous.(Coffey 27)

The speech which initiates the *njakiri* duel discussed here, for example, "I did not know you would be here for this occasion", is delivered melodramatically with a great deal of gesturing and mimicry. The rhetoric of the session includes direct verbal attacks and caricature. N is described as perching on the seat of his car "like a woman with a painful waist"; accused of having "lost his senses" and of having a head "like a vulture's". Z too is insulted as a "wretch" and E is called a "bugger", a "tout" and a miser. Figures of speech and idioms drawn from the Igbo culture and environment abound. The metaphor of "the old man who wastes soup" is traditional, and so are the idioms "a child born yesterday" and "to kill a fly with a mortar"; the proverb "Let no one touch the leopard by the tail, whether he is alive or dead" and the ironic reference to "the wisdom of a young man who tells his father that he got a son before him". The latter not only echoes an Igbo proverb with the same content (*A makam ihe sịrị nna ya na ya e burula ya ụzọ mụta diọkpara*), but is also a popular Igbo anecdote. Together with the sense of the ironic which runs through the whole exchange, they enhance the literary content of the text. *Njakịrị* can thus be regarded as the quintessence of a traditional Igbo sense of satire in two senses: first, a great many of the satiric practices of the culture reveal an underlying *njakịrị* spirit, and secondly, it is built into the poetics of the language.

A few illustrations of this observation are called for. Before colonial contact and the subsequent establishment of modern court and legal institutions, the traditional Igbo communities relied, among other things, on ritualized verbal and non-verbal satiric practices for punishing citizens who committed certain types of offence, for example, stealing certain categories of property. The thief, costumed in a particular degrading manner, would be forced to dance round the community to the rhythm of a special type of music, with a large crowd trailing him and jeering.[9]

Though these highly functional devices of judicial ridicule had verbal content, each was circumscribed by the ritual structure of the judicial process and was, therefore, not very amenable to artistic license. In any case, the contemporary scholar of traditional humour has no opportunity of studying these practices in context, since modern courts and para-judicial establishments have replaced these traditional practices as instruments of legal control.

But there are other forms of punitive satiric practices in the culture which are almost entirely verbal and are related to the spirit of *njakiri*. One such is the large repertoire of Igbo women's songs which have remained popular even in contemporary times. These songs lend themselves to various taxonomic delineations,[10] but this paper will concern itself with their function among Igbo village women as a medium for criticizing what they consider to be the follies and vices of their community. About these songs Sylvia Leith-Ross had observed:

> 'making a song' i.e. shame and ridicule on the victim by means of more or less ribald improvisations concerning his or her appearance, character, and conduct is a popular and very effective form of Ibo punishment. (97)

One such song, reproduced below, was made by the women of Amasiri, an Igbo community in the Afikpo Local Government Area of Ebonyi State. These women generally consider their men very chauvinistic, and a great many of their songs are targeted at the menfolk (though some are directed at the women themselves or at the younger members of the community). This community, like any typical Igbo community, is male-dominated; even though the women exercise an appreciable degree of economic independence, they do not feel as free as the men to spend their money the way it pleases them. There are structured socio-political arrangements which enable the women to express their views and fight for their rights publicly, but these arrangements do not provide a regular forum in which both sexes can engage in democratic debate.

The women, therefore, tend to revert to the medium of art—their satirical songs—to make public their criticism of the menfolk and the rest of society.

Although these Amasiri-Afikpo songs can be performed at every moment the women feel appropriate, especially at festivals, the most distinguished occasion for singing them and for releasing new ones is during the annual festival of Igwo Iyi ("The Cleansing of the Stream")[11].

The song quoted below is from the repertoire of *egwu igwo iyi*. Functionally it is a work song; the women sing it in unison while they weed and sweep clean the stream and its environs, and occasionally use their working tools as rhythmic percussion. Some of the women use obscene gestures to demonstrate the antics of the men who are ridiculed in the song. These demonstrations often lack restraint, especially since the ritual of the cleaning of the stream is wholly a women's affair and no man would be expected to be present. (In practice, though, a handful of men pass by, ostensibly going about their normal business; they observe the performance with feigned indifference, but go back to the village and talk about it.) The occasion usually produces new compositions which are added to the corpus of women's satirical songs. At the end of the event, the women go back to the village with the songs, which are then gradually diffused into the society as a whole as individual women and groups of children sing them informally and as other women's groups incorporate relevant aspects of the songs into their own repertoire of the satirical songs which are performed during childbirths, ceremonies, festivals and other female group outings. Here is the song:

Igbo (Afikpo Dialect)

We hụnụ nwanyi kpuru ekpu, taa maama

Ha jụwa diya,

Ị na-ajụ ma I lụrụ?

Ị ma akpo eku?

Ị ma akpọ eku dari peni?

O meche onye ọzọ a wamomuo

O meche onye ọzọ a maghị onye ụlọ eme,

Onye ụlọ a kụa yaa.

O meche onye ọzọ

Mgbe dum nwunye gi ma mkpekere eku.

Lụchaa nke ilụụ n'ụlọ

M'ichoje onye ọzọ

English Literal translation

If they see any woman gorgeously dressed

They inquire to know who she is,

Do you ask so that you will marry her?

Can you buy dresses?

Can you buy a pennyworth of dresses?

Admirer of outsiders.

Every time your wife is seen in tattered dresses.

Care for the wife you have in the house

Before admiring an outsider (Okpara, Appendix, Song 1)

In the song, the women ridicule men who are unfaithful to their wives. They say that these men admire other women who are beautiful and well dressed, but do not care to provide their wives with good clothes so that they can look pretty too. Instead, the men keep mistresses outside the home and lavish on them the attention they fail to give to their wives. Even though the song is performed by a group of women, there are indications that it originated in the first place in a particular marital experience (note, for example, the shift in line 3 from the third-person plural pronoun to the second-person singular pronoun).

Thus there are four discernible characters or groups of characters in the song: a specific woman who accuses her husband of waywardness; a specific husband who indulges in extra-marital affairs; the menfolk of Amasiri of whom the specific man is only a representative and who are therefore all branded with the same faults; and the women of Amasiri who satirize the man's marital irresponsibility and neglect. Throughout the song the *njakiri* spirit is evident in these respects:

(a). The festival enables the women to openly confront the men (and perhaps the particular husband whose actions initiated the song);
(b). The women indulge in personal abuse;
(c). In turn, passing men shout back at the singers;
(d). Even though the women are serious both in their condemnation of infidelity and in their expectation that the men will reform, there is no animosity;
(e). There is a good deal of humour, especially when the women invoke a variety of histrionic and comic markers to strengthen their ridicule.

Because the context of this particular song invests it with a greater degree of universality than the particular experience which gave rise to it, it is less hard-hitting than a typical *njakiṛi* duel. But the women do have many songs in their repertoire in which their satire is less mellow. A good example is the following in which the target of attack is not disguised at all:

Igbo (Afikpo Dialect)

Akpu onye aṛụrala.

Zụta ncha peni.

Isi ha gị ka igbe ozu

Ha muo na a laamue.

Ọnụ dịghị ka nkapị

Onye ogbomgbo isi.

Dahụ banụnụ na owue m ewu.

Ihe Akpu meri nwa nnem nta,

Ọ na ewem iwe.

A magi m ekwe.

English Translation

Akpu the wicked.

Buy a pennyworth of soap you can't.

With a head as big as coffin.

Leave me alone; you have messed me up.

Your mouth is like that of a rabbit.

The large-headed one,

(Head) too large to be shifted without discomfort.

The thing Akpu did to my younger sister,

It pains me.

I will not forgive him. (Okpara, Appendix, Song 59)

Here, the target of the song, Akpu, is attacked for putting the complainant's younger sister in the family way. The singer's resentment and discomfort at the consequent scandal is shown by the sudden switch of mood between the comic and the mournful. The comic element is sustained by constant name-calling and denigration of Akpu's integrity, and his appearance alike is attacked. However, this personal resentment is transformed the moment the events become material for the satiric song of *igwo iyi*. Within this performance ambience, Akpu's offence becomes a matter for public concern. The women have taken over the case, and their business is, not so much to forgive him, as to expose him. He becomes a representative of the meanness of the menfolk.

In a similar satirical song by a different group of Igbo village women, the target of the attack is not the man who has put a girl in the family way but the girl who is pregnant (Ezejideaku 45): she had shifted the blame for her situation to another man who had to prove his innocence by swearing to a ritual oath and surviving the ordeal. The song, which is a narrative, ridicules the girl for her waywardness and wickedness. The women mention the names of all the three persons involved, but it is the girl who is satirized: she is called a sheep and derided as the plaything of all young men in the community. This direct naming of the objects of ridicule is characteristic of the quintessential *njakiri*, in which it is imperative that the target of attack be accused in person.

Most theorists and practitioners of the art of satire as a written form, from Archilochus through Aristophanes to Juvenal, Horace, Moliere, Voltaire, Johnson, Pope and Swift, in differing degrees all emphasize the corrective end of the satiric exercise. The Igbo women, too, insist that the ultimate aim of their songs is to attract the attention of "everybody" to the "bad things" being practiced in the society.

It is significant that most "women satirical songs" in Amasiri are composed in the process of ritual cleansing of the community's stream, a source of life, fertility and regeneration. The moral purpose of the songs—to cleans the society—is thus symbolized by the ritual event during which they are composed. The women's expectation establishes an immediate link between these songs and the quintessential *njakiri*.

In everyday conversation in Igbo society, one finds that a great deal of the humour derives from bits of *njakiri* now and then unobtrusively slipped in to cause amusement and occasional roars of laughter. Though they are totally inoffensive, these pieces retain some essentials of satire. For example, a man is visited by a relation who has not paid this kind of visit for quite some time. The host, while greeting the visitor with warmth, says: "Well, it looks as if I am going to win some raffle today. I had thought I had become a feeder on human flesh".[12] To which the visitor replies: "You have always been a feeder on human flesh; the size of your carnivorous teeth shows it". Both parties laugh, join hands and move into the house. Satiric comments have been made about people who do not visit others and about people with protruding teeth, but nobody takes offence.

It is from this kind of folk-satiric tradition that many Nigerian Igbo novelists, especially of Chinua Achebe's generation, have derived their comic strength: as much as possible they cushion into their narratives witty and humorous expressions and dialogue that appear to have been lifted from live conversations.[13] When characters in their everyday life, in fiction and out of fiction, make *njakịrị*-derived utterances in speeches and conversations, they are not usually involved in overtly satirical practices; but the exercise bestows on their language a peculiarly humorous colour which can only really be appreciated in relation to Igbo satiric tradition. In this specific context, direct criticism loses its power to provoke a serious reaction, and instead assumes the status of an apparently inconsequential joke. It is a tribute to the high tolerance ethic of Igbo society that a people who otherwise have an extremely serious view of life can thus deny words their provocative value.

Conclusion

In modern times, when the Nigerian society is becoming increasingly complex and cosmopolitan—when individuals more and more adopt their own private ethical codes, when religions impose their own canons of decorum, and governments legislate to ensure human rights and establish laws of libel—it is necessary to raise the question of the future of *njakịrị*, a verbal practice that derives its semantic and rhetorical resources from communities that hold certain beliefs, practices and moral codes in common. In a multi-ethnic country like Nigeria, such a question is very relevant. Some individuals are known to have objected to an *njakiri* session on the basis that its occasional bawdiness is unchristian. Others, especially people who have lived for a long time outside the Igbo culture area, tend to resent the practice and regard it as both abusive and libellous. Conversely, Igbo people who live in other parts of the country and who have tried to export the *njakiri* spirit to non-Igbo people have been accused of arrogance, indiscretion and boastfulness: what would have been acceptable behaviour within their own culture is deemed evidence of insensitivity by some other ethnic groups in the country. Chinua Achebe aptly articulates the situation:

> This kind of success [of the Igbo in Nigeria's socio-economic system] can carry a deadly penalty: the danger of *hubris*, over-weening pride and thoughtlessness, which invite envy and hatred; or even worse, which can obsess the mind with material success and dispose it to all kinds of crude showiness.

There is no doubt at all that there is a strand in contemporary Igbo behaviour which can offend by its noisy exhibitionism and disregard for humility and quietness (46).

In this kind of situation, *njakiri* is likely to lose some of its potency as a satirical instrument and some of its effectiveness as humour: on the one hand, practitioners of this vernal art are becoming more sensitive about the context, especially the sort of people present in a particular potential *njakiri* situation; and on the other hand, the practice is increasingly leading to cases of interpersonal and inter-group misunderstanding. It is unlikely that *njakiri* in its oral form will be entirely phased out, but one suspects that written literature will increasingly become the custodian of the spirit of the tradition. For, as long as creative writers from the Igbo culture, writing in the Igbo language or in English, continue to draw their resources of rhetoric and humour from what Wordsworth called the "very language of men", so long will they capture in the rhythm of their dialogues and expressions nuances of *njakiri*. The quality and intensity of these nuances will depend on the quality and intensity of the dynamic interplay between the oral and the written word.

NOTES

1. It is the failure to distinguish between the religio-magical curse and the humour-bound "deflated curse" of mundane utterances that renders defective Nwoga's argument on the origin of the "satirical urge" among the Igbo. See Nwoga, "The Concept and Practice of Satire among the Igbo" (34).

2. In the Igbo culture, it is customary for any member of a patrilineage who has had some striking good luck, usually of a material nature, to host a party for the patrilineage or a section of it with a consanguineous relationship no more distant than first patrilineal cousins. The opportunities for such parties include child-birth, title initiations, marriages, dedication of new houses, purchase of cars, etc. The participants invariably become a natural cast in which the rituals of celebration evoke a high degree of communal consciousness.

3. I shall use only a single initial to refer to each person. Since I knew all those present closely, I had no problem identifying the voices when I played back the tape. Indeed, it was only my membership of the group that enabled me to do the recording in the first place; I explained that I was studying the way people said certain things in the Igbo language. The recording was then in Igbo, with English words and expressions thrown in here and there. In translating the transcript, I have tried to retain as much as possible certain Igbo speech nuances in the utterances, without undermining the intelligibility of the English translation.

4. K, in his sixties, is the eldest in the group, and is generally regarded as the most traditional in that section of the patrilineage.

5. The Igbo idiomatically refer to an adult who is playing children's pranks as "the elder who wastes soup". In Igbo cuisine, each meal of pounded cassava (often called 'foo'foo' in Pidgin English) is accompanied by a helping of soup sufficient for the *foo-foo*. To waste the soup also wastes the *foo-foo*— only a child would not be aware of this fact. The elder who wastes soup is therefore an adult who is as uninformed as a child.

6. "Fabricating a lie" is a literal translation. It may sound tautological, but is reflective of the nature of the relationship between some Igbo verbs and

their objects. For example, whereas "He is eating [some] food" may sound tautological in English since whatever is "eaten" is in any case some kind of food, this expression would be the perfect translation of *O na-eri nri,* which is the normal way Igbo expresses the act of feeding.

7. The age-old spirit of competition through the structure of age-grade organizations persists in modern times. When members of one's age-grade begin to achieve certain successes, it is considered slothful for one to lag behind; one should be able to boast that one has also achieved what most of one's age-mates have achieved.

8. That is, "passenger tout". In Nigeria, the expression is generally used to refer to layabouts in motor stations who often harass passengers in an attempt to induce them to patronize particular commercial vehicles. They are notorious for their crude behaviour and general bawdiness. Incidentally, they are experts at *njakiri* and do occasional settle scores with fists.

9. D.I. Nwoga mentions the evolution of satire among the Igbo from this rituastic, judicial context to the purely verbal context characterized by humour and amusement in "The Igbo Poet and Satire", (Abalogu, Ashiwaju & Amadi-Tshiwala (1981). Some anthropologists on the Igbo have discussed the pre-colonial Igbo use of ritual satire as an instrument of punishment of judicial offences. See Meek 217; Leith-Ross 97 and Nsugbe 64.

10. Chapter eight of this book has discussed the thematic and stylistic features of Igbo women's birth and maternity songs. See also D.I. Nwoga's "Mma nwayi Wi Nwa: Poetic Images of Childbirth Among the Igbo" (142–165).

11. I am obliged to one of my former students, Mrs. Veronica Okpara, for the painstaking research she did on these songs under my supervision. See also Veronica Okpara 1986.

12. "Not being a *feeder on human flesh*" (*Ori anu mmadu*), which literally means "not being a cannibal" is an Igbo idiomatic expression often used by someone to protest over his or her being isolated or feared. Such a person could say to a child afraid to approach him or her, "Come on, I will not eat you. I do not eat human beings". The expression features most often in humorous conversations and comments. The English equivalent might be "I won't bite you!".

13. For comments on the folkloric quality of the dialogues and speeches in the works of these novelists from Eastern Nigeria, see: O.R. Dathorne 103; Moore 91; Obiechina 26; Lindfords 93 and *passim.*

Works Cited

Achebe, Chinua. *The Trouble with Nigeria*. Enugu: Fourth Dimension Publishers, 1983. Print.

Afigbo, A.E. "The Indigenous Political System of the Igbo". *Tarikh* 4.2(1973). 13–23. Print.

Bullit, J.N. "Jonathan Swift and the Anatomy of Satire". *A Study of Satiric Technique*. Cambridge M: Harvard University Press, 1996. Print.

Coffey, Michael. *Roman Satire*. London: Methuem, 1976. Print.

Darthone, O.R. *African Literature in the Twentieth Century*. London: Heinemann, 1976. Print.

Egudu, Romanus. "Social Values and Thought in Traditional Literature: The Case of Igbo Proverbs and Poetry". *Nigerian Librarian* 8. 2 (1972). 74–90. Print.

Ezejideaku, Emmanuel. "Satirical Songs Among Igbo Women: the Nnokwa Example". B.A. Long Essay in Linguistics/Igbo, Imo State University, Okigwe. June, 1986.

Leith-Ross, Sylvia. *African Women*. London: Faber & Faber, 1939. Print.

Lindfors, Bernth. *Folklore in Nigerian Literature*. New York: African Publishing Company, 1973. Print.

Meek, C.K. *Law and Authority in a Nigerian Tribe*. London: Oxford University Press, 1939. Print.

Moore, Gerald. *The Chosen Tongue*. Harlow: Longman, 1969. Print.

Nsugbe, P.O. *Ohafia, A Materilineal Igbo People*: London: Oxford University Press, 1974. Print.

Nwoga, D.I. "Mma Nwayi Wụ Nwa: Poetic Images of childbirth Among the Igbo". *Folklore* 84 (1973). 142–165. Print.

—. "The Concept and Practice of Satire Among the Igbo". *The Conch* III. 2 (1971). 30–45.

—. "The Igbo Poet and Satire". *Oral Poetry in Nigeria*. Ed. Abalogun, U.N,G. Ashiwaju and Amadi-Tshiwala. Lagos: Nigeria Magazine, 1981. 230–246. Print.

Obiechina, E.N. *Culture, Tradition and Society in the West African Novel*. Cambridge: Cambridge University Press, 1975. Print.

Okpara, Victoria. Satire in Amasiri Afikpo Women's Songs, B.A. Long Essay Project. School of Humanities Imo State University, Okigwe. August, 1086.

PART SIX: ACROSS THE GENRES

Chapter Seventeen

The Role of Women in Three African Epics: A Feminist Reading of Sundiata, the Ozidi Saga and the Mwindo Epic

Chinyere Nwahunanya

INTRODUCTION

Recent studies of the epic in African (such as those by Okpewho, 1979) focused on challenging the claims of western scholars (like Finnegan, 1970) that the epic does not exist in Africa. Such research was geared towards proving that contrary to commonly-held western opinions, Africa has tales of the exploits of heroic men (and women) comparable to those found in the West, tales told or sang by bards like those A.B. Lord (1960) describes as "the singer of tales". That the epic exists in Africa is therefore no longer in doubt, although it has uneven provenance across the continent. However, in spite of the provenance of the epic in Africa, even afro-centeric scholars who have promoted the scholarly interest in the African epic have tended not to highlight the role of women in such epics. Although women characters play various vital roles in epics, scholars have tended to focus on the heroes, whereas their exploits start from the womb while they were undergoing gestation and continue throughout their lives in their relationship with their mothers and other women.

Feminist scholars have frequently lamented the second-fiddle position to which women are subjected as being the consequence of the conscious attempts to denigrate the image of women by patriarchy, where the shots are called by men. In patriarchal societies, feminists point out unrelentingly, women have no voice, and are so fettered that even their natural creative endowments are not allowed to develop and blossom because of male-imposed restrictions. Even the tradition of singing the epic in most cultures is a male art, and therefore the sidelining of women becomes inevitable.

While many of the feminist claims are largely true in many societies as sociologists have confirmed from studies of marriage systems, widowhood practices, inheritance and other social structures and institutions, we contend in this essay that the correct picture of the role of women which the epic really presents has not been properly analyzed by most scholars of the epic. The African epic and other epics indeed provide a contrary view of the image, roles and status of women, a picture which might even question the antagonism expressed by contemporary feminists in their writings.

We wish to argue in this essay that a closer study of *Sundiata, The Mwindo Epic* and *The Ozidi Saga,* three representative African epics, reveals that it is mainly in the epic, compared with other oral literary forms, that women are given recognition and a voice, because of the complementary role they play in their relationships with men, as opposed to the usual subordinate position they are assigned in many male-authored works in contemporary African literature. In fact the trend in reconstructing the female image in African literature in particular may be said to be inspired by the positive portraiture of women in the epic.

Scholars of orature and folklore agree that the songs a people sing constitute part of their folklore, and incorporate their general world view and attitudes to specific things or issues. So do these epics incorporate the traditional attitudes to women, which contradict the views being espoused by feminist jingoists. The negative portrait of women we see in a number of African novels, for instance, is a watering down of the female image, especially as women in some epics are made too powerful to the extent that the men they relate with have to depend almost absolutely on them for their successes.

Some heroic stories from the oral tradition which preceded written literature have an array of women who were not deficient in strong character traits ordinarily associated with men. The Moremis, the Queen Aminas, the Amazons of ancient Abomey, etc, had heroic qualities that isolated them for recognition and applause as role models, and like their biblical equivalents—Deborah, Abigail, Esther, etc,—they excelled like men in all the areas of endevour in which they found themselves.

Joseph Mbele is one of the few scholars who have taken interest in this positively strong image of women portrayed in the African epic. In his 2006 study, "Women in the African Epic" (RAL Vol. 37,2), he confirms our view that women characters play various roles in African epics, including heroic role, but audiences and scholars generally fail to note and appreciate the full extent of these roles, focusing, instead, on male characters and their actions. In most published studies, the experiences and actions of men get more attention than those of women. Notions such as heroism are seen and understood from a male perspective. And these biases are built into research tools such as motif-indexes and the archetypal hero pattern.

The truth however, as we contend here, is that women play more important roles in epics and heroic stories than scholars have been willing to admit or concede. To take one example from the Greek oral tradition, the story of Theseus and the labyrinth of Crete while highlighting the courage of Theseus in accepting to embark on the risky adventure of going into the labyrinth to confront and kill the monster, the minotaur, is incomplete until the role of the King's daughter Ariadne is brought in. In the Mesopotamian epic, *Gilgamesh*, it is the women (the maids of Uruk) who shout praises to Gilgamesh on his arrival in Uruk following the defeat of Humbaba, thereby inflating his ego (cf Sundiata's triumpthant entry into Niani after defeating Soumaoro). Although women are not so prominently featured in the epic of Gilgamesh referred to, legitimate and logical inferences can be drawn about the role of women in ancient Mesopotamia from the characters Nishun, Ishtar and the Harlot. According to a Wikipaedia entry, these women pump up the egos of the men they encounter. And each of them embodies a certain creativity and power untouched by the men they come across.

Similarly, despite the fact that Beowulf (in the old English poem of that title) is projected as a courageous hero who defeats three monsters for the sake of a nearby country, three major women play integral roles throughout the epic: these are Wealtheow, Grendel's mother and Hildeburh. These women, according to Summer Stewart (2010), "entertain, bring peace, and contradict social expectations of the female gender in a society where the major roles of women are those of hostess, peacemaker and monster".

In "Beowulf", the woman as peacemaker is responsible for uniting tribes and maintaining solid relations between these groups. The strongest model of the peacemaker in "Beowulf" is Hildeburh, the Danish princess who was married off to the king of the Jutes. Hildeburh is a gift from the Danes to the Jutes in hopes to bring peace between the countries and establish an alliance. Nicole Smith notes that Hildburh's main job as a "happily confined" queen is to act as a "mediator and a departure from male-dominated activities and relationships", which means that she eases tensions that may arise between men. (She can be compare with the wife of Fakoli who Soumaoro abducts in *Sundiata*).

The woman who plays the role of hostess is Wealtheow the queen of Daneland and wife of Hronthgar, who establishes a warrior's status by using the cup of mead. The hostess holds political power in the hall. Wealtheow demonstrates this power by publicly requesting the king not to allow Beowulf be the heir to the throne, but to remember that her sons are the rightful heirs to such a position. (Here, she resembles Sasouma Beret, the eldest wife of Nare Maghan in *Sundiata* who plots to ensure that Sundiata is displaced by her son Dankaran Touman by sending the latter as an emissary to the king of Mema).

Unlike the peacemaker and the hostess, the female monster embodies masculine energy and counteracts social expectations of a woman in society. She uses physical force and violence to solve conflict. For example, Grendel's mother is viewed as evil and monstrous; she attacks anyone that enters her cave without reason ("Beowulf" lines 1257–1260). As Porter (p.2) has noted, Grendel's mother is a "hostile hostess" who uses "the sword to rid her hall ... of unwanted guests" (quoted by Stewart). The behaviour is masculine and demonstrates that the female monster does not resolve conflict with words and pleadings (like the peacemaker's hostesses), but with physical action. The poet of "Beowulf" condemns this behaviour which he feels should never be tolerated regarding social status ("Beowulf" lines 1940–1943). Moreover, the female monster exhibits unexpected masculine energy by engaging in the customs assigned to a warrior. In this society, only men seek vengeance; therefore a woman that does so is considered villainous for disobeying the expected behaviour of the female in civilized society. (Oreame is in some respects comparable to the female monster who even the men in *Ozidi* find awesome.)

Generally speaking, in all patriarchal societies the role of women is frequently underplayed while the role of men is sublimated, if only to emphasize the point that it is men who call the shots. This has been the ground on which all feminist arguments are predicated. Even when women are presented as good mothers, hard working/industrious wives, daughters, sisters, courtesans, etc, feminists have argued that these patronizing portraitures still reduce the female to a subordinate position, a status of servitude from which she must be liberated. Many feminist writers have indeed found these pictures of women as the ":weaker sex" dependent on men, as presented in earlier African novels, unacceptable, and the new writers create women that exhibit a resourcefulness, independence and force of character that make it difficult for men to lord it over them. Thus, women's roles in the new emergent literature are being reevaluated.

We aver that this reevaluation partly derives from a consciousness derived from a better understanding of the roles of women in the epic. We know from the epic for example that the statement that "behind every successful man is a woman" in a truism. Even when women are presented as "femme fatale" we cannot underplay their role in ensuring the success of the men they come into contact with.

Most of the women who appear in the African epic are defined by their relationships to men. Their actions are considered important chiefly by the ways they impact male characters. Is not a subservient relationship, but rather a complimentary one devoid of the element of dependency.

The heroes in epics are usually destined for greatness, and their careers inexorably and inevitably build up towards fulfilling such destinies, which may involve restoring or salvaging a nation or tribe. A number of obstacles, however, often show up to prevent the hero from fulfilling his destiny. Most of these obstacles are life threatening, and the heroes find themselves having to depend on the women in their lives.

In their early childhood, epic heroes are often weak, feeble and fragile, and despite the prodigious risks which they would take later in life, are often targets for destruction in their infancy (eg Jesus Christ and Moses). This is the first plane at which the role of women manifests. It is the duty of their mothers and other women to protect such heroes until they can stand on their own, or help them fulfill their destiny. This is a role and responsibility from which women have never abdicated.

Although in Muslim societies, of which the Mandinka of Mali is typical, women are not recognized as important, the women in *Sundiata* stand out, especially in their roles as mothers. Although no wife or lover of Sundiata is mentioned specifically, the women in that epic are nevertheless very influential because of the variety of roles they play.

To start with, Maghan Kon Fatta marries Sogolon Djata because he realizes that she is destined to bear a very special son, and he tried to make Sundiata his heir even though Dankaran Touman, his older son by his first wife, can muster more support because of his mother's royal blood (cf Absalom and Solomon). Sassouma Berete, (like Athaliah and Bathsheba) uses her connections to make Dankaran Touman king despite his dead father's wishes, only to have Dankaran prove too weak to defend the country against Soumaoro Kante's invasion.

Quite early, Sassouma Berete, Nare maghan's first wife, sees Sundiata as a threat to her son Dankaran Touman's ambition to get to the throne, and she sends nine witches to kill Sundiata by directing them to illegally harvest from Songolon's vegetable garden, in the hope that Sundiata would come to defend the violation of his mother's rights.

Sundiata however survives the plot by showing kindness to the old hags and elicits their sympathy. Their leader Soumosso Konkomba later confesses to Sundiata: "We were sent by the queen mother to provoke you and draw the anger of the nocturnal powers upon you" (p. 26). They instead hail him "child of justice" and promise to watch over him. Not deterred by his failure, Sassouma still uses her son to hijack the throne of Mali, and persuades the elders to confirm her son as king of Mali. Like Athlaliah in the Bible, she was desperate to acquire power and secure her son's future, and she kept mocking Sologon her co-wife (in a manner comparable to Penniah's constant mockery of the barren Hannah) because Sologon petitions the gods and gets a staff from the apple custard tree which liberates Sundiata from infirmity.

In his controversial *Anatomy of Female power*, Chinweizu has made the following perceptive observation:

Because every man has as boss his wife or his mother, or some other women in his life, men may rule the world, but women rule the men who rule the world. Thus, contrary to appearance, woman is boss, the overall boss of the world.

The import of Chinweizu's observation would be lost to us unless we consider it against the background of the roles which women play in traditional society, especially as noted by Simone de Beauvoir, and manifested in the African epic:

She (the early woman) was the one who cultivated the land around the village setting, she was in charge of all forms of domesticity—pottery, maintaining the flock, providing utensils and keeping the economic and religious life of the race (de Beauvoir 78).

As de Beavoir concludes,

"through them, therefore, the clan was maintained and extended. They were the soul of the community".(78)

Even in the sexual act, the woman proves stronger. For while a man "collapses" after ejaculation, the woman lasts longer to enjoy her post-orgasmic stimulation. It is often the woman therefore who has to "wake up" the man after intercourse.

The powers that the woman wields over the life of the race, and her more-than-ordinary affinity with the land "inspired in man a respect mingled with fear which was reflected in their worship" (78). When we add to this the kind of influence which women wield over their children, especially male children, who constitute the future generation that would ensure the continuity of the race/tribe, it becomes clear that this may be found in the design of women's clothes during the Victorian period. Women's dresses designed by men were deliberately crafted so as to weigh women down with their bulk, and to make locomotion virtually impossible; or "slow them down" so as to justify the male demand that women should behave properly as ladies.

Despite these restrictions, the influence of women has remained in many areas of male female interaction. One such area is in their position as domestic advisers. Men who have habitually refused to listen to good counsel from their wives have tended to end up badly, or make costly mistakes, for example Nabal. This is why king David is to be commended for heeding Abigail's advice. David was on the verge of taking a rash action following Nabal's provocative insult on him in the presence of David's messengers (1 Sam. 25:10–11). But Abigail intervenes wisely (1 Sam. 25:23–31). David heeds the advice and confesses: "…and blessed by thy advice, and blessed be thou, which hast kept me this day from coming to shed blood, and from avenging myself with mine own hand" (1 Sam. 25:32–34) Obviously, David's withdrawal allows God to deal with Nabal Himself.

In *The Ozidi Saga* Orea pleads with Ozidi Snr not to honour the invitation of the townspeople (in a manner comparable to Calpurnia's advice to Julius Caesar not to step out on the Ides of March as the soothsayer had advised). Unfortunately, as stubbornly as Caesar spurns his wife's advice, Ozidi Snr rejects Orea's advice and gets killed. Similarly, Agbogidi's wife, in *The Ozidi Saga* too, seeing her husband's reactions, advises him to suspend the battle for some other day. He too bluntly refuses and meets his doom.

Women in the epic show themselves as very influential in the kind of advice they give and their consequences. For example, Sassouma Berete, for all her destructive ambition in *Sundiata*, is regent with unquestioned authority to distribute public funds, proving the point that women in the epic are perhaps more powerful than the men they help or support. Thus, according to Afonja, African historians and anthropologists who have recorded African epics have aided in correcting "the image of the African woman as a chattel and identity women and women's institutions that were active in social and political life" (3).

Sassouma Berete was definitely a bad influence, so her activities are not commendable. But they are important to the extent that they also bring out the best in Sogolon's resourcefulness. When on his mother's advice Dankaran Touman takes away Sundiata's griot by sending him away as an embassy to the court of Soumaoro (27), Sogolon pacifies Sunadiata who wanted to revenge immediately, and advises and insists on the path of self-exile, an option that saves Sundiata from an ultimately tragic end which would have aborted his destiny. And while they are in exile, Sogolon arranges for Sundiata's apprenticeship, negotiating with foreign sovereigns on his behalf.

In Many respects, these women resemble certain female characters in the bible. For example following the advice of Nathan the prophet, Bathsheba (1 Kings 1:15–21) pleads with David and persuades him into anointing her son Solomon to be king in his stead. David consequently reaffirms his promise to her on oath to the lord in 1 Kings 1:30. In verse 34, David directs Zadok the priest and Nathan the prophet to anoint Solomon king at Gihon, and they carry out the directive in verse 39.

The political influence of Sassouma Berete is also comparable to that of Athaliah and her desperation is gunning for the throne: "Sundiata's popularity was so great that the queen mother (Sassouma) became apprehensive for her son's throne ... At the age of eighteen [Dankaram Touman] was still under the influence of his mother ... it was Sassouma Berete who really reigned in his name" (p. 24). Similarly, "when Athaliah the mother of Ahaziah saw that her son was dead, she arose and destroyed all the seed royal" (2 Kings 11:1). She is described as "that wicked woman" (in 2 Chron. 24:7), a kind of evil genius that shares the attributes of Sassouma Berete; and "Athaliah reigned over the land" for six years before she is killed in 2 Chron. 23:154 on the orders of Jehu who had the divine mandate to execute her.

Thus these women in the epic are political strategists who are interested not just in steering the ship of state, but also in determining the political direction of their societies by influencing the men with whom their lives are linked. The basic platform for their control of power is their position as mother, co-wife or consort. Sologon especially, in spite of seeming a calm and non-volatile character, is a political strategist and diplomat par excellence. Sogolon's strength of character keeps the remainder of her family together in exile and gives Sundiata the resolve to return home to rid the country of the usurper.

But beyond their political influence the women's other roles are also highlighted. Repeatedly in the text, Sundiata is referred to as "son of Sogolon" (pp. 16, 22, 24, 26, 27, 28, 29, 38, 42, 47, 50, 52, 54, 69, 69, etc), to emphasize the recognition given to his mother as an important factor in the story of the hero. When Sundiata himself hears of the escape of his half-sister, Nana Triban and his griot, Balla Fasseke, from Soumaoro, he says: "If my sister and Balla have been able to escape from Sosso, Soumaoro has lost the battle" (p. 57). We should also note that the bard, in spite of being a griot, deliberately mentions Sundiata's sister before his griot, suggesting an unusual order of precedence in traditional protocol.

We are already aware that Sassouma Berete's daughter, Nans Triban was married by Soumaoro, apparently to strengthen the latter's hold on Mali, but she becomes a Delilah figure who wheedles out of him the secret of how he can be defeated, and then defects to Sundiata at the first opportunity and tells him.

For the seven crucial years during which Sundiata is incapacitated after birth, it is Sogolon that takes the responsibility of his upbringing as his mother, in spite of the taunting and mockery of his co-wife, Sassouma Berete. So, beyond carrying him in her womb, Sogolon extends her role in protecting the royal child from early death, almost in the same manner that Mary protects Jesus, or Moses' mother and Miriam protect Moses, thus preparing them for their divinely ordained responsibility as leaders of their people.

In the course of their interaction, Sundiata observes that Manding Bory his half-brother had become "fond of that daughter of Mansa Konkon's" (p.29). Mansa Konkon was the socerer king of Djedaba in whose land Sogolon and her children had sojourned. During the game of wori with the murderous Mansa Konkon (pp 30–31), it is "the king's daughter" that "had revealed the secret to Manding Bory", Sundiata's half-brother, who quickly conveys the necessary information to Sundiata that enables Sundiata defeat Mansa Konkon and save his life.

It is through Sogolon's daughter Koloukan that the plot of Sassouma to destroy Sundiata by engaging the nine witches is foiled. She "saw them at night hatching their scheme" after being briefed by Sassouma. But Kolonkan was well versed in the art of witchcraft and watched over her brother without his suspecting it" (26). Through this same Kolonkan the mystery of how to contact Sundiata in exile is solved for the emissaries from Niani on espionage on their arrival at Mema. At the market in Mema it was Kolonkan who "noticed a woman [a member of the search party] who was offering for sale nafiola and genounou, condiments unknown to the people of Mema … and she recognized baobab leaves and many other vegetables which her mother used to grow in her garden at Niani" (43).

We are also informed by the griot that Kelaye, the wife of Fakoli Koroma, Sassouma's cousin, "was a great magician like her husband" (p. 42). Her incestuous relationship with Soumaoro deals a big blow on Soumaoro's camp, as it leads to the defection of her husband, Fakoli Koroma, to Sundiata before Sundiata's final and main battle against Soumaoro at Krina.

For Sogolon, however, we should note her all-encompassing roles played from her vantage position as Sundiata's mother. She contributes to Sundiata's physical protection, and his mental development, especially in the manner she initiates him into tribal wisdom in the use of proverbs (p .29). She also provides spiritual guidance for him, and helped him build up his confidence while they are in exile, a factor that enables Sundiata look the king Soumaba Cisse of Wagadou in the face and compel the latter to confess: "There's one that would make a great king. He forgets nobody". If he has a kingdom one day everything will obey him because he knows how to command" (34). And all her advice and suggestions provide effective counter to the wicked plots of Sassouma Berete.

It is for this reason that Sundiata finds it difficult to severe himself from her when she becomes sick and too weak to travel back to Niani. Sundiata still listens to her counsel and has to wait for her to die and bury her before he leaves for home. Even when she dies, the king of Mema wanted to rubbish her image by refusing to give Sundiata land to bury her properly; but after being threatened, he gives Sundiata the land he asked for, and "Sogolon received her funeral honours with all regal obsequies" (p. 47). Thus the bard of Sundiata manipulates the story in such a way that he dispenses with her and allows her die only after Sundiata has been established and proves he can manage his own affairs, that is, when he no longer needed his mother's influence. We rest assured at this point that even her buried remains will not be tampered with.

The women who feature in *The Ozidi Saga* are also portrayed as exerting a lot of influence over their men. In fact the power and influence of women is extolled. Ozidi's mother, Orea strives to protect her young son from Azezabife and his murderous allies who have killed Ozidi's father. In a similar manner, Ozidi's grandmother, Oreame, does all in her power to protect him after his father's death. Being a witch with mystical powers, she arranges and takes her daughter Orea back home from her husband's town after confirming her pregnant. She in fact tells Orea that the child in her womb would be greater than his father, a prophecy that endorses Ozidi's position as a post-humous avenger.

From the day of Ozidi's birth, Oreame takes the responsibility to see to it that Ozidi does not develop into a weakling. She has him bathed with magic herbs, puts him through various initiations, and makes him pass a number of trials of courage and endurance tests intended to steel him and prepare him for his future encounters with formidable opponents. Aware that Ozidi could not face his numerous enemies and opponents if he was not fortified, she initiates him into the world of magic and charms, taking him in the process from one native doctor to another to stuff him with magical/spiritual powers. Finally, with the magical power in the magic fan she invokes a blacksmith out of the bowels of the earth to forge a sword for Ozidi, the sword that becomes his weapon of invincibility. To cap it all, she acquires a retinue of drummer and horn blower for Ozidi, to give a royal touch to his personality.

We never see her sleep a wink, as she is always there to give Ozidi support in his campaigns and encounters. On one occasion she says: "My son, even if it is the whole city fighting you, I am standing by" (p. 64). As Ozidi's metaphysical prop, Oreame is "she that surpasses a city" (p. 73). "The woman is the boy's strength" (p. 81), and men like Azeza confess Oreame's greatness (p. 81). Of Oreame in the story, it is also said: "this woman really is great" (p. 127); "this witch is indeed powerful" (p. 126). It is Oreame who discovers the secret of Ogueren's resistance (p. 124); and Azeza, one of Ozidi's enemies confesses, "if you don't include this witch in your plans, then you have plotted against none ... Once we neutralize the woman, it should be over. For after we have neutralized her, neutralized them as group, we shall of course have disarmed the child too" (p. 81). This confirms that Oreame is the human metaphysical prop of Ozidi.

Oreame herself is aware of Ozidi's limitations and ensures that she is always available whenever he needs her assistance. Because Ozidi is a posthumous avenger who does not have the benefit of tutelage under a biological father, Oreame occupies a front burner position in his life, because she is in custody of certain vital family information and tribal secrets which Ozidi needs to incite him to fight the battles he must. (The magical ritual initiations which Oreame makes Ozidi go through are comparable to the efforts of Sogolon to initiate Sundiata into Mandinka lore and customs.) And she provides him the necessary prompting at the crucial moments to ginger him into action. At a point in the story following Azezabife's "show of force", "Oreame flew off straight to God—scaled the skies until she arrived and asked God...: "This battle my son is fighting with the people of Orua, what do you yourself think of it? Do you think that my son should die on top of his father's head, do you think so?" (p. 82). It is only after she gets reassurance from God that "the fight is a just one" (p. 82) that she flies back to earth to prod on Ozidi to fight. Thus she is also the link between Ozidi and the realm of the gods.

To cap up this discussion, we may now turn to *The Mwindo Epic*. This story from the Nyanga of the Congo is about the birth of Mwindo to a family where male children are not desired, and the subsequent conflict that arises between Mwindo and his father who does not want a male successor. In this epic, women also play prominent roles in the life of the hero, but two are outstanding.

The first set of women whose actions are significant are the midwives who attend to Mwindo's mother when she is in labour and deliver her of the child. Thereafter, they collude and hide the sex of the new born child from his father since they know he would want to destroy the child. Next are Iyanangura, and Kahindo.

Iyanguara is Mwindo's aunt whose story is structurally placed strategically to open the epic. Because she would play a major role in the story later, her marriage to Mukiti the water serpent is elaborated upon, and in the process her relationship with Mwindo's father, Shemwindo, is established, in order for the audience to accept the intercessory role she plays to enable Mwindo seek "asylum" in her place of abode. In some sense, Mwindo's journey in search of his aunt is structured to parallel his search for his fleeing father.

Mwindo's journey starts after the drum in which he was thrown away to die fails to sink and drown him. The injustice in Shemwindo's act is manifested in the cosmic turmoil: "it rained for seven days: hailing left the earth no more; that rain brought much famine in Tubondo" (p. 60).

Mwindo's first major obstacle on his way is Musoka who he overcomes with ease, before encountering Mukiti, his aunt's husband.

Mukiti's obstacle is quite formidable, for Mukiti says: "…here never anybody passes, who would have crossed over these logs and dried leaves; so then you never go to sleep thinking! You alone are (the man) who in spite of all will (be able to) pass here where I am!" (p. 69). During the altercation between Mwindo and Mukiti, word gets to Iyangura from the maidens that "there is a little man saying that Mukiti should release him, that he is Mwindo, that he is going to encounter Iyangura, his paternal aunt" (p. 69). When she hears this Iyangura screams, "Lo! That is my child, let me first go to where he is" (p. 69). The incantatory statements of Iyangura, and the song by Mwindo from the drum which follows, releases the entrapped drum, and it moves towards where Iyangura is, confirming for her that Mwindo is indeed her nephew. It is then that the drum leaves the water and Iyangura, seizing the drum and taking hold of a knife, slashes the drum, removes the hide and releases Mwindo.

From this point Iyangura's helping in Mwindo's life becomes more apparent. Most of her references to Mwindo from this point are as "my son", implying that she has taken responsibility for his custody and protection, in a manner comparable to Oreame's take-over of all responsibility for Ozidi's affairs. When Mwindo arrives at Iyangura's house, she discourages him from eating, aware as she is of her husband's deceitful plans. Instead she urges him to dance, as requested by Kasiyembe. Mwindo dances successfully and sings provocatively, in the process agitating his conga-scepter, which, with the help he receives from spider's bridges, gives him a double immunity. (*Mwindo Epic*. p. 26, 74–75).

When eventually Mwindo decides to return to his home village to fight his father, his aunt, skeptical, decides to accompany him together with her servants. According to her, "I also shall go with you to see how your father will be eating you into pieces". (79). Along the line Mwindo finds out by some form of clairvoyance, that his father fled to the realm of Muisa. This is where Kahindo, Muisa's daughter, plays a significant role in helping Mwindo escape Muisa's tricky invitation to sit down, drink banana beer and eat banana paste. Thereafter, an intimate relationship that culminates in Mwindo healing Kahindo of her yaws develops. Mwindo, however, rejects Muisa's proposal that Mwindo marry Kahindo.

As the tale races to its end, Iyangura is portrayed as a stabilizer. We would recall that once Mwindo submits to the divine power of Nkuba the lighting god and gets his cooperation, he is able to totally destroy the village of Tubondo, whichhad allied with his father, with the seven lightning flashes supplied by Nkuba. All the while Iyangura remains in touch with Mwindo through the rope she had got bells attached to (p. 10).

Mwindo's destiny is to become a chief in his father's stead, but he has to rule over people, and not in an uninhabited domain. After catching up with and reconciling with his father, Mwindo's aunt reminds him: "You, my son, shall we go on living always in this desolate village, (we) alone, without other people? I, Iyangura, I want you first to save all the people who lived here in this village; when they have resuscitated it is then only that I shall know to ask the young man, Shemwindo, to tell me some of the news of the ways in which he acted, all the evil that he did against you" (p. 118). This is because she considers Mwindo the "eternal savior of people" (p. 118). This appellation from his aunt inspires Mwindo into incantatory poem that begins their resuscitation that repopulates Tubondo, in a manner reminiscent of the valley of dry bones in Ezekiel 37:1–4:

> each one who died in pregnancy resuscitated with pregnancy;
> each one who died in labor resuscitated being a labor
> each one who was preparing paste resuscitated stirring paste;
> each one who died defecating resuscitated defecating;
> each one who died setting up traps resuscitated trapping;
> each one who died copulating resuscitated copulating;
> each one who died forging resuscitated forging;
> each one who died cultivating resuscitated cultivating
> each one who died while making pots and jars resuscitated shaping;
> each one who died carving dishes resuscitated carving
> each one who died quarreling with a partner resuscitated quarreling.

Subsequently, Iyangura presides over the final scene of reconciliation between Mwindo and his father. After Shemwindo confers kingship on his son (p. 127), Iyangura gives the benediction in a solemn advisory rendition worth quoting in full:

> Oh, Mwindo, hail!
> Blessing, here, hail!
> If your father throws you into grave, hail? Don/t habor resentment,
> Hail!
> May you stand up and make your first step hail!
> May you be safe, may you be blessed, hail!
> And your father and your mother, hail!
> May you bring forth tall children, boys and girls.
> Be strong, my father, as for me, there is nothing ominous left, hail!
> (p. 129).

After this, Iyangura returns to her husband, having established Mwindo, and restoring peace in Tubondo.

For the three epics we have examined, it is significant to note that each of the three principal female characters who work with the heroes—Sogolon, Oreame and Iyangura—is destined to conduct the heroes through their regal lineage to the thrones they are destined to sit on, before they take charge of the kingdoms or empires they are destined to reign over. Without them the destinies of these heroes would never have been fulfilled. They prove to be effective props, in accordance with the popular saying that "behind each successful man there is a woman". Part of the implication of this structural pattern and moral summation of these stories is that the men, even in those societies, are being advised to tap into the resource which women constitute, in order to give society the needed stability and direction.

From all the above it is clear that contrary to the image of the woman in many contemporary African novels where she is portrayed as dependent, unresourceful and voiceless, the African epic presents women who occupied revered positions in traditional African societies. Whatever roles they played by virtue of their gender only complemented or grew out to the central position they already occupied in their society. Their strength of character, however, may have led men to set up certain institutional structures and customs aimed at limiting their powers, which is what contemporary feminist writers are kicking against. Part of the process of reestablishing the woman's original position must start from taking a detailed look at the extent of the power wielded by women in the epic and other traditional oral literature forms, and the extent of the damage already done to the female image by patriarchy. Thereafter, the rebuilding process already started by Nwapa (in *Efuru*), Elechi Amadi (*Alekiri*), Buchi Emecheta (*Debbie Ogedemgbe*), Adichie (*Kainene*), Akachi Ezeigbo and a host of other writers would receive a perfect finish. Thus, women would be allowed to fully develop their potentials, play their natural roles, unfettered, and help stabilize and advance society in a manner that would ensure equity and security for everyone.

WORKS CITED

Afonja, S. *Gender and Feminism in African Development*. Bloomington: Indiana University Press, 2005. Print.

Belcher, S. P. *Epic Traditions of Africa*. Bloomington: Indiana University Press, 1999. Print.

Biebuyck, Daniel P. "The African Heroic Epic". *Journal of Folklore Institute*. 13. (1) (1976). 5–36. Print.

—. & Mateene, C.K. *The Mwindo Epic*. Berkeley: University of California Press, 1969. Print.

Chinweizu. *Anatomy of Female Power: A Masculinist Dissection of Matriarchy*. Lagos: Pero Press, 1990. Print.

Clark, J.P. *The Ozidi Saga*. Ibadan: University Press, 1977. Print.

Confrad, David C. "Oral Sources on Links Between Great States: Sumanguru, Servile Lineage, the Jariso, and Kariaga". *History in Africa* 11 (1984). 35–55. Print.

De Beavoir, S. *The Second Sex*. New York: Vintage Books, 1974. Print.

Deme, M.K. *Heroism and the Supernatural in the African Epic*. Taylor and Francis, 2010. (Especially Chapter 6, "Women as bearers of Supernatural Powers in the African Epic".) Print.

Hale, T.A. "Griottes: Female Voices from West Africa". *Research in African Literatures*. 25. 3 (Autumn 1994) pp. 71–91. Indiana University Press. Print.

Ejakaitpapa, C. "Women in Oral Literature". *Women, Ecology and the Scientif-*

ic Revolution. New York: Harper Collins, 1980. Print.

Finnegan, R. *Oral Literature in Africa.* London: Oxford University Press, 1970. Print. Holy Bible (King James Version).

Izevbaye, D.S. "J.P. Clark-Bekederemo and the Ijo Literary Tradition". *Research in African Literatures* 25, 1, (Spring 1994). 1–21. Print.

Janson, Marlue, "The Narration of the Sunjata Epic as Gendered Activity". Jansen, *Epic Adventures: Heroic Narrative in the Oral Performance Traditions of our Continents.* Jan.; Mair, Henk M.J. Munster: Lit Verlag (2004). 81–88. Print.

Johnson, J.W., Thomas A. Hale, Stephen Belcher, Ed. *Oral Epic From Africa: Vibrant Voices from a Vast Continent.* Bloomington: Indiana University Press, 1977. Print.

Kermode, F. et al. *The Oral Anthology of English Literature.* Vols. 1 & 2. London: OUP, 1973, Print.

Lord, A.B. *The Singer of Tales.* Cambridge, Mass.: Harvard University Press., 1960. Print.

Mbele, J. "Women in the African Epic". *Research in African Literatures.* New York: Barnes and Noble Classics, 2005. Print.

Merchant, C. *The Death of Nature: Women, Ecology and the Scientific Revolution.* New York: Harper, Collins, 1980. Print.

Niame, D.T. *Sundiata: An Epic of Old Mali.* London: Longman, 1979. Print.

Okpewho, I. "Does the Epic Exist in Africa?" *Research in the African Literatures* 8,.14 (1977). 171–200. Print.

Okpewho, I. *"The Epic in Africa: Towards a Poetics of Oral Performance.* New York: Columbia University Press, 1979, print.

—. *African Oral Literature: Backgrounds, Character and Continuity.* Bloomington and Indianapolis: Indiana University Press, 1992. Print.

Porter, D. "The Heroic Age: The Social Centrality of Women in Beowulf'. Western Michigan University, 2002. Web. 10 April 2010.

Stewart, S. "Beowulf: Roles of Women". Web. April 30, 2010, Accessed 28/8/12.

Smith, N. "Representations of Women in Medieval Literature: Margey Kempa, Gawain and Beowulf". *Article Myriad.* 2008. Web. 01 April 2010.

Tsaaior, James Tar "Webbed Words: Market Meanings: Proverbiality and Narrative/Discoursive Strategies in D.T. Niane's Sundata: An Epic of Mali". *Proverbium 27* (2010). 339–362. Print.

Chapter Eighteen

Essential Stylistic Features Of Oral Literature

G.I.N. Emezue

INTRODUCTION
ORAL LITERATURE: ISSUES OF DEFINITION

The term, *oral literature,* has been variously referred to as folklore, folk literature, oral narrative, oral tradition, traditional literature and orature. But in recent times, advocates of the use of the terms orature and oral literature seem to be unrelenting in their request to impose either of the terms as the more appropriate. The promotion of the use of orature is hinged on the Eurocentric thinking that literature, strictly speaking, is any written artistic-cum creative work. And since oral literature is principally verbally narrated (spoken) and not written, it should not be associated with literature.

However, advocates of oral literature as the more appropriate term argue that 'being written' is not all that gives literature its distinctiveness, for every literature—whether written or oral—is a product of some ingenious creativity. This later groups argue further that both written and oral literatures involve some dexterous handling of language, thus subscribing to the view that there is an obvious link between language and literature; that all literature is expressed through language and that literature is a manifestation of verbal culture and cannot be filtered out of, or separated from, language (D. Williams 234; H, Brian 47).

Before Williams and Brian, Roger Fowler had posited that the life of anything that can pass as literature is in language and without language, no literature can be said to really exist (3). It is in the fact of words (language use) being an inevitable raw material for the production of both forms of literature that we subscribe more to the use *oral literature* than *orature*. Also, oral literature is not in any way inferior to written literature. After all, all literature began as oral. As Ronald Carter and John McRae put it:

> Literature is as old as human language, and as new as tomorrow's sunrise…. The first literature in any culture is oral. The classical Greek epics, the Asian narratives of Gilgamesh … the earliest version of the Bible … were all communicated orally, and passed on from generation to generation—with variations, additions, omissions and embellishments until they were set down in written form in versions which have come down to us. (3)

Same goes for African oral literature most of which we study today in its written form. What then is oral literature?

According to Mbunda, oral literature "…is the verbal art of essentially non-literate societies composed extemporaneously before a traditional audience and transmitted from one generation to another by word of mouth…". (125) Oral literature would also include those artistic and imaginative compositions that are spoken or sung with the aim of informing, teaching and entertaining. Through its performance important truths and information are told and transmitted from one generation to another. Defined in a simple manner, oral literature is "literature delivered by word of mouth" (Isidore Okpewho 3).

From a historical and cultural perspective, Ime Ikideh expresses the fact that "literature, particularly of the oral mould, is a social product that has its roots in a defined cultural context" (59). In other words, oral literature does not operate in a vacuum. To a large extent it is the medium for artistic expression of a people's culture. This explains why a non-member of the particular cultural society may not fully appreciate the particular performance.

This chapter is a discussion of the major stylistic features of oral literature. In doing this, it ought to be noted that oral literature, unlike its written opposite number, is not rigidly fossilized. There are improvisations that guarantee unlimited artistic dynamism, vivid imagination, vigour, suppleness and consummate aesthetic and communicative effects. Generally, any genre of oral literature "depends on a performer who formulates it in words and there is no other way in which it can be related to literary product" (Ruth Finnegan 2). Put another way, it is the performer who repackages known stories into something new and refreshing and entertaining.

Oral literature may be broadly categorized into two: ritual and non-ritual. The ritual-oriented oral literature, as the name implies, is used for ritual purposes. They are often employed and limited to recitations for ritual purposes. The notable performers here are traditional priests and healers. Generally, this genre of oral literature comes in the form of incantations such that it is difficult for the uninitiated to understand what is recited. It is in this regard that some critics have tended to see them as secret codes and as such not qualified to be categorized as literature.

The non-ritual oral literature is rendered in simple ordinary language of the people. By ordinary we do not have in mind that it is bereft of any artistry or aesthetic value and so could be easily understood by everybody. It is just that the language can be identified as the known language of the community or a semblance of it. This explains why-non-ritual oral literature is classified into two:

i. Folk poems and tales use the language which are difficult to understand and so require to be interpreted by the tutored, usually someone of the older generation.

ii. The poems and folktales embody a language which is commonly understood and its performance comprehended and enjoyed by all. Because the language of performance is the common language of the community, it can be linguistically analyzed.

2.0 STYLE AND STYLISTICS

In considering the essential or fundamental stylistic characteristics of oral literature, there is the need to have some understanding of what constitutes 'style' and consequently, stylistics. This is because it is nearly always imperative to discuss style in every discussion of stylistics. A simplistic way of explaining the concern of stylistic studies is that the emphasis is on style; where style is taken to be the way artists employ the subtle nuances of their language to make meaning and communicate intension while also exhibiting their individual, peculiar artistry. But in order to give the present enterprise direction, style has been approached from two perspectives:

(i). Style as an artist-related phenomenon (i.e. style as a characteristically unique manner an artist or a griot performs) and,

(ii). Style as text-related phenomenon; that is, style as something that is intrinsically related to meaning.

While (i) is informed by the reasoning that artists can—and do, in fact—have their characteristic manner or performance as distinct individuals, (ii) is premised on the understanding that each genre of oral literature has its peculiar style which the artist is expected to appropriate to a very considerable extent, such that a distinct deviation from the 'norm' is adjudged as aberration.

Our views expressed about style in (i& ii) above are in tandem with Dan Ben-Amos' position that, "while there is a personal style in the delivery of folklore, it is subject to the cultural constraints and conception of excellence in narrative and poetic performance" (in Bernth Lindfors 12). It is, therefore, obvious that in considering the stylistic features of oral literature we are engaged in examining the linguistic and non-linguistic features that give oral literature its distinctive quality as an art. But it should be reiterated that it is in the unique handling of the language in use that the style of the individual artist is adjudged great or mediocre.

J. Hawthorne sees stylistics as a discipline situated in the borderline between the study of language and the study of literature and concerned technically with the study and analysis of manners of expression (248). In the stylistics of oral literature, close attention is paid to the artists, taking into cognizance their "manners of expression" in terms of diction (word choices), sentences patterns, sound patterns and paralinguistic accompaniments. Our notion of stylistics should therefore be understood as a consideration of some symbiotic relationship between literary artistry and language. Thus, when we speak of the stylistic essence of oral literature we speak in regard of the ways language and other means of communication have been used by the oral artist to perform in such sub-genres of oral literature as ritual and curative chants, musical genres, folktales, epic-poems, creation tales, myths, life histories, historical narrative, tongue-twisters, proverbs, songs, riddles, *njakiri*, etc.

STYLISTIC FEATURES

Essential stylistic features of note are many, but for space only a few shall be considered. As we have noted earlier, the stylistic features of oral literature are most evident in language. Here we consider the employment of such linguistic elements as syntax (evident in parallelism as in lexical and lyrical repetitions) and phonology (sound effects). We intend to show that the language of oral literature could be as rich, complex, intricate and absorbing as that for the written form of literature. While written literature could be rigidly fossilized, same cannot be said of oral literature with its improvisations that ensure the continuity of its dynamism, vivid imagination, as well as the vigour, suppleness and subtlety of contrivance that contribute to the aesthetics of its performance. This is evident in the use of such figures of speech as personification, symbolism, imagery, metaphor, allusion, etc. all of which give oral literature its beauty and aesthetic value.

PARALLELISM

Parallelism performs three basic functions in oral art: (i) it is used to shape and organize the particular verbal art as text; (ii) It reveals the structuring principles of the language [of the poem] itself; and (iii), it expresses parallelisms in cultural thinking (Fabb 144). Parallelism is evident in repetition, refrain, formulaic expressions, etc. Let us consider the following songs:

War Song

1

Onye akpala nwa agụ aka n'ọdụ	One, touch not the tail of a leopard
Ma ọdị ndụ, ma ọnwụrụ anwụ	Whether it is alive or dead
Onye akpala nwa agụ aka n'ọdụ	One, touch not the tail of a leopard

Dirge

2

Ọnwụ eme m arụ	Death has done me evil
Ọnwụ na eme m arụ	This death has done me evil
O buru ọgbalaga.	It carried and raced away

3

Anyị n'achọ anyị n'achọ, anyị n'achọ	We're searching, we're searching, we're searching
Anyị n'achọ nwanne anyị kamgbe	We're searching for our brother/sister since
echi	yesterday
Anyị n'achọ nwanne anyị furu efu	we're searching our lost brother/sister
Onye ọbụla chọọ, kanyi mara ebe	Everybody, search so that we know where
anọ	he/she is
Onye ọbụla chọọ k'anyị mara ebe	Every body search so that we know where s/he
ọnọ	is
Anyi n'achọ anyị n'acho anyị n'achọ	We're searching, we're searching, we're searching

LOVE

4

Me kwa onye dimma enyi o	Befriend a good-looking person o
Me kwa onye dimma enyi o	Befriend a good-looking person o
Adamma, mekwa onye dimma enyi o	Adamma Befriend a good-looking person o
Adamma, mekwa onye dimma enyi o	Adamma Befriend a good-looking person o
Adamma, mekwa onye dimma enyi o	Adamma Befriend a good-looking person o
Nnenna, mekwa onye dimma enyi o	Nnenna, Befriend a good-looking person o
Nnenna, mekwa onye dimma enyi o	Nnenna, Befriend a good-looking person o
Ina eme enyi,	When you desire a friend,
Me kwa Onye dimma enyi maka olulu	Befriend a good-looking person because of marriage

REPETITION

Geoffrey Leech lends credibility to his position that repetition as a literary device is very important in oral literature based on his observation that humans are wont to express themselves expansively on matters which affect them deeply (79), given this natural tendency to say and repeat matters of deep personal concern many times over. Thus, for Leech, the repeated hammering of the same issue in the same manner and using the same words, sounds, etc is a veritable way of relieving inner feelings of sadness or of joy.

Okpewho shares the same view about the artistic and communicative importance of repetition:

Repetition is no doubt one of the most fundamental characteristic features of oral literature. It has both aesthetic and a utilitarian value: in other words, it is a device that not only gives a touch of beauty or attractiveness to a piece of oral expression (whether song a narrative or other kind of statement) but also serves certain practical purposes in the overall organization of the oral performance. (71)

Earlier, J.N. Kwabena Nketia has stated that repetition in oral literature is not a padding device or attempt at filling the gap. He posits that, "On the contrary, they may have a musical mode of meaning or they may be a means of emphasizing points that mourners might wish to make" (104). In other words, these repetitions are not a product of forgetfulness or any lapse in the performance. They are often deliberate in order to achieve intense musicality.

It is in the same mode of thinking that Okpewho goes on to emphasize that:

It is necessary to grasp first the aesthetic value of repetition in a piece of oral performance. In a fundamental way, the repetition of a phrase, a line, or a passage does have certain sing-song quality to it; if the repetition occurs between intervals in, say a song or a tale, the audience is often delighted to identify with it and to accompany the performer in going over a passage that has now become familiar. (71)

Refrain

Another form of repetition in oral literature (especially, in dirges) is the use of the refrain. Here, the lead singer sings a part and other singers including, of course, the audience most of whom usually know how to sing the particular song, join the chorus and repeat what the lead singer has sung. In the singing of most Igbo dirges, there is the utilization of the antiphonal form, which involves the collaboration of the lead singer and the chorus. Here, key phrases are repeated many times. Usually, it is the lead singer who begins the dirge by singing the first verse, which is then repeated by the chorus:

Lead singer:	Ọnwụ eme m arụ	Death has done me evil
	Ọnwụ na eme m arụ	This death has done me evil
	Ọbụrụ ogbalaga	It carried and raced away

Chorus:	Ọnwụ eme m arụ	Death has done me evil
	Ọnwụ na eme m arụ	This death has done me evil
	Ọbụrụ ogbalaga	It carried and raced away

What is basic is the employment of antiphonal elements, the main characteristic being the repetition of key phrases. We notice the repetition of parallel constituents with the same semantic implication. Apart from creating the rhythm in the song, the somber voice of its rendition and the repetition enforce and reinforce the sense of loss and the helplessness of the bereaved which is evident in their inability to catch or arrest death and save the victim by bringing him/ her back to life. Thus, the rhymes are defined both by the repetition of same words and phrases coupled with the phonic aspects (dulled, saddened voices) and give the song its aesthetic value and communicative effect. Well simulated, the song could draw tears from the eyes of the audience.

Finnegan explains that:

> ...the antiphonal form provides scope for far more flexibility, rich elaboration, and varied interpretation than is immediately apparent from the bald statement that this is the characteristic structure of African songs. It is also a most suitable form for the purposes to which it is put. It makes possible both the exploitation of an expert and creative leader, and popular participation by all those who wish or are expected to join in. The repetition and lack of demand on the chorus also make it particularly appropriate for dancing. Finally the balanced antiphony both give the poem a clear structure and adds to its musical attractiveness. (262)

Generally, as Adeboye Bablola says of the Yoruba *ijala*, the language of the song is organized poetically "so as to create impressions and fulfill functions of poetic rhythm" (344).

FORMULAIC EXPRESSIONS IN FOLK TALES

The telling of Igbo folk tales is usually preceded by some prefatory statement made by the narrator (N). The narrator makes a statement and the audience (A) responds. We have qualified these statements as formulaic because they follow the same pattern nearly all the time. The following are examples:

N:	Otii	Otii
A:	Ọyọọ	Oyoo
N:	Onwere akụkọ m ga akọrọ unu	There is a story I will tel you
A:	Kọọrọ anyị k'obi dị anyị mma	Tell us so that we shall be happy

Or

N:	*Chapkii*	*Chakpii*
A:	*Woo*	*Woo*
N:	*Nkịta nyara akpa*	*[When] a dog caries a bag*
A:	*Nsị agwụla n'ohịa*	*Faeces disappear from the bush*
N:	*Ohịa ogwu mara ọkụkọ*	*In a bush where a thorn pricks a fowl*
A:	*Anaghi epio ye epio*	*No human can enter [that bush]*
N:	*Agwọ turụ mbe*	*A snake that bites a tortoise*
A:	*Ọtụrụ okpokoro ya*	*Only [harmlessly] bites the shell*
N:	*Oruru otu mgbe*	*Once upon a time*
A:	*Otu mgbe eruharia*	*Atime upon once*

The beauty of these formulaic expressions that introduce the tale lies in the truth embodied in the imagery. For instance, local dogs are known to feed on faeces; no matter how thick a thorny a bush is, fowls enter and feed there and the venom of a snake cannot penetrate the shell of a tortoise. If the pictures created were true, then it behoves the audience to willingly suspend their disbelief and enjoy the about-to-be-told tale.

These formulaic expressions act as summons, a signature tune of a kind the aim of which is to draw the attention of the audience and also urge them to be quiet.

PARALINGUISTIC ACCOMPANIMENT

In oral performance, speech (or the use or words) are often accompanied by gestures, gesticulations, etc. This mode of communication through ways other than words is examined within the purview of paralinguistics. Here, facial expressions, voice modulations, movements of the hands and legs accompany words in the communication act and help dramatize the action expressed in words. To a large extent, dancing is part of the paralinguistic accompaniments.

IDEOPHONE

As a stylistic device that relies on the effect of sounds, Okpewho says that ideophone means "idea-in-sound". The idea is that from the sound of words, one can get the message or have some inkling about the object, thing or event under reference. But we hesitate to liken it to onomatopoeia, for it is not onomatopoeic in the strict sense of its use. Consider the following:

Miri nezo, anwu n'acha	*[when] it is raining, [when] it is shining*
Ehi na umu giridim gidim	*The cow and his 'children' giridim gidim*

Giridim gidim describes the noise of stamping feet of the running elephants. Another is:

Mgbe ogbu nkwu n'egbu,	*When the palm harvester seek to cut palm fruits*
O na waghari	*He scouts through the bush*
Mgbe ohuru nkwu chara acha,	*When he sees a ripe palm, his heart rejoices*
Kpotikpo, fururu biam, furubiam	*Kpotikpo, fururu biam, furubiam*

Kpotikpo has no meaning of its own except it echoes the sound of the knife as it is used to cut the palm fruit. And *fururu biam* is the sound made by the palm fruit as it drops ("fururu") from the palm tree and falls to the ground ("biam").

Musical instruments can also be ideophonic, for example, the *tichanchan-tichanchan* sound of the nkwatankwa.

USE OF MUSICAL INSTRUMENTS

Another stylistic device is the use of musical instruments. Among the Igbo, Yoruba and other ethnic groups in Nigeria an instrument like *Ogene (Igbo) and agogo* (Yoruba) can be used as "solo in ritual ceremonies or in orchestral ensembles to perform rhythmic (poetic) and colouristic functions" (Samuel Akpabot 15). During *ofala* festival in parts of the present Anambra State of Nigeria, *oja* is used not just to announce the presence of the Igwe but also to sing his praises. In Ohafia war dance, for instance, the *nkwatankwa* (special stick carved from bamboo stem) is a major instrument that gives percussion and direction to the leg, shoulder and arms movements.

RHYTHM

Achievement of musical rhythm is stylistic in the performance of oral literature. Rhythm is achieved, basically, through drumming, ringing of bells, and the playing of assorted musical instruments as expressed in dance. Dance steps, waste-wriggling, hand movements and facial expressions all project the particular performance as that of joy (celebration) or sorrow (mourning). For instance, in the Ohafia war dance, the spasmodic movement of the shoulders and the stamping of the feet are done in mockery of the dead enemy in the course of war. They mimic the last spasm, jerking and rigour that overtake the human body when the head is suddenly cut off and death strikes.

ARTIST, PERFORMANCE AND AUDIENCE

It will be quite inadequate to consider the essential stylistic features of oral literature without giving a thought about the artist, the performance and the audience. The artist or performer in folktale, poetry, epic, may be called a folklorist, griot, or bard. And it is his/her performance that constitutes the literature in question. An essential feature of oral literature is, therefore, its performance. It will not be an exaggeration to posit that no genre of oral literature is worth its name without its practical performance. Ben-Amos emphasizes the significance of *performance* when he avers that an oral poem is essentially a fleeting work of art and it is performance that gives it its essence (qtd. in Mbunda 127).

The audience is a very important aspect of oral performance. Most of the time, the audience cease to be spectators and become active participants. This is essentially true in such instances in the course of narrative folk tales and singing dirges when the audience/participants take in the songs or other forms of antiphonal acts. J.S. Nketia aptly observed that, "...the presence and participation of the audience influences the animation of the performance, the spontaneous selection of music, the range of textual improvisation and other details and this stimulus to creative activity is welcomed and even sought by the performer" (33). Abrahams considers performance as very paramount when he states that in examining traditional expressive literature, there is a need to emphasize all aspects of the aesthetic performance and audience participation (144). These authoritative sources inform our presentation of the role of performance and audience in oral literature.

CONCLUSION

Every artist seeks to communicate and entertain the target audience. To achieve this, the oral artist makes use of some stylistic devices so that the audience can appreciate his/her performance. What we have made clear is that stylistics is the application of linguistic and non-linguistic "manners of expression" for artistic and communicative function effects. But we must reiterate as Be-Amos points out that even though there is a personal style in the performance of oral literature, there are still some cultural constraints and conformity to these cultural or conventional stylistic demands influences the notion of excellence in narrative and poetic performance. In discussing some stylistic features, we have relied on our knowledge of the language of performance, which is Igbo. It should be emphasized that without the knowledge of the native language of the oral performers, our translation and/or judgment about what is stylistic becomes somewhat flawed.

WORKS CITED

Abrahams, R.D. "Introductory Remarks to Rhetorical Theory of Folklore". *Journal of American Folklore, 81* (1988). 44–145. Print.

Akpabot, Samuel Ekpe. "Musicological Approach to Efik/Ibibio Oral Poetry". *Oral Poetry in Nigeria.* Ed. Abalogu, U, Garba Ashiwagu and Regina Amadi-Tshiwala Lagos. (1981). 86–95. Print.

Babalola, Adeboye. *The Content and Form of Yoruba Ijala.* Ibadan: Oxford University Press, 1966. Print

Brian, H. *English as a Second and Foreign Language.* London: Edward Arnold, 1993. Print

Carter, Ronald & John McRae. *The Routledge History of Literature in English.* London & New York: Routledge Ltd, 2001. Print

Fabb, N. *Linguistics and Literature.* Oxford: Blackwell Publishers Ltd., 1997. Print

Finnegan, Ruth. *Oral Literature in Africa.* Nairobi: Oxford University Press, 1970. Print

Hawthorne, J. *A Glossary of Contemporary Literary Theory.* New York, 1994. Print.

Ikideh, Ime. *Historic Essays on African Literature, Language and Culture.* Uyo: Minders, 2005 Print.

Lindfors, Bernth. *Forms of Folklore in Africa: Narratives, Poetic, Gnomic, Dramatic.* Austin & London: University of Texas Press, 1977. Print.

Mbunda, F.M. ed. *Oral Literature In Contemporary Society. Essays and Literary Concepts in English.* (Ed), S. Onuigbo. Nsukka: Afro-Orbis Publications Limited. (2006). 125–139, Print

Nketia, J.S. *The Music of Africa.* New York: Norton, 1975. Print

Okpewho, Isidore, *African Oral Literature: Backgrounds, Character, and Continuity.* Bloomington: Indiana University Press, 1992. Print.

Nketia, Kwabena. *Funeral Dirges of the Akan People.* Exeter: Achimota, 1955. Print

Williams, D. *English Language Teaching:* Ibadan: Spectrum Books Limited, 1990. Print.

Chapter Nineteen

The Researcher And African Oral Literature

Emma Ngumoha

The field of oral literature is known to be a very vast one and an apt taxonomy for describing its formal inclination is an important starting point in its study. Such an approach, as Okoh has rightly pointed out, presents us with a highly tricky, if not entirely elusive situation as it is a particularly slippery phenomenon in oral litera-ture. "A crucial fact here is that considerable overlapping is involve, and no water-tight compartments can be envisage in the business of classification". (113) The proverb and the riddle, for instance, are important oral literary forms which are not as extensive as stories to be called prose or as rhythmic as poetry to be called poems. With anticipation of exact taxonomical and terminological equations, we follow, for our purpose, the classification scheme delineated by some scholars of oral literature, notably W.H. Whitely and Ruth Finneg-an who advocate generic distinctions that are relatively convenient. These include "what is said", "what is sung and what is acted".

They sum up to the three-pronged literary division (the Prose Genre, the Poetic Genre and the Dramatic Genre) with which we are already familiar in written literature. Oral literature then, as Onue-kwusi classified it, is shown below:

Oral Literature

A. What is Spoken (Oral Prose)

B. What is sung (Oral Poetry)

C. What is acted (Drama)

What is spoken could be further subdivided into:

A. Proverbs

B. Riddles

C. Narratives

The narratives can be further divided into:

A. Myths

B. Legends

C. Folktales

Folktales can further be subdivided into:

A. Animal Stories

B. Stories with human supernatural characters.

C. Stories that combine animal, human and supernatural characters.

What is sung could be subdivided into:

A. War songs

B. Works songs

C. Birth songs

D. Children's songs

E. Title-taking songs

F. Funeral songs

G. Praise songs or poems

H. Tale songs

There are other songs coined according to their occasion of use. What is acted could be subdivided into:

A. Ceremonial drama

B. Funeral drama

C. Masquerades

D. Festival drama (14–15)

II

The search for knowledge in oral literature exposes the scholar to rigours and problems that the scholar of written literature may avoid. This is predicated on the fact that one major area of difference between written and oral literature is that written literature is fixed in its outlook while oral literature is fluid by nature.

Written literature is easily locatable and retrievable especially by the literate audience who have acquired the skill of reading. In a fundamental sense, then, the primary instinct that lies at the root of written literature is a recrudescence, a transposition of the story-telling instinct. What gives written literature, as we have come to know it, a Western or African stamp is not the newness of the act and art of extended narration or presentation of collective or individual experience. It is in the technological revolution of printing and the mass production of the printed word which now presented the extended narrative in the form of a bound volume (a finished product) which could be bought, borrowed or stolen and consumed by the literate individual in the privacy of his or her home. Therefore, that which is Western or African etc. about written literature in general is its present physical format, not its ontological essence. This is confirmed by Walter Benjamin:

> What distinguishes the novel from the
> Story (and from the epic in the narrower sense)
> Is its essential dependence on the book (87).

In turn, the conversion of the story into a book was a product of determinate changes in the mode of literary production from the oral through the hand-written to the machine-printed modes, necessitated by the industrial revolution and the advent of political economy of capitalism.

From the foregoing and as scholars and critics of written literature, we would have little or no problem investigating, for instance, the folktale as structural strategy or morality and political symbolism in Achebe's *A Man Of The People*. Why, we have the book, the text to interrogate and interact with for full critical analysis. The situation in oral literature is totally different. The "Text" does not exist and there is nothing to "read" or to subject scholarly critical analysis. This is because

> an oral piece cannot make an impact or have an existence, much less maintain its continuity, outside the process of perfor- mance. More importantly, even such is reflective and, in more ways than one. Scheub captures the situation succinctly and ex- actly when he applies to oral literature the term, an evanescent phenomenon. (Okoh 158)

The problem of oral literature study is therefore that of conducting research in an area which is not easily empirically recoverably in ad- dition to being "evanescent". This is the kind of research that cannot be practiced without field work and recording because it is literature that hardly moves. Some oral performance are linked to certain fes- tivals and the researcher must determine from his/her preliminary investigation of the oral art concerned, the specific period in which the festival or oral performance is held and the remoteness of scenes where such festivals take place. This is to ensure that the researcher moves into the field with a background knowledge of the language(s) of the intended social milieu(x) as well as a good idea of the oral art form he/she wants to work on. At this preliminary stage, the researcher must make sure that he/she has procured the necessary materials and equipment for field research. Filming and recording equipment such as camcorders, discs and tapes as well as batteries in adequate quantity are essential for rewarding field trips. It must be emphasized that batteries are essential needs as most of the per- formances take place in remote scenes lacking electricity/light sup- ply. In addition to gadgets and equipment, a lot of money is needed for transportation, accommodation, payments to porters, assistants, translators and interpreters if he/she does not share a common lan- guage with the subjects.

For a researcher dealing with chanting and/or dramatic perfor- mance, recording and filming are made first hand during the festival during which these oral forms occur. Oral literature is by nature, circumscribed by occasion, and so the performance is not there all the time. The probability of simulation of the performance is almost non-existent vis-à-vis the cost-benefit implication. In addition , the performers themselves may turn down request to perform in stimulatory theatrics of their own much cherished oral arts/performances which are determined by peculiar situations and occasions in the culture of the people. To this end, the researcher must have a schedule that accommodates the convenience of his/her subjects.

The oral literature researcher may elect to join the enactment of the songs and dances if he/she has the skill. The researcher's assumption of a distinctive investigator status serves the good purpose of establishing a rapport between the researcher and the performer. Thus, by participating in the performance, the researcher is enlisted as a person who identifies with the significant elements in the people's aesthetics rather than someone prying into the secret lore of the people or a mere interested outsider. However, the researcher's participatory role should not distract him from the significant investigative duty of attentive observatory roles.

The researcher does not only watch and make notes or record the songs or chants, he also photographs the costumes, masks and other paraphernalia used in the performance. The photographs would be useful later for stylistic and content analysis of the particular oral art. Sometimes, difficulty may be encountered in the process of photographing the materials used in the performance because the researcher may be refused access to some vital materials used as accompaniments in the poetic or dramatic performance unless he/she is initiated. The informants or the people should be made to see the role which folk literature plays in the education of their children. Directly or indirectly, the introduction or appreciation of oral literature in Adult Education Programmes for rural communities and the involvement of local government councils for Arts and Culture in collecting oral literature materials should be seriously encouraged.

After the recording, the researcher proceeds to the interview stage where an interpreter can be used if the researcher lacks a basic understanding of the local dialect. The researcher would need the aid of one or two interpreters who are fluent in English or any other language which the researcher may want to work with. Many things arc taken into consideration with regard to the selection of informants and interpreters. Of special importance is their names, ages and bio-data which in one way or the other influence the research. The degree of competence of informants certainly relates to age and experience. The average age of the informants for the historical or oral literary perspective could be from sixty-five to seventy-five years or more. Other informants are chosen according to their special knowledge concerning the oral arts being studied. It is better to conduct the interview at the venue of the performance so as to give the whole exercise an aura of freshness and creative authenticity. The interpreters should be able to render a direct translation into English without adding their own ideas or emotions.

The recordings and interviews having been completed, the next level is that of transcribing, translating and analyzing the various items, facts and statistics as collected during the oral literature research. For every effective transcription, a good knowledge of the phonological, semantic and syntactic forms of the language of the people who produce the oral literature is inevitable. The details of tone, stress and syllable timing must be noted and marked as they contribute immensely to the general evaluation of the oral narration. The researcher should be very careful in writing his/her report because there may crop up some difficulties in transcribing the oral renditions accurately. Problems of transcribing and translation can be effectively solved by two interpreters. One interpreter should translate into English while the second interpreter cross-checks the translation to make sure that the subtle nuances of meaning and patterns of thought of the informants or narrators in their original and native contexts are captured in the translation.

Oral literature research opens for African scholars the avenue for the preservation and transmission of our oral tradition. Writing about the early Greeks who were presumed the first to preserve their myths in plays, Etherton states as follows:

> The dramatization of the myths and legends brings performance and oral tradition together and this dramatization

becomes questioning and interpretative ... the desire to give these performances at the festivals a semantic quality which is intellectualized and precise, requires that the new bits be written down ... *there was need to write down or record what was being used unchanged in the the performance. (66)*

The burden of this paper is that every effort should be made by researchers of African oral literature to record oral traditions as oral literature is one field of study where scholars have not done as much research as they should. It is one clear case, as Onuekwusi points out, where "the harvest is plentiful but the labourers are few". (207) It therefore behoves every African oral literature researcher to contribute his/her quota in the battle to record, preserve and perform our oral tradition especially African oral performances some of which have been investigated but which still invite further studies in them. These African oral performances, as pointed out by Ebeogu, are

Of various scopes and degrees of importance,
ranging from the new yam festival performances
in remote African communities, to the Kwagh
hir puppet theatre of the Tiv and those of Bornu,
both of Nigeria, to the mythic enactments of the exploits of the
Yoruba Ogun (god of iron) or Sango (god of thunder), to the Khamani (so-called bushman)
representational plays in South Africa, to the comedies
of the Mande-speaking peoples of West Africa, to the
Ekpe masquerade performances of Southern Nigeria,
To the heroic war dance of the Igbo Ohafia and Abiriba,
To the Ozidi epic performance of Nigeria's
Ijaw, to the Sundiata epic of Mali and so on. (8)

J.P. Clark, no doubt, is an outstanding scholar who is to be seriously credited with significant contribution towards the realization of an important responsibility of recording and dramatizing (in literary textuality) our oral tradition. The *Ozidi* Saga was, for instance, first heard by J.P. Clark when he was nine years and in school far from his home. It was narrated by a story-teller called Afolua and it made a deep impression on him. Many years later after his university and when he made literary scholarship and creativity his career, he wanted to rediscover the story. But he could not find the story-teller Afolua who had become a seaman. When, however, he succeeded in tracking him down, it was a terrible disappointment. The man had forgotten the saga. Fortunately, he was introduced to another story-teller named Okabou. He told the saga in its entirety in one long day and night in Ibadan, and this time Clark recorded it on tape. In 1964 while working on the Okabou transcriptions, Clark travelled to Orua town, in the Delta region with the film-maker Francis Speed and made a film of the *Ozidi* saga. The enactment of the saga was performed by one Erivini. The film was made on 16mm, in colour was titled *Tides of the Delta*, lasts 45 minutes. So, Clark had two versions of the saga: the narrative by Okabou and the enacted version by Erivini[1].

The example of Clark has been drawn to demonstrate a typical and qualified return to oral literature research. What better manifestation of his dedication to the preservation of our oral tradition could there be than this? He turned his eye backwards in time to prospect in archaic fields for the forgotten gems which would dazzle and enrich the present. His was a distinguished effort.

As a postscript to this chapter, it should be stressed that the exposition and globalization of various oral literatures remains an important challenge. As the challenge still exists, the unexplored oral literature of African societies should be well studied, investigated, recorded and preserved by scholars and researchers in African oral literature, for, as Okpi has slightly pointed out, "the Ijaw people of today may not be here in a hundred years time but J.P. Clark's play *Ozidi* will outlive them all, it will even outlive Nigeria" (59).

NOTE

1. See, J.P. Clark, *The Ozidi Saga*. Ibadan. OUP, 1977, Pp. xv–xxxvii.

WORKS CITED

Benjamin, Walter. *Illuminations*. Ed. & trans. Hannah Arendt. Glasgow: Fontana/Collins, 1973. Print.

Ebeogu, Afam. "Domestication Processes in African Literary Drama" *Trends in African Drama and Theatre*. Ed. Uzoma Nwokochah. Owerri: Crystal Publishers, 2000. 1–19. Print.

Etherton, Michael. *The Development of African Drama*. London: Hutchinson University Library for Africa, 1982. Print.

Okoh, Nkem. *Preface to Oral Literature*. Onitsha: Africana First Publishers, 2008. Print.

Okpi, Kalu. "Folklore onto the Stage: The example of *Ozidi*". *Nka*. 2 (1988). 53–59. Print.

Onuekwusi, Jasper Ahaoma. *Fundamentals of African Oral Literature*. Owerri: Alphabet, 2001. Print.

Index

Azuonye, Nnorom: 259

www.ingramcontent.com/pod-product-compliance
Lightning Source LLC
Chambersburg PA
CBHW010650100726
47901CB00012B/2501